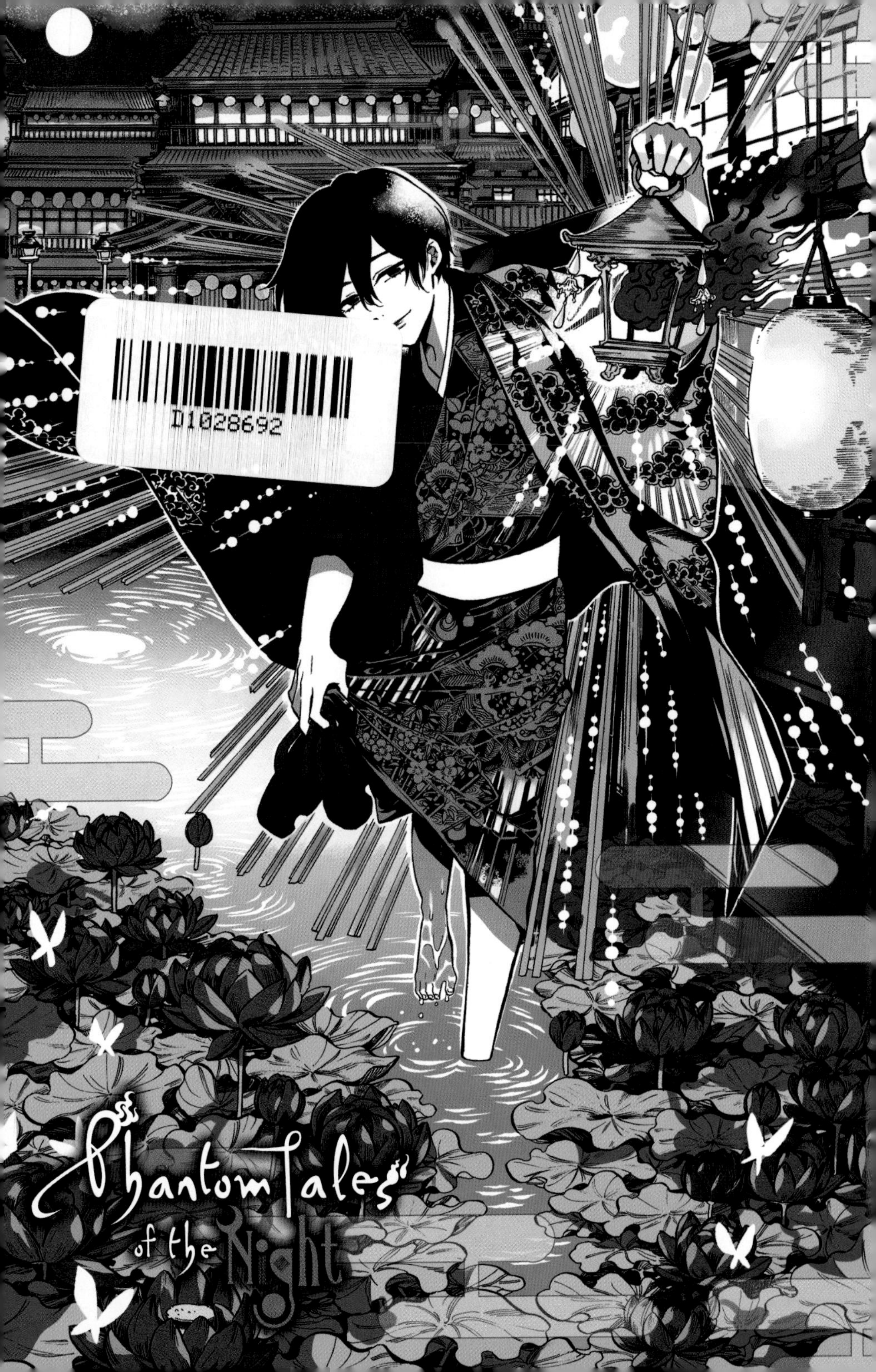
Phantom Tales of the Night

CONTENTS

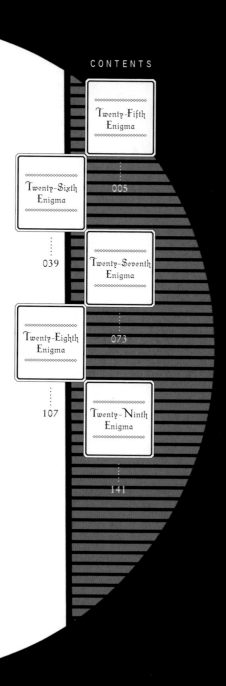

Twenty-Fifth
Enigma

005

Twenty-Sixth
Enigma

039

Twenty-Seventh
Enigma

073

Twenty-Eighth
Enigma

107

Twenty-Ninth
Enigma

141

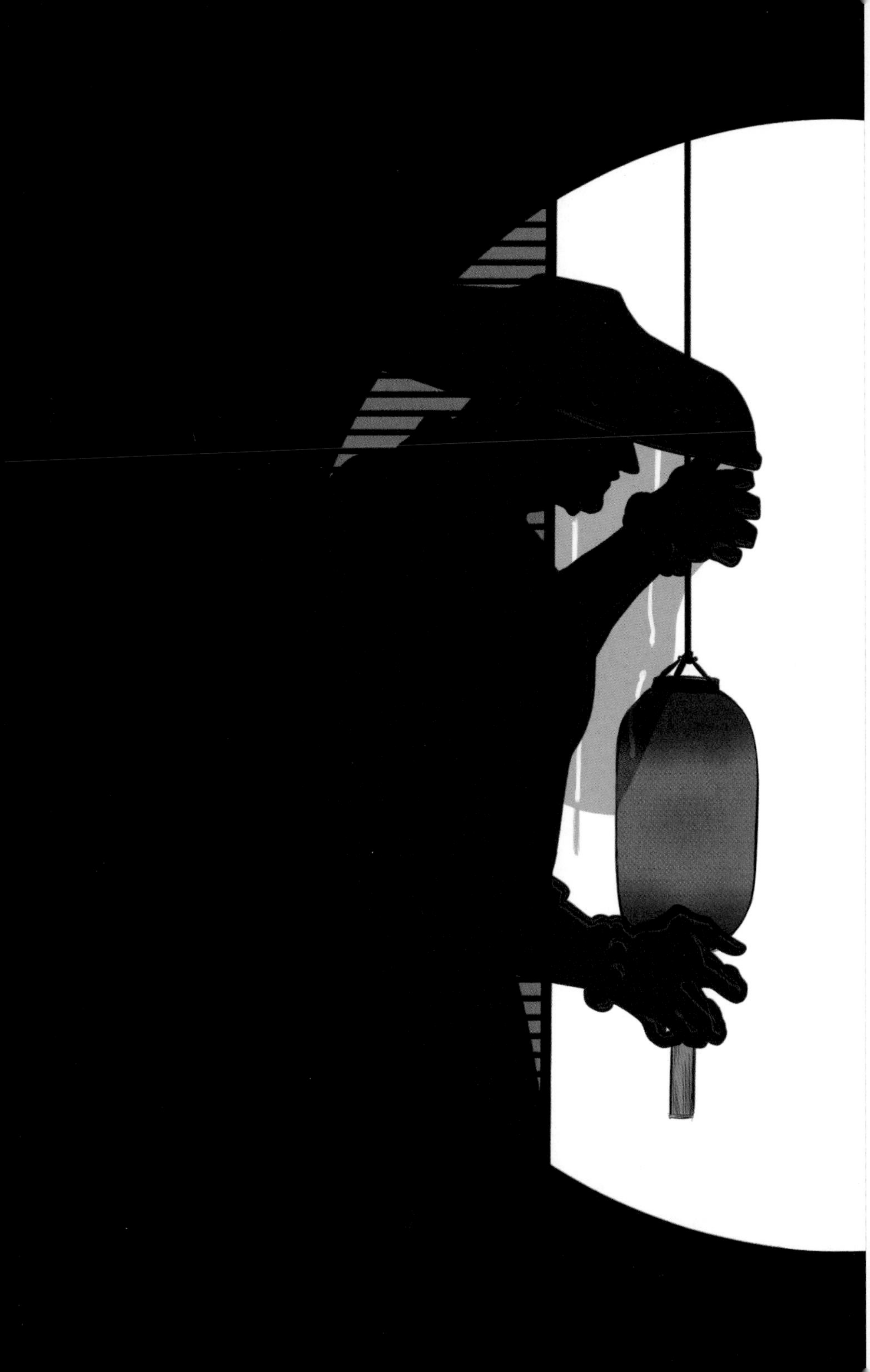

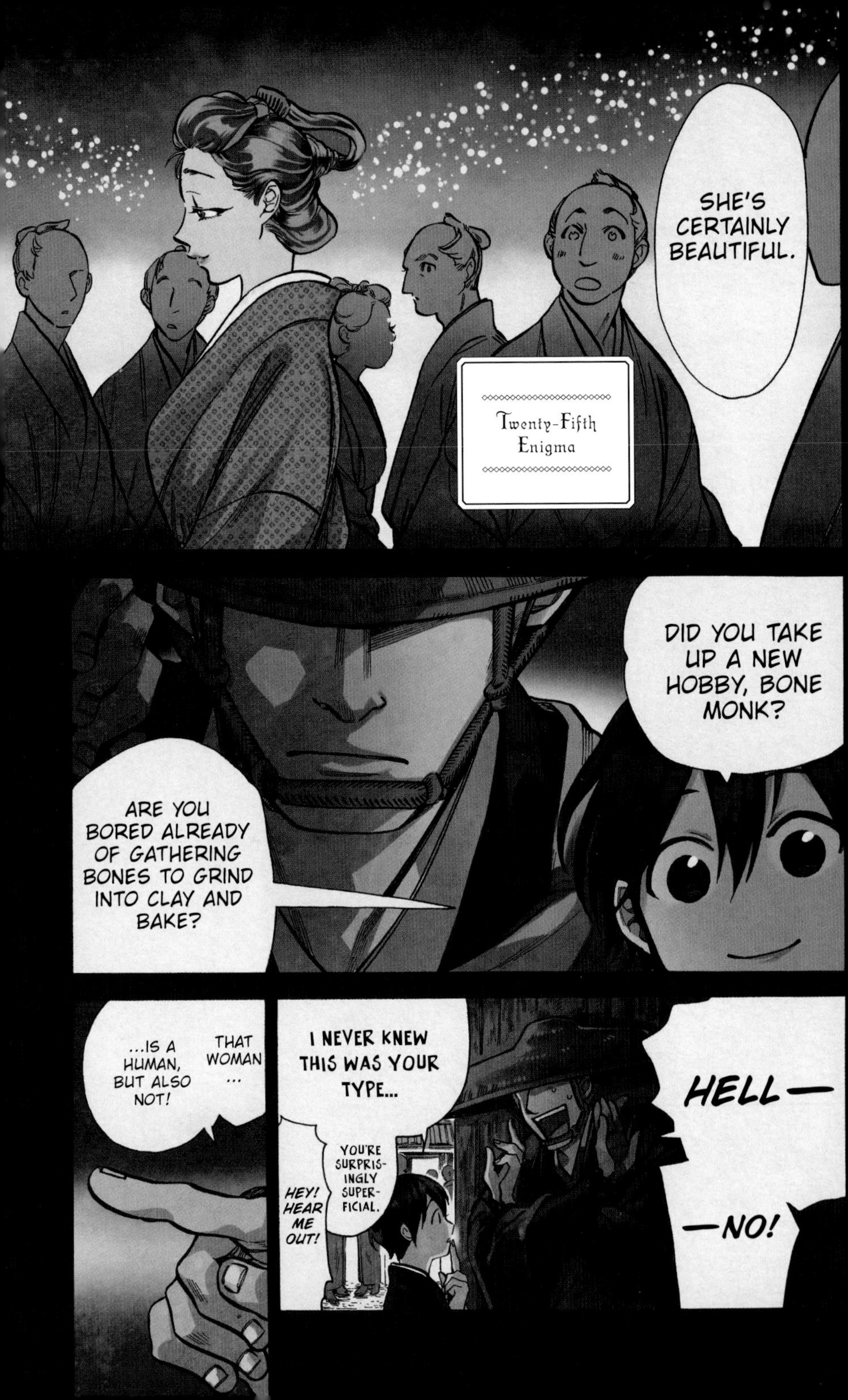
SHE'S CERTAINLY BEAUTIFUL.
Twenty-Fifth Enigma
DID YOU TAKE UP A NEW HOBBY, BONE MONK?
ARE YOU BORED ALREADY OF GATHERING BONES TO GRIND INTO CLAY AND BAKE?
HELL—
—NO!
I NEVER KNEW THIS WAS YOUR TYPE...
YOU'RE SURPRISINGLY SUPERFICIAL.
HEY! HEAR ME OUT!
THAT WOMAN...
...IS A HUMAN, BUT ALSO NOT!

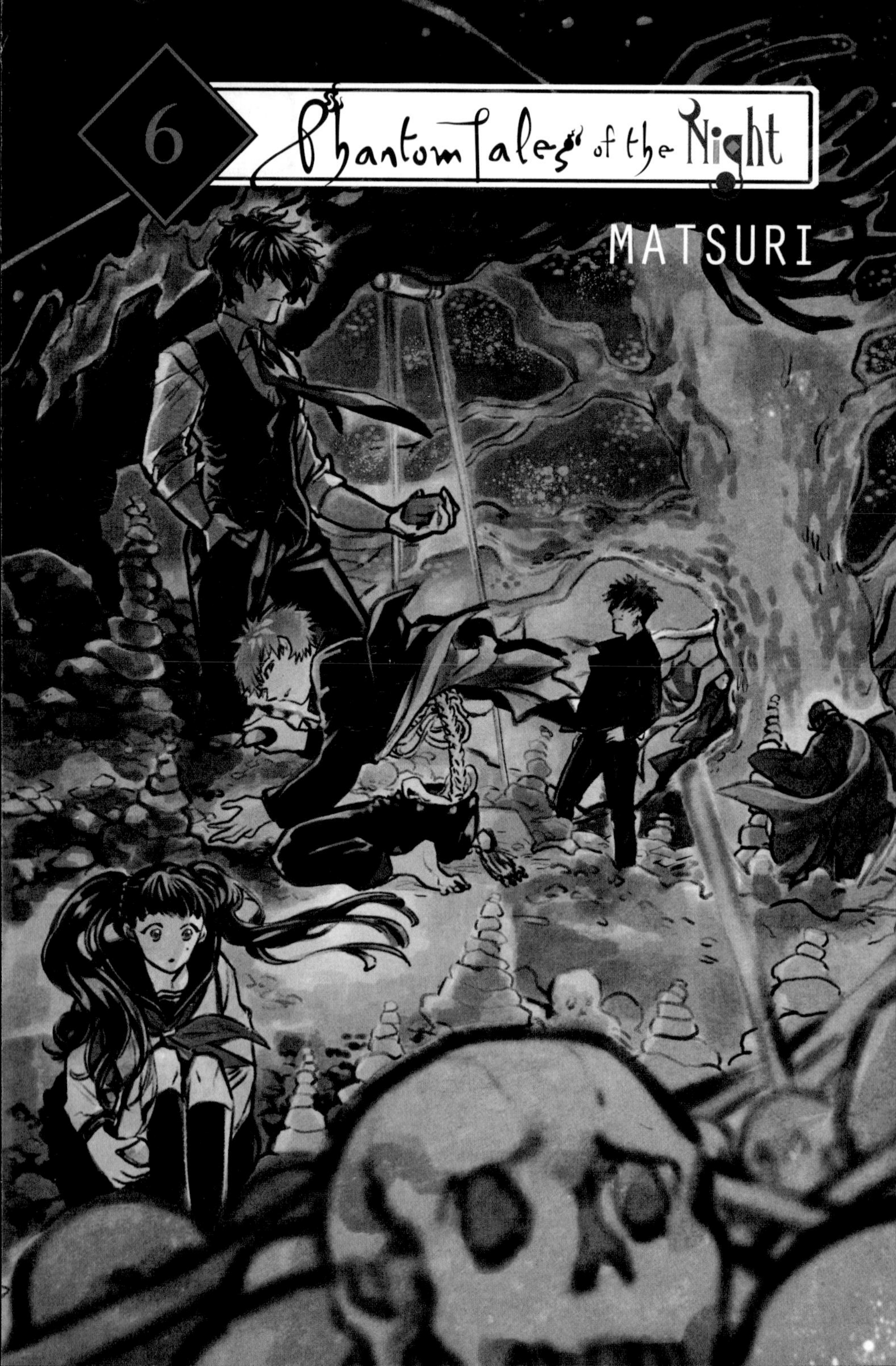
6
Phantom Tales of the Night
MATSURI

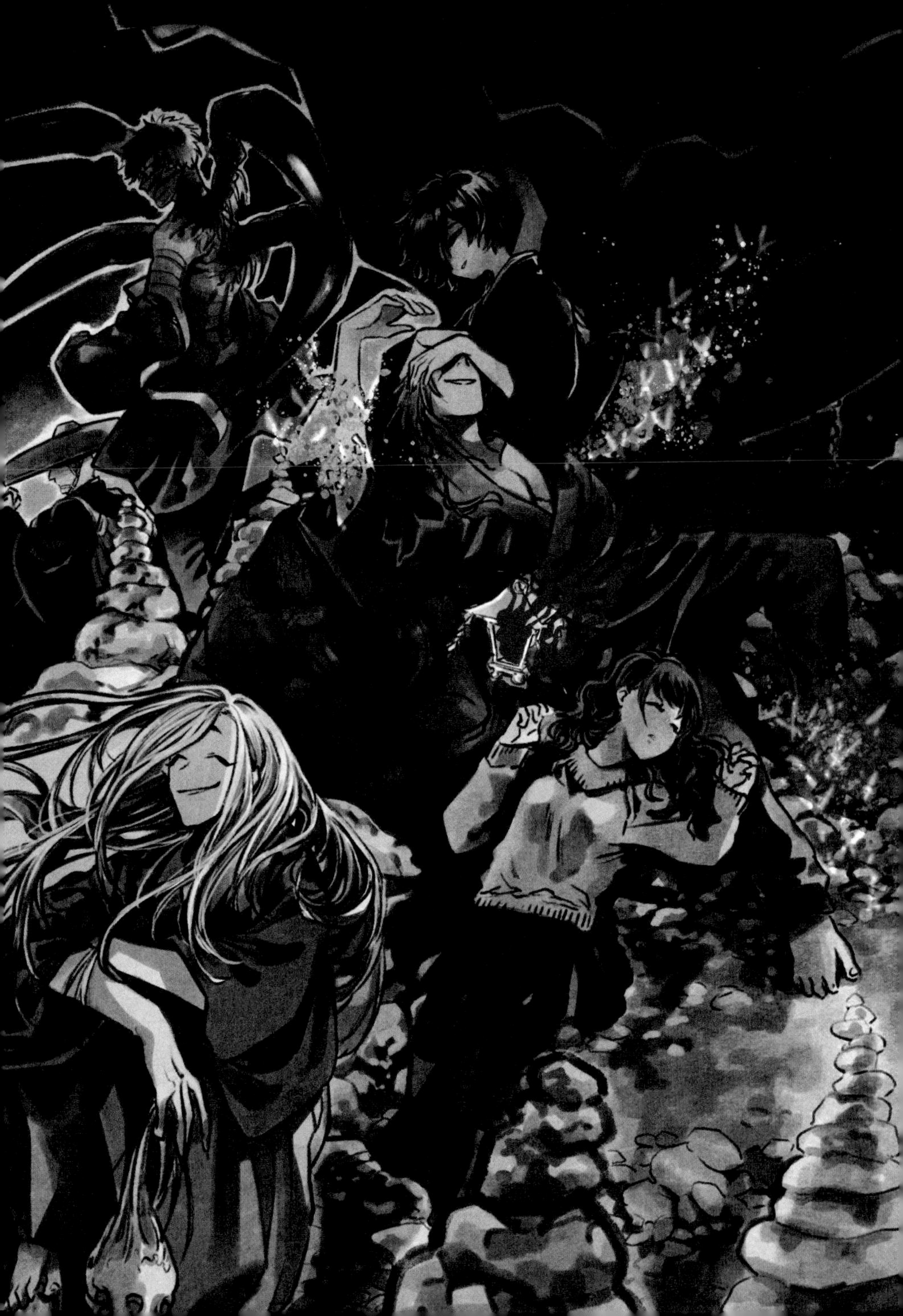

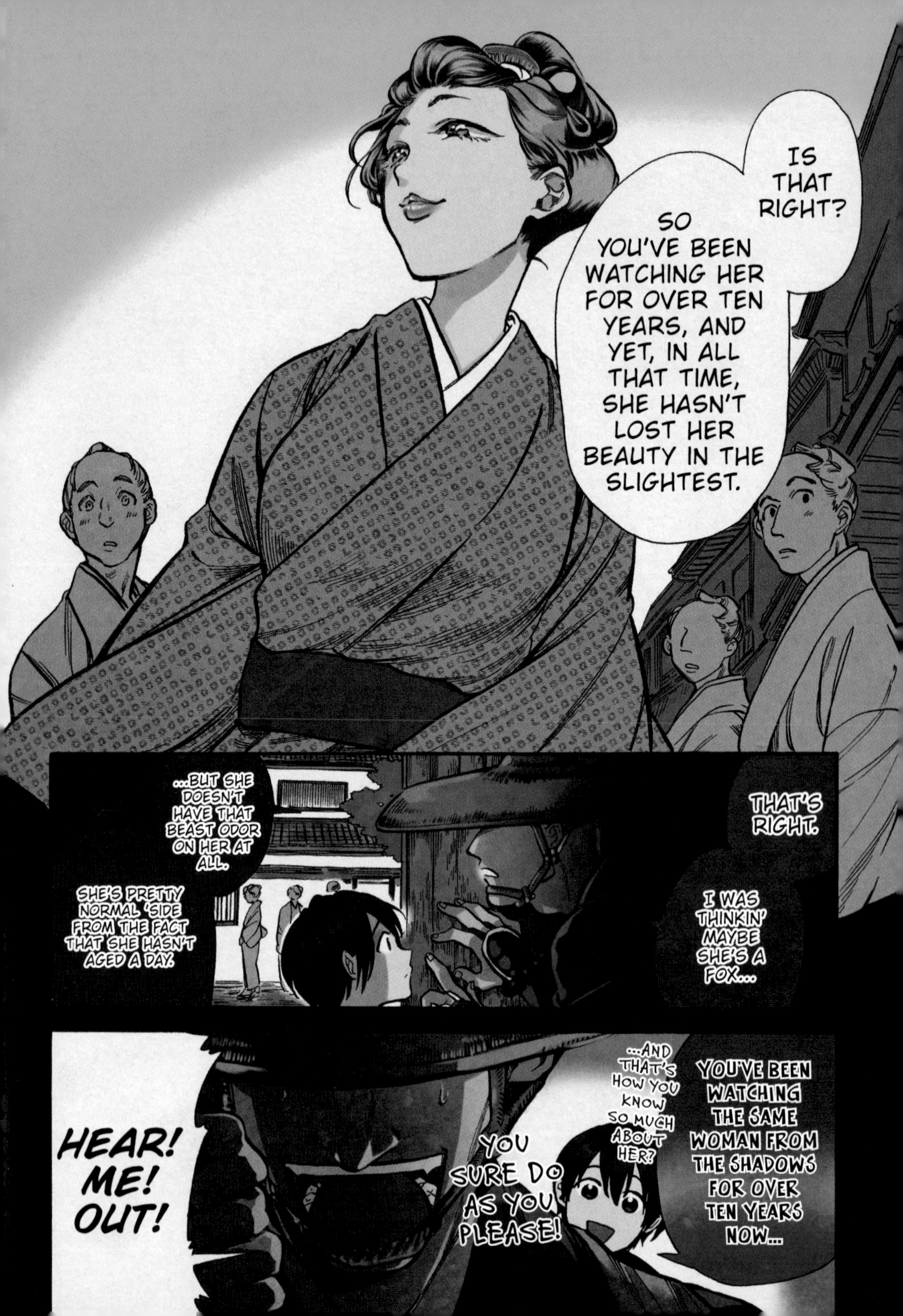
IS THAT RIGHT?
SO YOU'VE BEEN WATCHING HER FOR OVER TEN YEARS, AND YET, IN ALL THAT TIME, SHE HASN'T LOST HER BEAUTY IN THE SLIGHTEST.
THAT'S RIGHT.
I WAS THINKIN' MAYBE SHE'S A FOX...
...BUT SHE DOESN'T HAVE THAT BEAST ODOR ON HER AT ALL.
SHE'S PRETTY NORMAL 'SIDE FROM THE FACT THAT SHE HASN'T AGED A DAY.
YOU'VE BEEN WATCHING THE SAME WOMAN FROM THE SHADOWS FOR OVER TEN YEARS NOW...
...AND THAT'S HOW YOU KNOW SO MUCH ABOUT HER?
YOU SURE DO AS YOU PLEASE!
HEAR! ME! OUT!

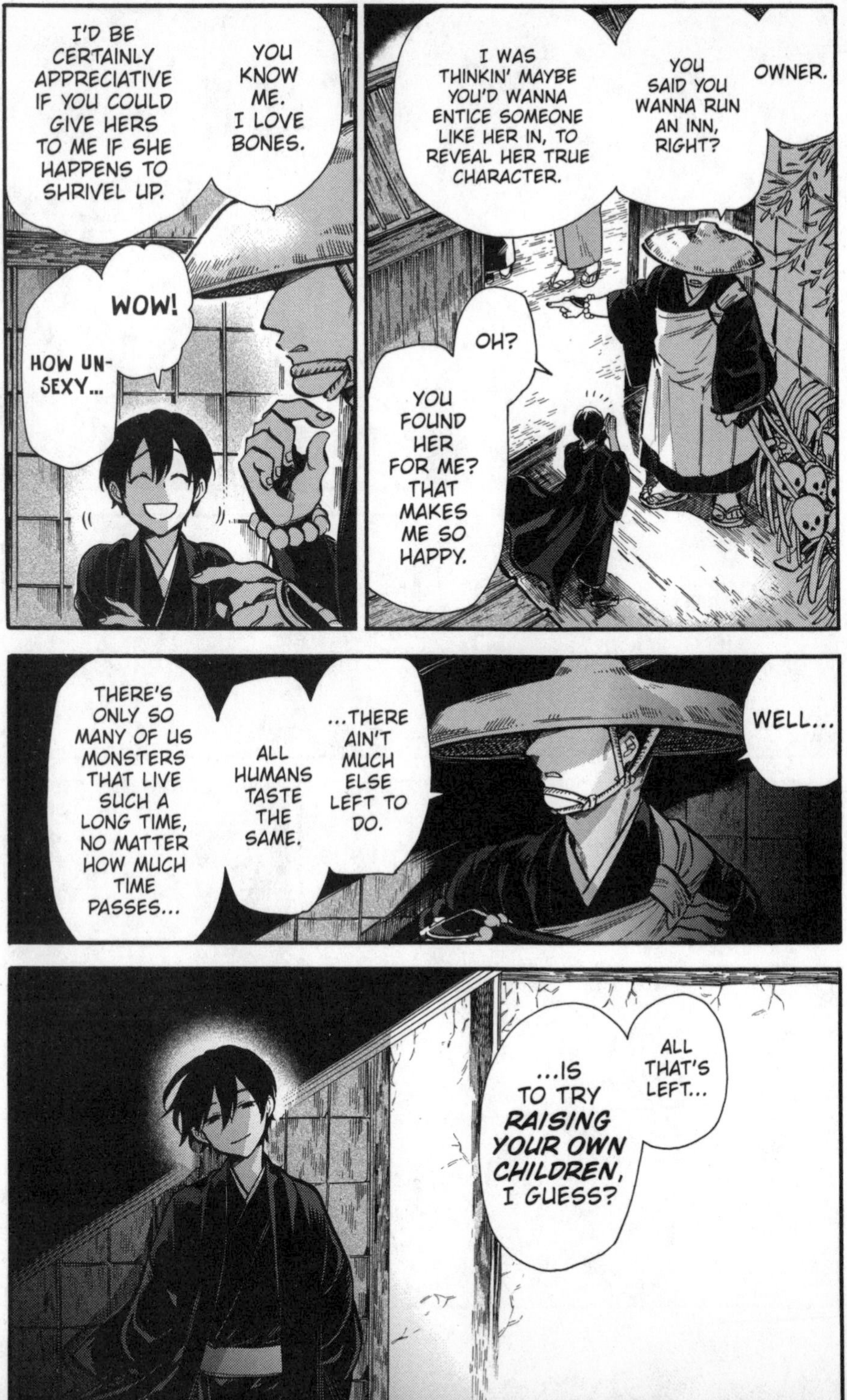
OWNER.
YOU SAID YOU WANNA RUN AN INN, RIGHT?
I WAS THINKIN' MAYBE YOU'D WANNA ENTICE SOMEONE LIKE HER IN, TO REVEAL HER TRUE CHARACTER.
OH?
YOU FOUND HER FOR ME? THAT MAKES ME SO HAPPY.
YOU KNOW ME. I LOVE BONES.
I'D BE CERTAINLY APPRECIATIVE IF YOU COULD GIVE HERS TO ME IF SHE HAPPENS TO SHRIVEL UP.
WOW!
HOW UN-SEXY...
WELL...
...THERE AIN'T MUCH ELSE LEFT TO DO.
ALL HUMANS TASTE THE SAME.
THERE'S ONLY SO MANY OF US MONSTERS THAT LIVE SUCH A LONG TIME, NO MATTER HOW MUCH TIME PASSES...
ALL THAT'S LEFT...
...IS TO TRY *RAISING YOUR OWN CHILDREN*, I GUESS?

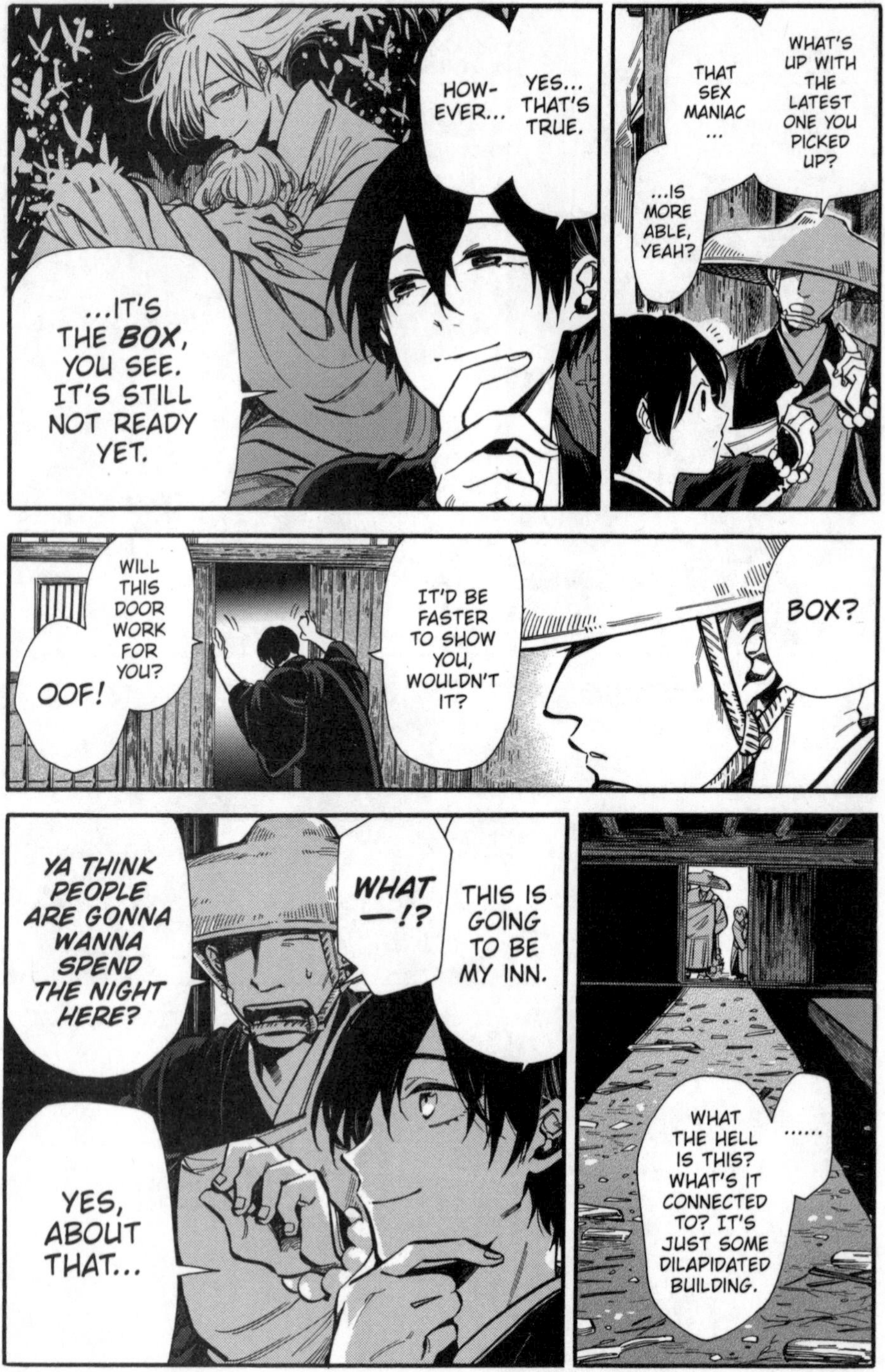
WHAT'S UP WITH THE LATEST ONE YOU PICKED UP?
THAT SEX MANIAC ...
...IS MORE ABLE, YEAH?
YES... THAT'S TRUE.
HOW-EVER...
...IT'S THE BOX, YOU SEE. IT'S STILL NOT READY YET.
BOX?
IT'D BE FASTER TO SHOW YOU, WOULDN'T IT?
WILL THIS DOOR WORK FOR YOU?
OOF!
......
WHAT THE HELL IS THIS? WHAT'S IT CONNECTED TO? IT'S JUST SOME DILAPIDATED BUILDING.
THIS IS GOING TO BE MY INN.
WHAT—!?
YA THINK PEOPLE ARE GONNA WANNA SPEND THE NIGHT HERE?
YES, ABOUT THAT...

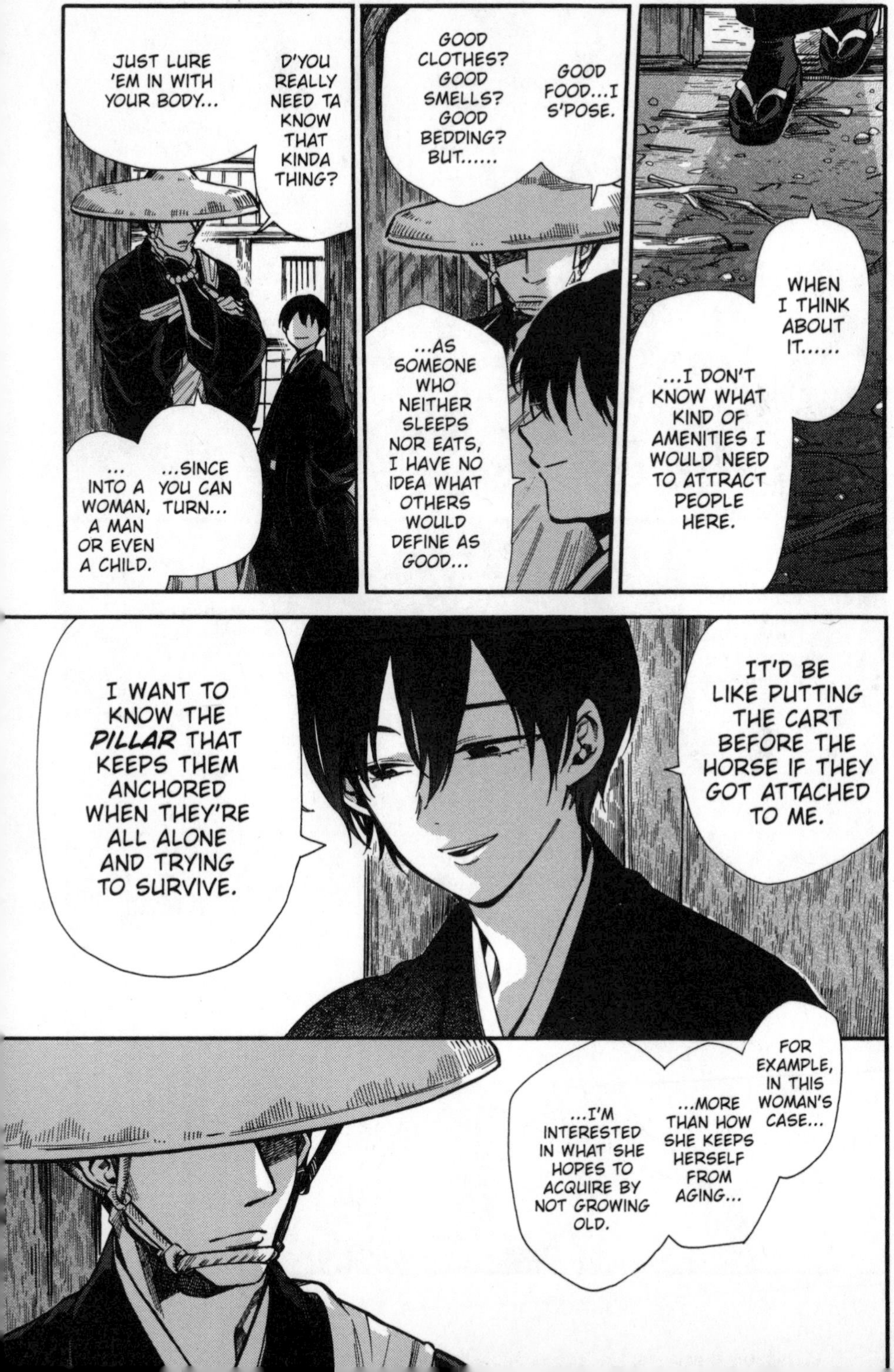
WHEN I THINK ABOUT IT......
...I DON'T KNOW WHAT KIND OF AMENITIES I WOULD NEED TO ATTRACT PEOPLE HERE.
GOOD FOOD...I S'POSE.
GOOD CLOTHES? GOOD SMELLS? GOOD BEDDING? BUT......
...AS SOMEONE WHO NEITHER SLEEPS NOR EATS, I HAVE NO IDEA WHAT OTHERS WOULD DEFINE AS GOOD...
D'YOU REALLY NEED TA KNOW THAT KINDA THING?
JUST LURE 'EM IN WITH YOUR BODY...
...SINCE YOU CAN TURN...
... INTO A WOMAN, A MAN OR EVEN A CHILD.
IT'D BE LIKE PUTTING THE CART BEFORE THE HORSE IF THEY GOT ATTACHED TO ME.
I WANT TO KNOW THE *PILLAR* THAT KEEPS THEM ANCHORED WHEN THEY'RE ALL ALONE AND TRYING TO SURVIVE.
FOR EXAMPLE, IN THIS WOMAN'S CASE...
...MORE THAN HOW SHE KEEPS HERSELF FROM AGING...
...I'M INTERESTED IN WHAT SHE HOPES TO ACQUIRE BY NOT GROWING OLD.

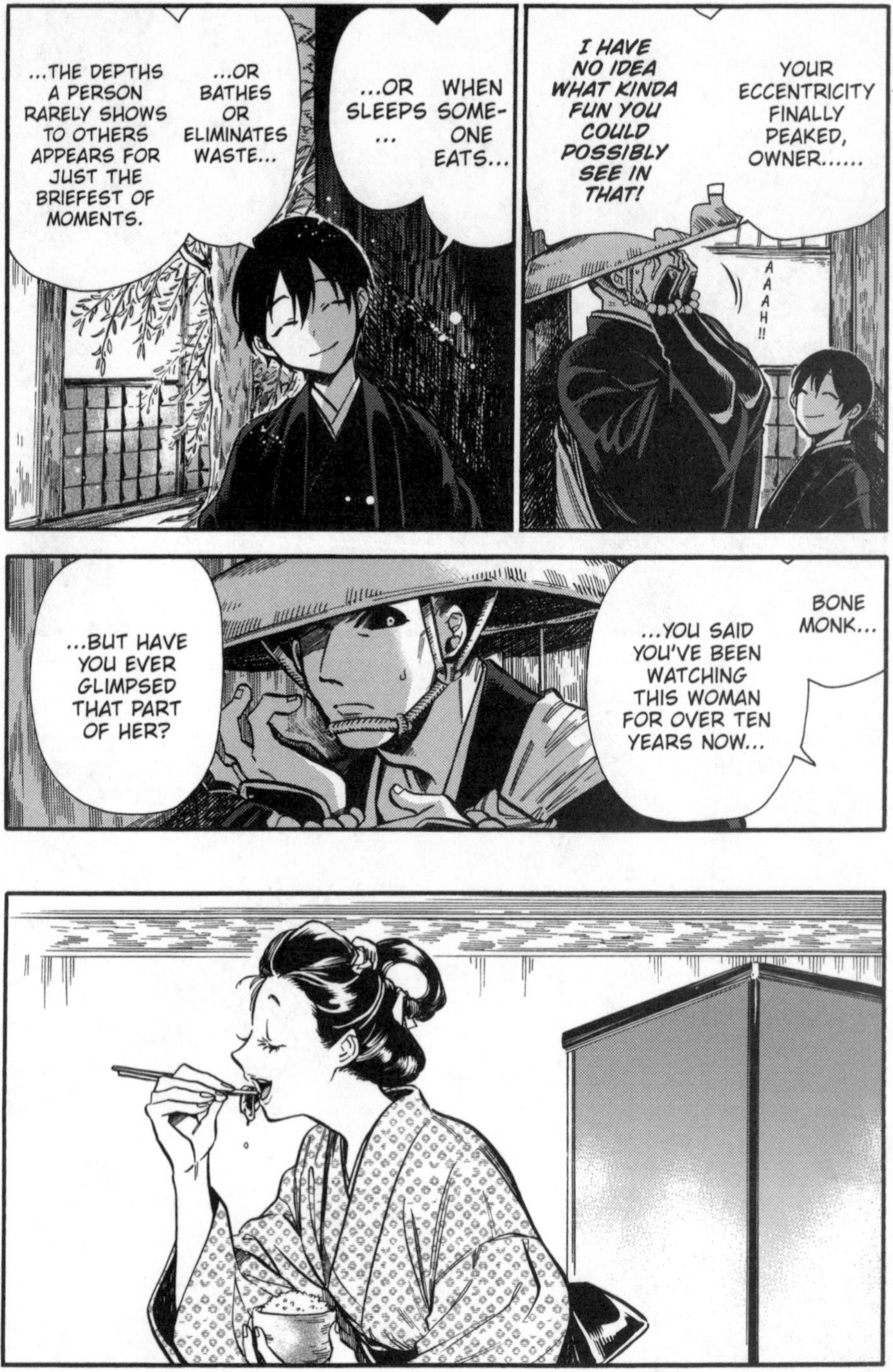
YOUR ECCENTRICITY FINALLY PEAKED, OWNER......
I HAVE NO IDEA WHAT KINDA FUN YOU COULD POSSIBLY SEE IN THAT!
AAAH!!
WHEN SOMEONE EATS...
...OR SLEEPS...
...OR BATHES OR ELIMINATES WASTE...
...THE DEPTHS A PERSON RARELY SHOWS TO OTHERS APPEARS FOR JUST THE BRIEFEST OF MOMENTS.
BONE MONK...
...YOU SAID YOU'VE BEEN WATCHING THIS WOMAN FOR OVER TEN YEARS NOW...
...BUT HAVE YOU EVER GLIMPSED THAT PART OF HER?

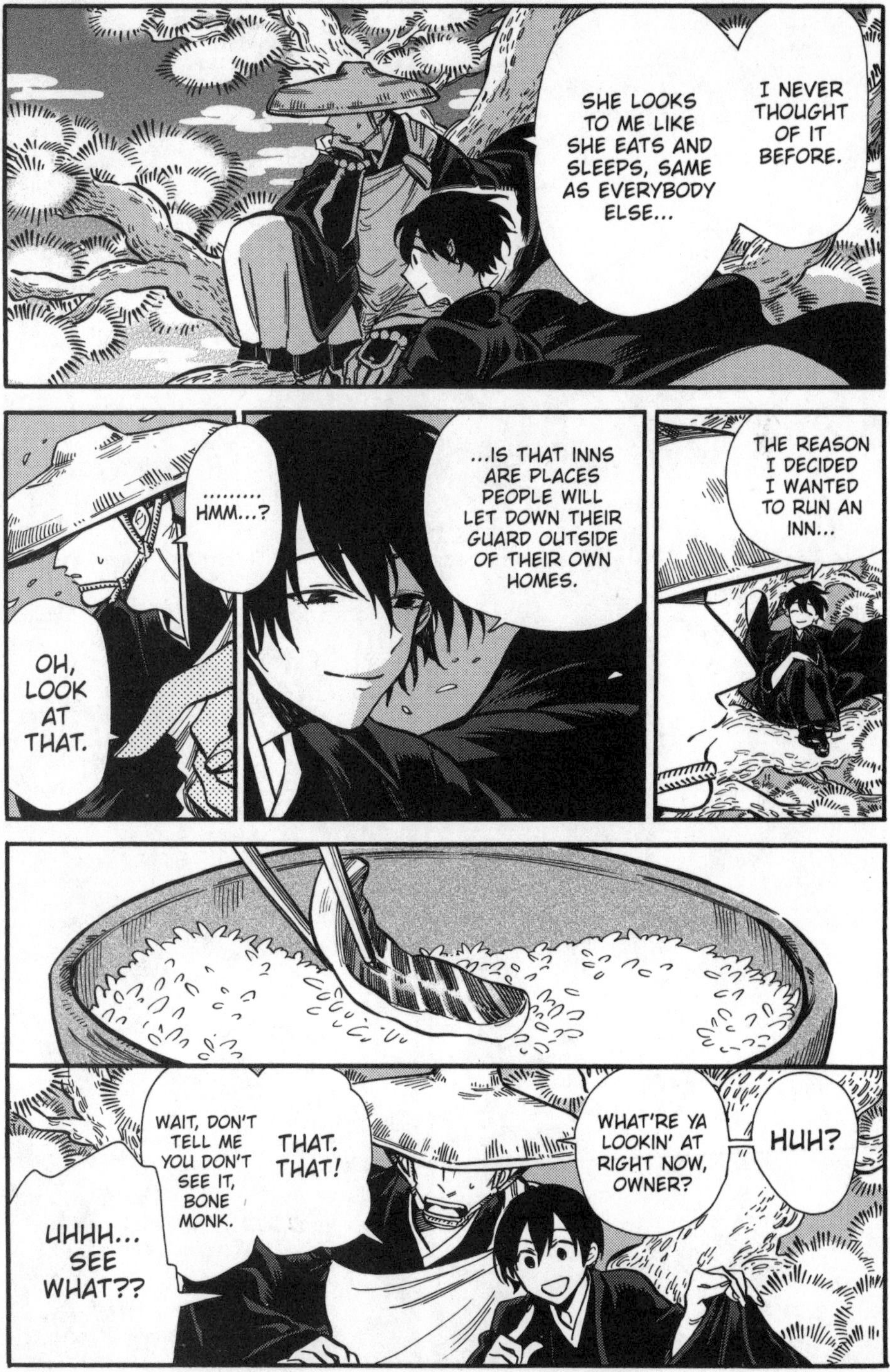
I NEVER THOUGHT OF IT BEFORE.
SHE LOOKS TO ME LIKE SHE EATS AND SLEEPS, SAME AS EVERYBODY ELSE...
THE REASON I DECIDED I WANTED TO RUN AN INN...
...IS THAT INNS ARE PLACES PEOPLE WILL LET DOWN THEIR GUARD OUTSIDE OF THEIR OWN HOMES.
.... HMM...?
OH, LOOK AT THAT.
HUH?
WHAT'RE YA LOOKIN' AT RIGHT NOW, OWNER?
THAT. THAT!
WAIT, DON'T TELL ME YOU DON'T SEE IT, BONE MONK.
UHHH... SEE WHAT??

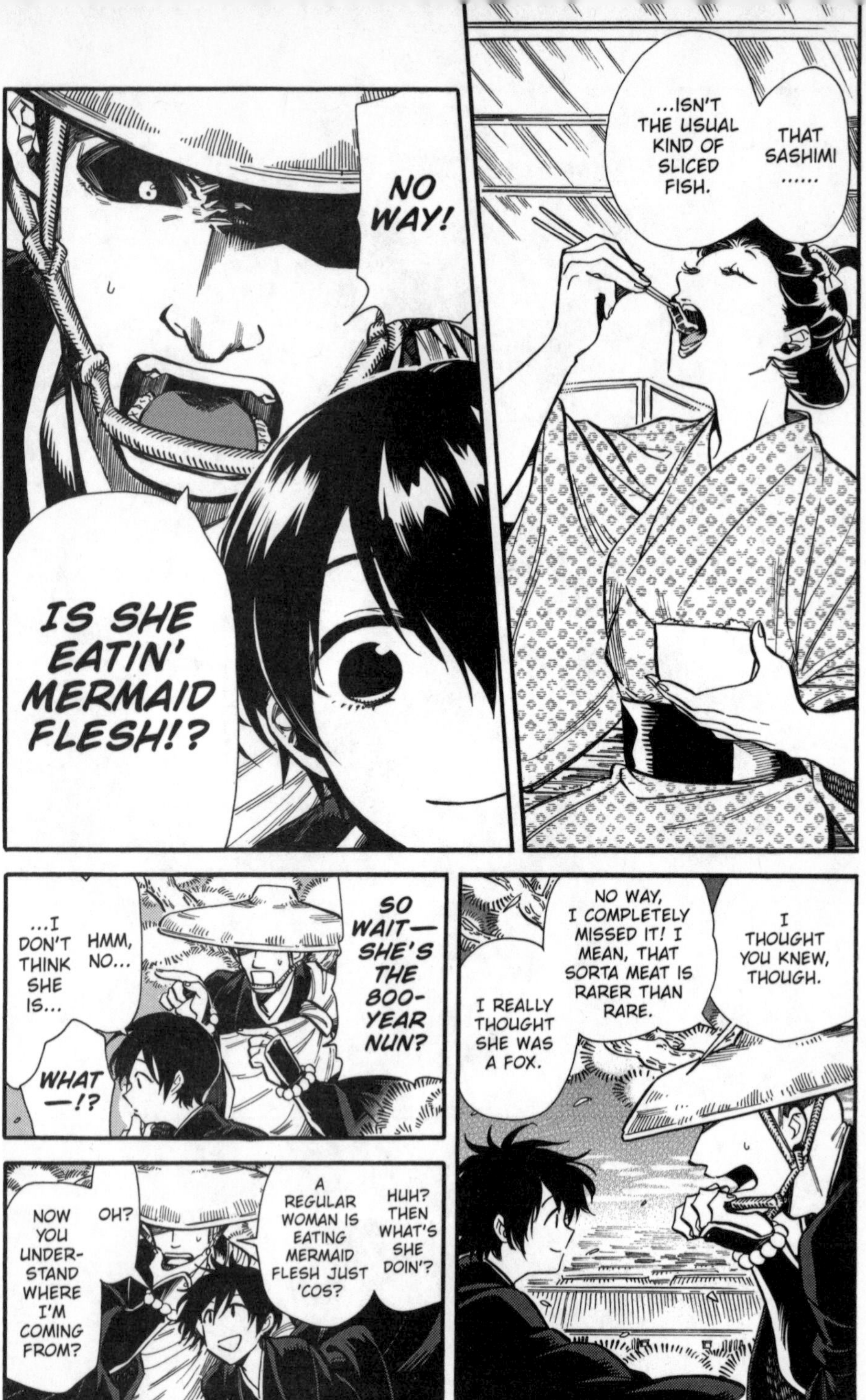
THAT SASHIMI ......
...ISN'T THE USUAL KIND OF SLICED FISH.
NO WAY!
IS SHE EATIN' MERMAID FLESH!?
I THOUGHT YOU KNEW, THOUGH.
NO WAY, I COMPLETELY MISSED IT! I MEAN, THAT SORTA MEAT IS RARER THAN RARE.
I REALLY THOUGHT SHE WAS A FOX.
SO WAIT—SHE'S THE 800-YEAR NUN?
HMM, NO...
...I DON'T THINK SHE IS...
WHAT—!?
HUH? THEN WHAT'S SHE DOIN'?
A REGULAR WOMAN IS EATING MERMAID FLESH JUST 'COS?
OH?
NOW YOU UNDERSTAND WHERE I'M COMING FROM?

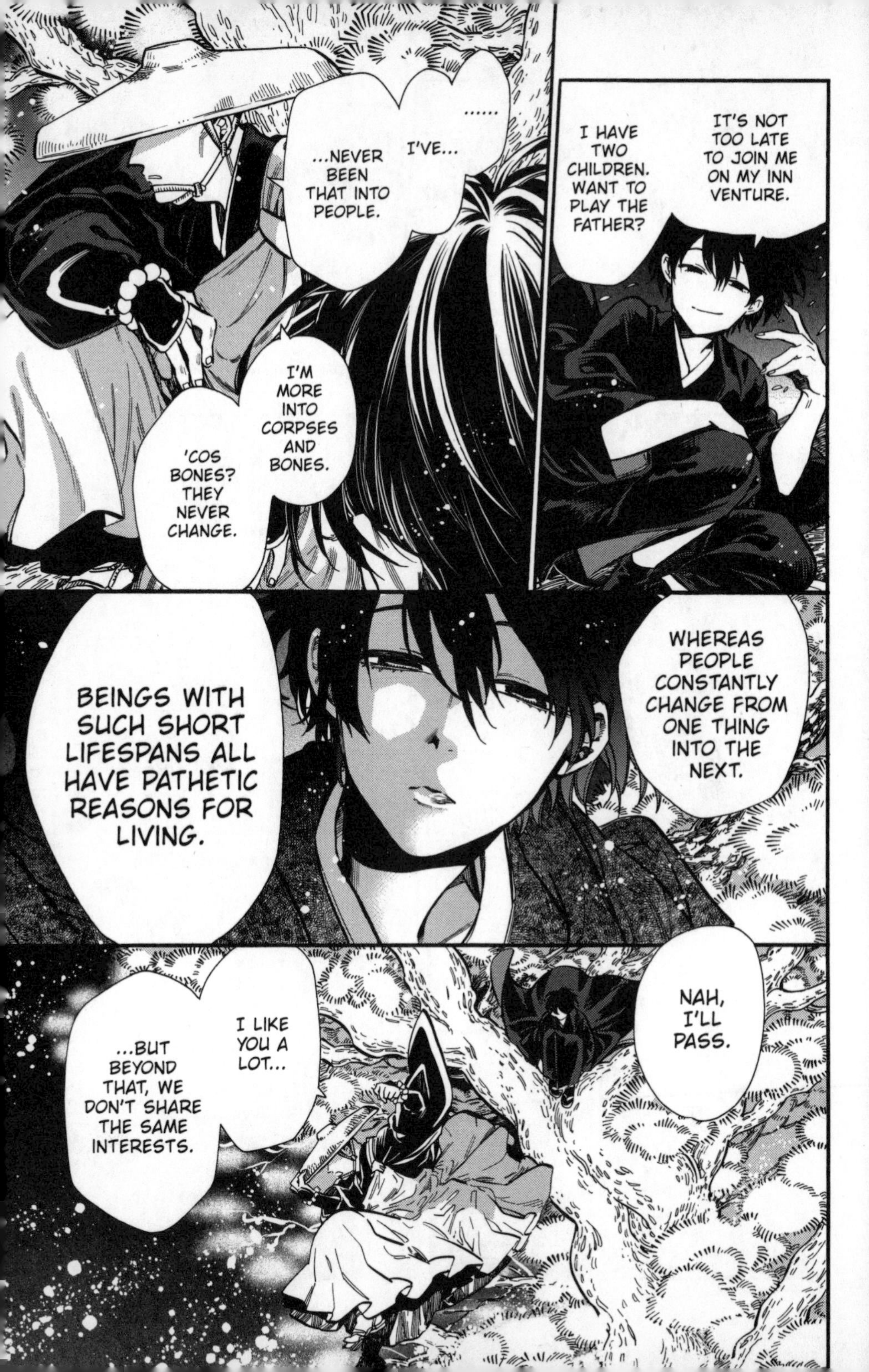
IT'S NOT TOO LATE TO JOIN ME ON MY INN VENTURE.
I HAVE TWO CHILDREN. WANT TO PLAY THE FATHER?
......
I'VE...
...NEVER BEEN THAT INTO PEOPLE.
I'M MORE INTO CORPSES AND BONES.
'COS BONES? THEY NEVER CHANGE.
WHEREAS PEOPLE CONSTANTLY CHANGE FROM ONE THING INTO THE NEXT.
BEINGS WITH SUCH SHORT LIFESPANS ALL HAVE PATHETIC REASONS FOR LIVING.
NAH, I'LL PASS.
I LIKE YOU A LOT...
...BUT BEYOND THAT, WE DON'T SHARE THE SAME INTERESTS.

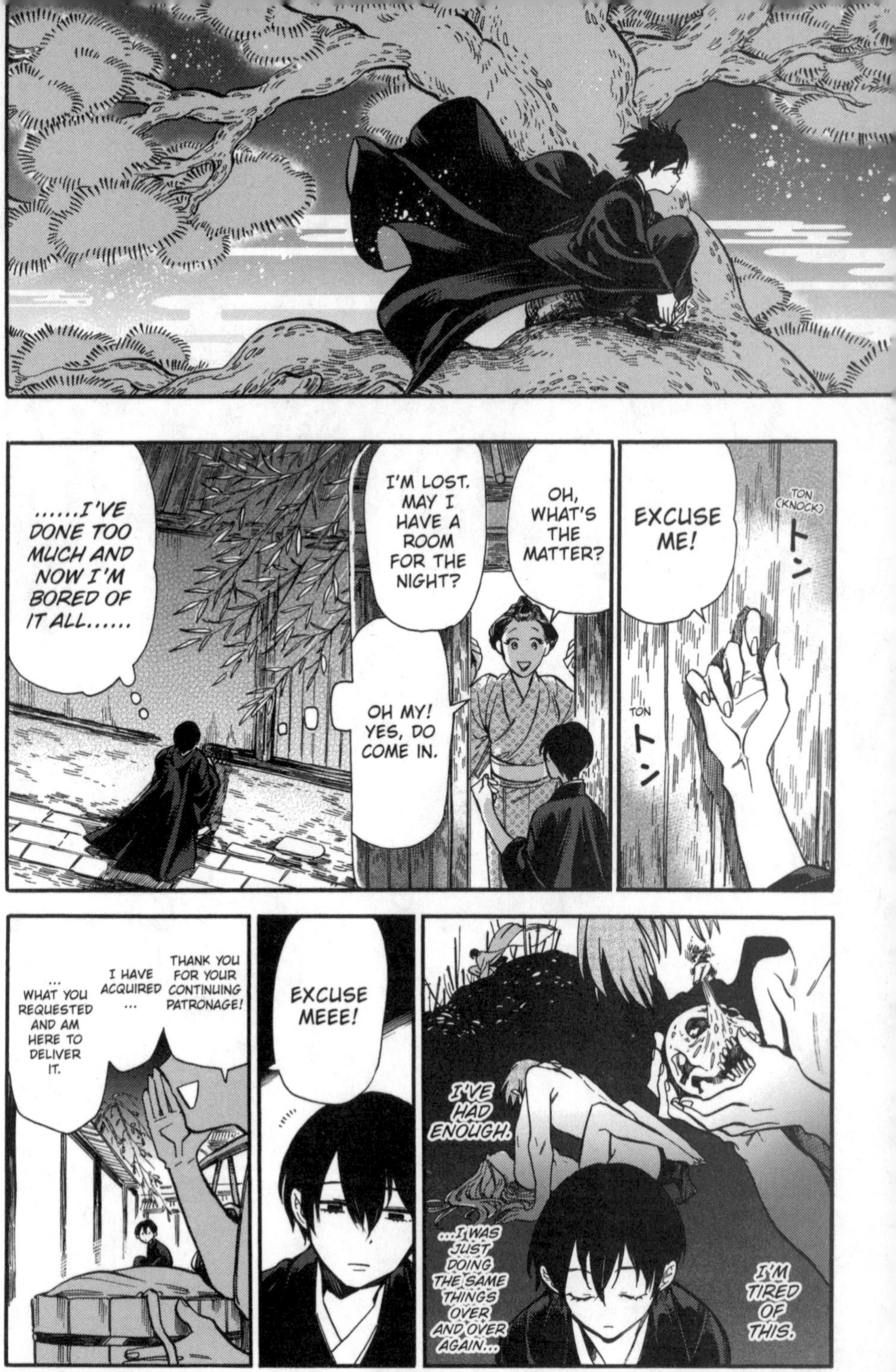
TON (KNOCK)
トン
TON
トン
EXCUSE ME!
OH, WHAT'S THE MATTER?
I'M LOST. MAY I HAVE A ROOM FOR THE NIGHT?
OH MY! YES, DO COME IN.
......I'VE DONE TOO MUCH AND NOW I'M BORED OF IT ALL......
I'VE HAD ENOUGH.
I'M TIRED OF THIS.
...I WAS JUST DOING THE SAME THINGS OVER AND OVER AGAIN...
EXCUSE MEEE!
THANK YOU FOR YOUR CONTINUING PATRONAGE!
I HAVE ACQUIRED ...
... WHAT YOU REQUESTED AND AM HERE TO DELIVER IT.

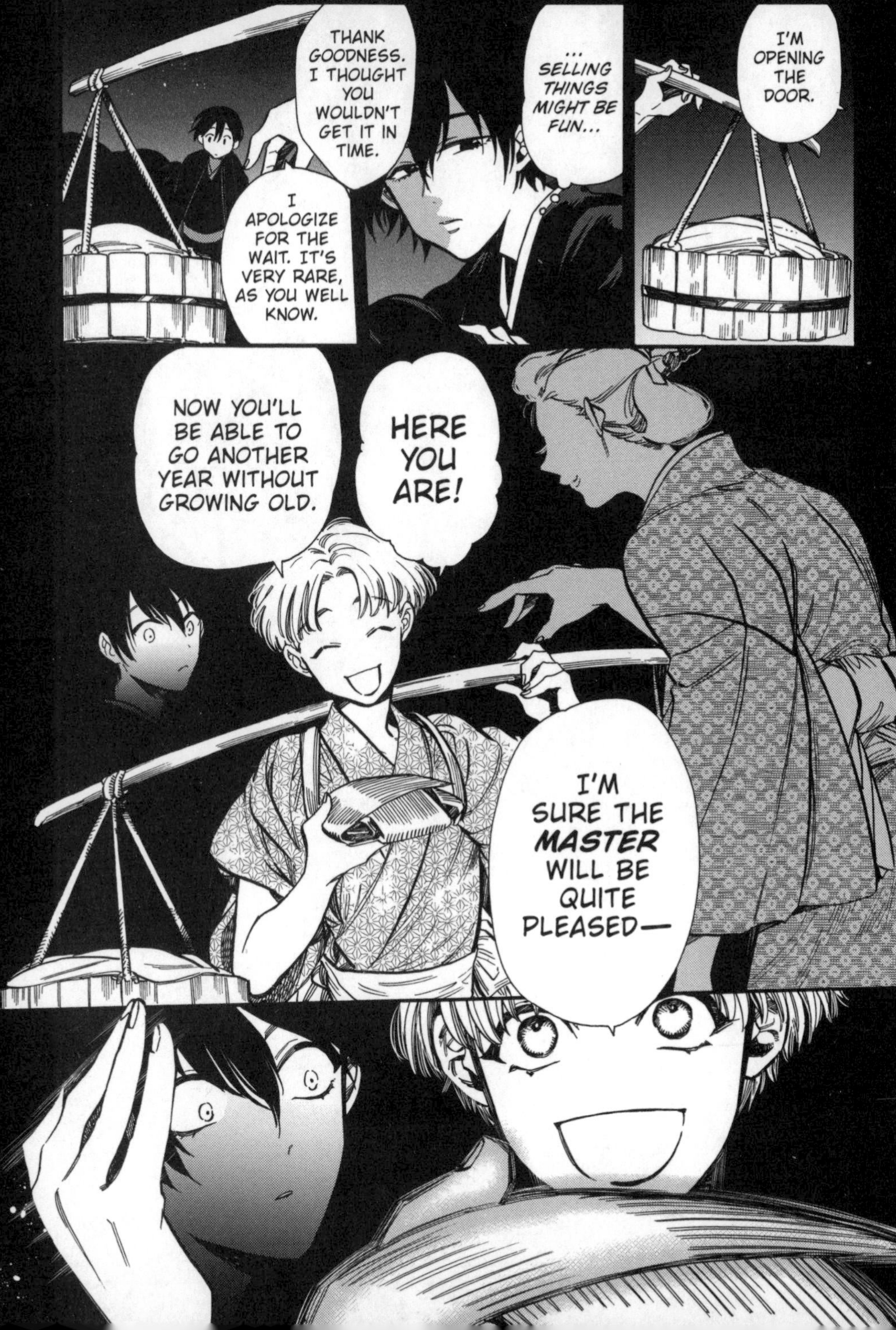
I'M OPENING THE DOOR.
... SELLING THINGS MIGHT BE FUN...
THANK GOODNESS. I THOUGHT YOU WOULDN'T GET IT IN TIME.
I APOLOGIZE FOR THE WAIT. IT'S VERY RARE, AS YOU WELL KNOW.
HERE YOU ARE!
NOW YOU'LL BE ABLE TO GO ANOTHER YEAR WITHOUT GROWING OLD.
I'M SURE THE MASTER WILL BE QUITE PLEASED—

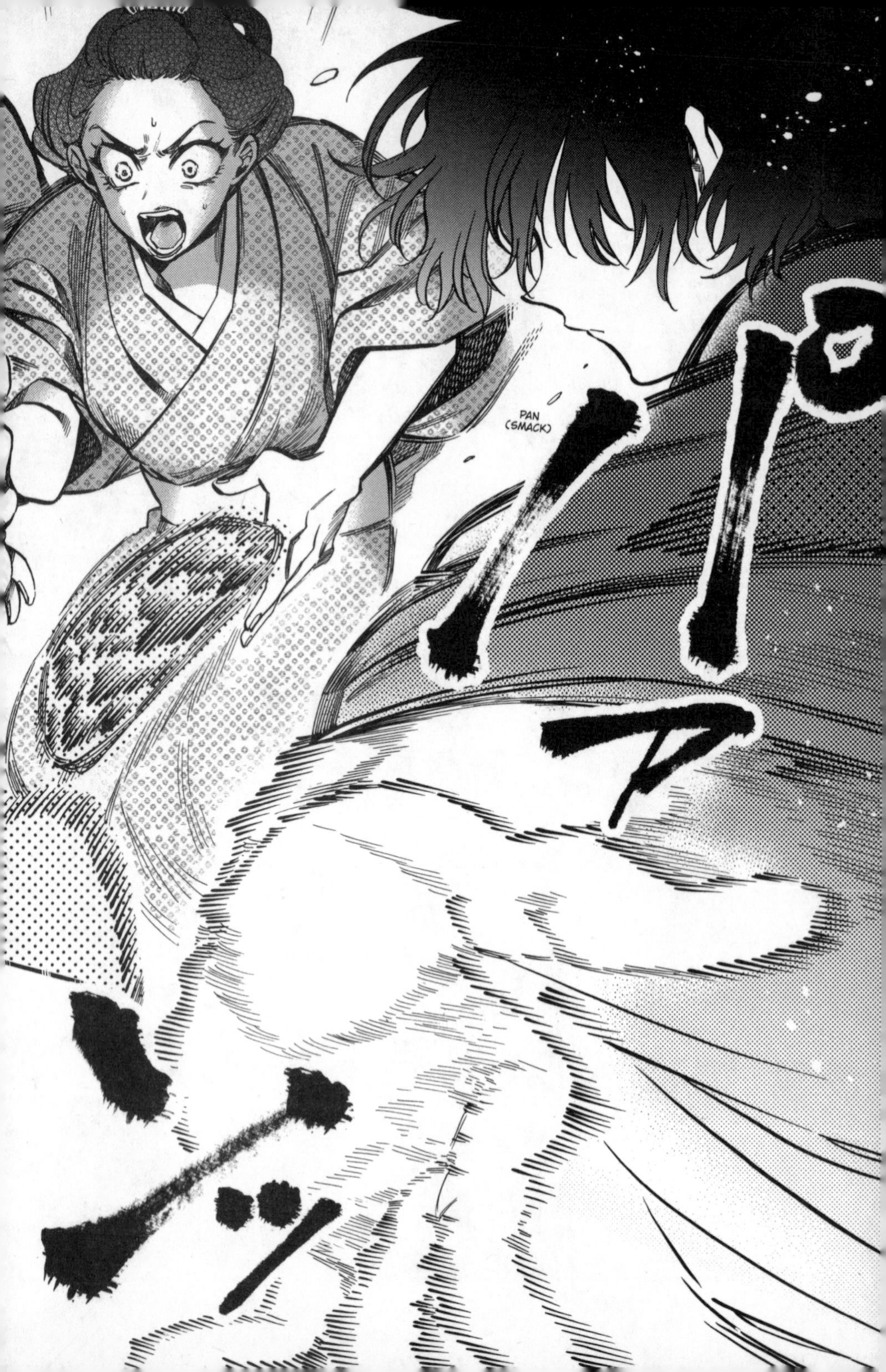
PAN
(SMACK)

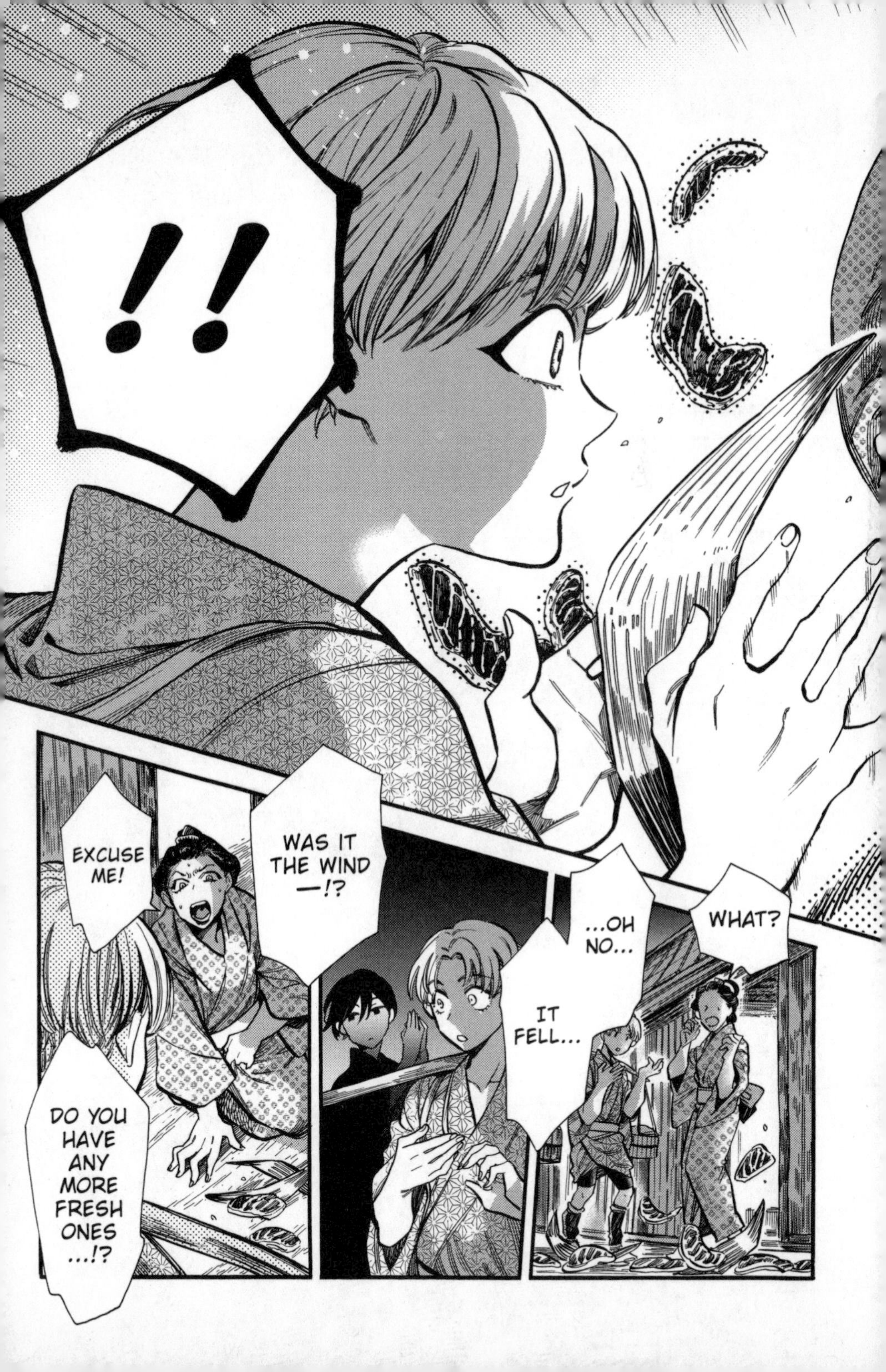
!!
WHAT?
...OH NO...
IT FELL...
WAS IT THE WIND—!?
EXCUSE ME!
DO YOU HAVE ANY MORE FRESH ONES ...!?

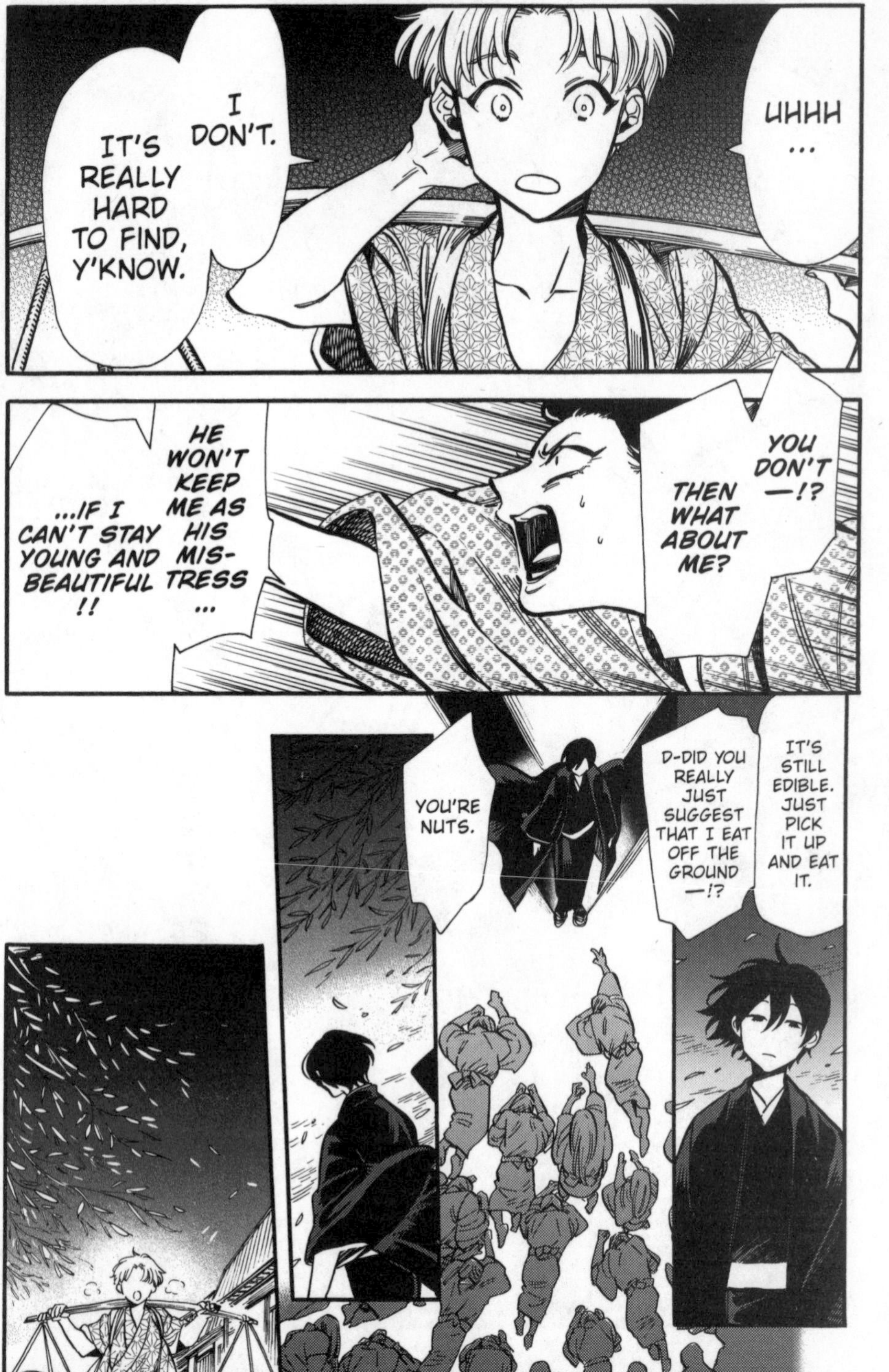
UHHH ...
I DON'T.
IT'S REALLY HARD TO FIND, Y'KNOW.
YOU DON'T —!?
THEN WHAT ABOUT ME?
HE WON'T KEEP ME AS HIS MIS-TRESS ...
...IF I CAN'T STAY YOUNG AND BEAUTIFUL !!
IT'S STILL EDIBLE. JUST PICK IT UP AND EAT IT.
D-DID YOU REALLY JUST SUGGEST THAT I EAT OFF THE GROUND —!?
YOU'RE NUTS.

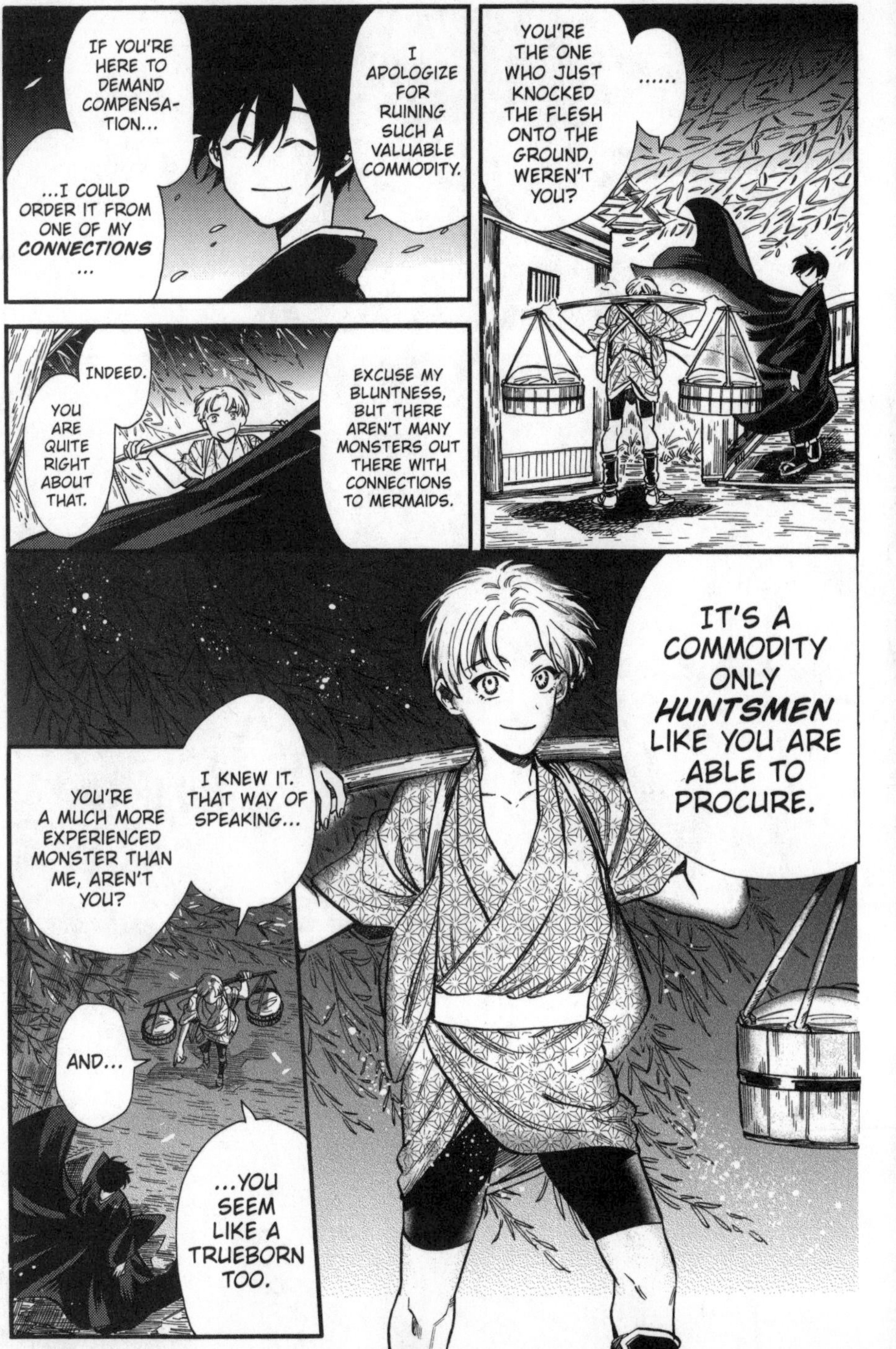
YOU'RE THE ONE WHO JUST KNOCKED THE FLESH ONTO THE GROUND, WEREN'T YOU?
......
I APOLOGIZE FOR RUINING SUCH A VALUABLE COMMODITY.
IF YOU'RE HERE TO DEMAND COMPENSA-TION...
...I COULD ORDER IT FROM ONE OF MY *CONNECTIONS* ...
EXCUSE MY BLUNTNESS, BUT THERE AREN'T MANY MONSTERS OUT THERE WITH CONNECTIONS TO MERMAIDS.
INDEED.
YOU ARE QUITE RIGHT ABOUT THAT.
IT'S A COMMODITY ONLY ***HUNTSMEN*** LIKE YOU ARE ABLE TO PROCURE.
I KNEW IT. THAT WAY OF SPEAKING...
YOU'RE A MUCH MORE EXPERIENCED MONSTER THAN ME, AREN'T YOU?
AND...
...YOU SEEM LIKE A TRUEBORN TOO.

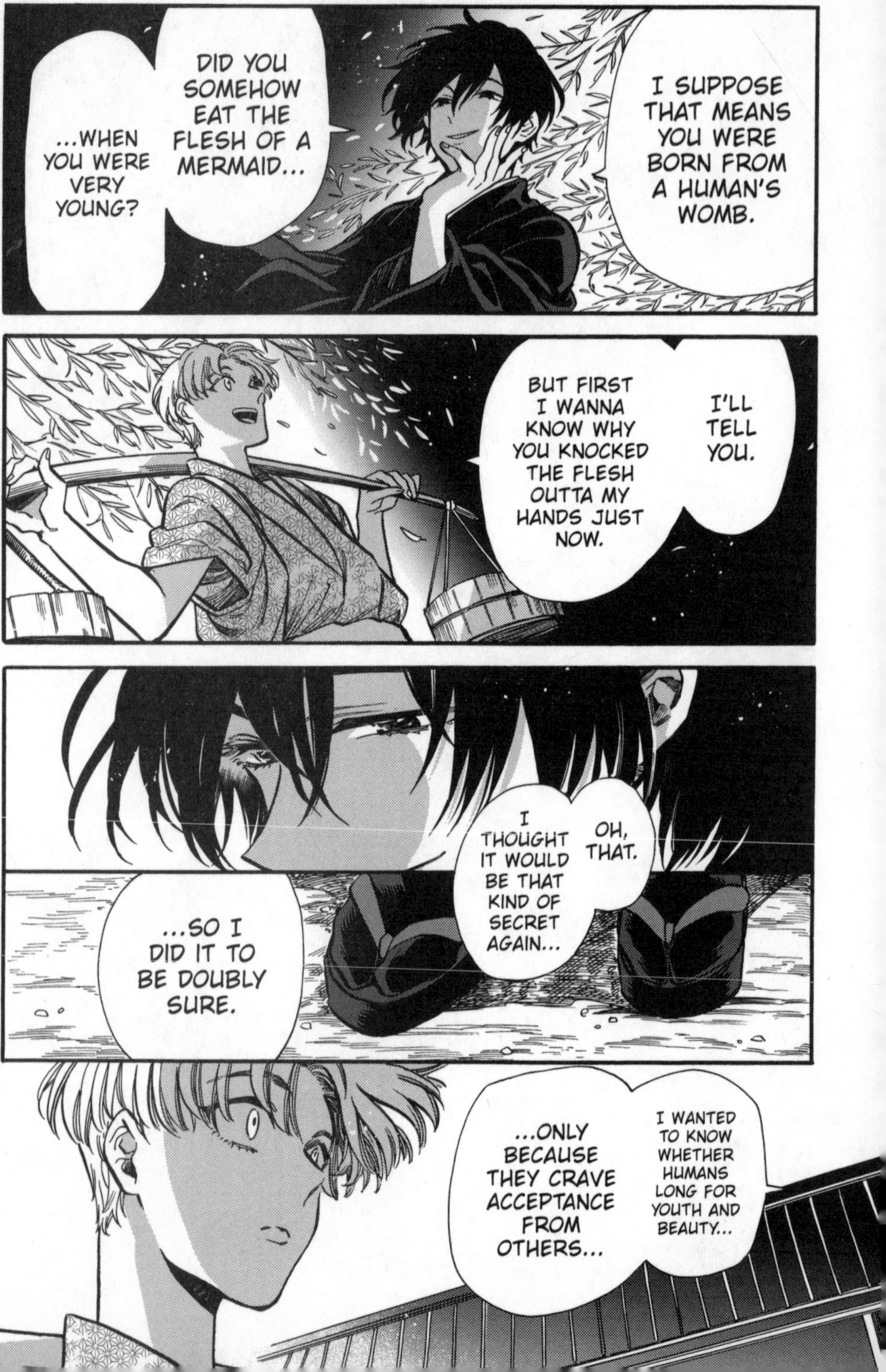
I SUPPOSE THAT MEANS YOU WERE BORN FROM A HUMAN'S WOMB.
DID YOU SOMEHOW EAT THE FLESH OF A MERMAID...
...WHEN YOU WERE VERY YOUNG?
I'LL TELL YOU.
BUT FIRST I WANNA KNOW WHY YOU KNOCKED THE FLESH OUTTA MY HANDS JUST NOW.
OH, THAT.
I THOUGHT IT WOULD BE THAT KIND OF SECRET AGAIN...
...SO I DID IT TO BE DOUBLY SURE.
I WANTED TO KNOW WHETHER HUMANS LONG FOR YOUTH AND BEAUTY...
...ONLY BECAUSE THEY CRAVE ACCEPTANCE FROM OTHERS...

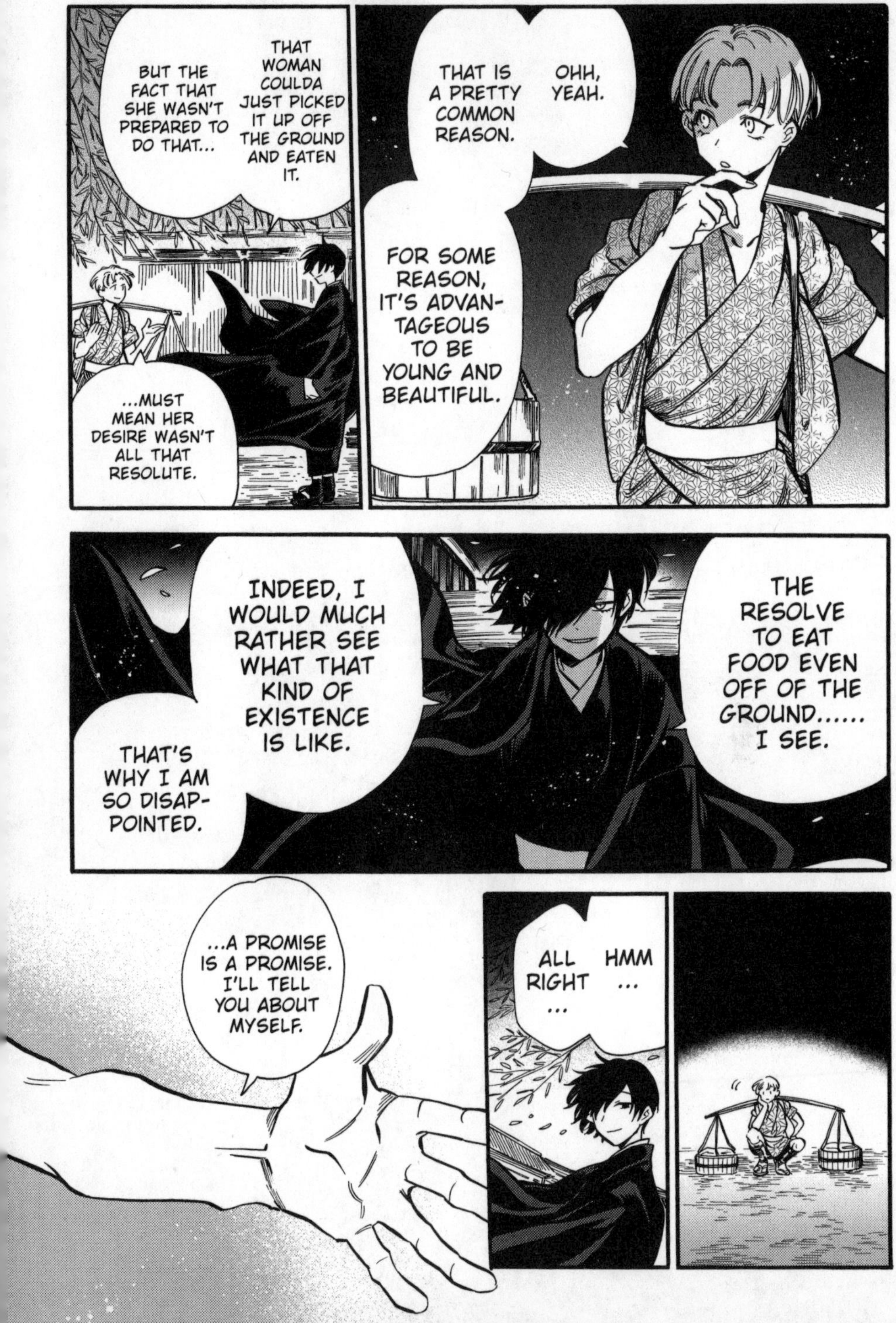
OHH, YEAH.
THAT IS A PRETTY COMMON REASON.
FOR SOME REASON, IT'S ADVANTAGEOUS TO BE YOUNG AND BEAUTIFUL.
THAT WOMAN COULDA JUST PICKED IT UP OFF THE GROUND AND EATEN IT.
BUT THE FACT THAT SHE WASN'T PREPARED TO DO THAT...
...MUST MEAN HER DESIRE WASN'T ALL THAT RESOLUTE.
THE RESOLVE TO EAT FOOD EVEN OFF OF THE GROUND...... I SEE.
INDEED, I WOULD MUCH RATHER SEE WHAT THAT KIND OF EXISTENCE IS LIKE.
THAT'S WHY I AM SO DISAPPOINTED.
HMM...
ALL RIGHT...
...A PROMISE IS A PROMISE. I'LL TELL YOU ABOUT MYSELF.

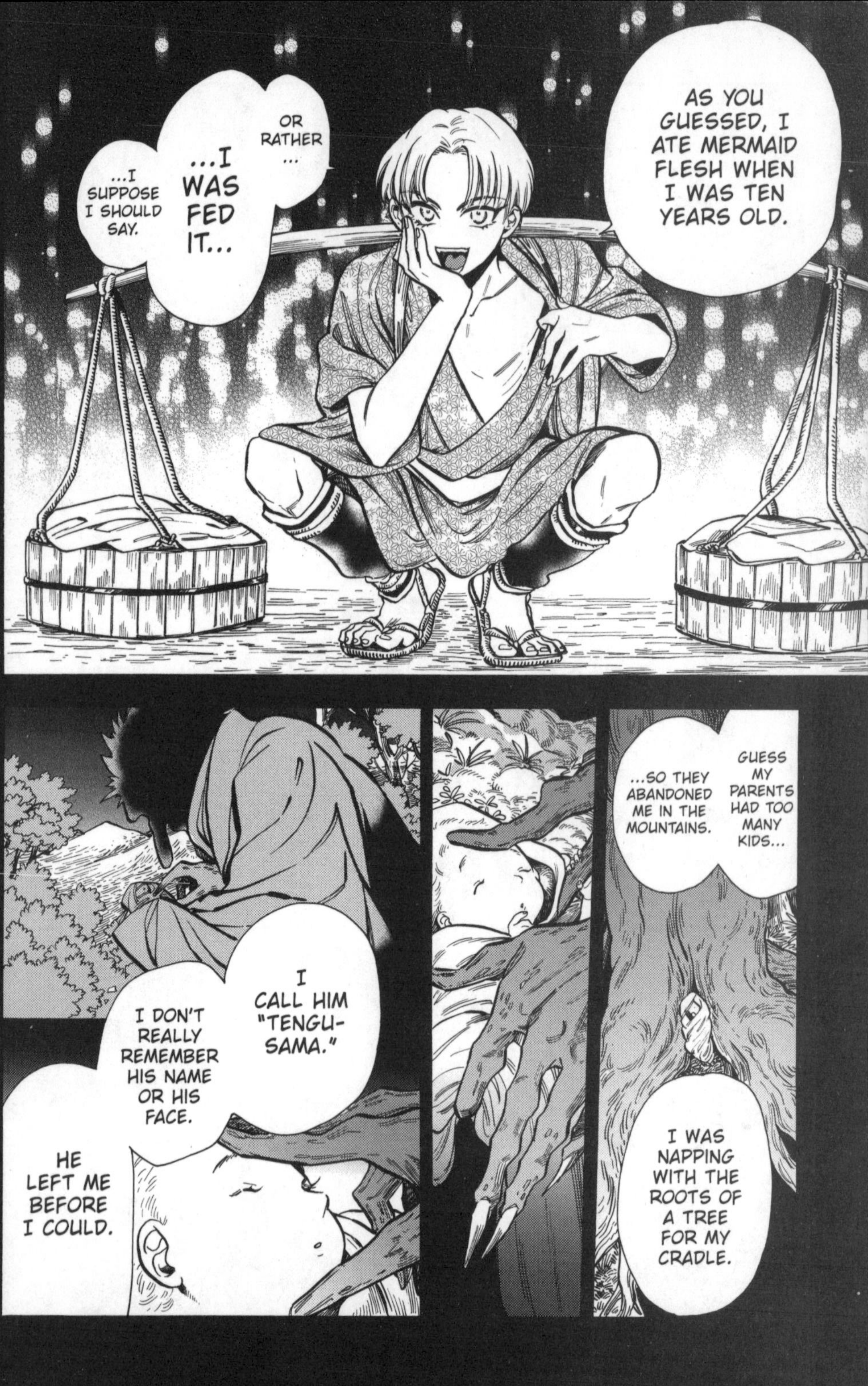
AS YOU GUESSED, I ATE MERMAID FLESH WHEN I WAS TEN YEARS OLD.
OR RATHER...
...I WAS FED IT...
...I SUPPOSE I SHOULD SAY.
GUESS MY PARENTS HAD TOO MANY KIDS...
...SO THEY ABANDONED ME IN THE MOUNTAINS.
I WAS NAPPING WITH THE ROOTS OF A TREE FOR MY CRADLE.
I CALL HIM "TENGU-SAMA."
I DON'T REALLY REMEMBER HIS NAME OR HIS FACE.
HE LEFT ME BEFORE I COULD.

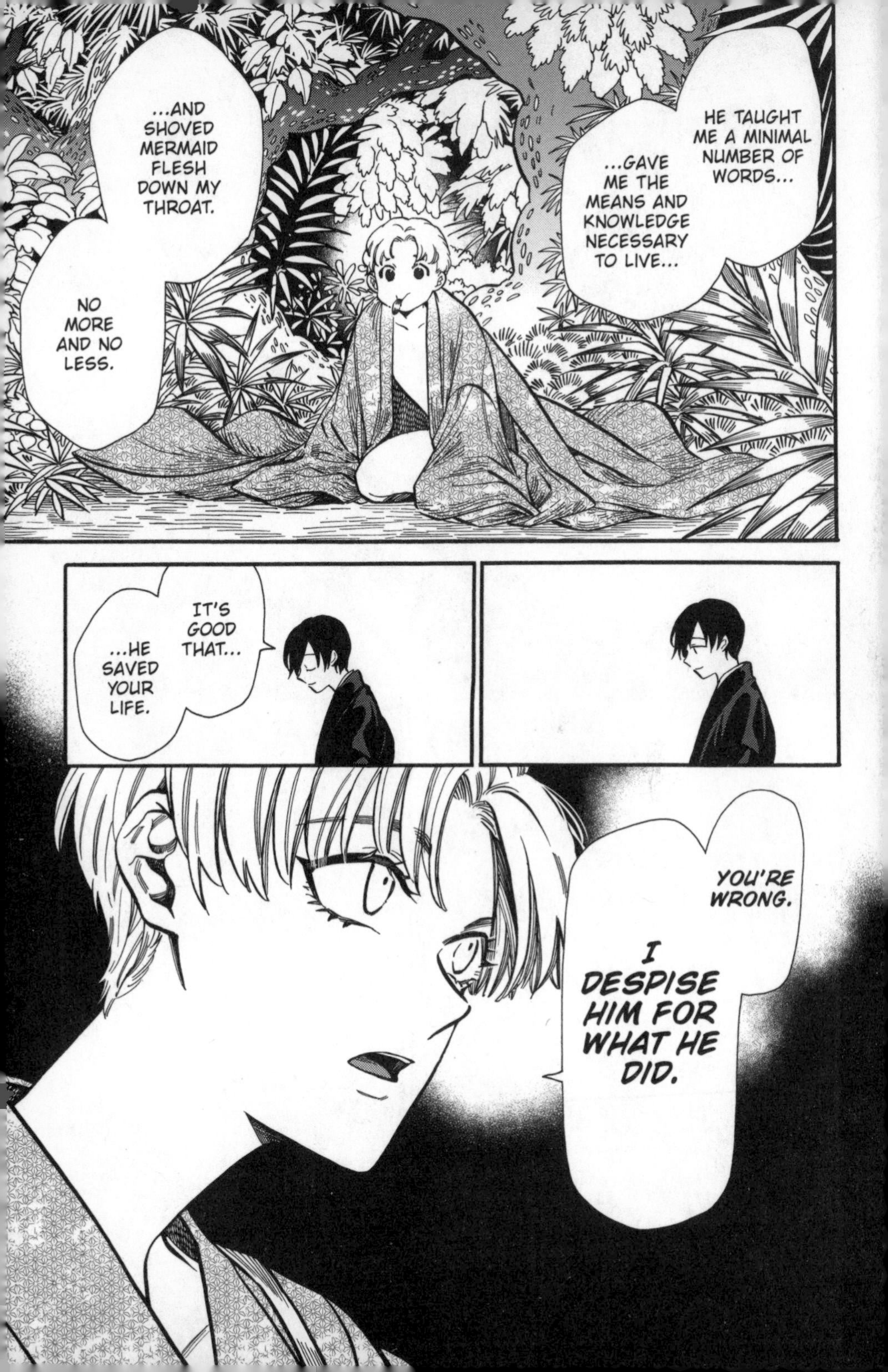
HE TAUGHT ME A MINIMAL NUMBER OF WORDS...
...GAVE ME THE MEANS AND KNOWLEDGE NECESSARY TO LIVE...
...AND SHOVED MERMAID FLESH DOWN MY THROAT.
NO MORE AND NO LESS.
IT'S GOOD THAT...
...HE SAVED YOUR LIFE.
YOU'RE WRONG.
I DESPISE HIM FOR WHAT HE DID.

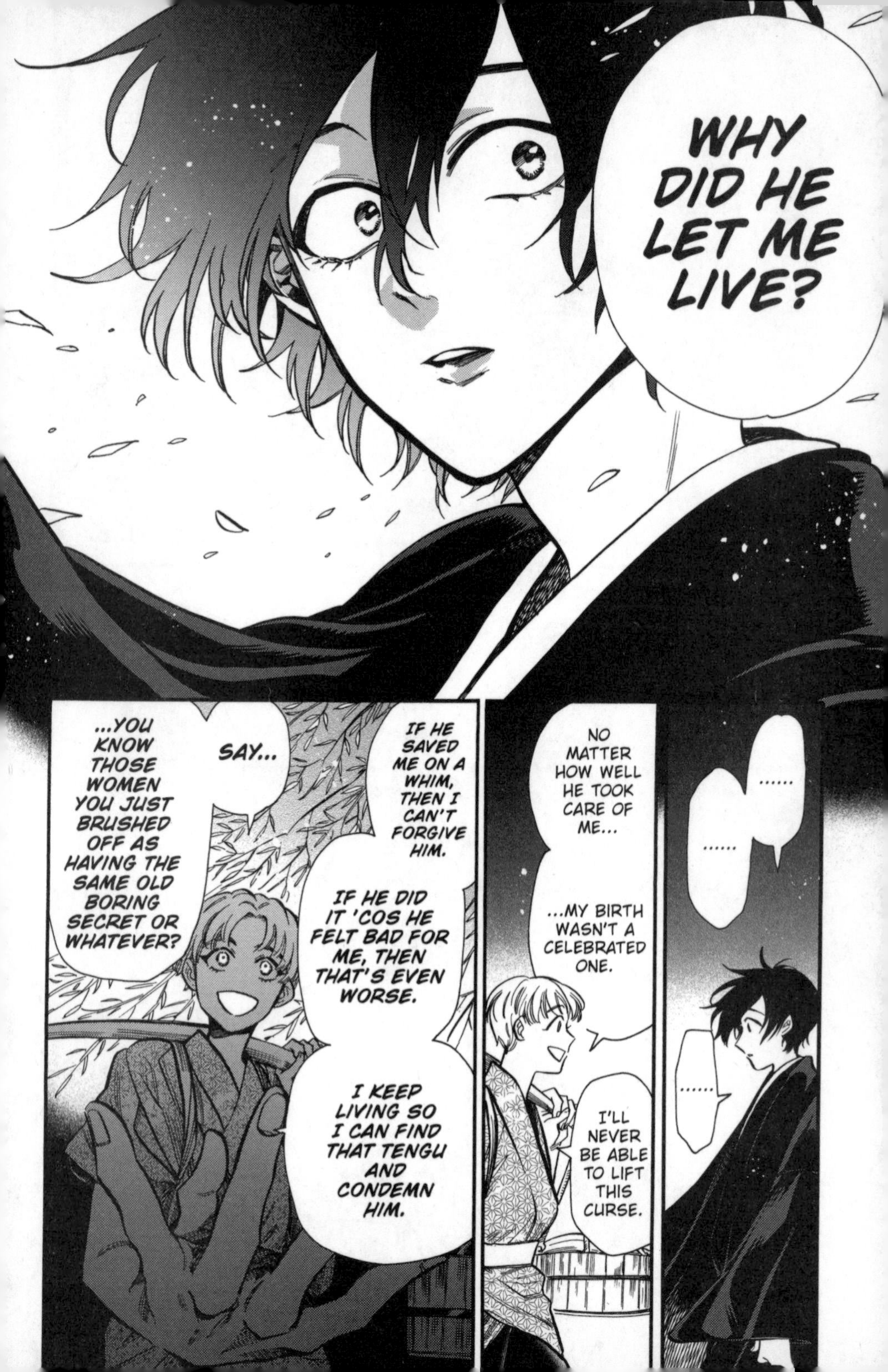
WHY DID HE LET ME LIVE?
......
......
......
NO MATTER HOW WELL HE TOOK CARE OF ME...
...MY BIRTH WASN'T A CELEBRATED ONE.
I'LL NEVER BE ABLE TO LIFT THIS CURSE.
IF HE SAVED ME ON A WHIM, THEN I CAN'T FORGIVE HIM.
SAY...
...YOU KNOW THOSE WOMEN YOU JUST BRUSHED OFF AS HAVING THE SAME OLD BORING SECRET OR WHATEVER?
IF HE DID IT 'COS HE FELT BAD FOR ME, THEN THAT'S EVEN WORSE.
I KEEP LIVING SO I CAN FIND THAT TENGU AND CONDEMN HIM.

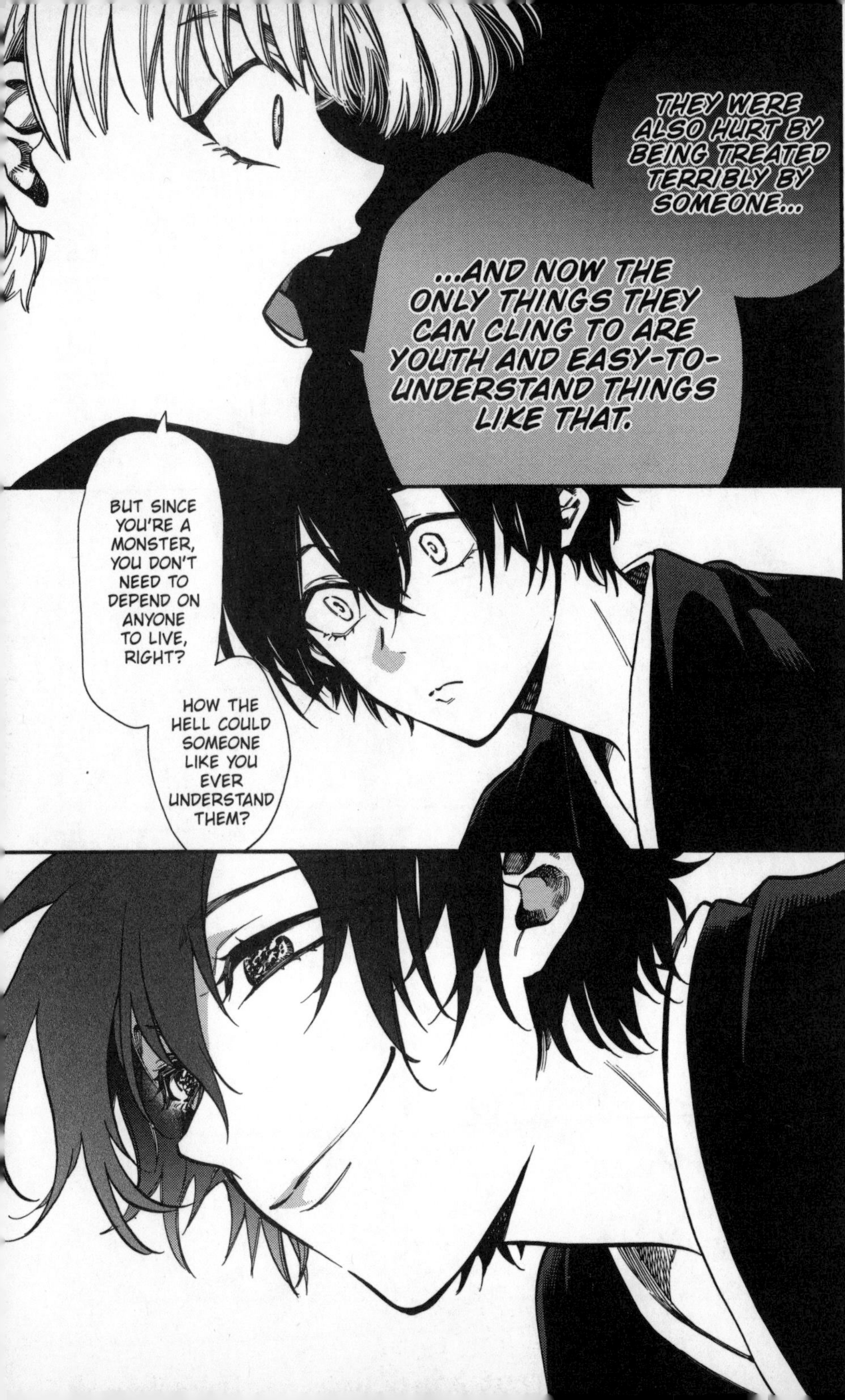
THEY WERE ALSO HURT BY BEING TREATED TERRIBLY BY SOMEONE...
...AND NOW THE ONLY THINGS THEY CAN CLING TO ARE YOUTH AND EASY-TO-UNDERSTAND THINGS LIKE THAT.
BUT SINCE YOU'RE A MONSTER, YOU DON'T NEED TO DEPEND ON ANYONE TO LIVE, RIGHT?
HOW THE HELL COULD SOMEONE LIKE YOU EVER UNDERSTAND THEM?

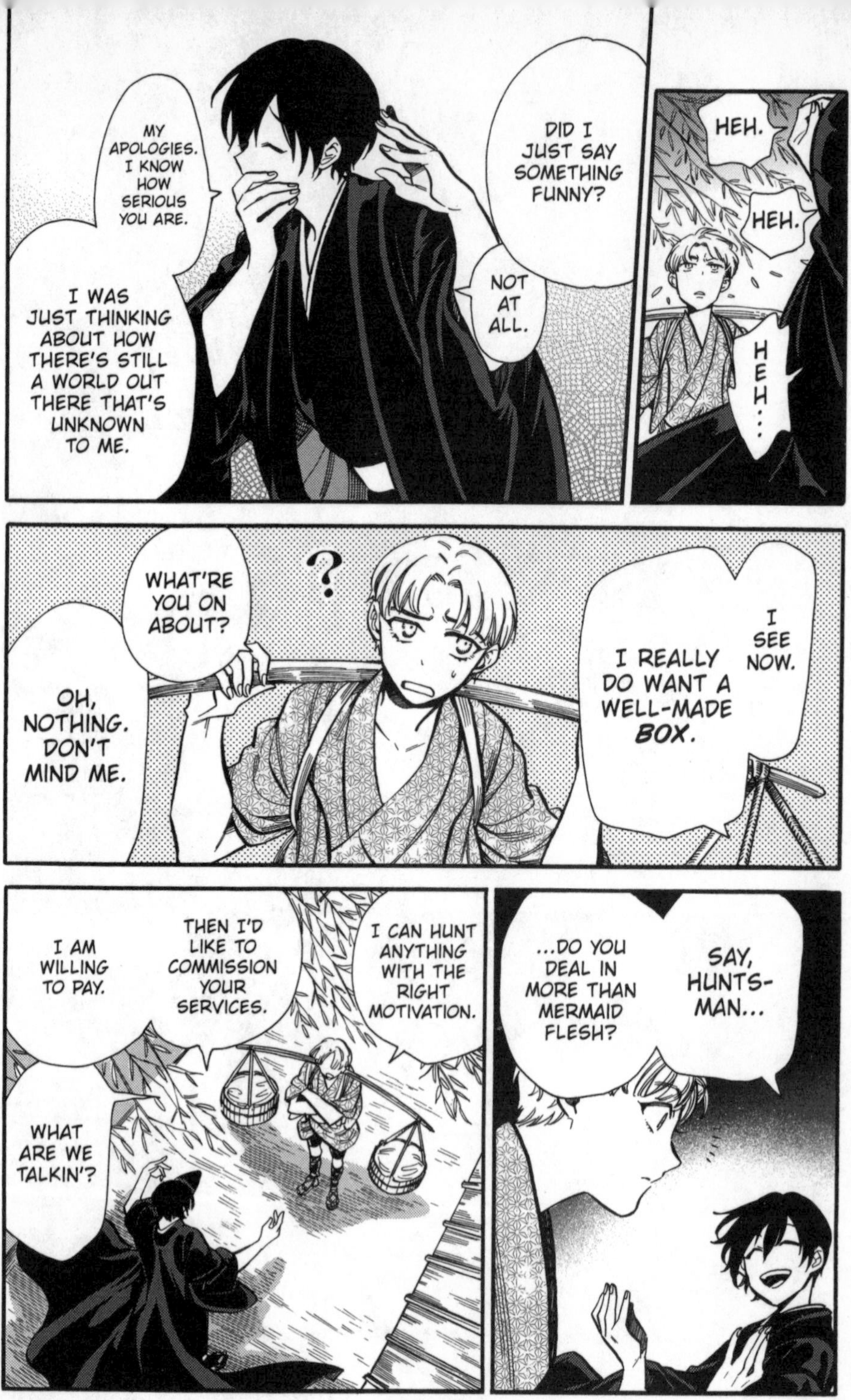
HEH.
HEH.
HEH...
DID I JUST SAY SOMETHING FUNNY?
NOT AT ALL.
MY APOLOGIES. I KNOW HOW SERIOUS YOU ARE.
I WAS JUST THINKING ABOUT HOW THERE'S STILL A WORLD OUT THERE THAT'S UNKNOWN TO ME.
I SEE NOW.
I REALLY DO WANT A WELL-MADE BOX.
?
WHAT'RE YOU ON ABOUT?
OH, NOTHING. DON'T MIND ME.
SAY, HUNTS-MAN...
...DO YOU DEAL IN MORE THAN MERMAID FLESH?
I CAN HUNT ANYTHING WITH THE RIGHT MOTIVATION.
THEN I'D LIKE TO COMMISSION YOUR SERVICES.
I AM WILLING TO PAY.
WHAT ARE WE TALKIN'?

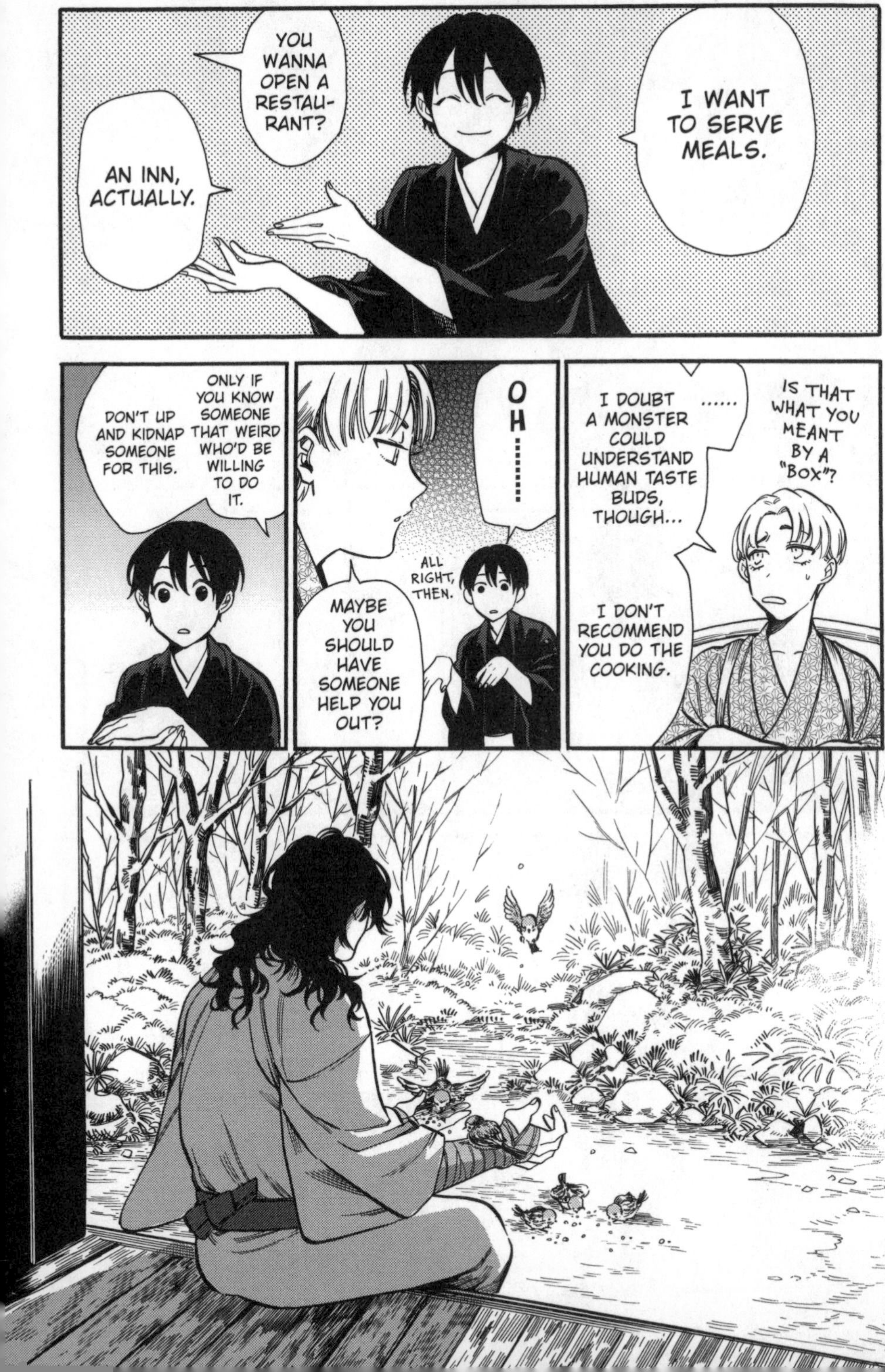
I WANT TO SERVE MEALS.
YOU WANNA OPEN A RESTAURANT?
AN INN, ACTUALLY.
IS THAT WHAT YOU MEANT BY A "BOX"?
......
I DOUBT A MONSTER COULD UNDERSTAND HUMAN TASTE BUDS, THOUGH...
I DON'T RECOMMEND YOU DO THE COOKING.
OH......
ALL RIGHT, THEN.
MAYBE YOU SHOULD HAVE SOMEONE HELP YOU OUT?
ONLY IF YOU KNOW SOMEONE THAT WEIRD WHO'D BE WILLING TO DO IT.
DON'T UP AND KIDNAP SOMEONE FOR THIS.

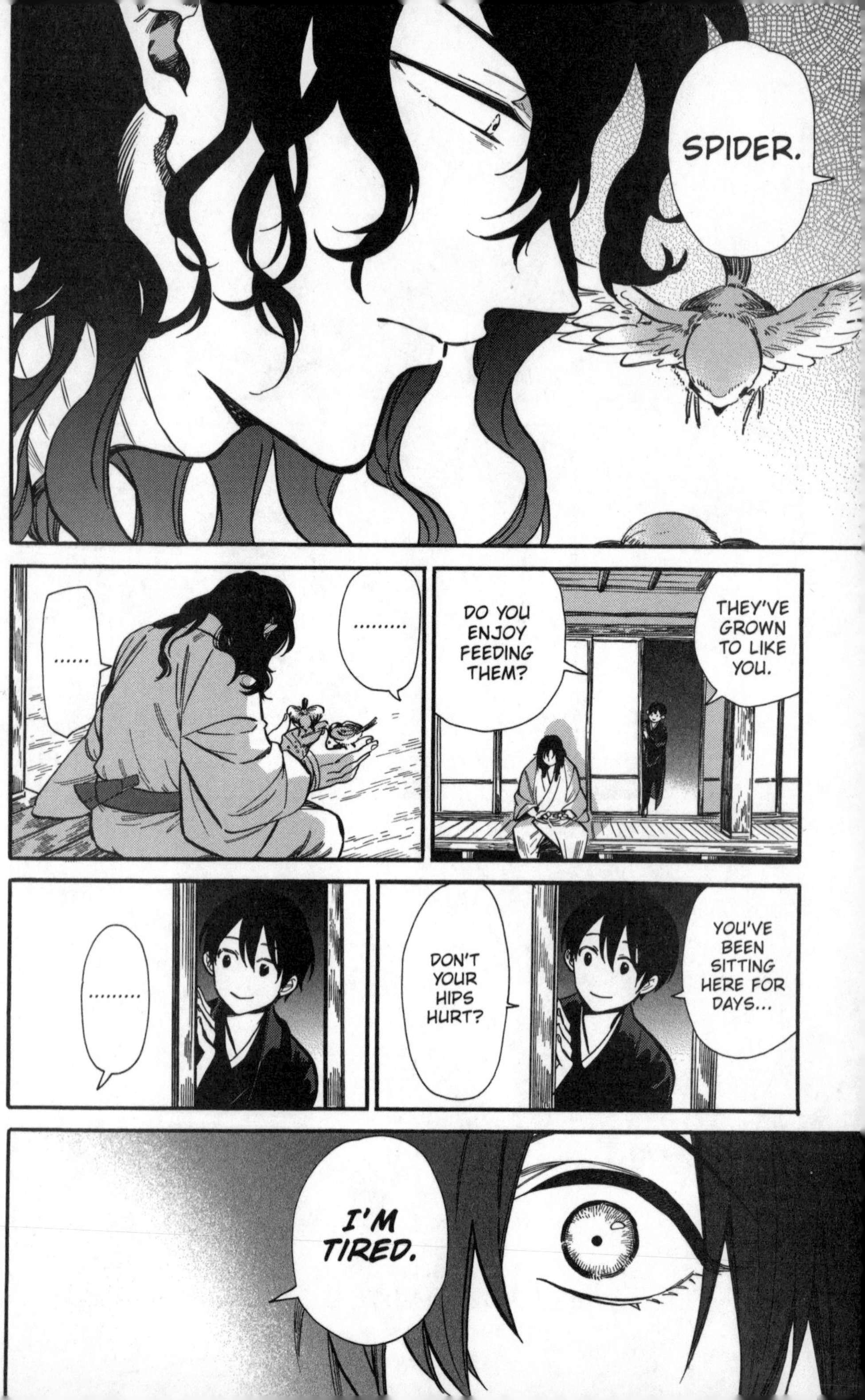
SPIDER.
THEY'VE GROWN TO LIKE YOU.
DO YOU ENJOY FEEDING THEM?
....
......
YOU'VE BEEN SITTING HERE FOR DAYS...
DON'T YOUR HIPS HURT?
....
I'M TIRED.

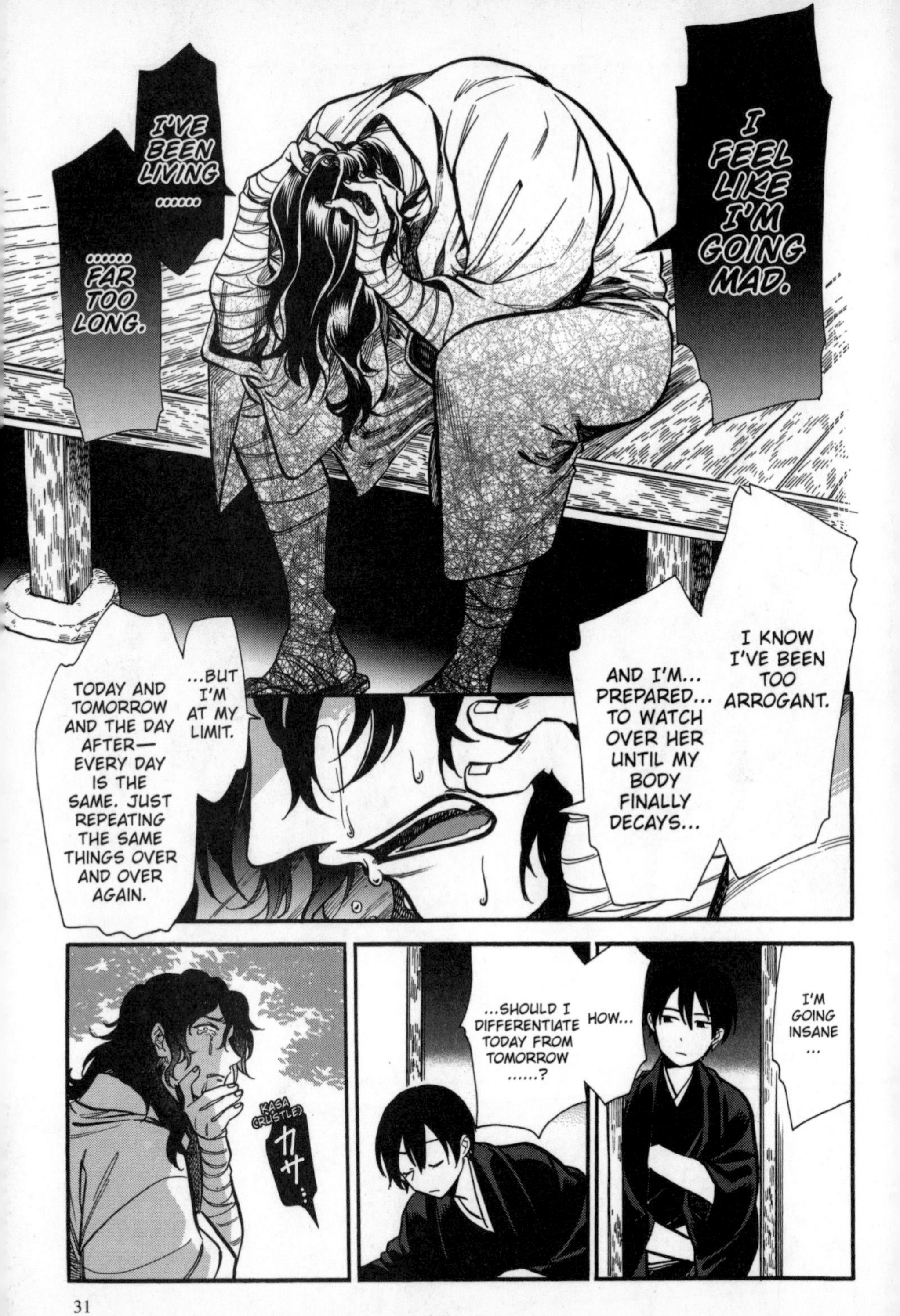
I FEEL LIKE I'M GOING MAD.
I'VE BEEN LIVING ......
...... FAR TOO LONG.
I KNOW I'VE BEEN TOO ARROGANT.
AND I'M... PREPARED... TO WATCH OVER HER UNTIL MY BODY FINALLY DECAYS...
...BUT I'M AT MY LIMIT.
TODAY AND TOMORROW AND THE DAY AFTER— EVERY DAY IS THE SAME. JUST REPEATING THE SAME THINGS OVER AND OVER AGAIN.
I'M GOING INSANE ...
HOW...
...SHOULD I DIFFERENTIATE TODAY FROM TOMORROW ......?
KASA (RUSTLE)
カサ…

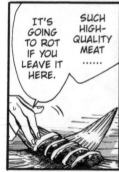

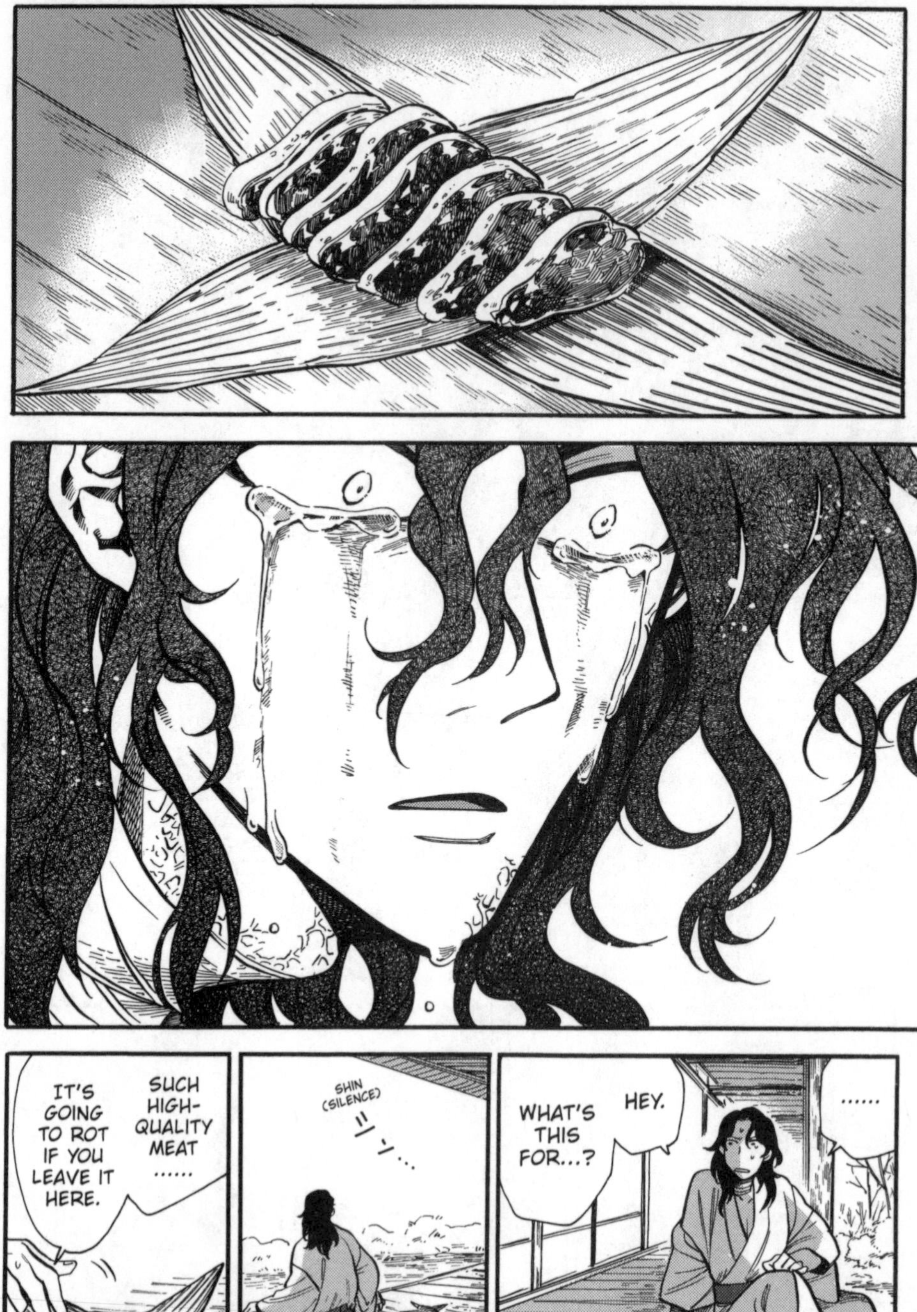
......
HEY.
WHAT'S THIS FOR...?
SHIN (SILENCE)
SUCH HIGH-QUALITY MEAT ......
IT'S GOING TO ROT IF YOU LEAVE IT HERE.

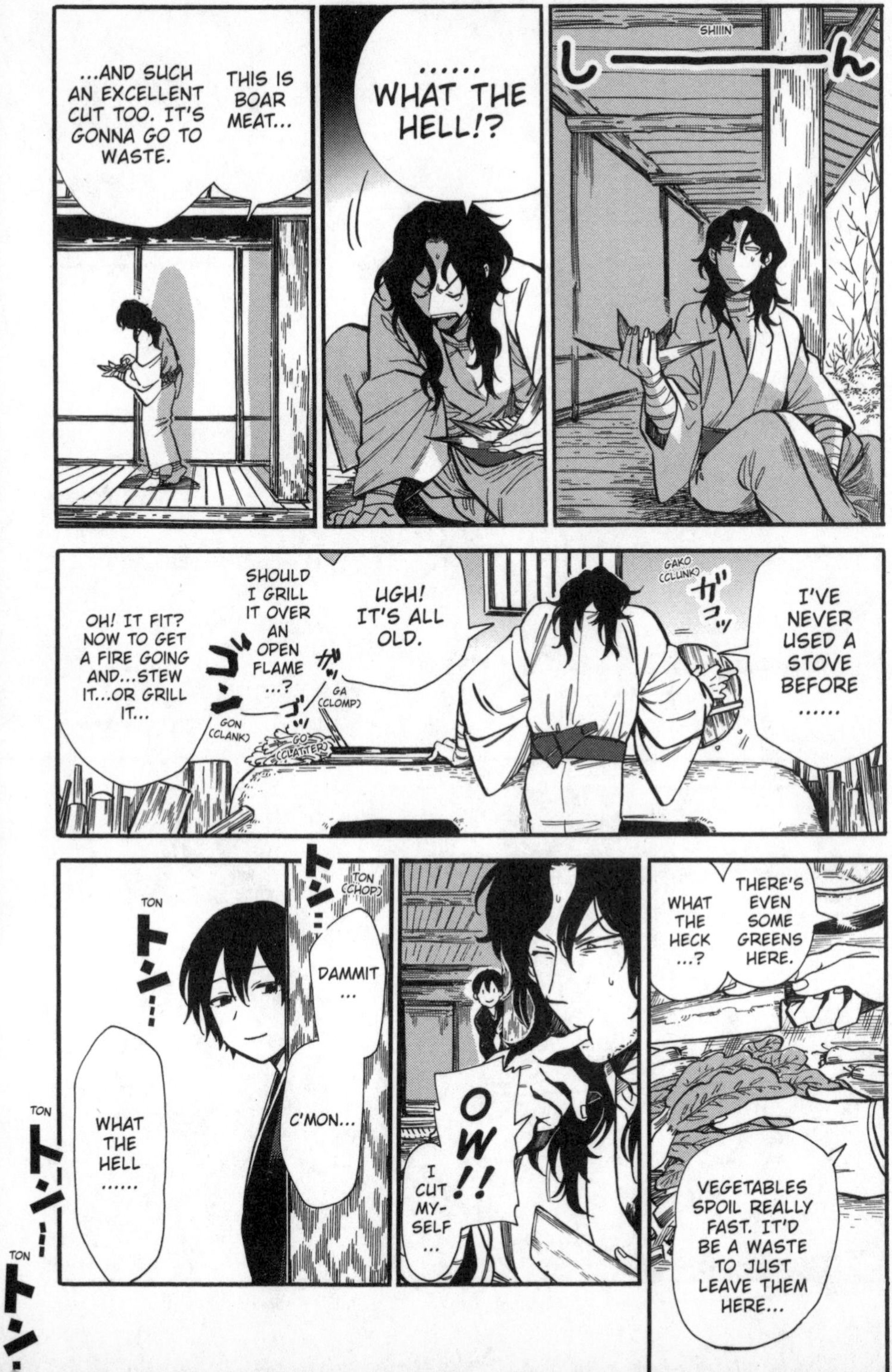
SHIIN
しーーーん
...... WHAT THE HELL!?
THIS IS BOAR MEAT...
...AND SUCH AN EXCELLENT CUT TOO. IT'S GONNA GO TO WASTE.
GAKO (CLUNK)
I'VE NEVER USED A STOVE BEFORE ......
UGH! IT'S ALL OLD.
SHOULD I GRILL IT OVER AN OPEN FLAME ...?
GA (CLOMP)
GO (CLATTER)
OH! IT FIT? NOW TO GET A FIRE GOING AND...STEW IT...OR GRILL IT...
GON (CLANK)
THERE'S EVEN SOME GREENS HERE.
WHAT THE HECK ...?
VEGETABLES SPOIL REALLY FAST. IT'D BE A WASTE TO JUST LEAVE THEM HERE...
DAMMIT ...
OW!!
I CUT MY-SELF ...
C'MON...
TON (CHOP)
TON
WHAT THE HELL ......
TON
TON

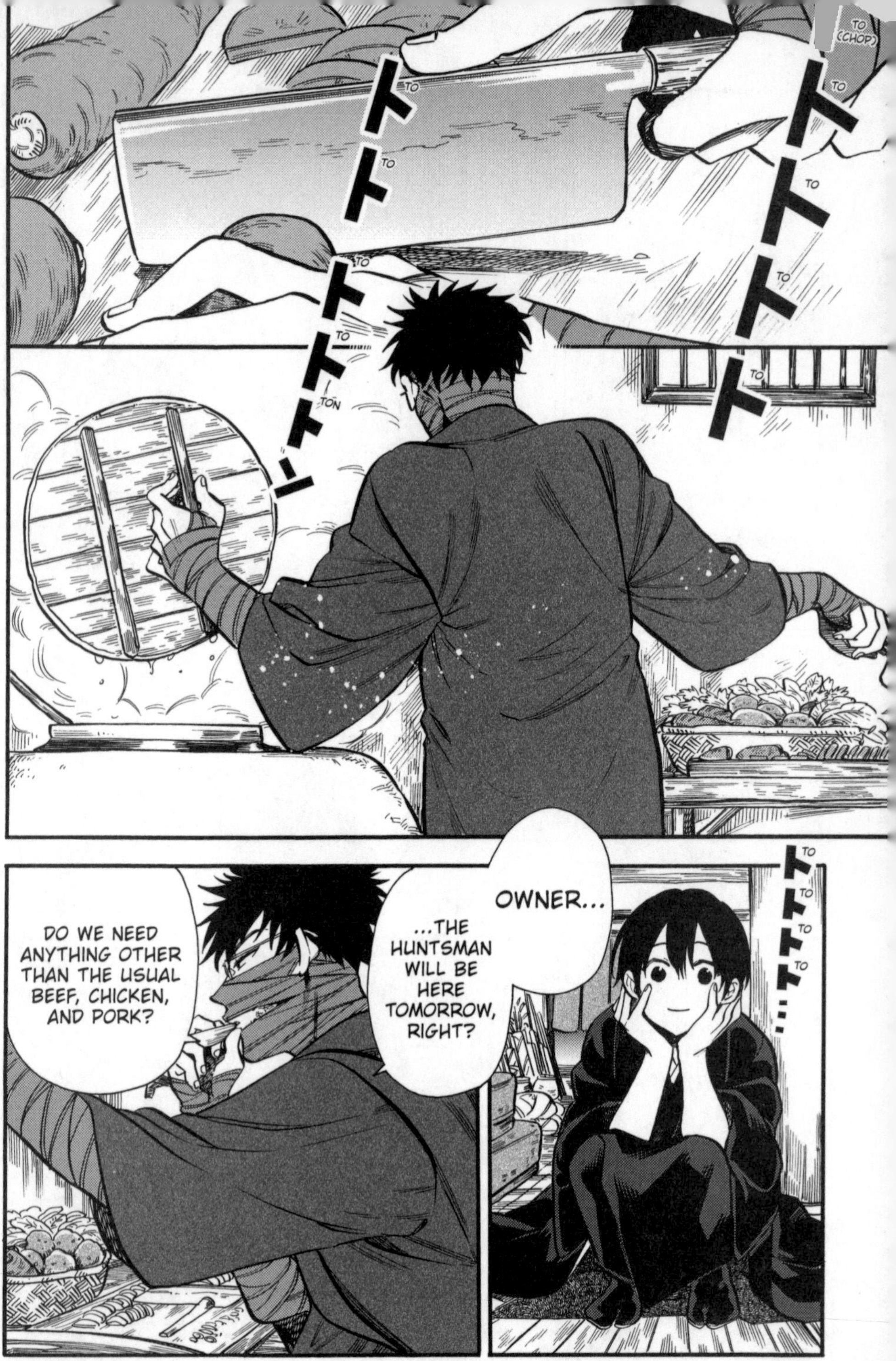

TO (CHOP)
TO
TO
TO
TO
TO
TO
TO
TON
TO
TO
TO
TO
OWNER...
...THE HUNTSMAN WILL BE HERE TOMORROW, RIGHT?
DO WE NEED ANYTHING OTHER THAN THE USUAL BEEF, CHICKEN, AND PORK?

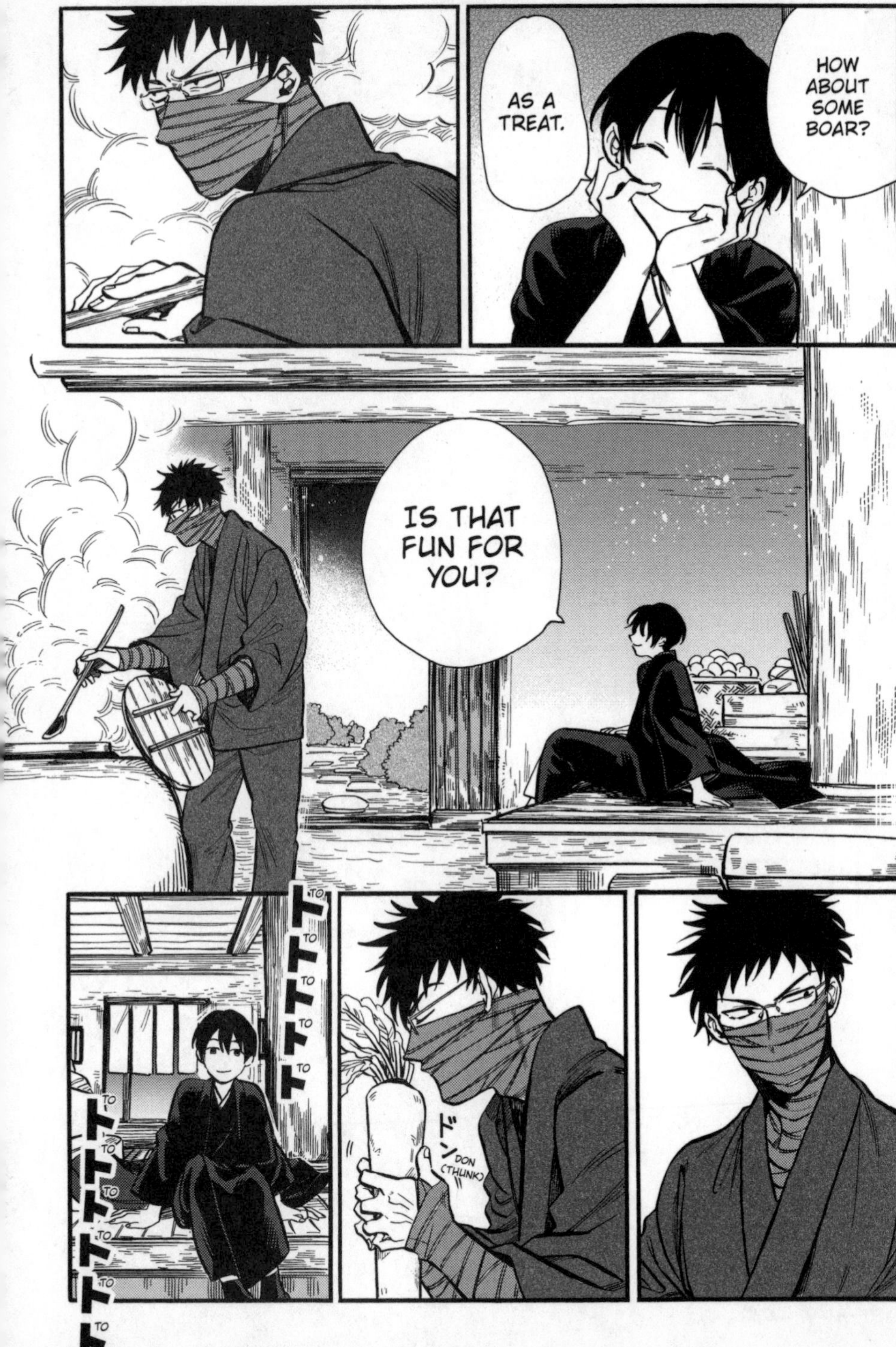
HOW ABOUT SOME BOAR?
AS A TREAT.
IS THAT FUN FOR YOU?
ドン DON (THUNK)
トトトトトトト TO TO TO TO TO TO TO
トトトトトトト TO TO TO TO TO TO TO

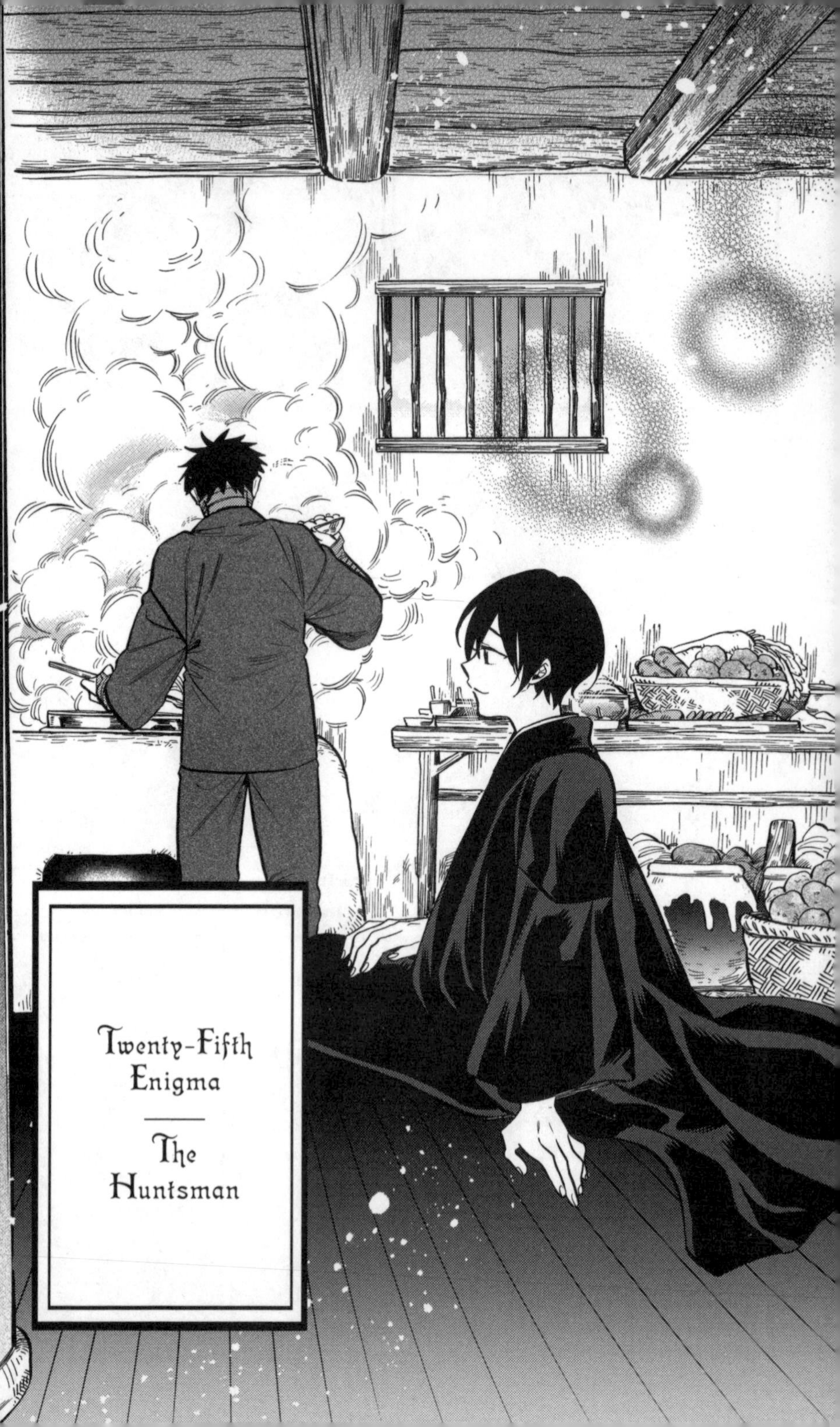
Twenty-Fifth Enigma
The Huntsman

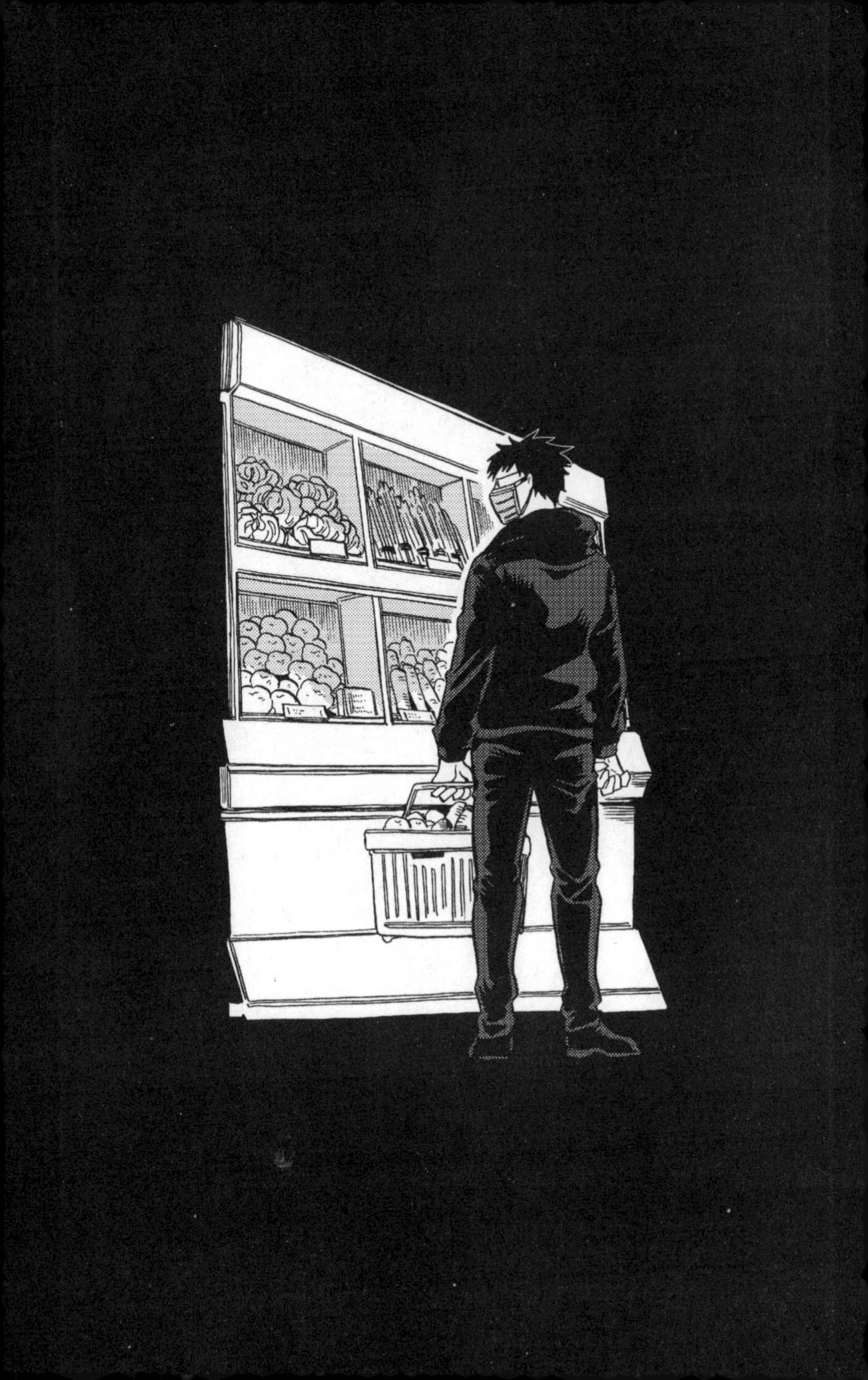

Phantom Tales of the Night

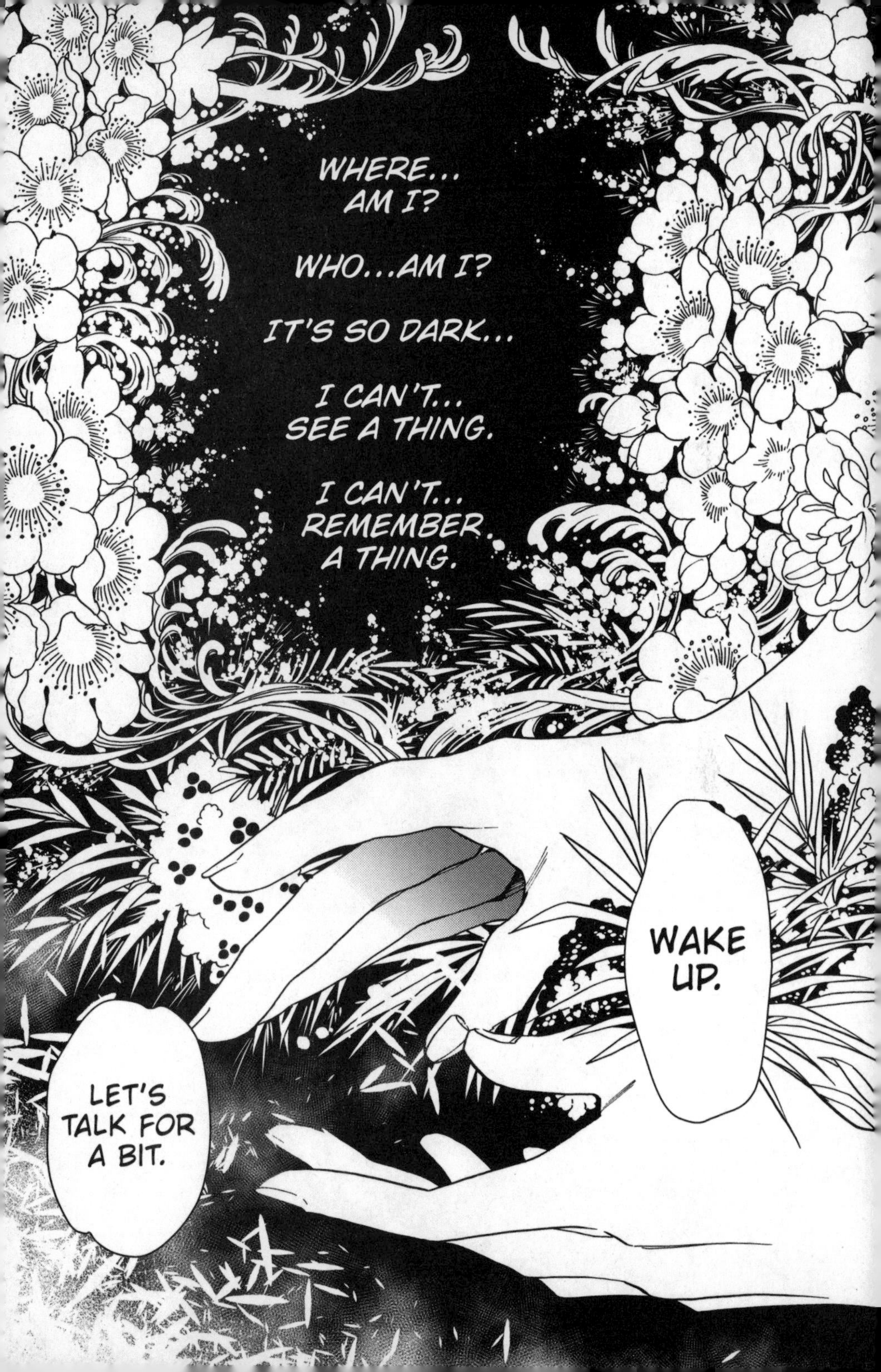
WHERE... AM I?
WHO...AM I?
IT'S SO DARK...
I CAN'T... SEE A THING.
I CAN'T... REMEMBER A THING.
WAKE UP.
LET'S TALK FOR A BIT.

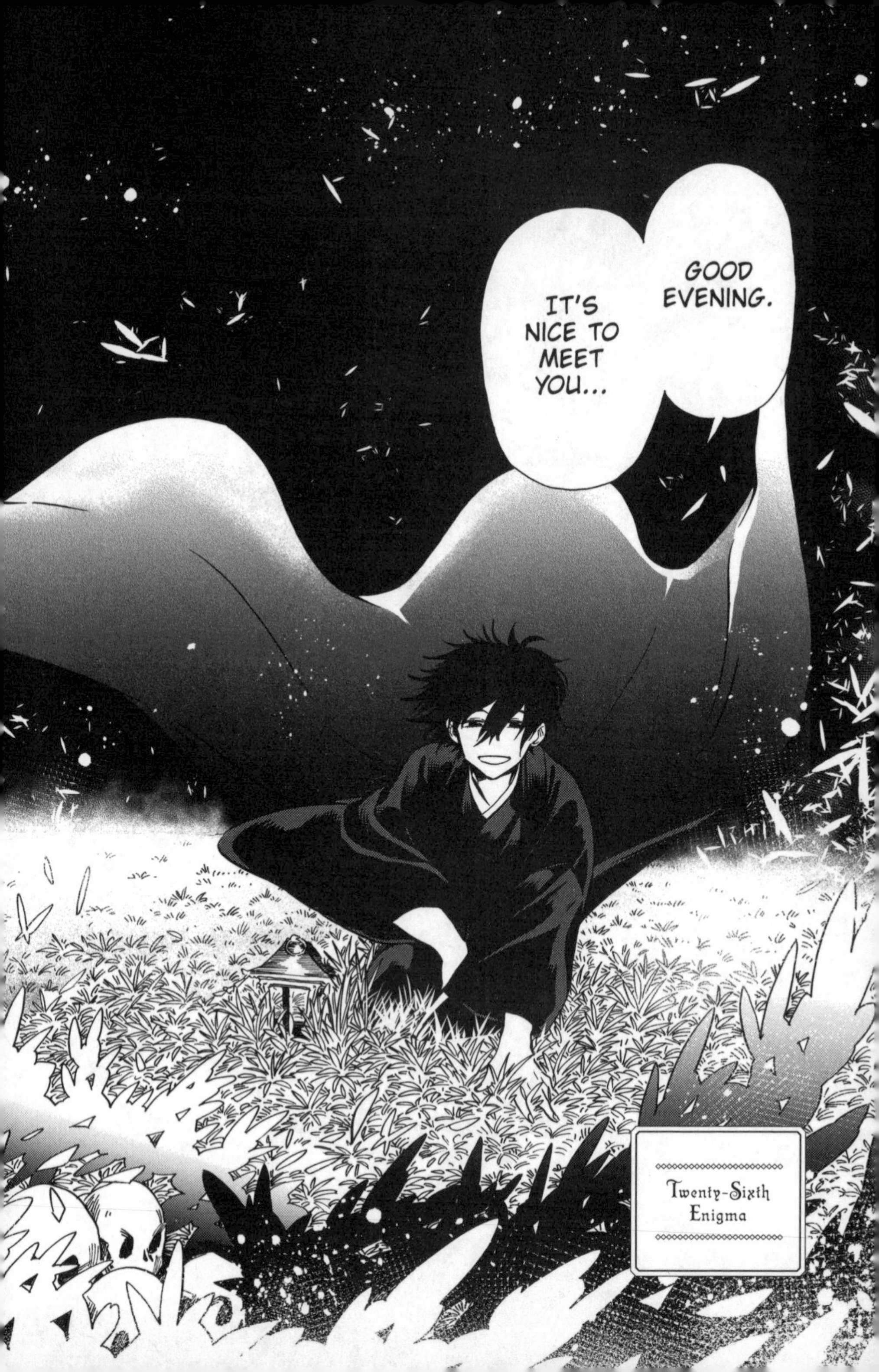
GOOD EVENING.
IT'S NICE TO MEET YOU...
Twenty-Sixth Enigma

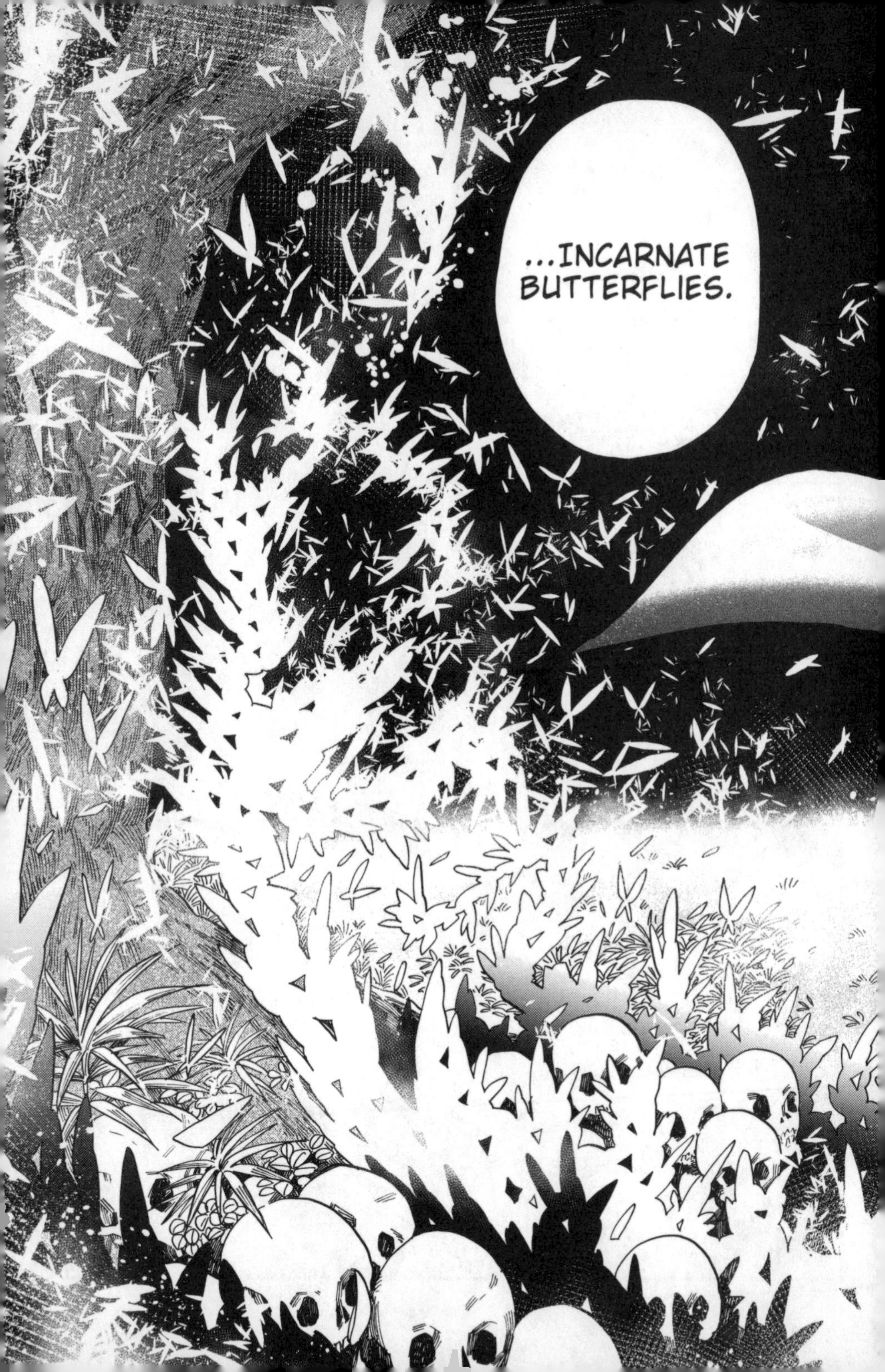
...INCARNATE BUTTERFLIES.

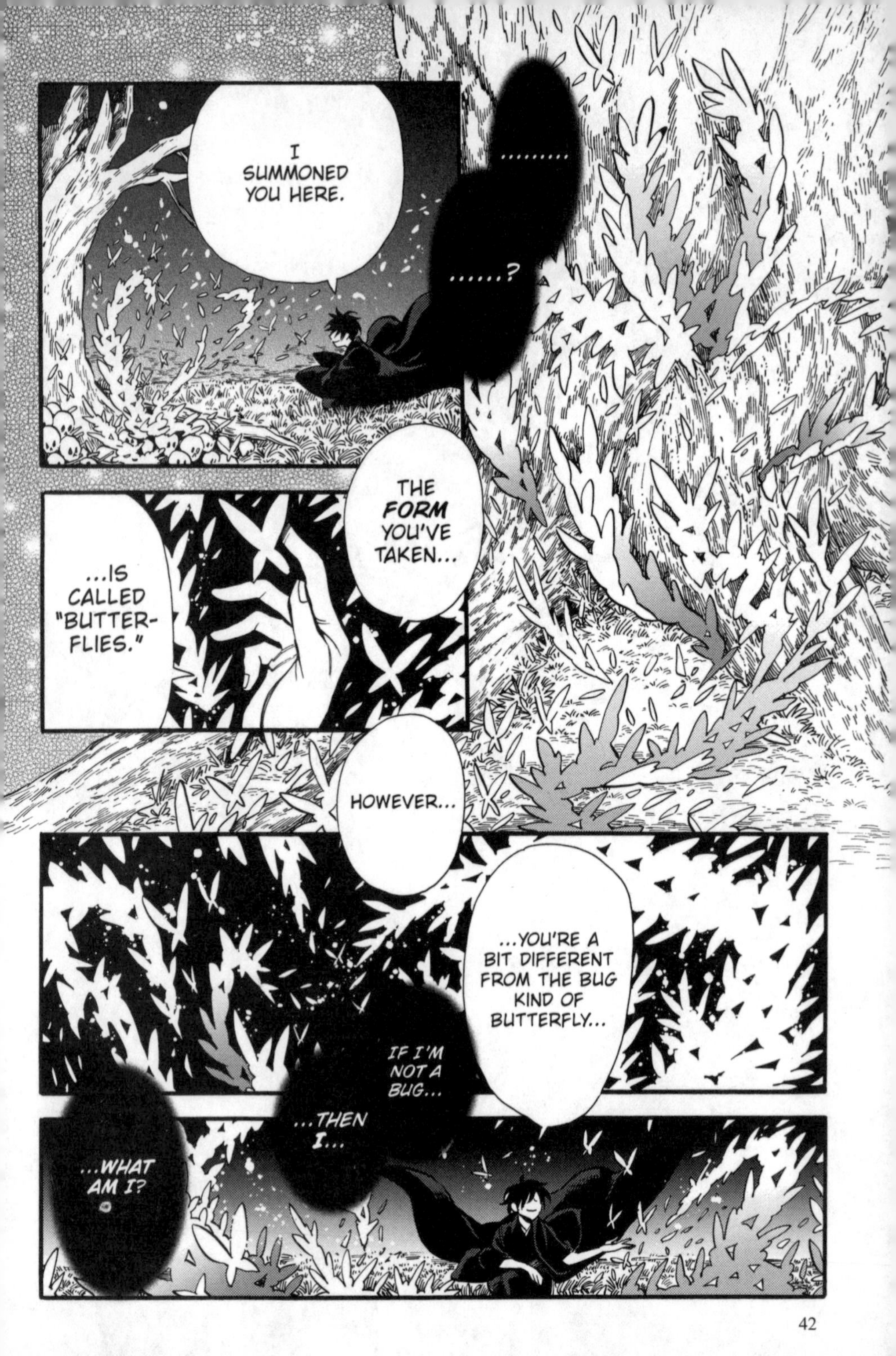
....
I SUMMONED YOU HERE.
......?
THE *FORM* YOU'VE TAKEN...
...IS CALLED "BUTTER-FLIES."
HOWEVER...
...YOU'RE A BIT DIFFERENT FROM THE BUG KIND OF BUTTERFLY...
IF I'M NOT A BUG...
...THEN I...
...WHAT AM I?

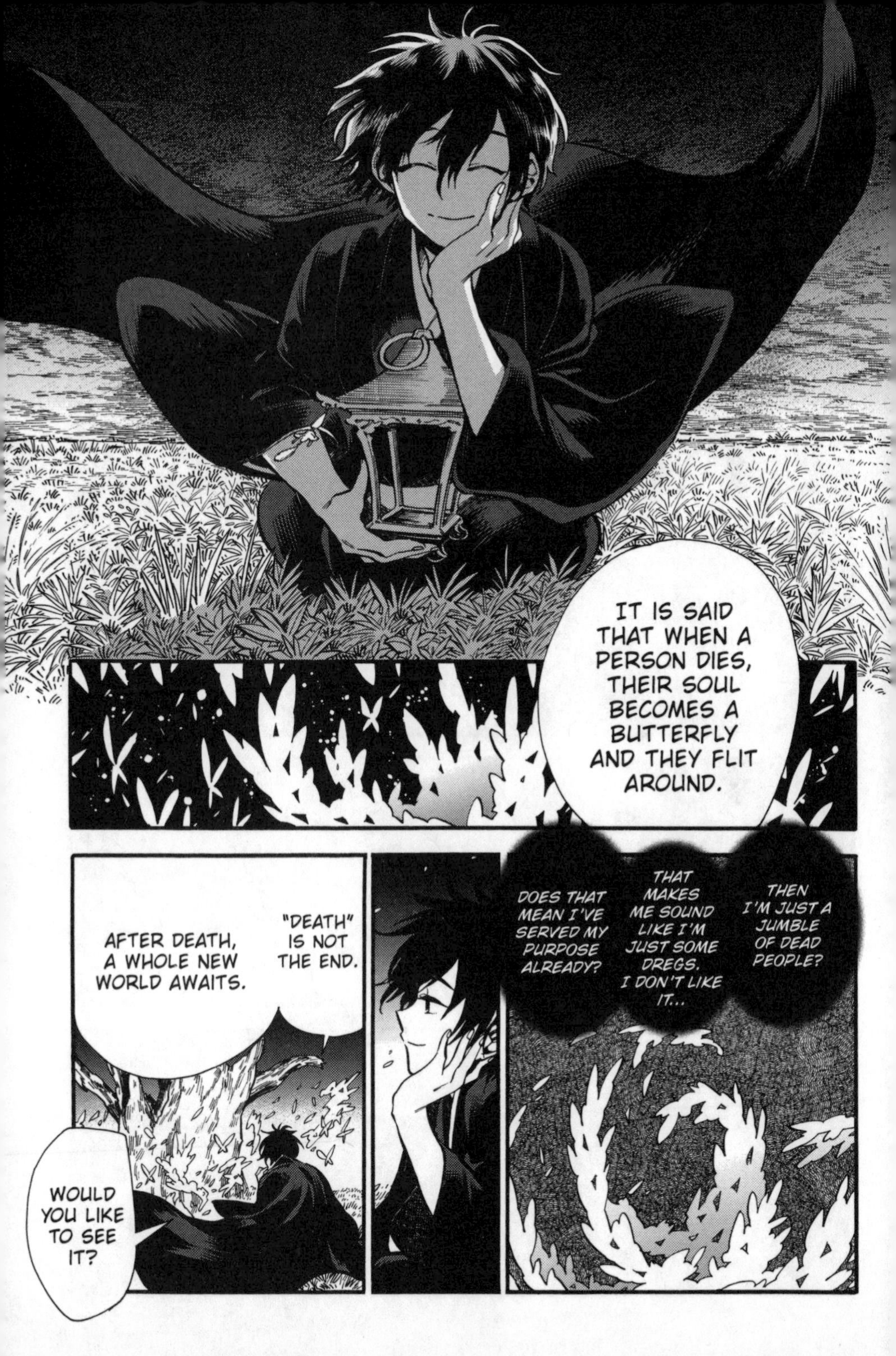
IT IS SAID THAT WHEN A PERSON DIES, THEIR SOUL BECOMES A BUTTERFLY AND THEY FLIT AROUND.
THEN I'M JUST A JUMBLE OF DEAD PEOPLE?
THAT MAKES ME SOUND LIKE I'M JUST SOME DREGS. I DON'T LIKE IT...
DOES THAT MEAN I'VE SERVED MY PURPOSE ALREADY?
"DEATH" IS NOT THE END.
AFTER DEATH, A WHOLE NEW WORLD AWAITS.
WOULD YOU LIKE TO SEE IT?

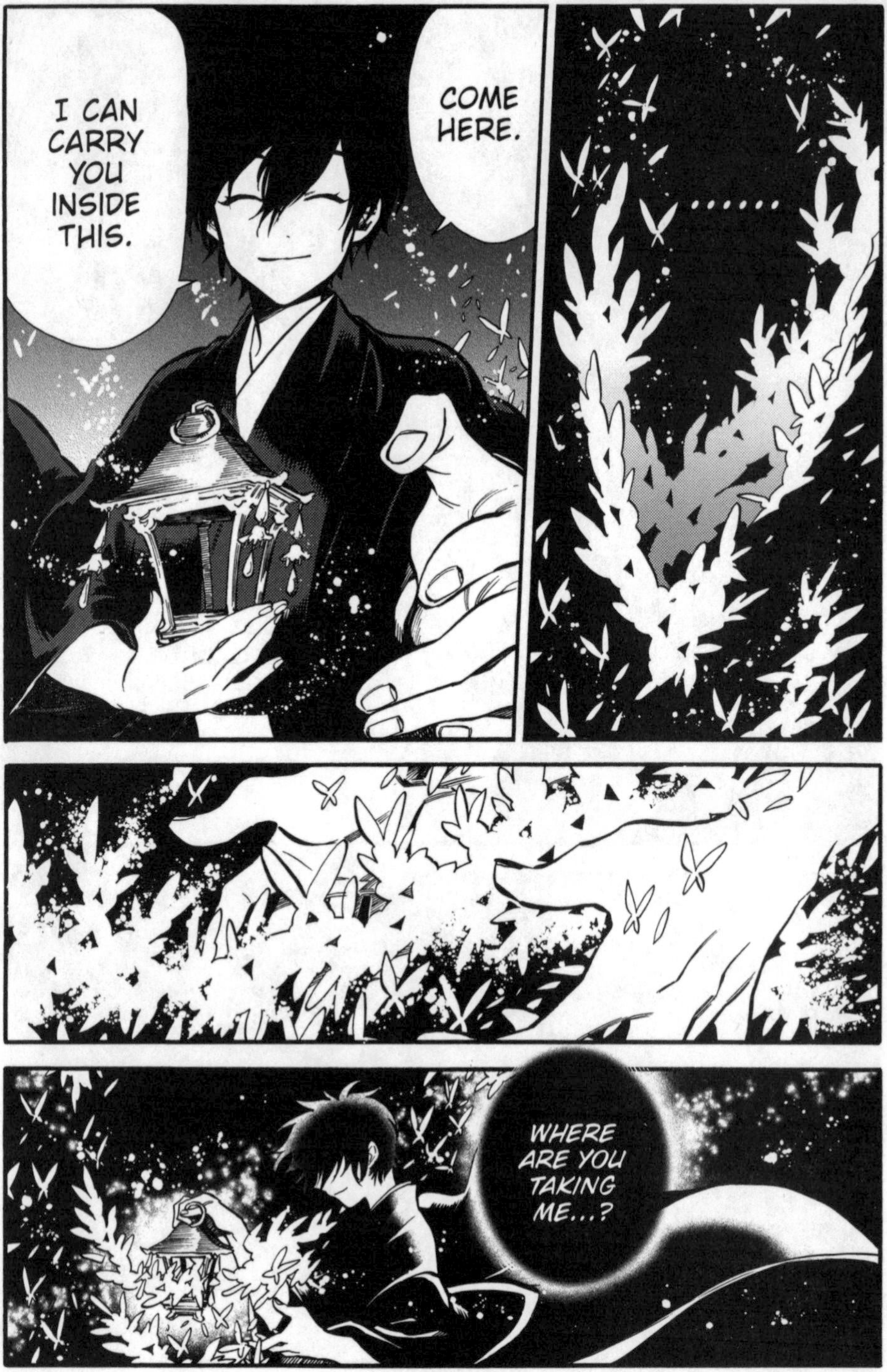
……
COME HERE.
I CAN CARRY YOU INSIDE THIS.
WHERE ARE YOU TAKING ME…?

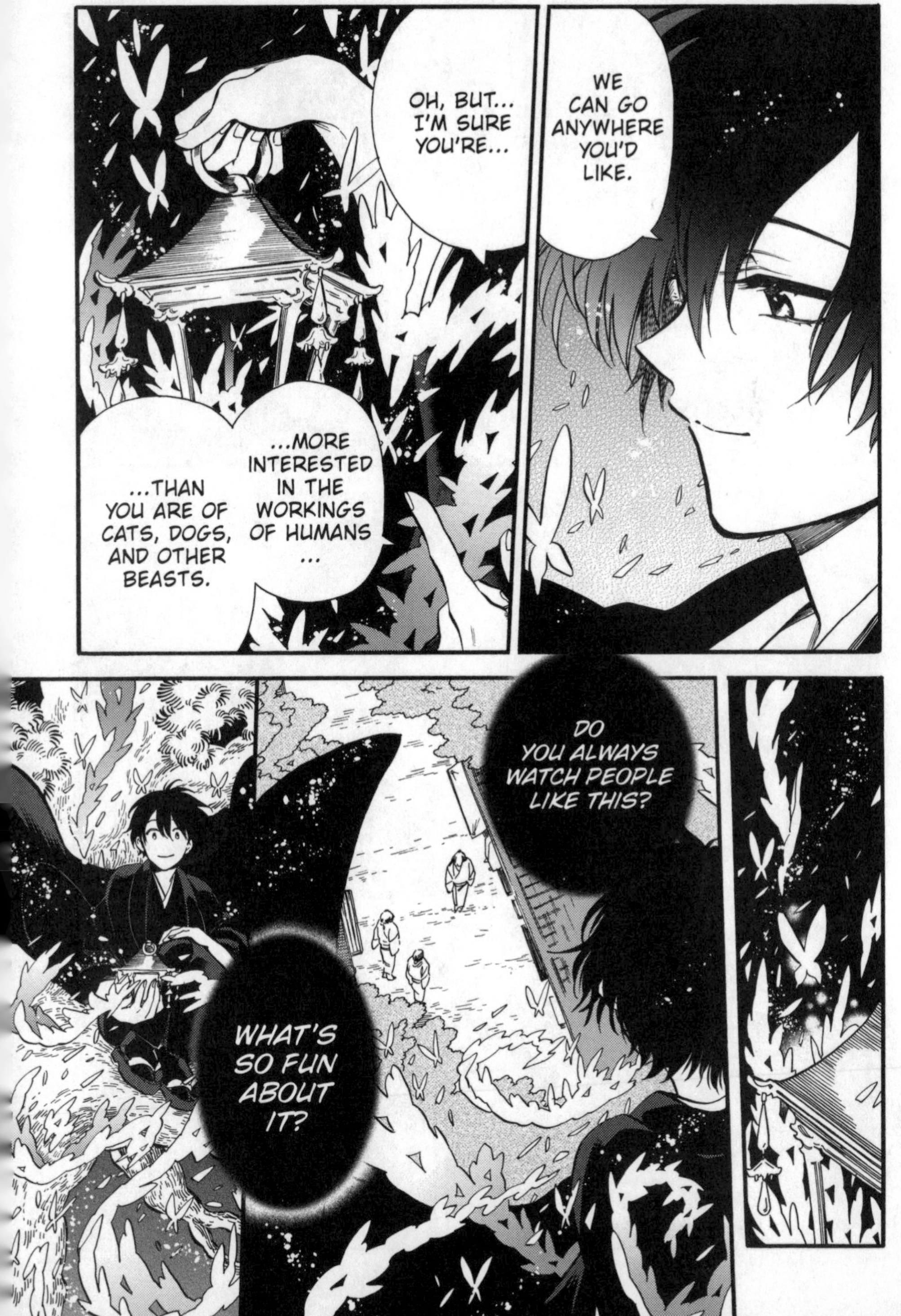
WE CAN GO ANYWHERE YOU'D LIKE.
OH, BUT... I'M SURE YOU'RE...
...MORE INTERESTED IN THE WORKINGS OF HUMANS ...
...THAN YOU ARE OF CATS, DOGS, AND OTHER BEASTS.
DO YOU ALWAYS WATCH PEOPLE LIKE THIS?
WHAT'S SO FUN ABOUT IT?

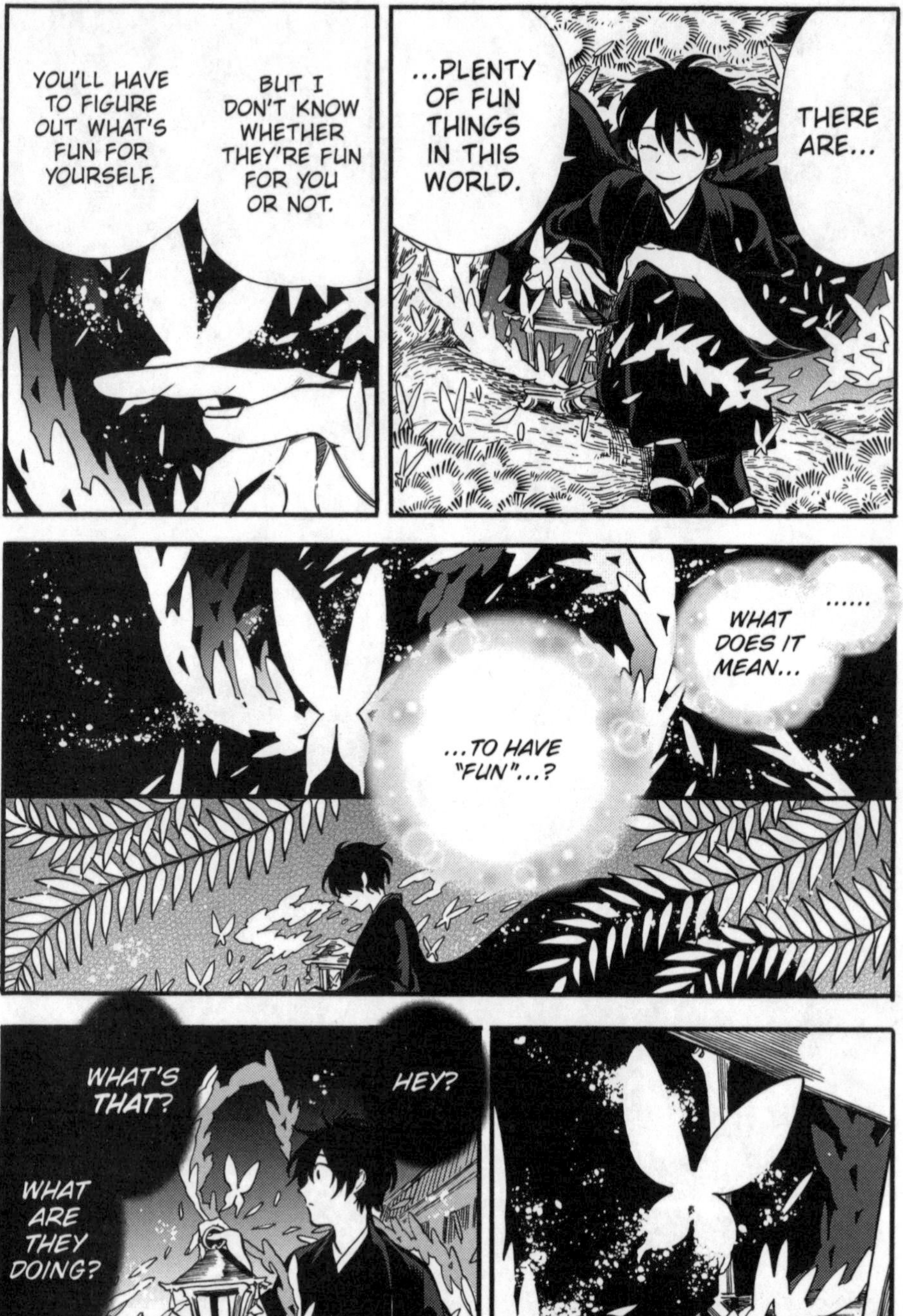
THERE ARE...
...PLENTY OF FUN THINGS IN THIS WORLD.
BUT I DON'T KNOW WHETHER THEY'RE FUN FOR YOU OR NOT.
YOU'LL HAVE TO FIGURE OUT WHAT'S FUN FOR YOURSELF.
......
WHAT DOES IT MEAN...
...TO HAVE "FUN"...?
HEY?
WHAT'S THAT?
WHAT ARE THEY DOING?

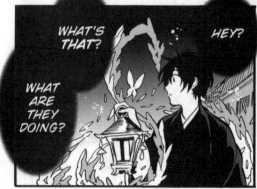

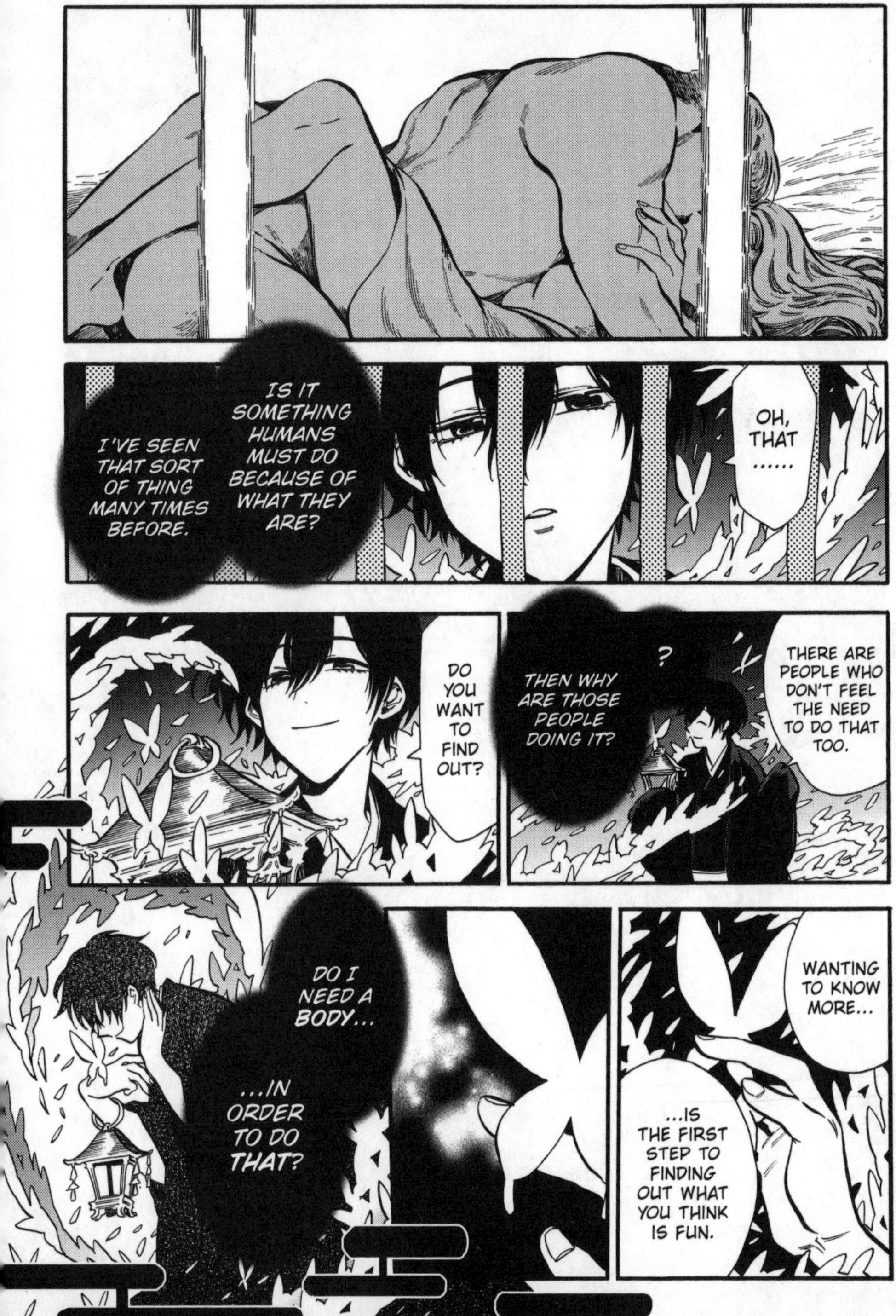
OH, THAT ......
IS IT SOMETHING HUMANS MUST DO BECAUSE OF WHAT THEY ARE?
I'VE SEEN THAT SORT OF THING MANY TIMES BEFORE.
THERE ARE PEOPLE WHO DON'T FEEL THE NEED TO DO THAT TOO.
?
THEN WHY ARE THOSE PEOPLE DOING IT?
DO YOU WANT TO FIND OUT?
WANTING TO KNOW MORE...
...IS THE FIRST STEP TO FINDING OUT WHAT YOU THINK IS FUN.
DO I NEED A BODY...
...IN ORDER TO DO THAT?

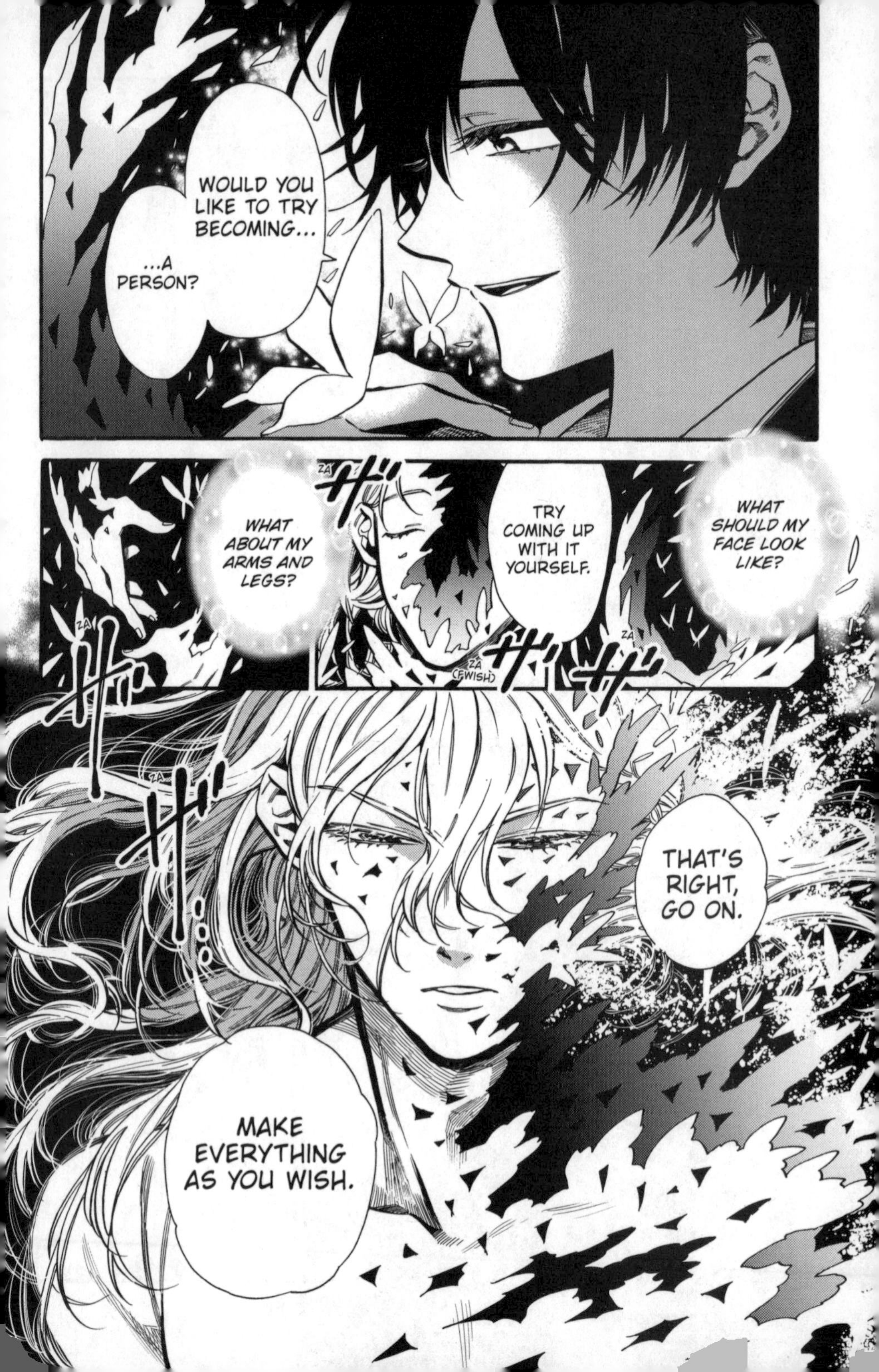
WOULD YOU LIKE TO TRY BECOMING...
...A PERSON?
WHAT SHOULD MY FACE LOOK LIKE?
ZA
TRY COMING UP WITH IT YOURSELF.
ZA (FWISH)
ZA
WHAT ABOUT MY ARMS AND LEGS?
ZA
ZA
THAT'S RIGHT, GO ON.
MAKE EVERYTHING AS YOU WISH.

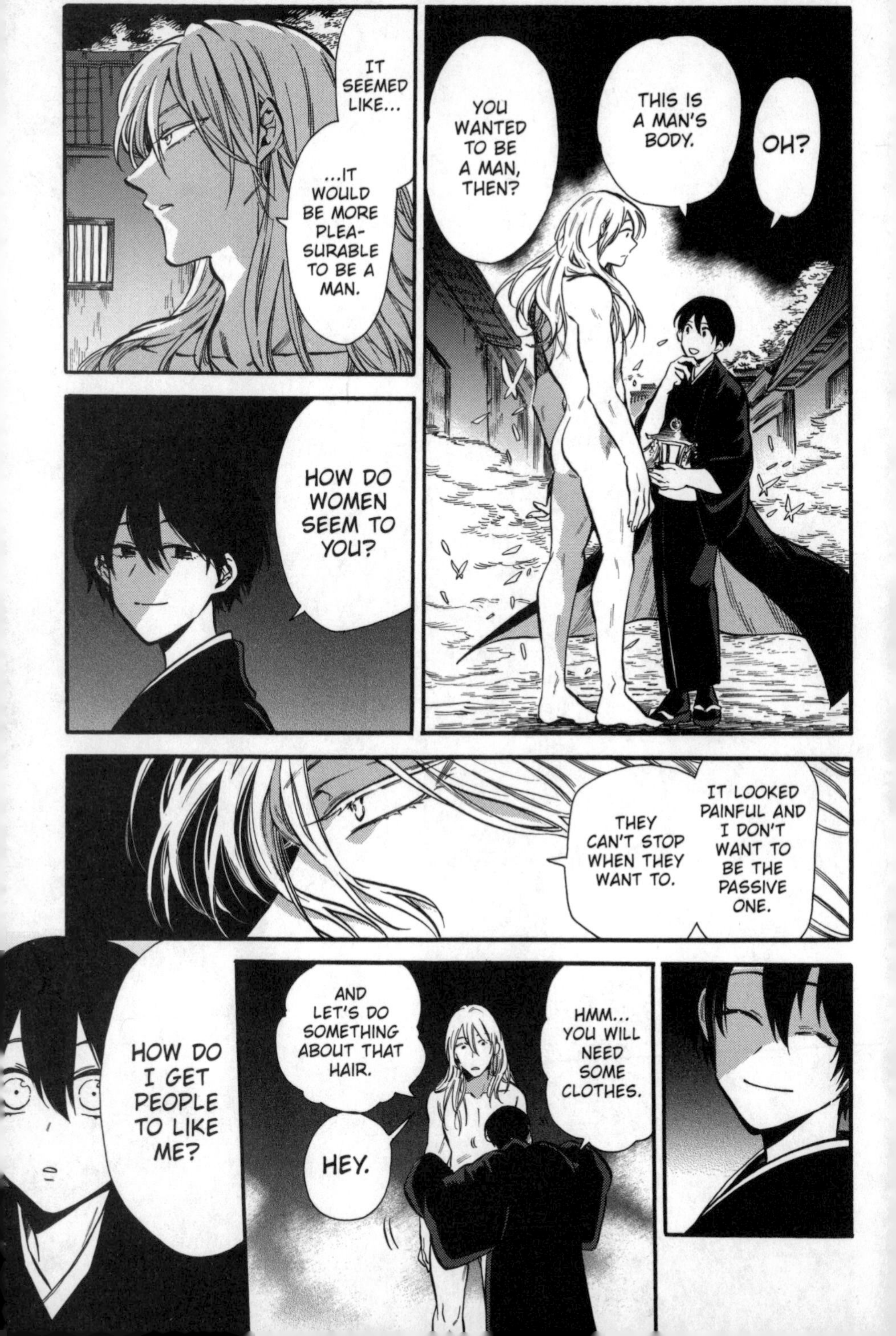
OH?
THIS IS A MAN'S BODY.
YOU WANTED TO BE A MAN, THEN?
IT SEEMED LIKE...
...IT WOULD BE MORE PLEA-SURABLE TO BE A MAN.
HOW DO WOMEN SEEM TO YOU?
IT LOOKED PAINFUL AND I DON'T WANT TO BE THE PASSIVE ONE.
THEY CAN'T STOP WHEN THEY WANT TO.
HMM... YOU WILL NEED SOME CLOTHES.
AND LET'S DO SOMETHING ABOUT THAT HAIR.
HEY.
HOW DO I GET PEOPLE TO LIKE ME?

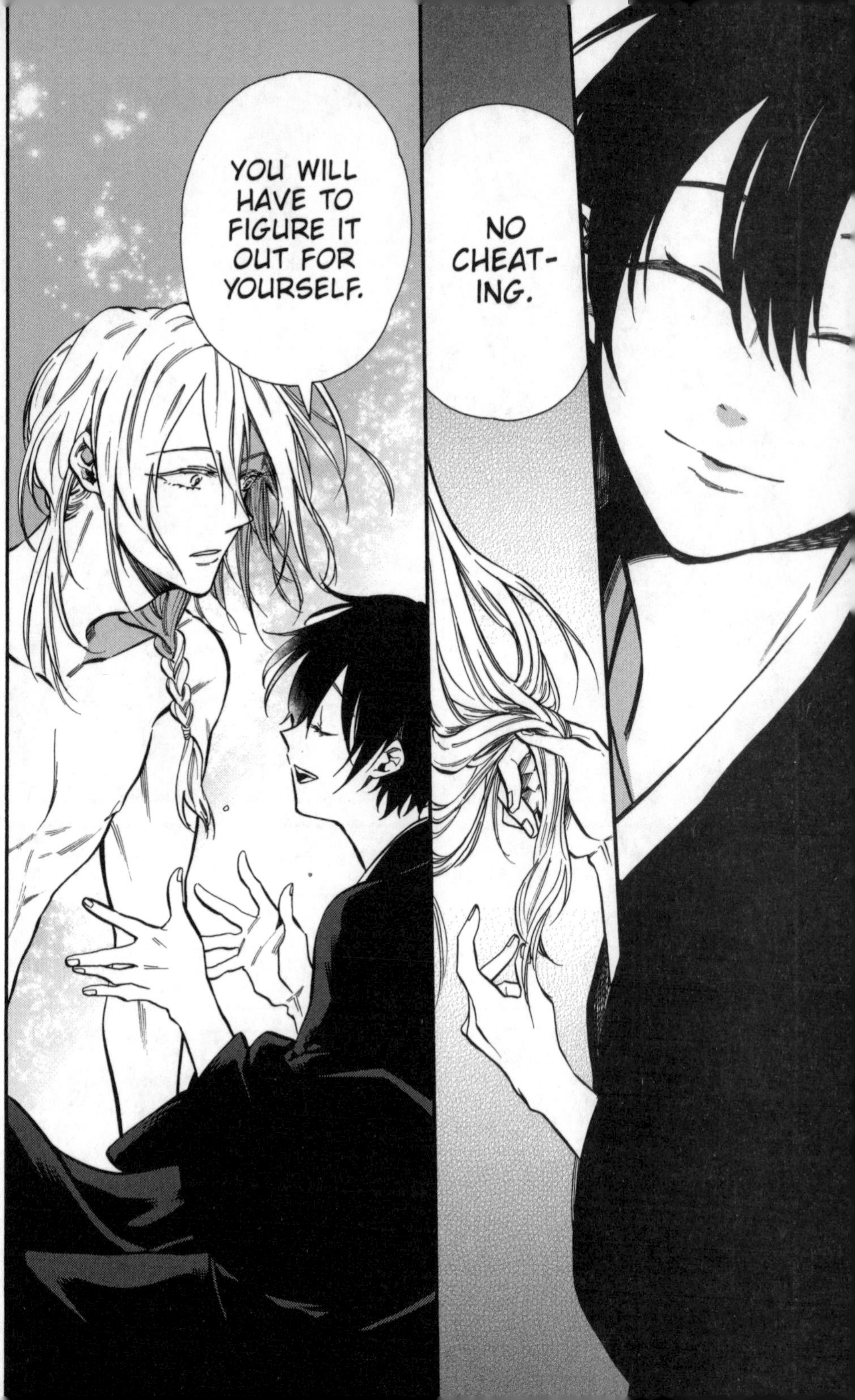
NO CHEAT-ING.
YOU WILL HAVE TO FIGURE IT OUT FOR YOURSELF.

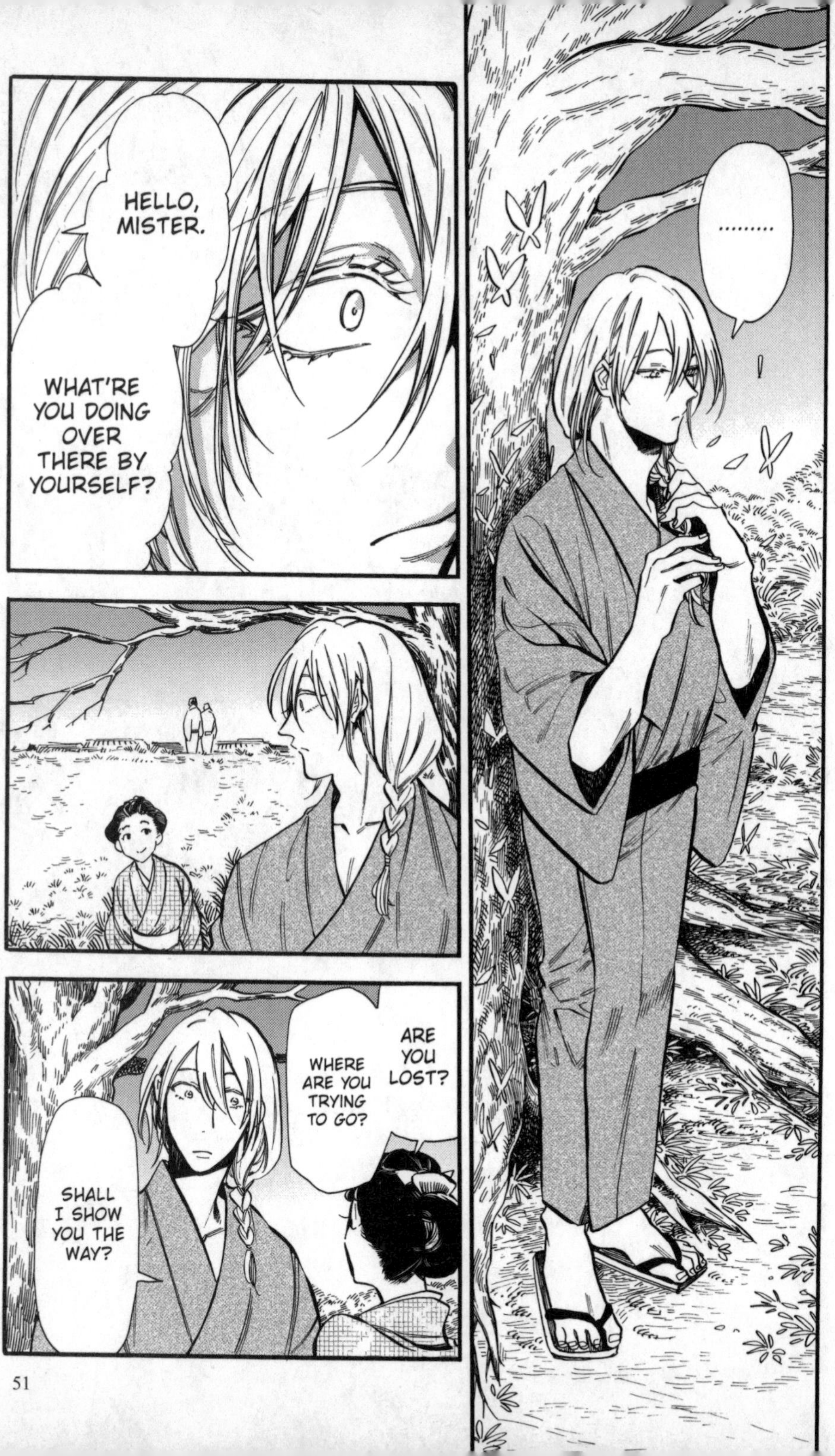
....
!
HELLO, MISTER.
WHAT'RE YOU DOING OVER THERE BY YOURSELF?
ARE YOU LOST?
WHERE ARE YOU TRYING TO GO?
SHALL I SHOW YOU THE WAY?

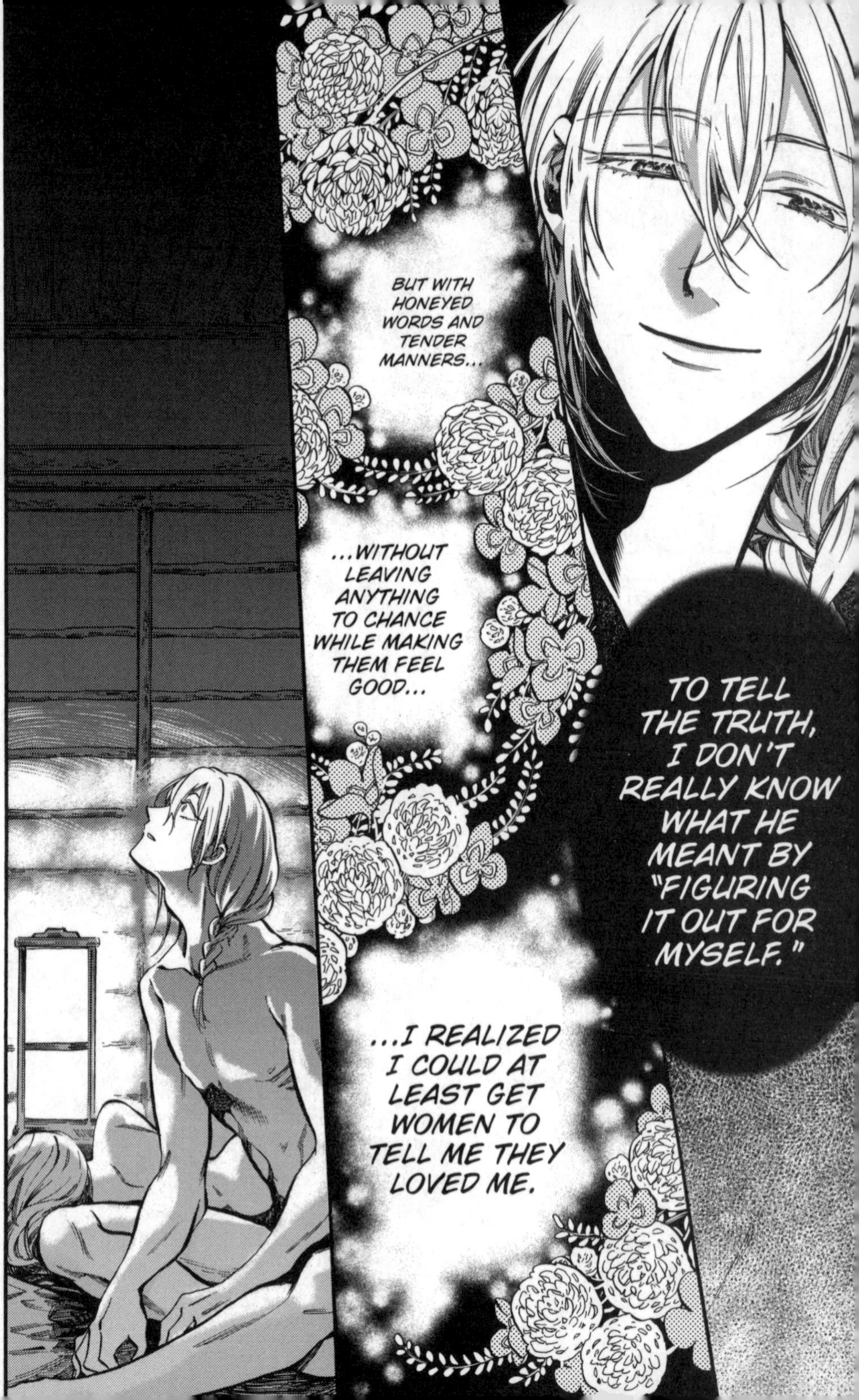
TO TELL THE TRUTH, I DON'T REALLY KNOW WHAT HE MEANT BY "FIGURING IT OUT FOR MYSELF."
BUT WITH HONEYED WORDS AND TENDER MANNERS...
...WITHOUT LEAVING ANYTHING TO CHANCE WHILE MAKING THEM FEEL GOOD...
...I REALIZED I COULD AT LEAST GET WOMEN TO TELL ME THEY LOVED ME.

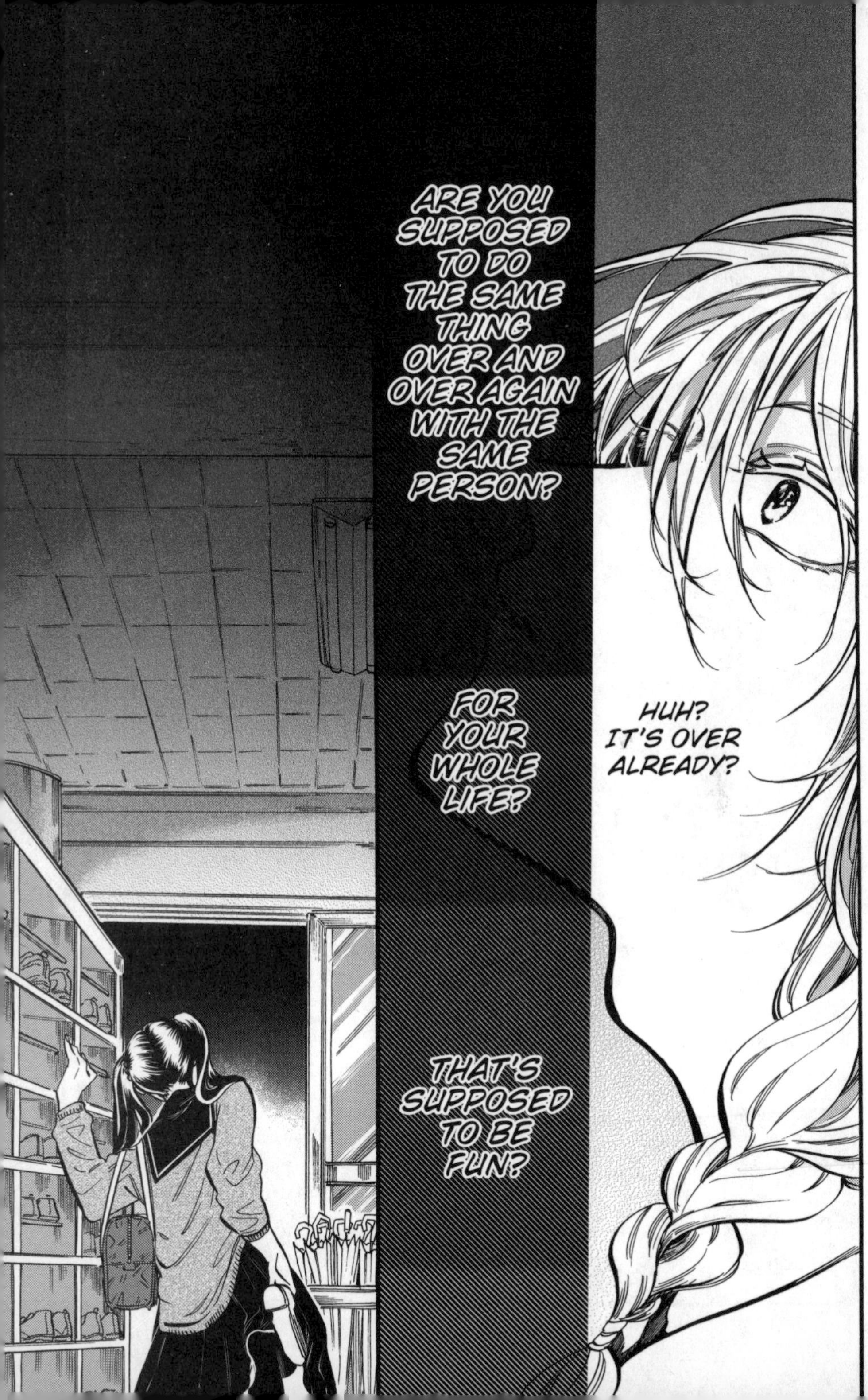
HUH? IT'S OVER ALREADY?
ARE YOU SUPPOSED TO DO THE SAME THING OVER AND OVER AGAIN WITH THE SAME PERSON?
FOR YOUR WHOLE LIFE?
THAT'S SUPPOSED TO BE FUN?

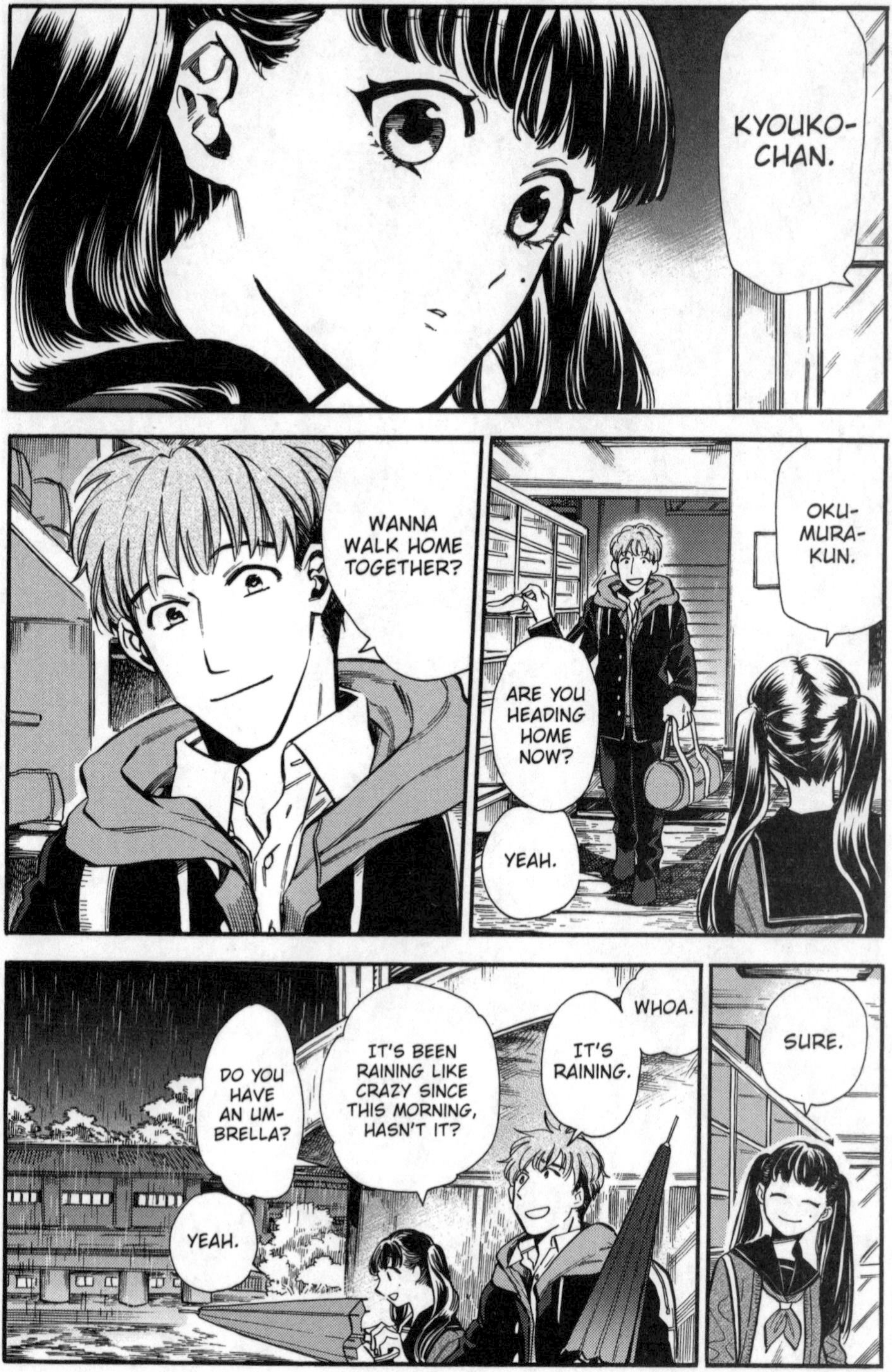
KYOUKO-CHAN.
OKU-MURA-KUN.
ARE YOU HEADING HOME NOW?
YEAH.
WANNA WALK HOME TOGETHER?
SURE.
WHOA.
IT'S RAINING.
IT'S BEEN RAINING LIKE CRAZY SINCE THIS MORNING, HASN'T IT?
DO YOU HAVE AN UM-BRELLA?
YEAH.

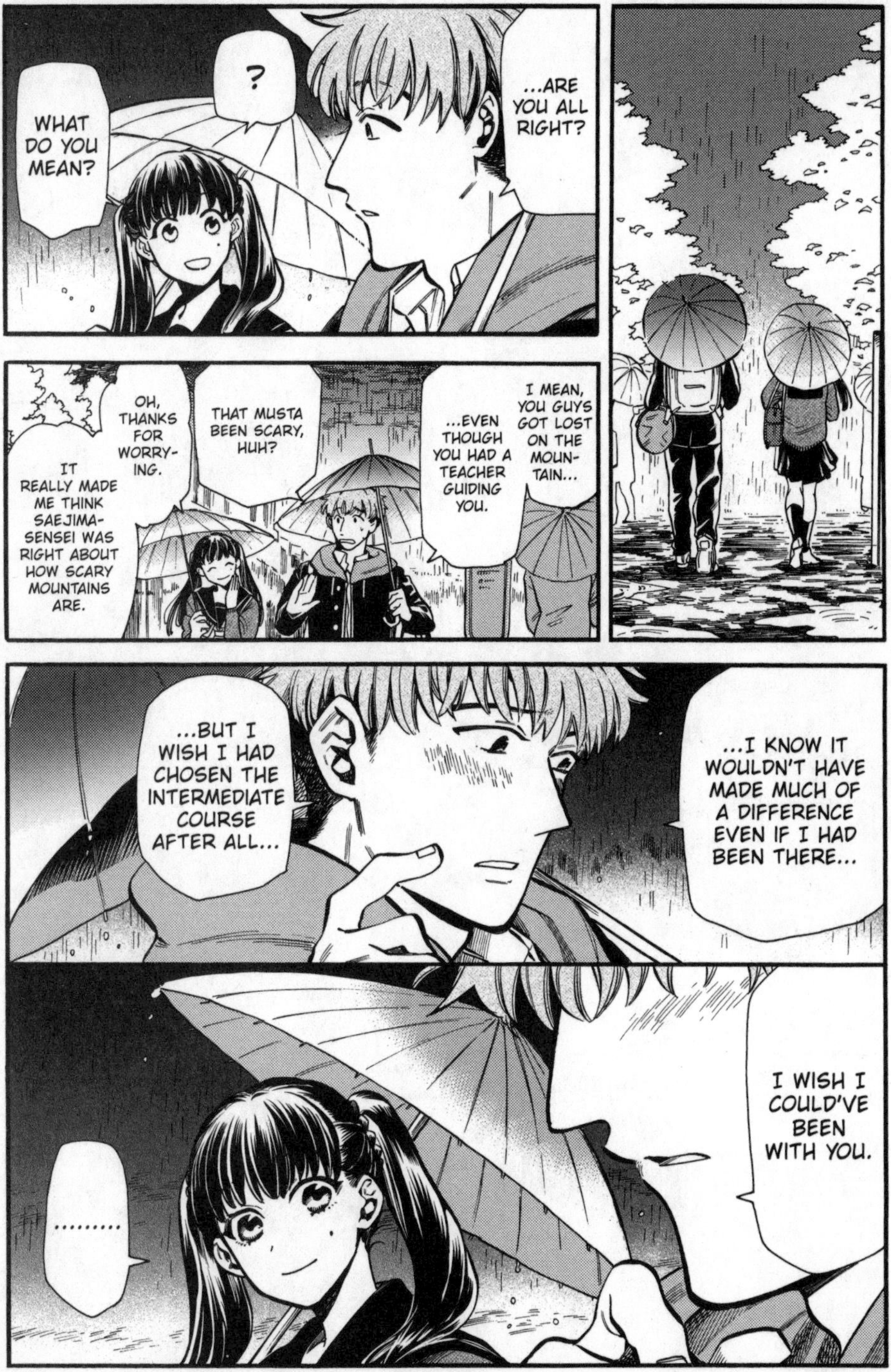
...ARE YOU ALL RIGHT?
?
WHAT DO YOU MEAN?
I MEAN, YOU GUYS GOT LOST ON THE MOUNTAIN...
...EVEN THOUGH YOU HAD A TEACHER GUIDING YOU.
THAT MUSTA BEEN SCARY, HUH?
OH, THANKS FOR WORRYING.
IT REALLY MADE ME THINK SAEJIMA-SENSEI WAS RIGHT ABOUT HOW SCARY MOUNTAINS ARE.
...I KNOW IT WOULDN'T HAVE MADE MUCH OF A DIFFERENCE EVEN IF I HAD BEEN THERE...
...BUT I WISH I HAD CHOSEN THE INTERMEDIATE COURSE AFTER ALL...
I WISH I COULD'VE BEEN WITH YOU.
....

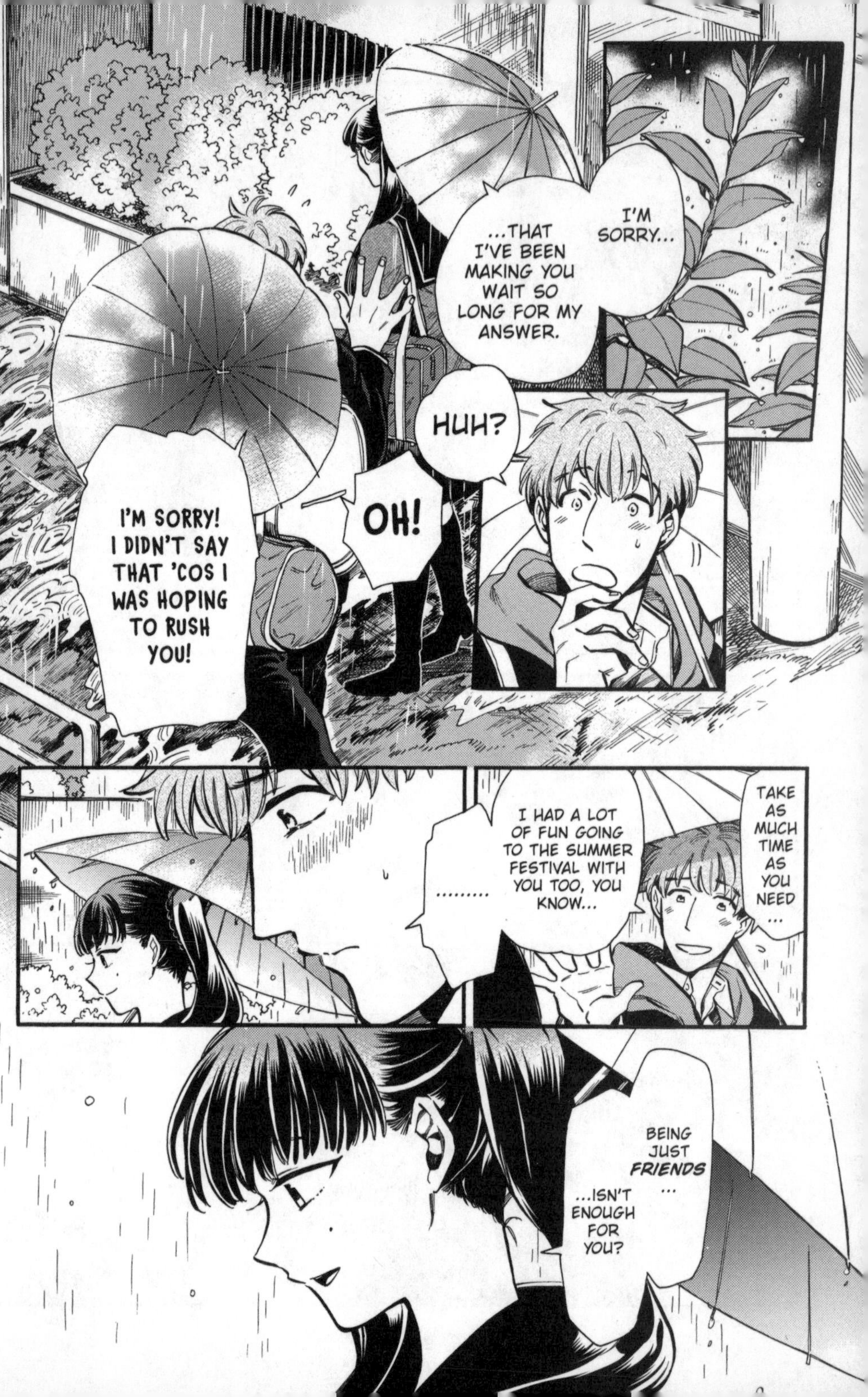
I'M SORRY...
...THAT I'VE BEEN MAKING YOU WAIT SO LONG FOR MY ANSWER.
HUH?
OH!
I'M SORRY! I DIDN'T SAY THAT 'COS I WAS HOPING TO RUSH YOU!
TAKE AS MUCH TIME AS YOU NEED ...
I HAD A LOT OF FUN GOING TO THE SUMMER FESTIVAL WITH YOU TOO, YOU KNOW...
....
BEING JUST FRIENDS ...
...ISN'T ENOUGH FOR YOU?

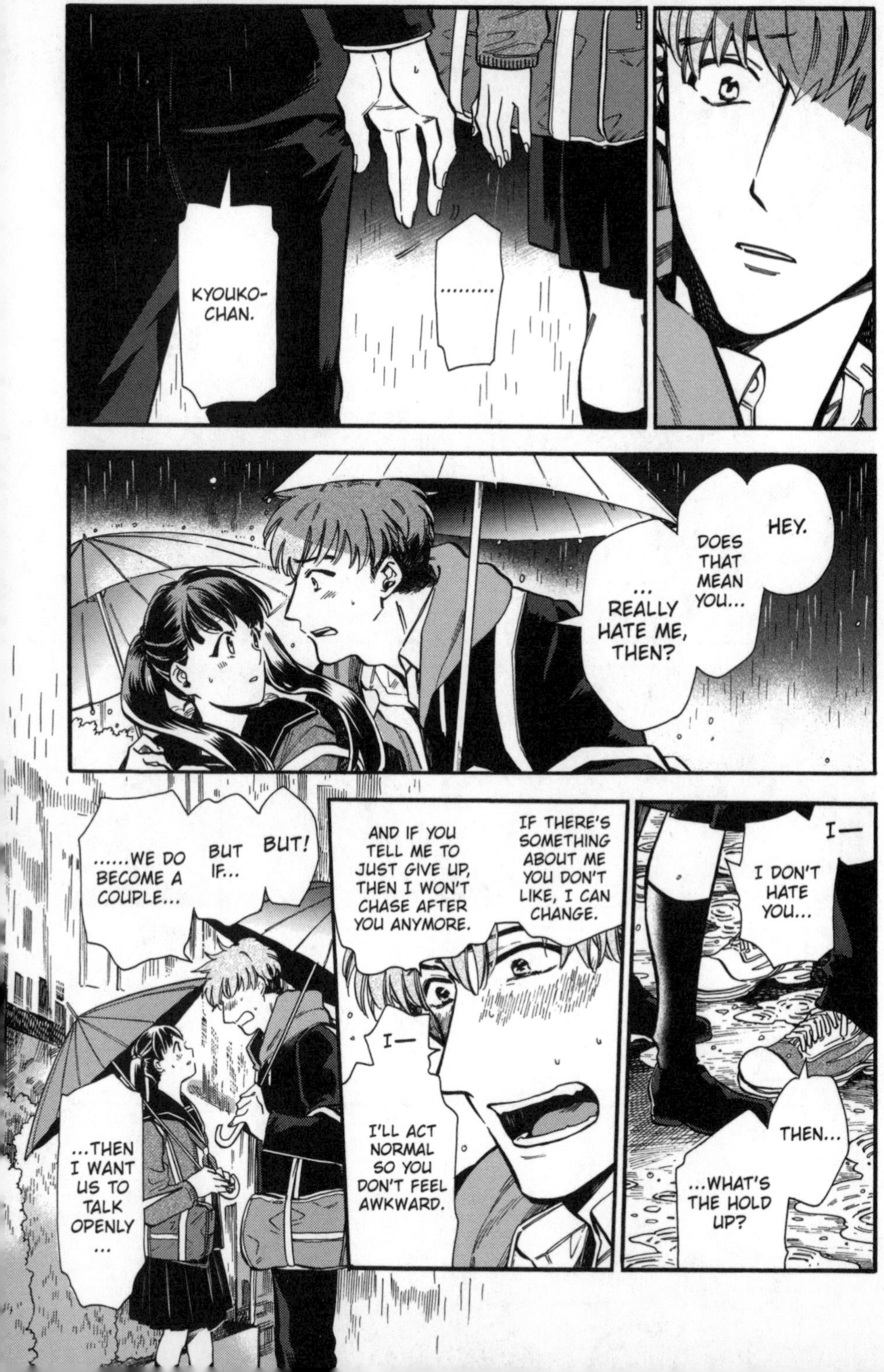
....
KYOUKO-CHAN.
HEY.
DOES THAT MEAN YOU...
...REALLY HATE ME, THEN?
I—
I DON'T HATE YOU...
THEN...
...WHAT'S THE HOLD UP?
IF THERE'S SOMETHING ABOUT ME YOU DON'T LIKE, I CAN CHANGE.
AND IF YOU TELL ME TO JUST GIVE UP, THEN I WON'T CHASE AFTER YOU ANYMORE.
I—
I'LL ACT NORMAL SO YOU DON'T FEEL AWKWARD.
BUT!
BUT IF...
......WE DO BECOME A COUPLE...
...THEN I WANT US TO TALK OPENLY...

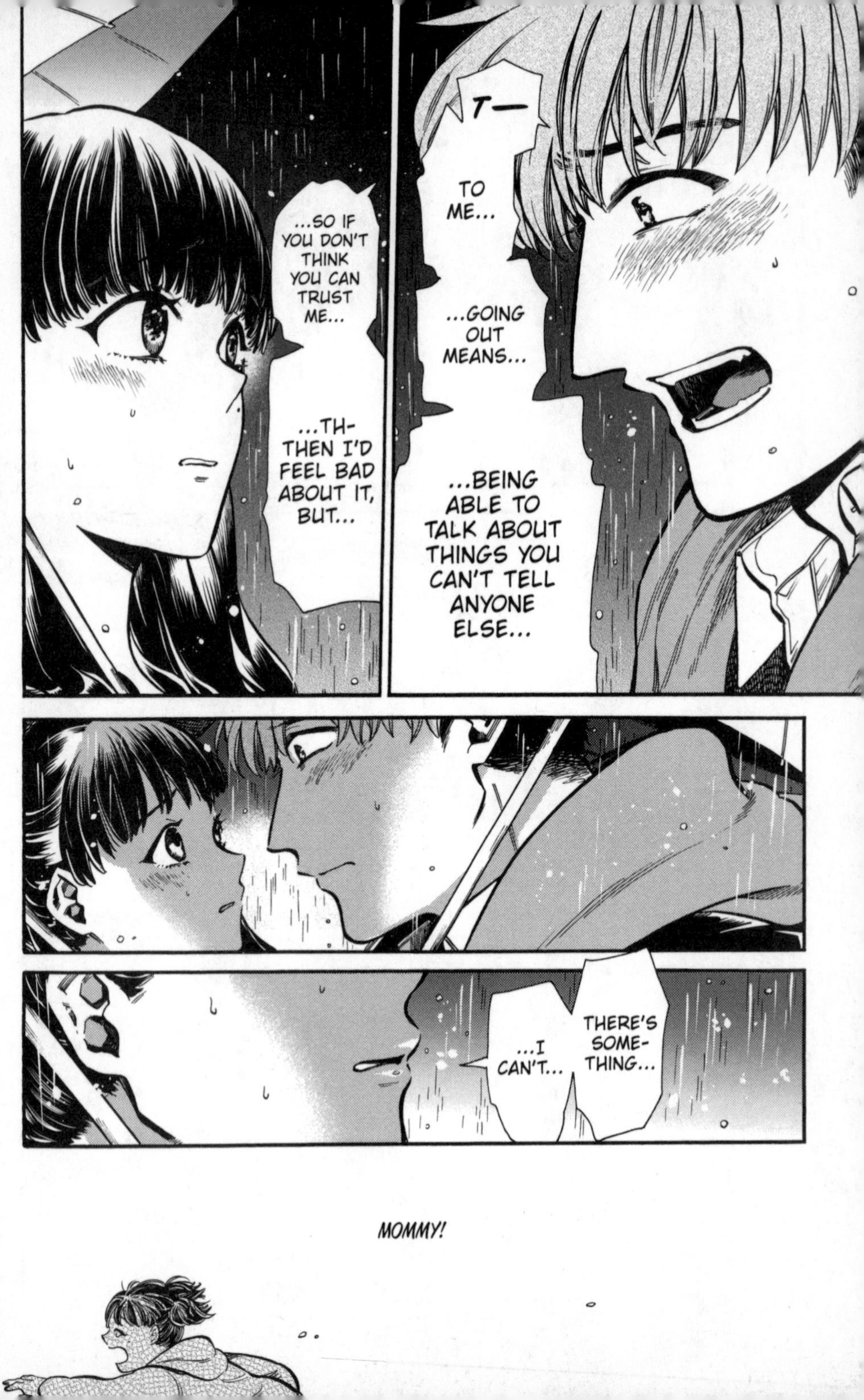
T—
TO ME...
...GOING OUT MEANS...
...BEING ABLE TO TALK ABOUT THINGS YOU CAN'T TELL ANYONE ELSE...
...SO IF YOU DON'T THINK YOU CAN TRUST ME...
...TH-THEN I'D FEEL BAD ABOUT IT, BUT...
THERE'S SOME-THING...
...I CAN'T...
MOMMY!

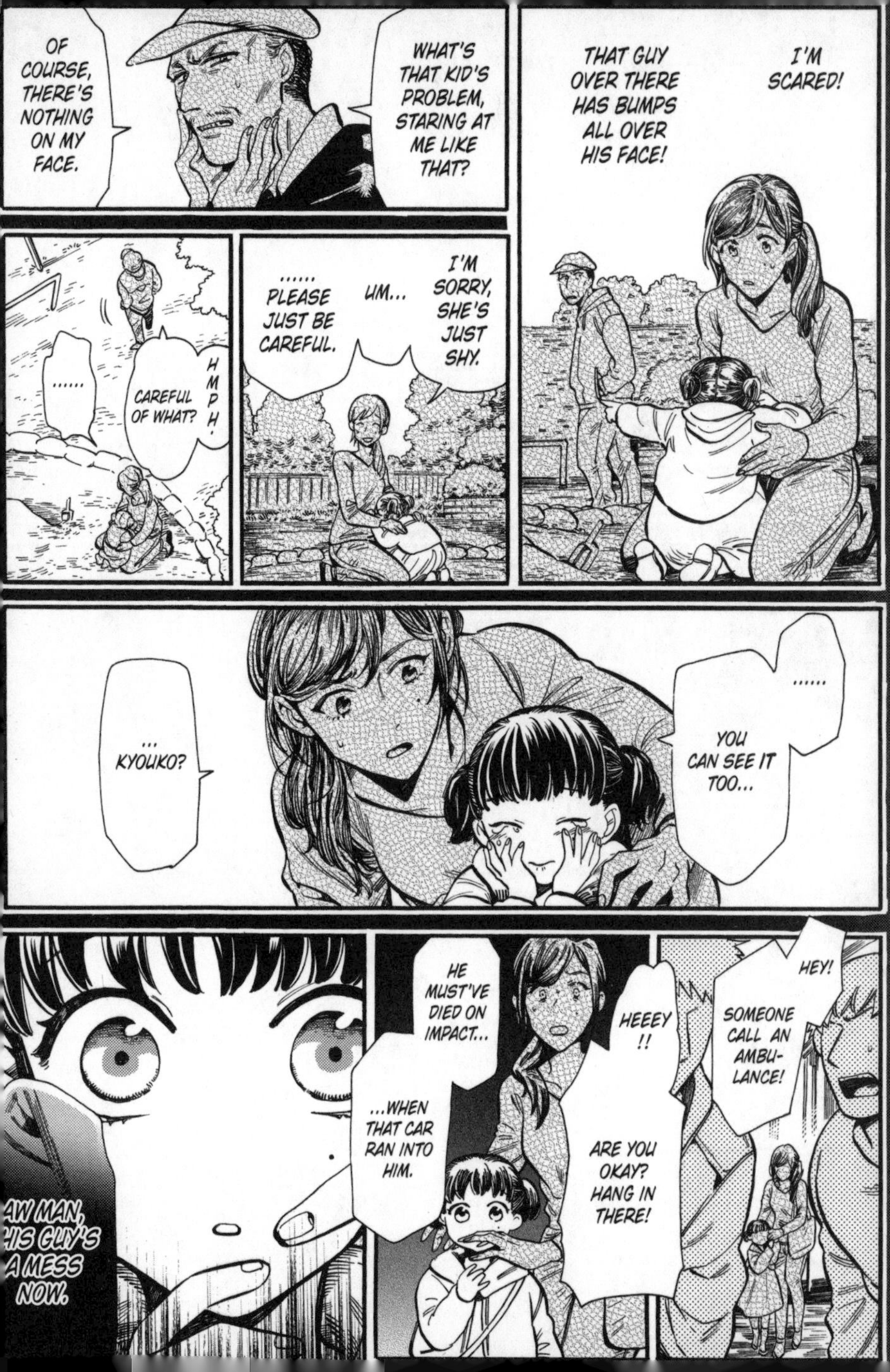
I'M SCARED!
THAT GUY OVER THERE HAS BUMPS ALL OVER HIS FACE!
WHAT'S THAT KID'S PROBLEM, STARING AT ME LIKE THAT?
OF COURSE, THERE'S NOTHING ON MY FACE.
I'M SORRY, SHE'S JUST SHY.
UM...
...... PLEASE JUST BE CAREFUL.
HMPH!
CAREFUL OF WHAT?
......
......
YOU CAN SEE IT TOO...
... KYOUKO?
HEY!
SOMEONE CALL AN AMBULANCE!
HEEEY!!
ARE YOU OKAY? HANG IN THERE!
HE MUST'VE DIED ON IMPACT...
...WHEN THAT CAR RAN INTO HIM.
AW MAN, HIS GUY'S A MESS NOW.

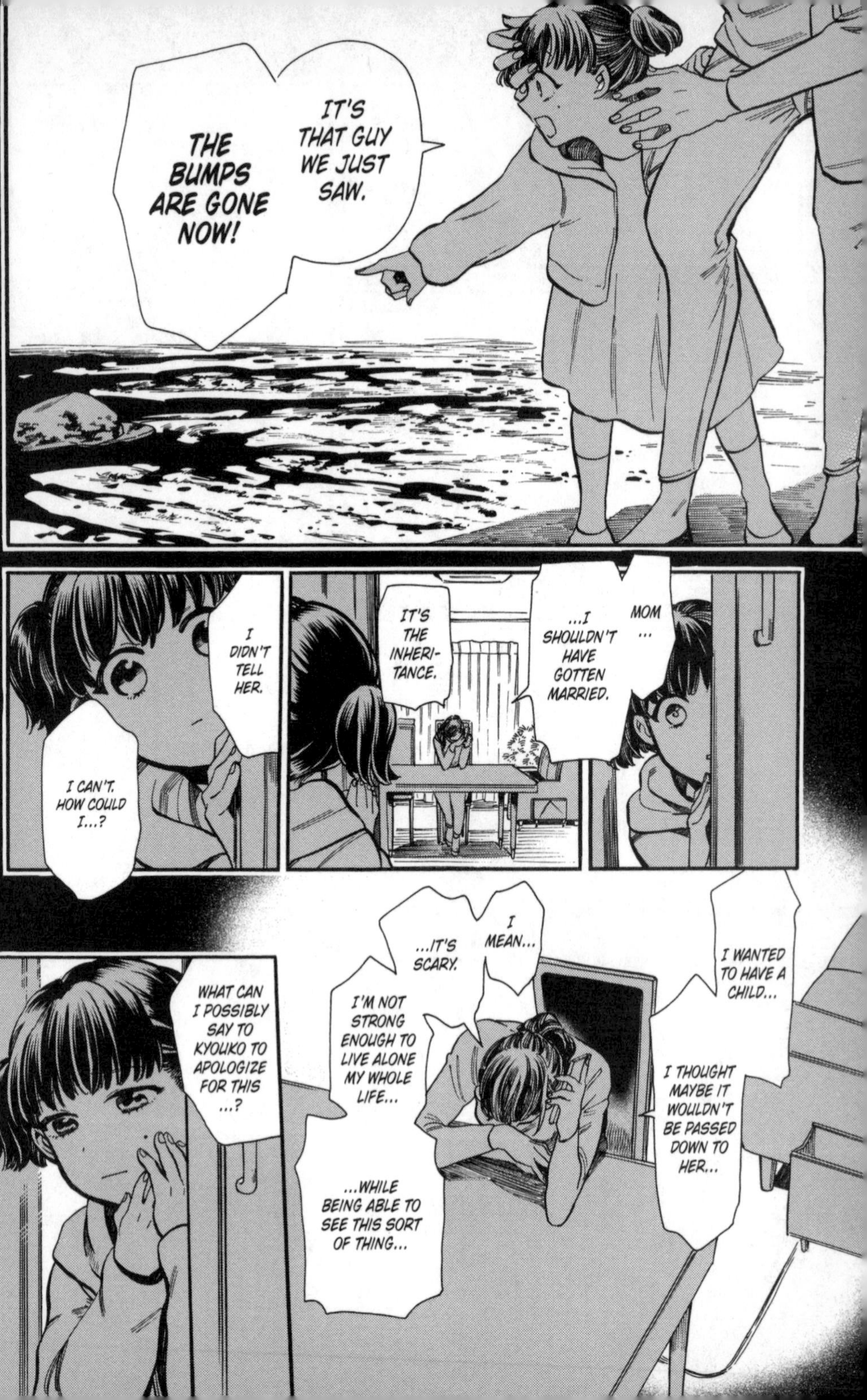
IT'S THAT GUY WE JUST SAW.
THE BUMPS ARE GONE NOW!
MOM ...
...I SHOULDN'T HAVE GOTTEN MARRIED.
IT'S THE INHERITANCE.
I DIDN'T TELL HER.
I CAN'T. HOW COULD I...?
I WANTED TO HAVE A CHILD...
I THOUGHT MAYBE IT WOULDN'T BE PASSED DOWN TO HER...
I MEAN...
...IT'S SCARY.
I'M NOT STRONG ENOUGH TO LIVE ALONE MY WHOLE LIFE...
...WHILE BEING ABLE TO SEE THIS SORT OF THING...
WHAT CAN I POSSIBLY SAY TO KYOUKO TO APOLOGIZE FOR THIS ...?

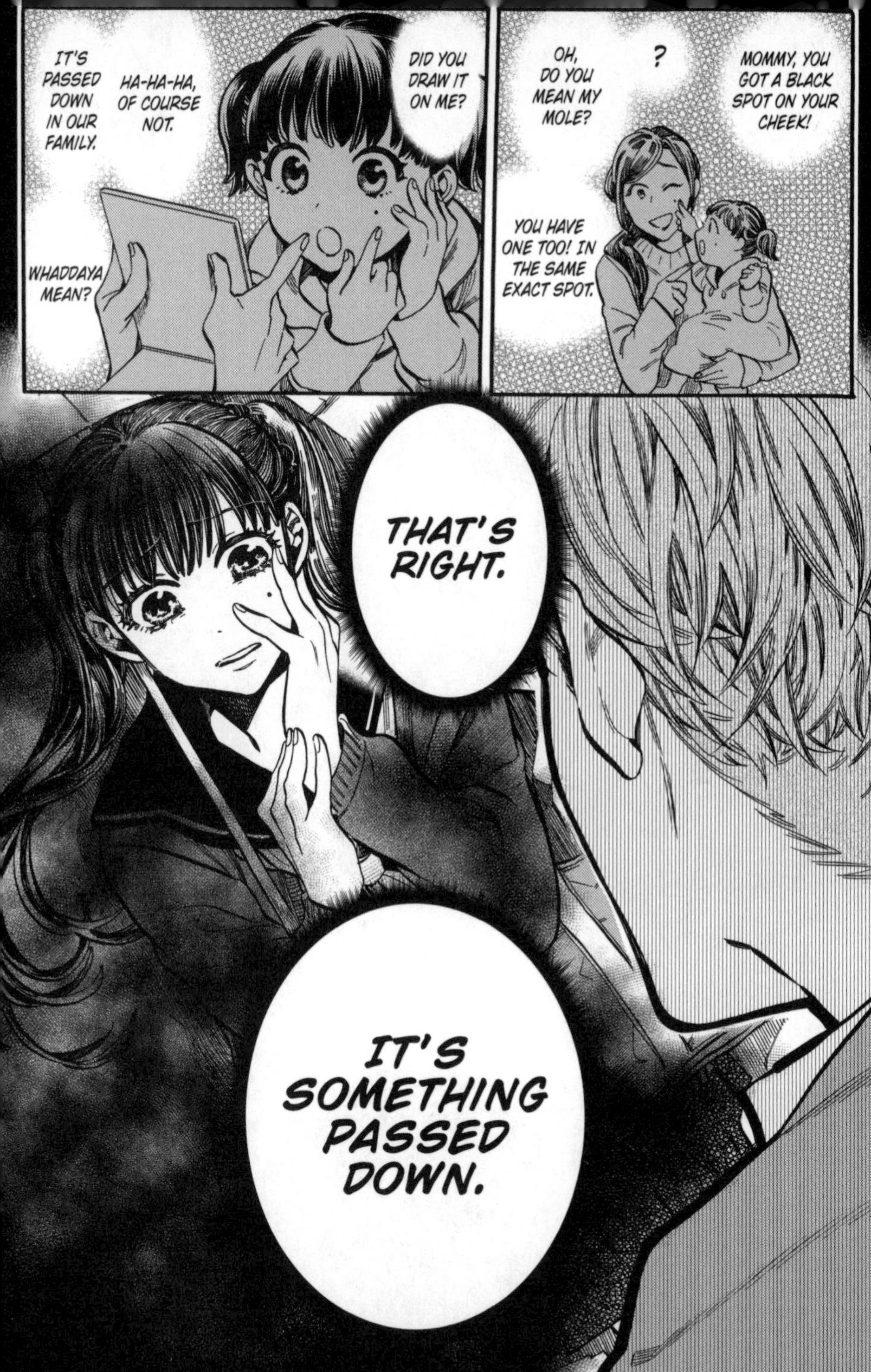
MOMMY, YOU GOT A BLACK SPOT ON YOUR CHEEK!
?
OH, DO YOU MEAN MY MOLE?
YOU HAVE ONE TOO! IN THE SAME EXACT SPOT.
DID YOU DRAW IT ON ME?
HA-HA-HA, OF COURSE NOT.
IT'S PASSED DOWN IN OUR FAMILY.
WHADDAYA MEAN?
THAT'S RIGHT.
IT'S SOMETHING PASSED DOWN.

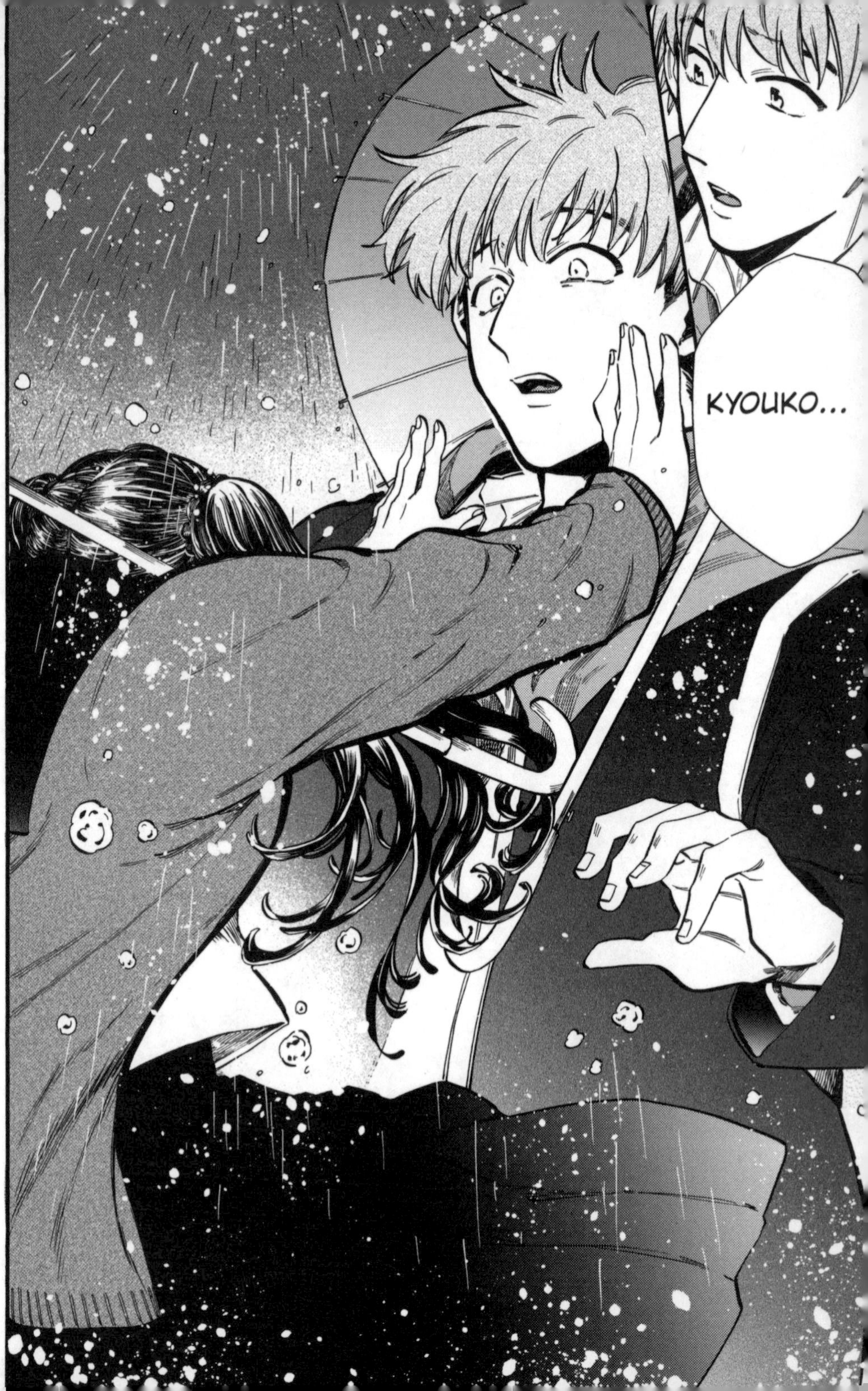
KYOUKO...

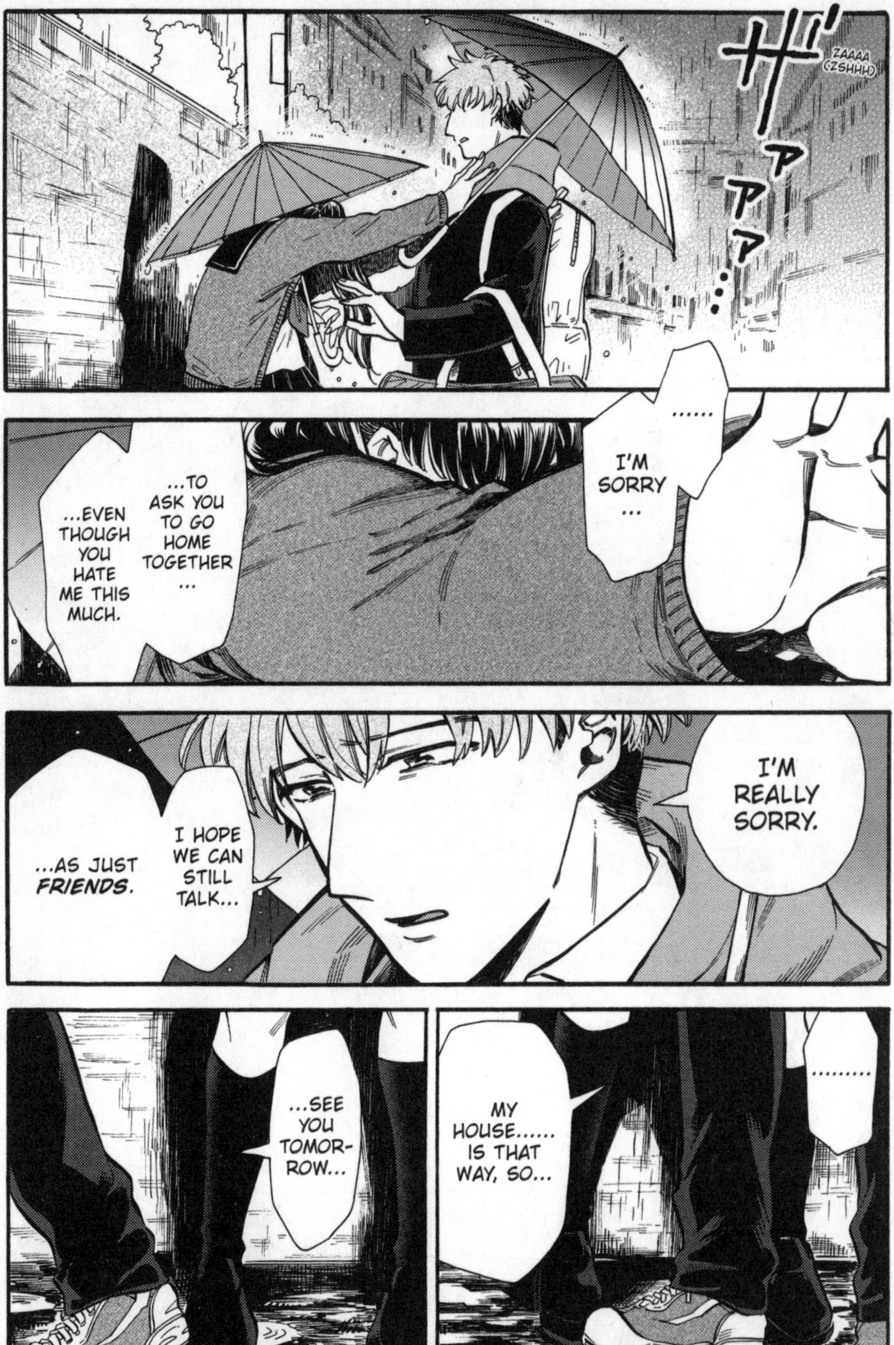
ザァァァ…
ZAAAA (ZSHHH)
...... I'M SORRY ...
...TO ASK YOU TO GO HOME TOGETHER ...
...EVEN THOUGH YOU HATE ME THIS MUCH.
I'M REALLY SORRY.
I HOPE WE CAN STILL TALK...
...AS JUST *FRIENDS*.
....
MY HOUSE...... IS THAT WAY, SO...
...SEE YOU TOMORROW...

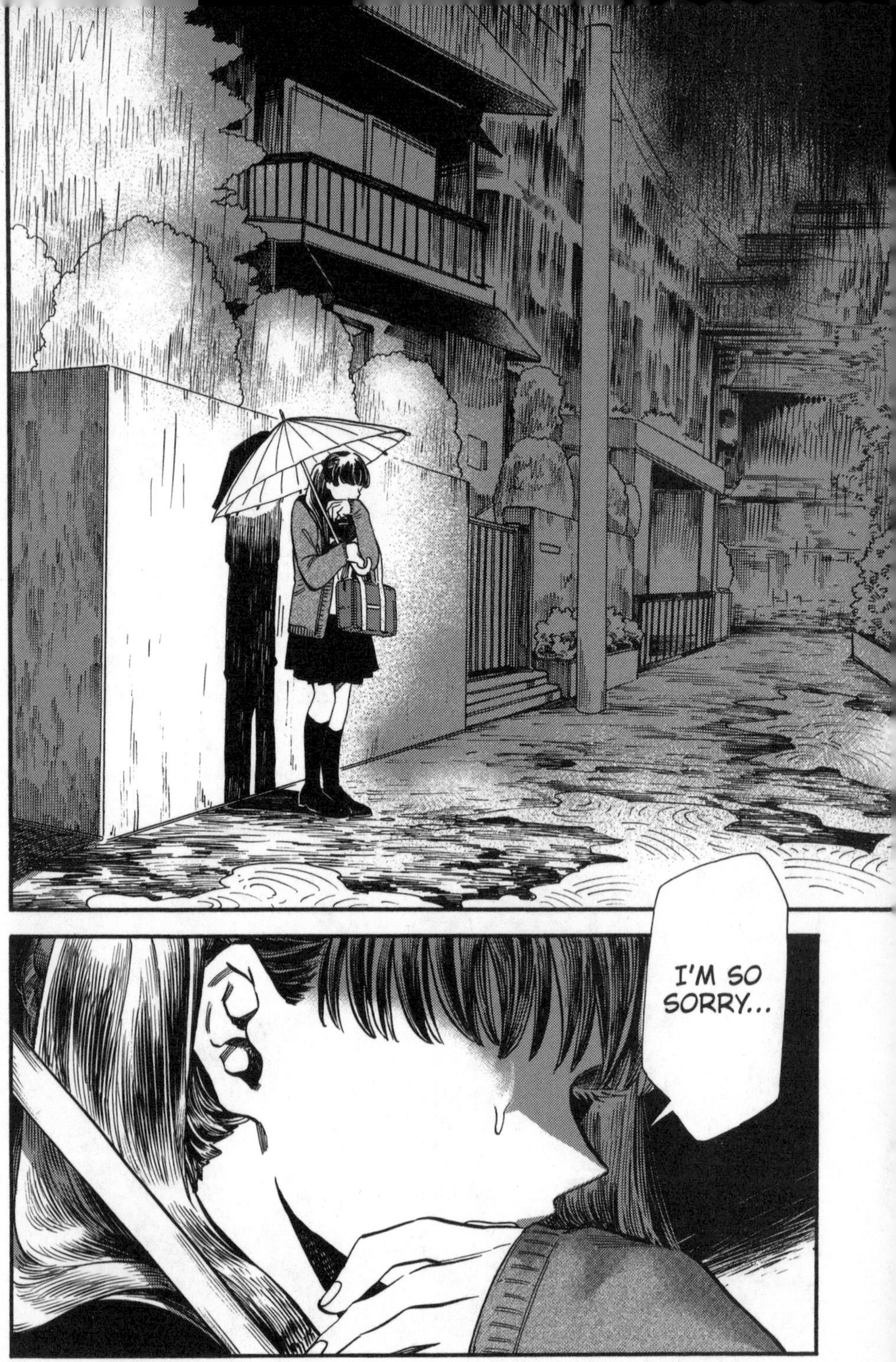
I'M SO SORRY...

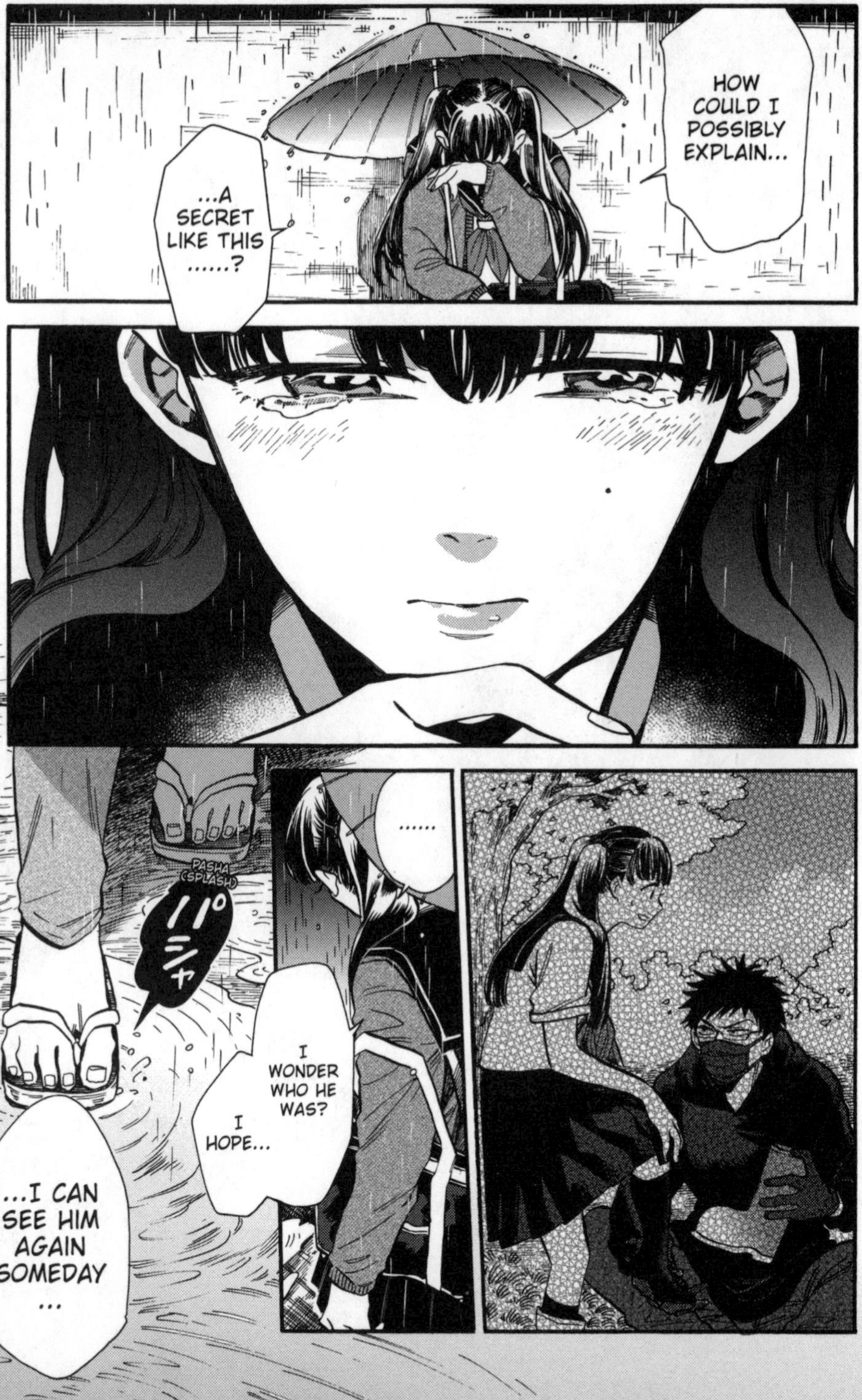
HOW COULD I POSSIBLY EXPLAIN...
...A SECRET LIKE THIS ......?
......
I WONDER WHO HE WAS?
I HOPE...
PASHA (SPLASH)
パシャ
...I CAN SEE HIM AGAIN SOMEDAY ...

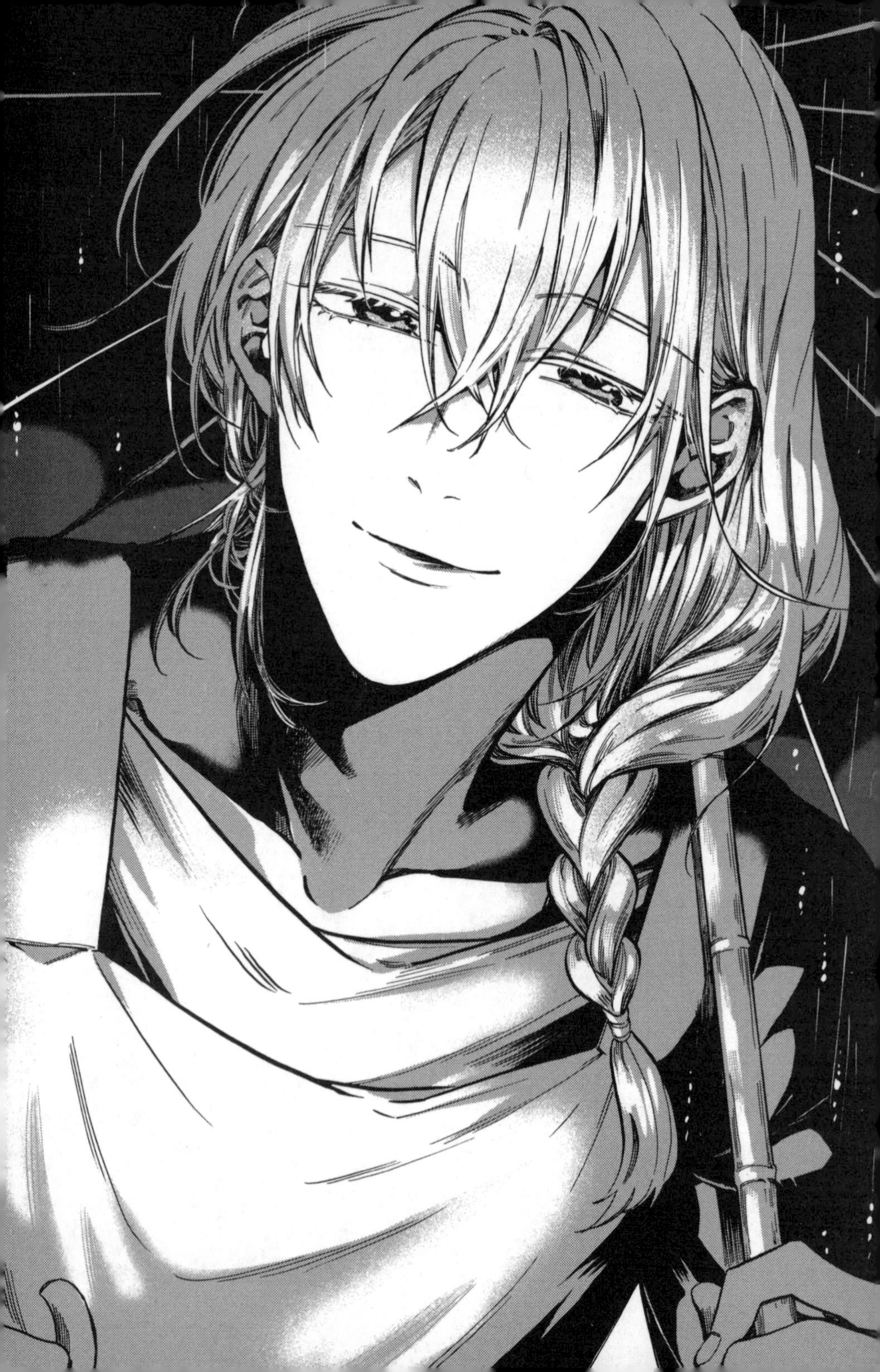

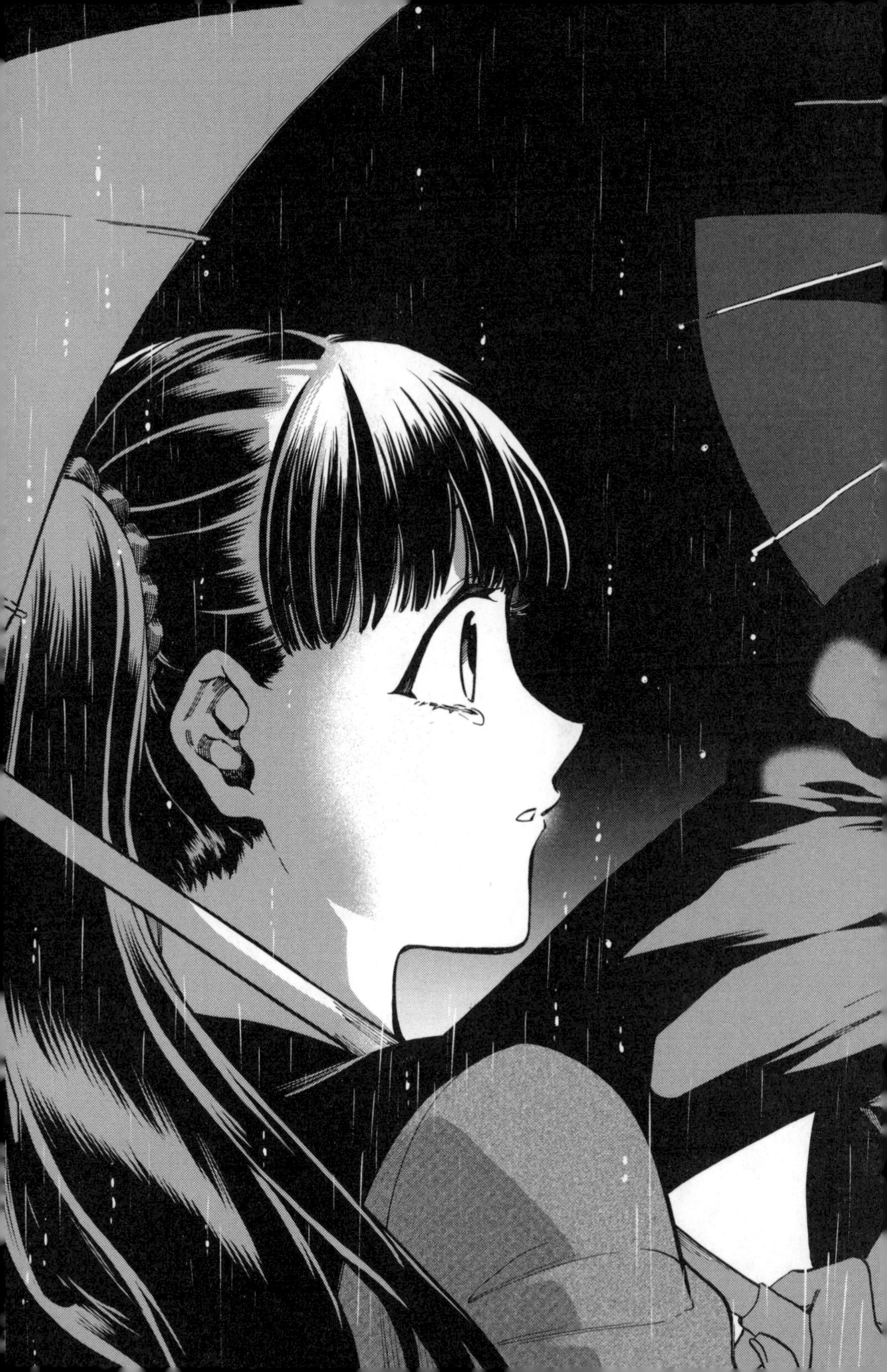

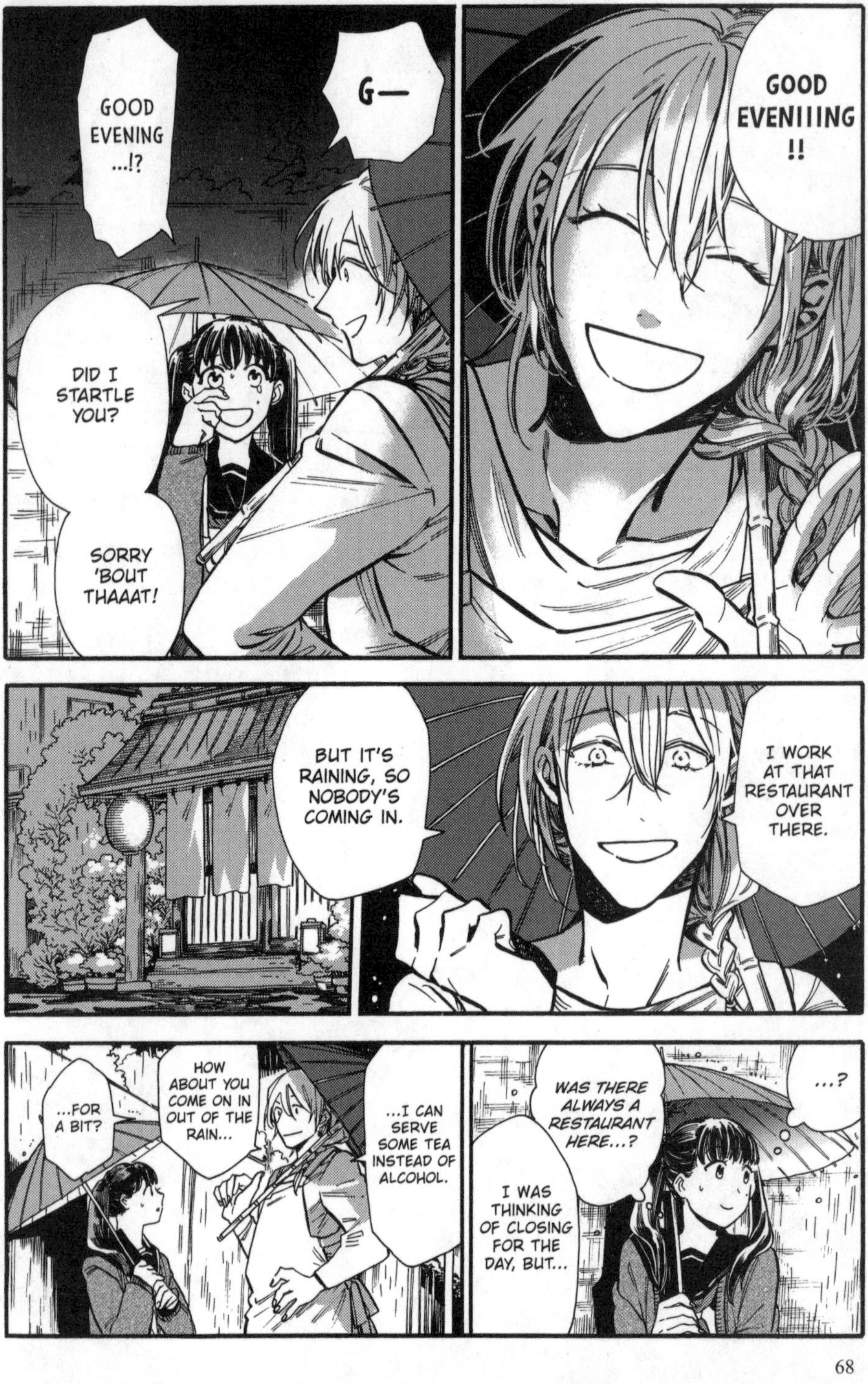
GOOD EVENIIING !!
G—
GOOD EVENING ...!?
DID I STARTLE YOU?
SORRY 'BOUT THAAAT!
I WORK AT THAT RESTAURANT OVER THERE.
BUT IT'S RAINING, SO NOBODY'S COMING IN.
...?
WAS THERE ALWAYS A RESTAURANT HERE...?
I WAS THINKING OF CLOSING FOR THE DAY, BUT...
...I CAN SERVE SOME TEA INSTEAD OF ALCOHOL.
HOW ABOUT YOU COME ON IN OUT OF THE RAIN...
...FOR A BIT?

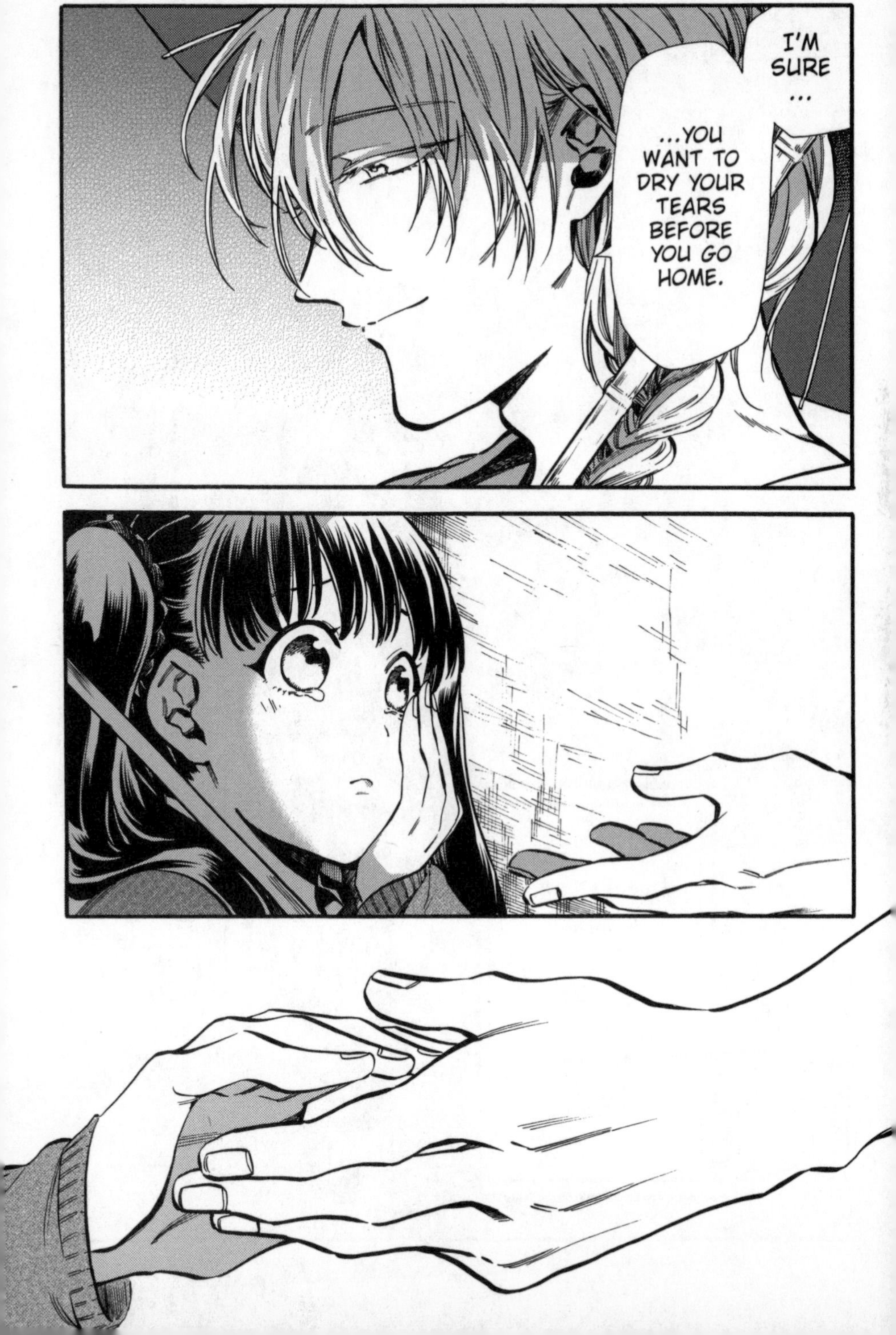
I'M SURE ...
...YOU WANT TO DRY YOUR TEARS BEFORE YOU GO HOME.

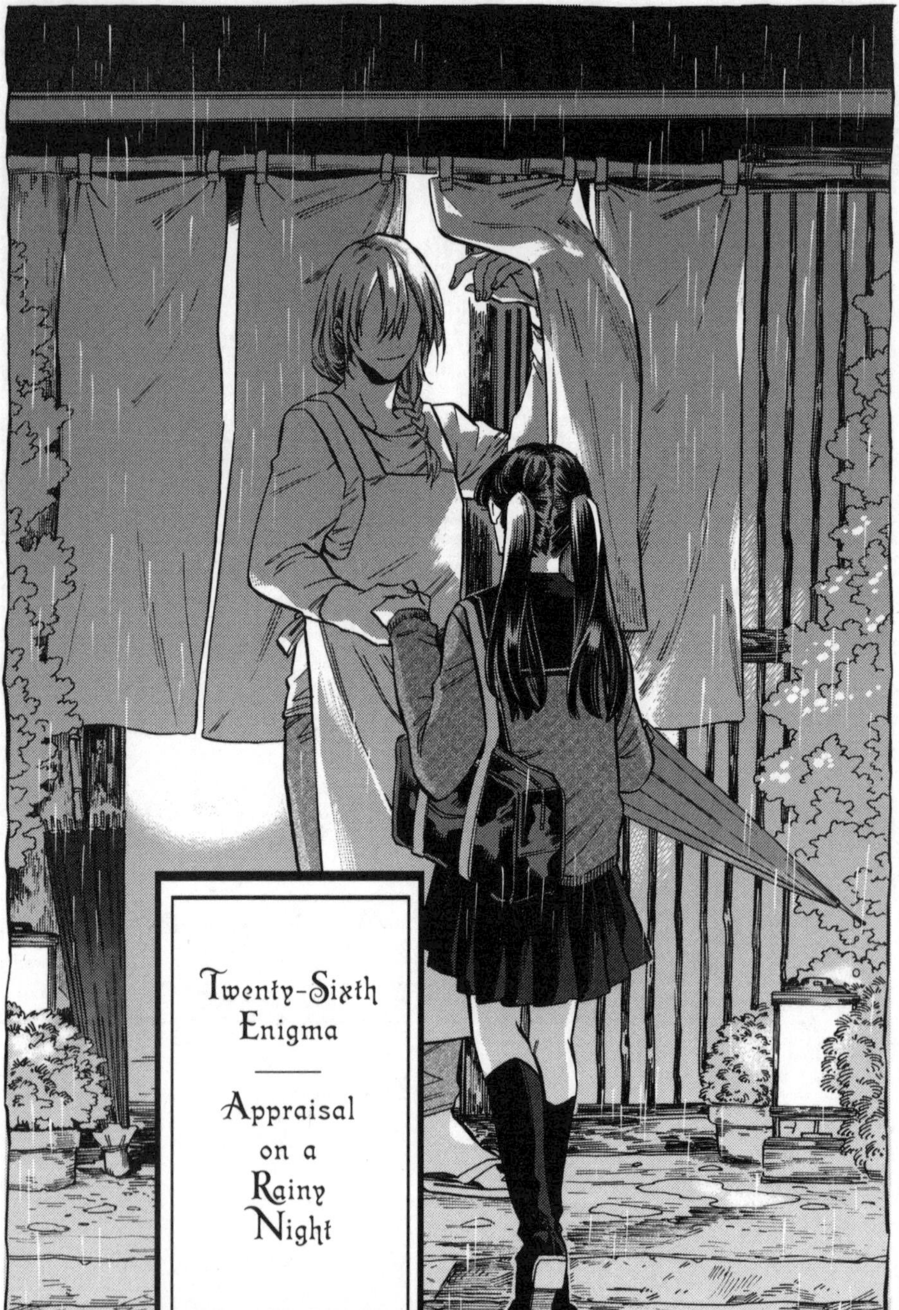
Twenty-Sixth Enigma
Appraisal on a Rainy Night

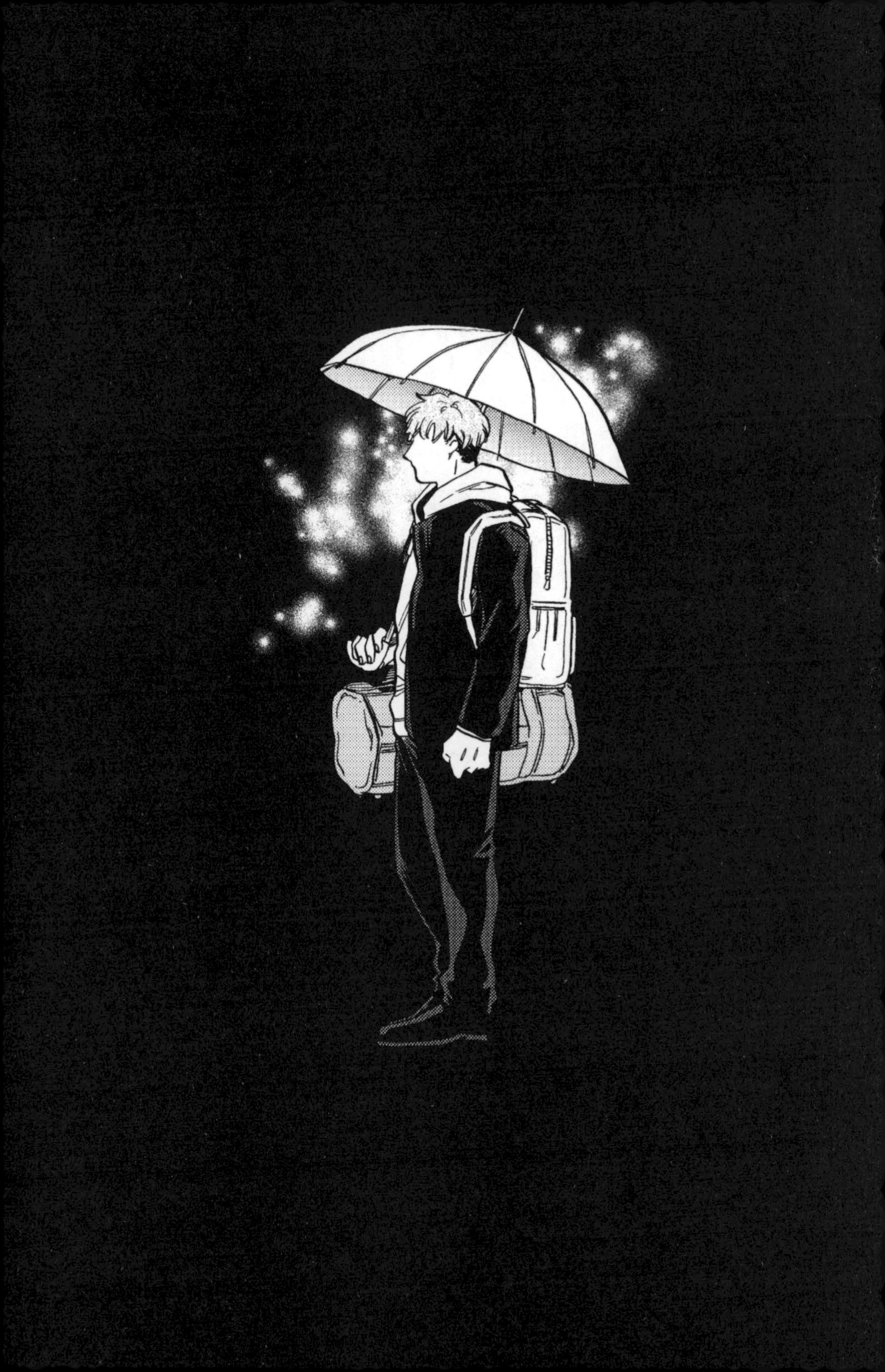

Phantom Tales of the Night

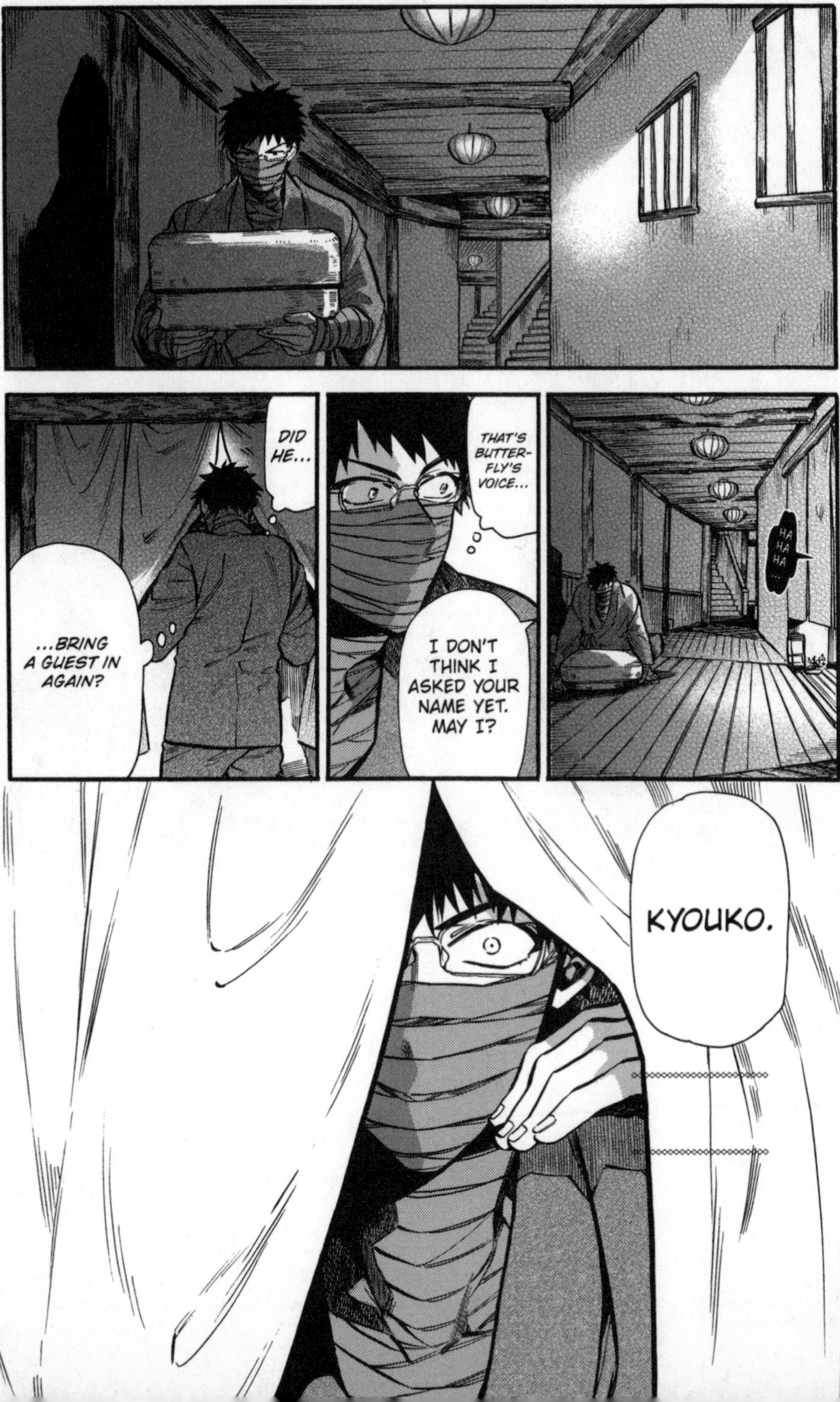
HA HA HA...
THAT'S BUTTERFLY'S VOICE...
I DON'T THINK I ASKED YOUR NAME YET. MAY I?
DID HE...
...BRING A GUEST IN AGAIN?
KYOUKO.

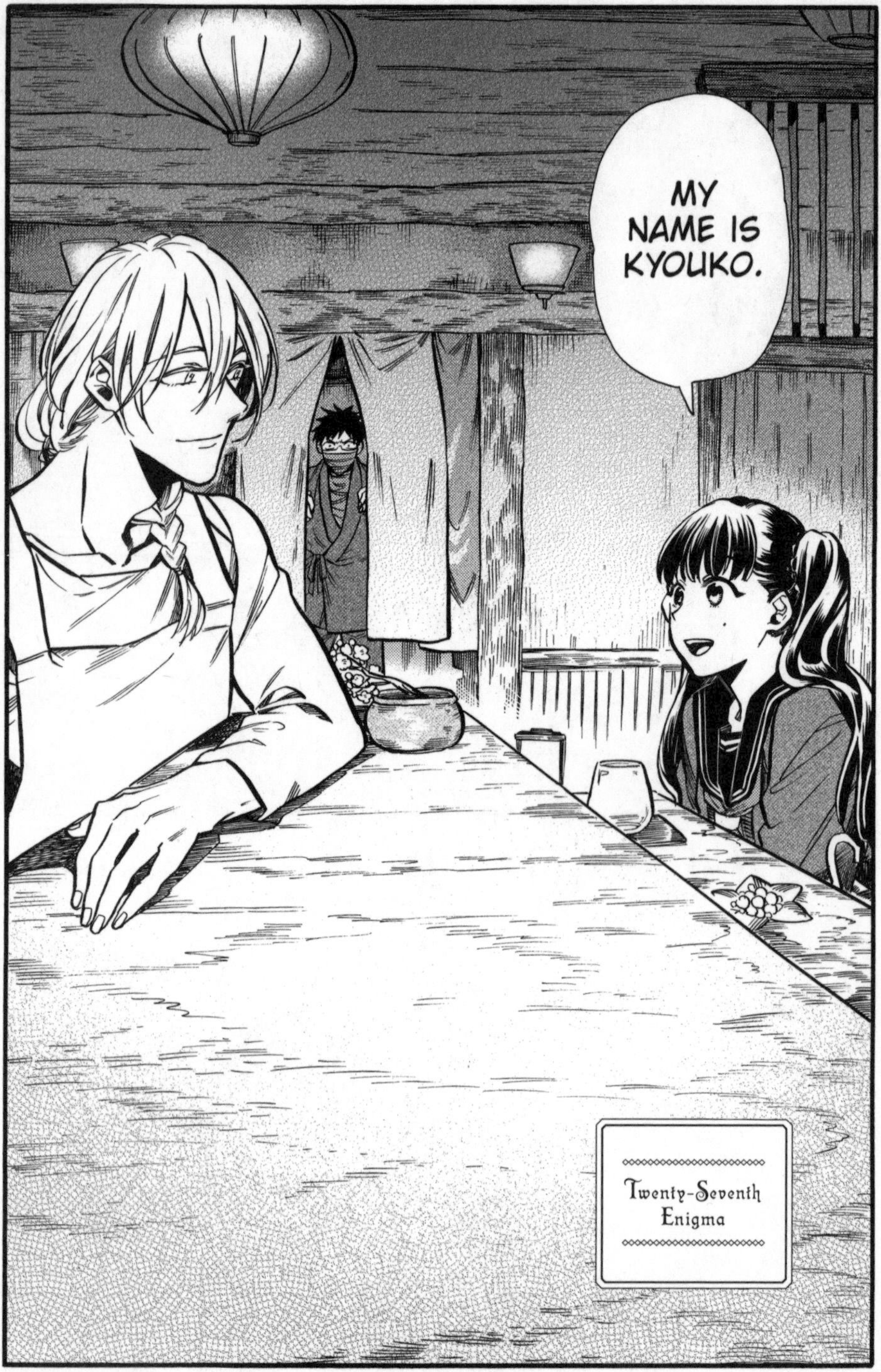
MY NAME IS KYOUKO.
Twenty-Seventh Enigma

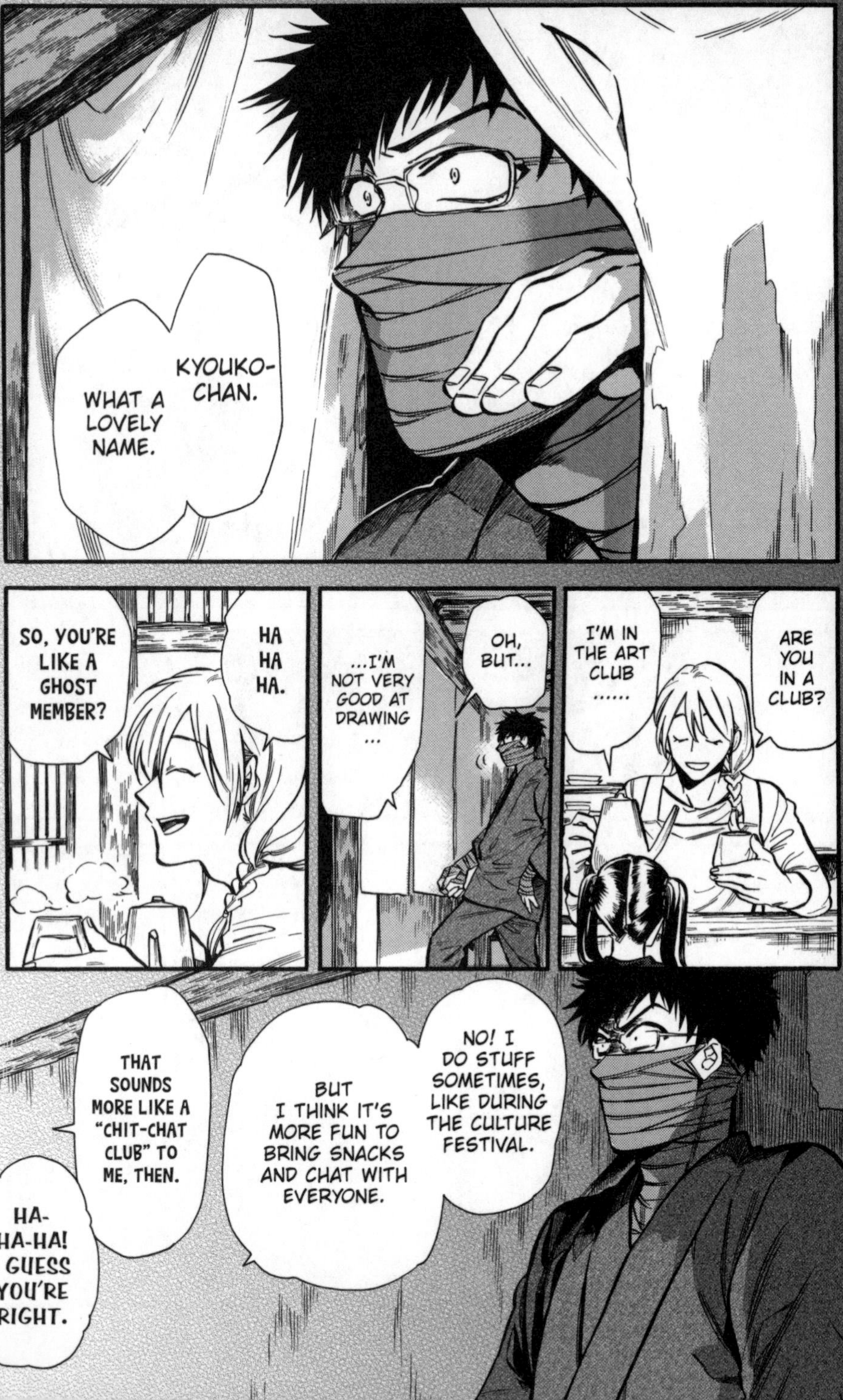
KYOUKO-CHAN.
WHAT A LOVELY NAME.
ARE YOU IN A CLUB?
I'M IN THE ART CLUB ......
OH, BUT...
...I'M NOT VERY GOOD AT DRAWING ...
HA HA HA.
SO, YOU'RE LIKE A GHOST MEMBER?
NO! I DO STUFF SOMETIMES, LIKE DURING THE CULTURE FESTIVAL.
BUT I THINK IT'S MORE FUN TO BRING SNACKS AND CHAT WITH EVERYONE.
THAT SOUNDS MORE LIKE A "CHIT-CHAT CLUB" TO ME, THEN.
HA-HA-HA! I GUESS YOU'RE RIGHT.

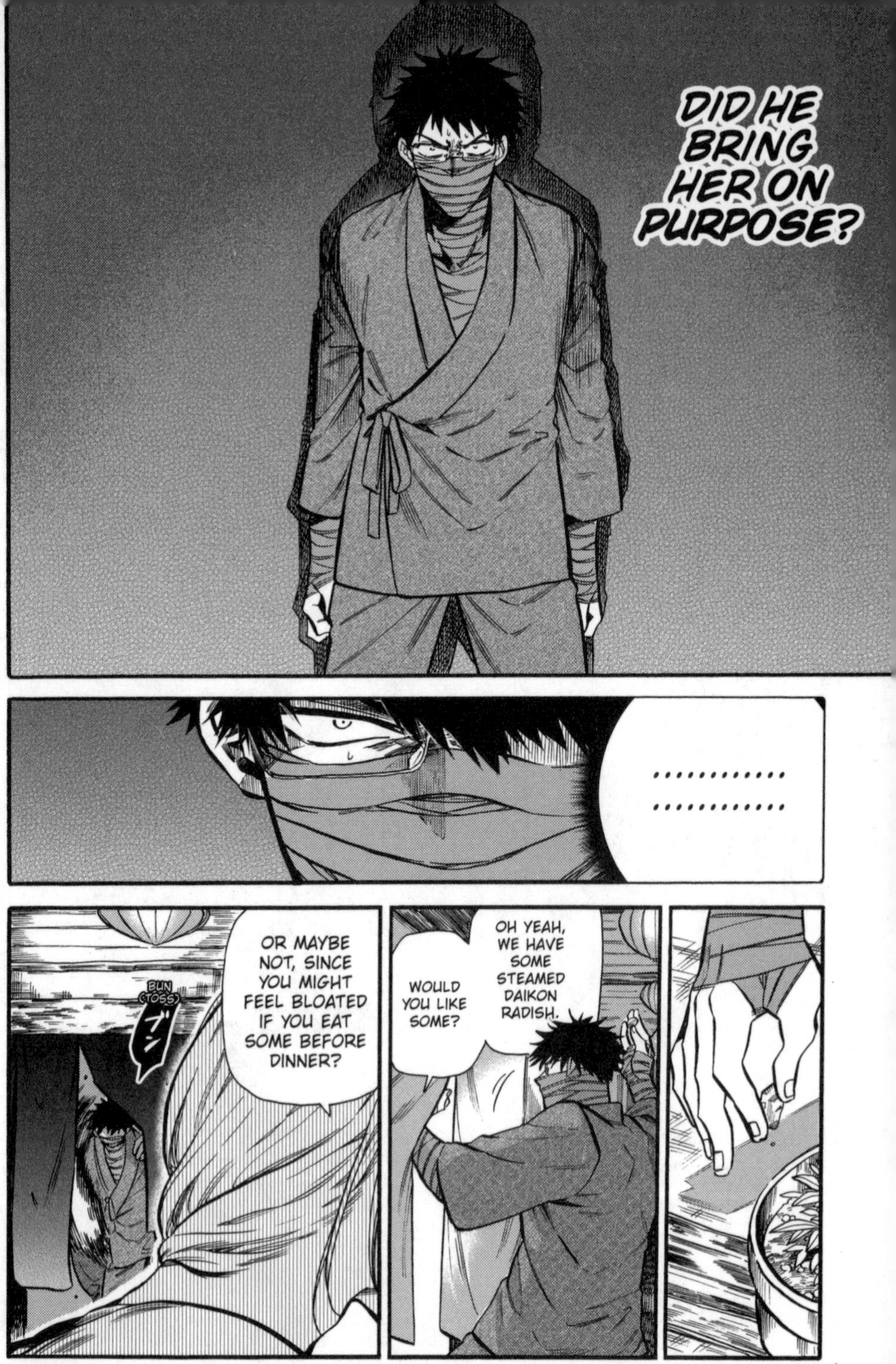
DID HE BRING HER ON PURPOSE?
....
....
OH YEAH, WE HAVE SOME STEAMED DAIKON RADISH.
WOULD YOU LIKE SOME?
OR MAYBE NOT, SINCE YOU MIGHT FEEL BLOATED IF YOU EAT SOME BEFORE DINNER?
BUN (TOSS)
ブン

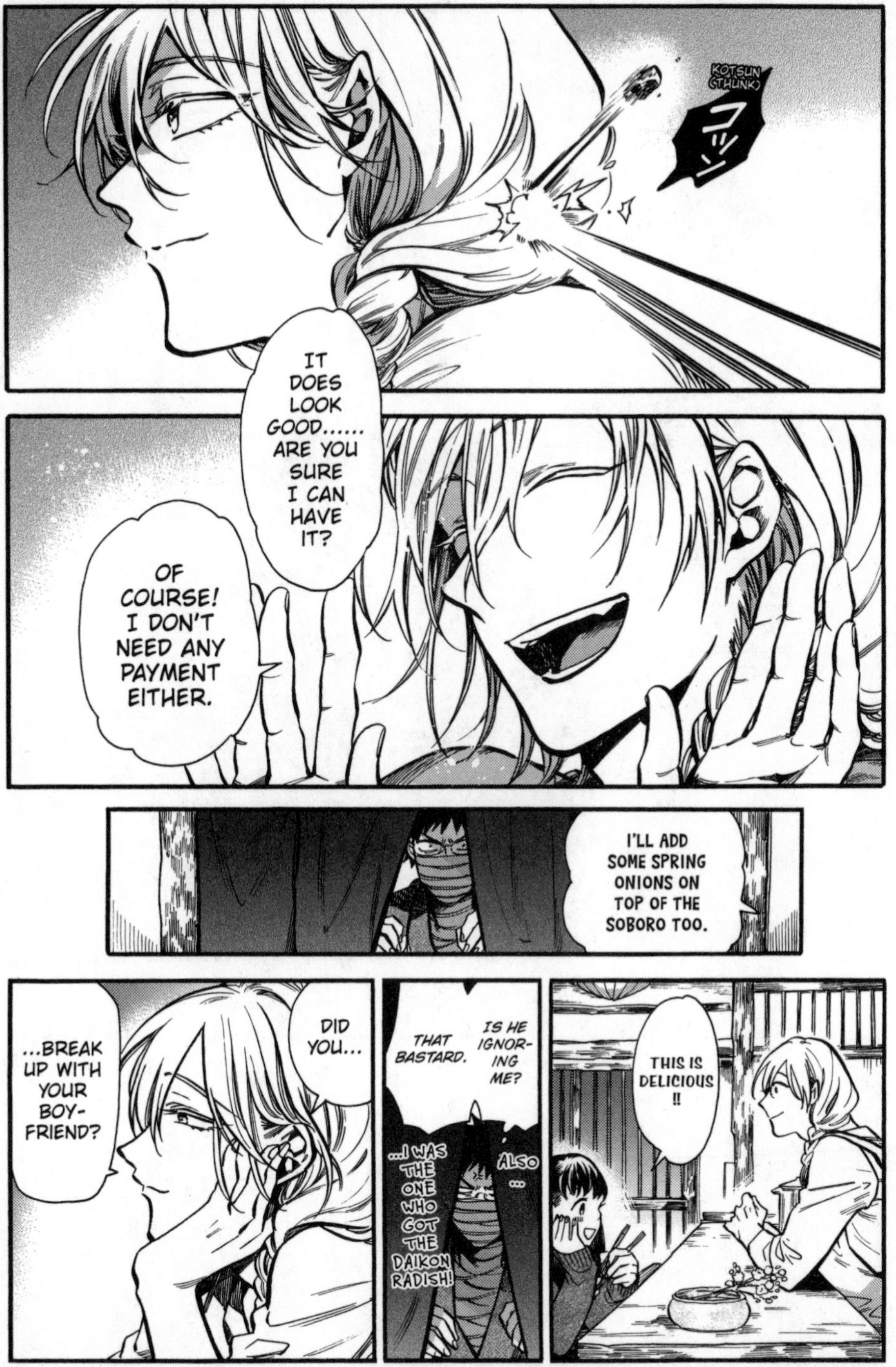
KOTSUN (THUNK)
IT DOES LOOK GOOD...... ARE YOU SURE I CAN HAVE IT?
OF COURSE! I DON'T NEED ANY PAYMENT EITHER.
I'LL ADD SOME SPRING ONIONS ON TOP OF THE SOBORO TOO.
THIS IS DELICIOUS!!
IS HE IGNORING ME?
THAT BASTARD.
ALSO...
...I WAS THE ONE WHO GOT THE DAIKON RADISH!
DID YOU...
...BREAK UP WITH YOUR BOY-FRIEND?

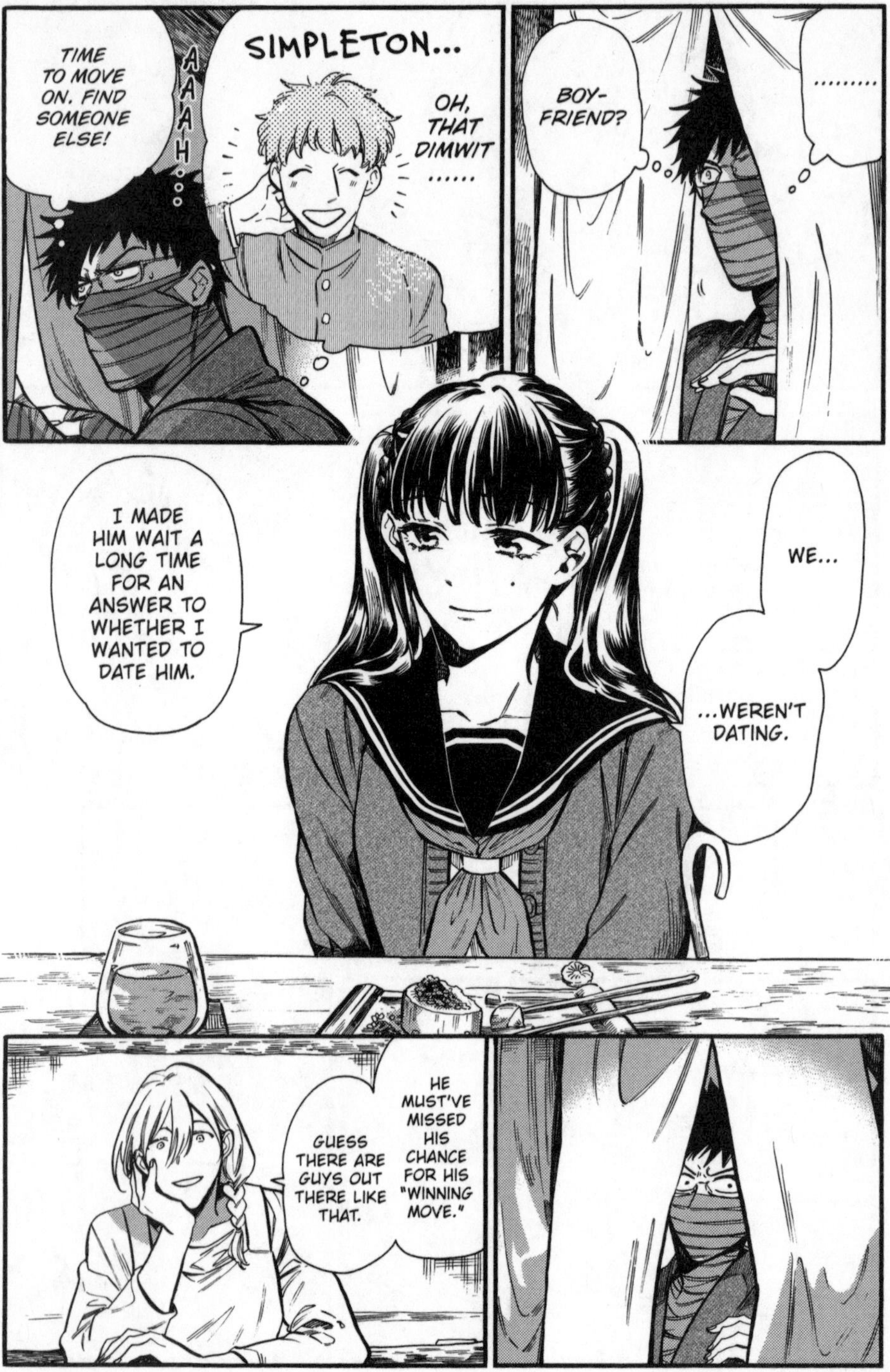
....
BOY-FRIEND?
SIMPLETON...
OH, THAT DIMWIT ......
AAAAH...
TIME TO MOVE ON. FIND SOMEONE ELSE!
WE...
...WEREN'T DATING.
I MADE HIM WAIT A LONG TIME FOR AN ANSWER TO WHETHER I WANTED TO DATE HIM.
HE MUST'VE MISSED HIS CHANCE FOR HIS "WINNING MOVE."
GUESS THERE ARE GUYS OUT THERE LIKE THAT.

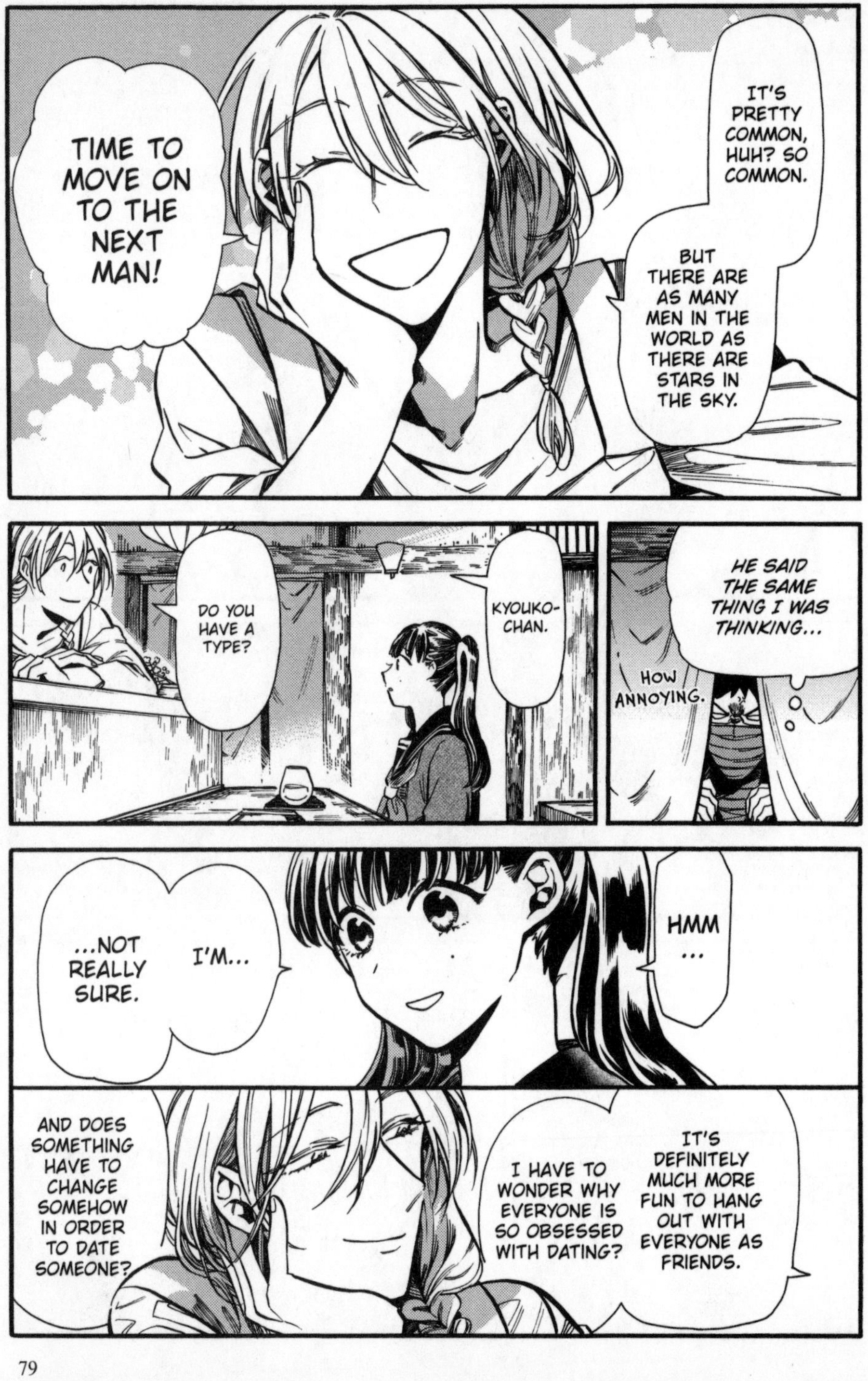

IT'S PRETTY COMMON, HUH? SO COMMON.
BUT THERE ARE AS MANY MEN IN THE WORLD AS THERE ARE STARS IN THE SKY.
TIME TO MOVE ON TO THE NEXT MAN!
HE SAID THE SAME THING I WAS THINKING...
HOW ANNOYING.
KYOUKO-CHAN.
DO YOU HAVE A TYPE?
HMM...
I'M...
...NOT REALLY SURE.
IT'S DEFINITELY MUCH MORE FUN TO HANG OUT WITH EVERYONE AS FRIENDS.
I HAVE TO WONDER WHY EVERYONE IS SO OBSESSED WITH DATING?
AND DOES SOMETHING HAVE TO CHANGE SOMEHOW IN ORDER TO DATE SOMEONE?

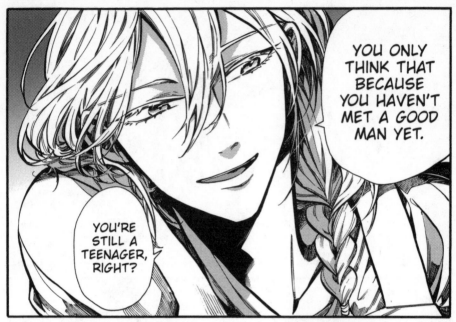

YOU ONLY THINK THAT BECAUSE YOU HAVEN'T MET A GOOD MAN YET.
YOU'RE STILL A TEENAGER, RIGHT?
IT'S FUN TO HANG OUT WITH FRIENDS...
...BUT A TIME WILL COME WHEN YOU'LL START TO WANT SOMETHING MORE.
SOME-THING MORE ...?
MAYBE IT'S EASIER FOR GUYS TO BE AWARE OF WHAT EXACTLY THAT IS.
THAT'S WHY A TIME COMES WHEN THEY DON'T HESITATE.
SOME-THING MORE.
...BY THAT...
...WHAT YOU MEAN IS *THAT*... RIGHT?
YEAH.
THERE MIGHT BE PEOPLE WHO WANT TO DO THAT TOO.
......
IF I MEET THE RIGHT PERSON ...
...I'LL START WANTING SOME-THING MORE TOO?
THAT'S RIGHT.
YOU'LL START FEELING THINGS LIKE WANTING TO TALK TO THEM WITHOUT ANYONE ELSE AROUND.
IT'S SOME-THING TO LOOK FORWARD TO.

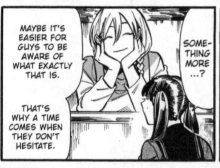

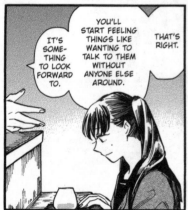

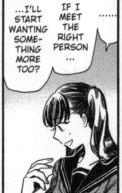

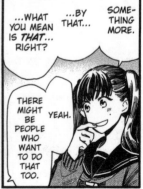

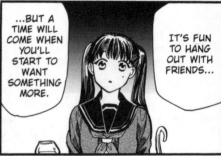

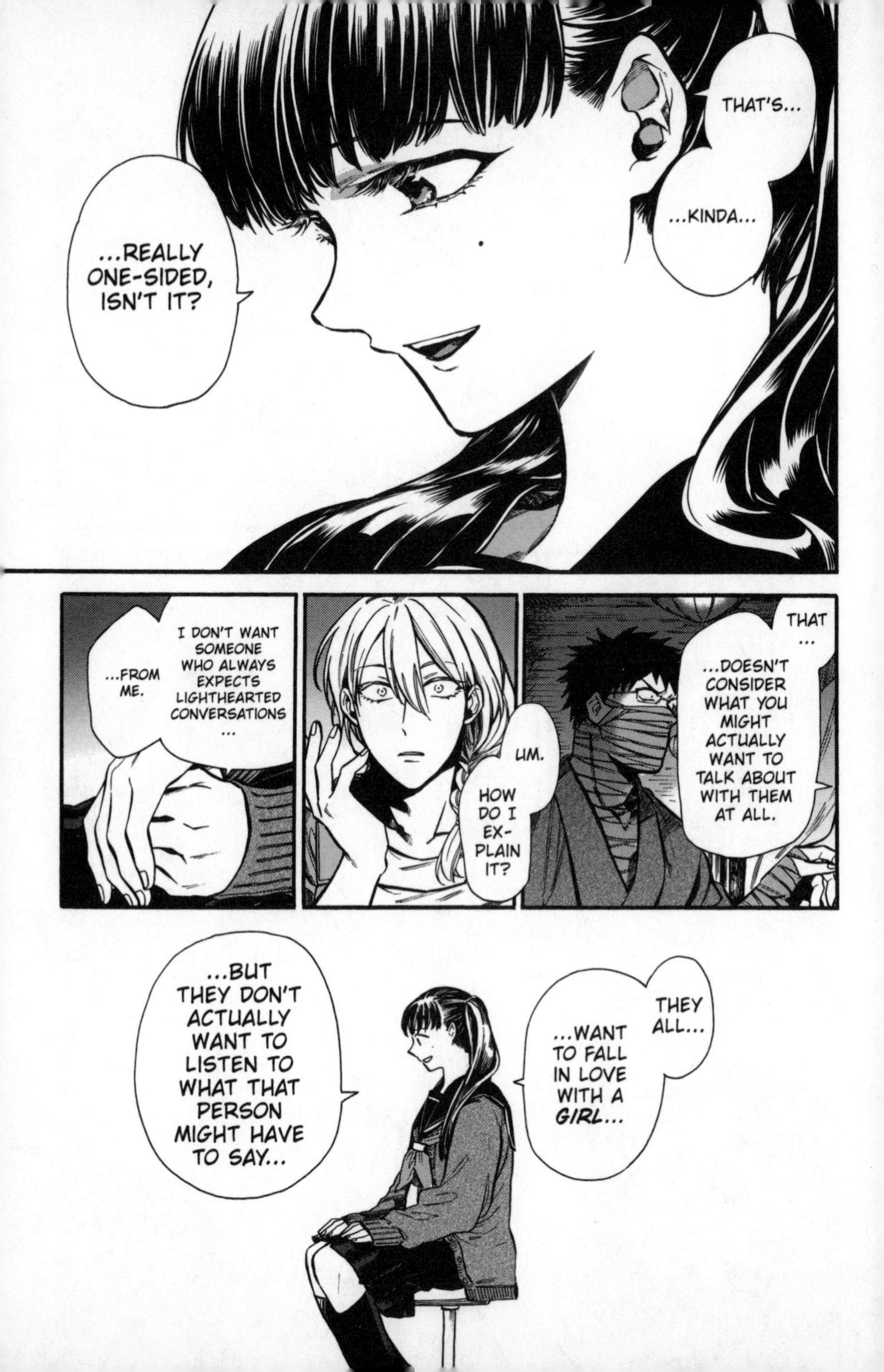
THAT'S...
...KINDA...
...REALLY ONE-SIDED, ISN'T IT?
THAT ...
...DOESN'T CONSIDER WHAT YOU MIGHT ACTUALLY WANT TO TALK ABOUT WITH THEM AT ALL.
UM.
HOW DO I EX-PLAIN IT?
I DON'T WANT SOMEONE WHO ALWAYS EXPECTS LIGHTHEARTED CONVERSATIONS ...
...FROM ME.
THEY ALL...
...WANT TO FALL IN LOVE WITH A *GIRL*...
...BUT THEY DON'T ACTUALLY WANT TO LISTEN TO WHAT THAT PERSON MIGHT HAVE TO SAY...

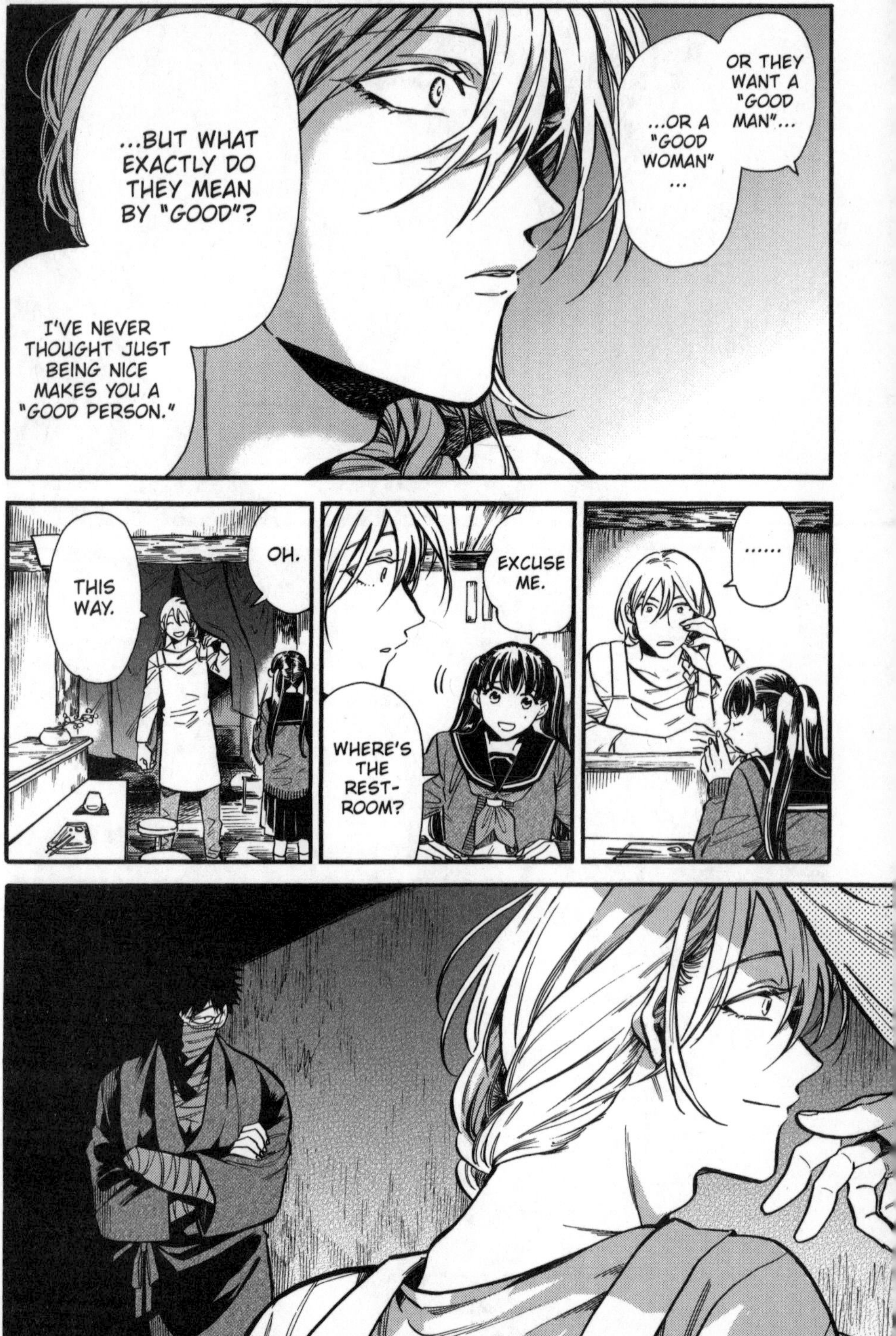
OR THEY WANT A "GOOD MAN"...
...OR A "GOOD WOMAN" ...
...BUT WHAT EXACTLY DO THEY MEAN BY "GOOD"?
I'VE NEVER THOUGHT JUST BEING NICE MAKES YOU A "GOOD PERSON."
......
EXCUSE ME.
WHERE'S THE REST-ROOM?
OH.
THIS WAY.

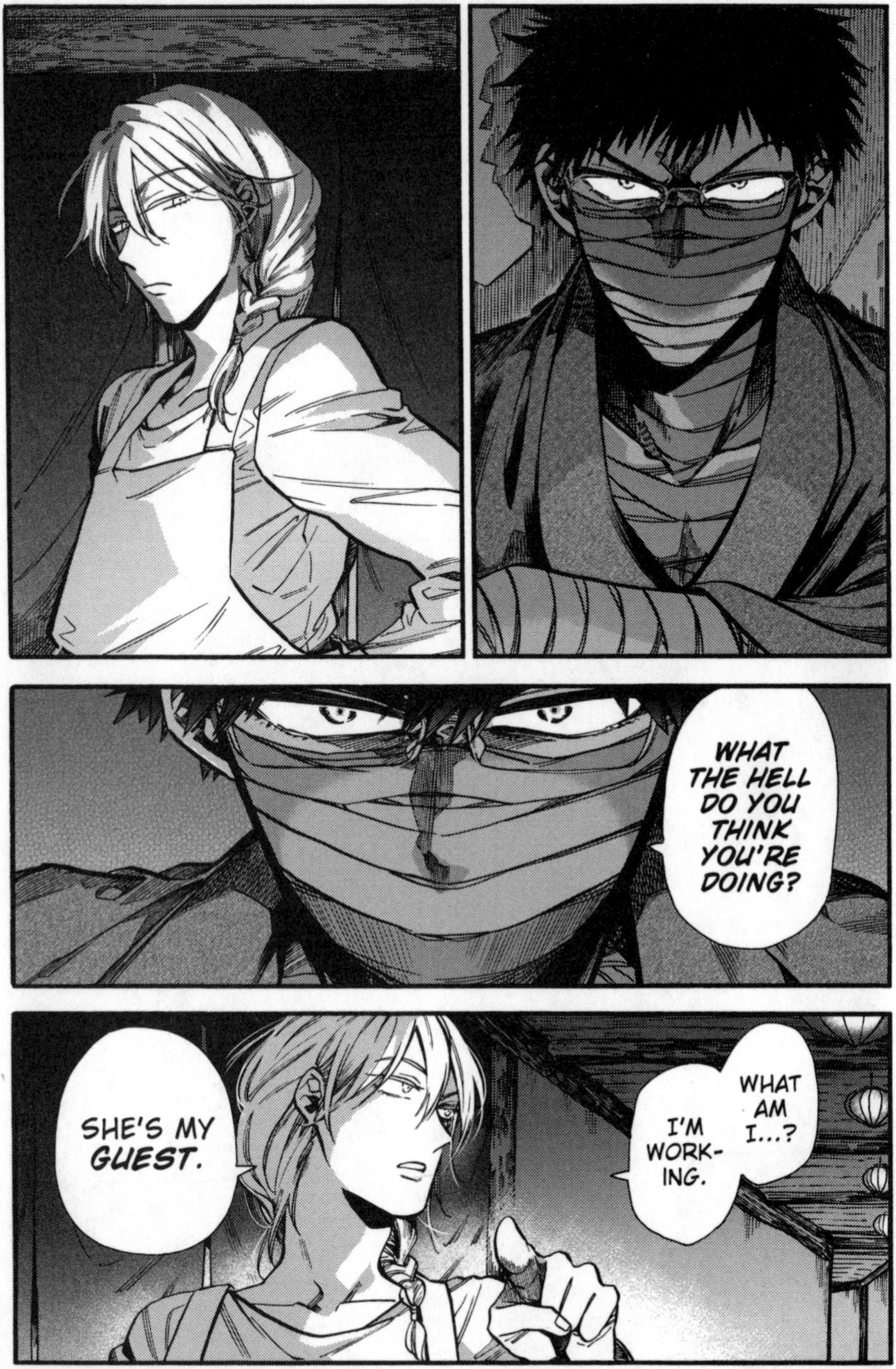
WHAT THE HELL DO YOU THINK YOU'RE DOING?
WHAT AM I...?
I'M WORKING.
SHE'S MY *GUEST*.

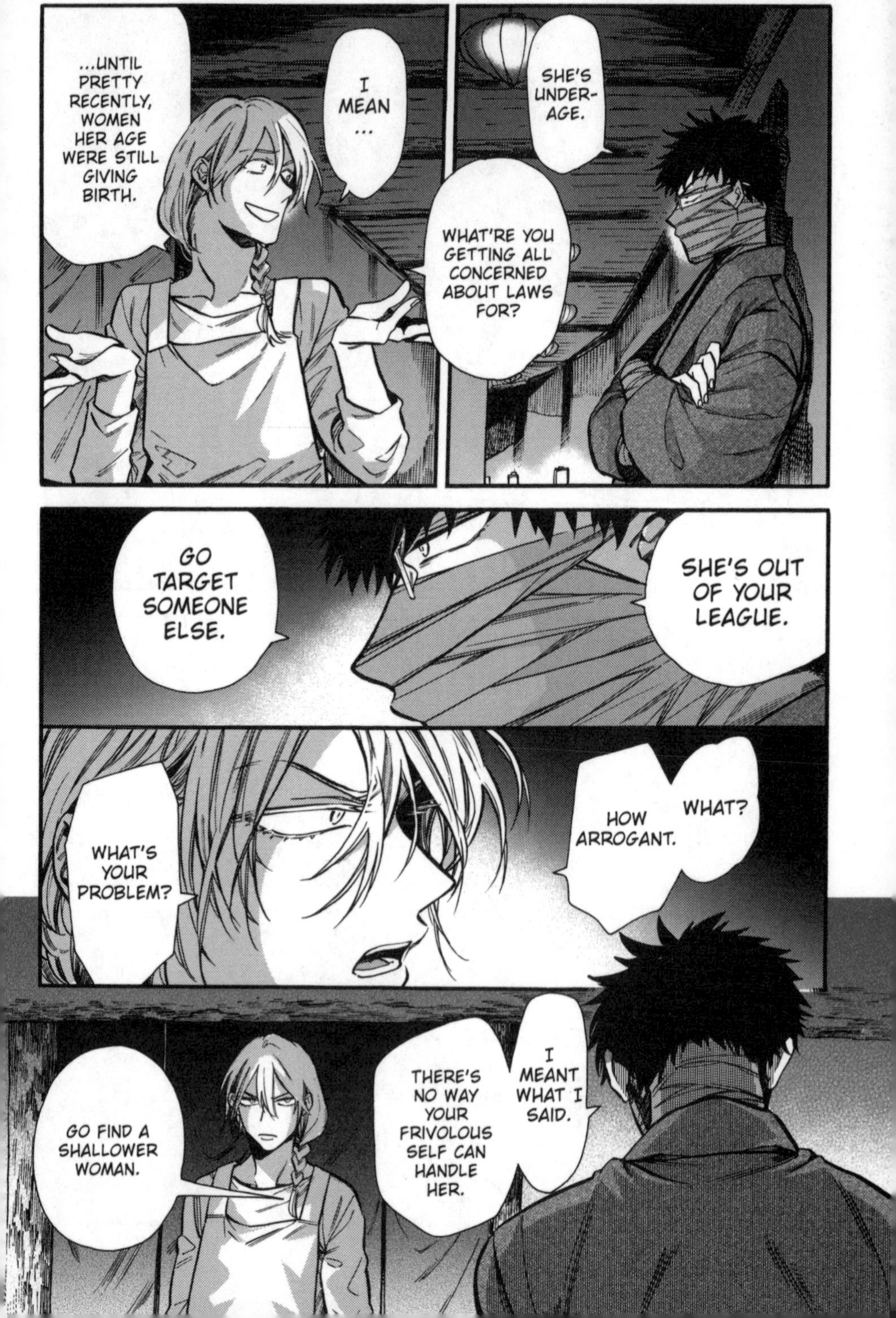
SHE'S UNDER-AGE.
WHAT'RE YOU GETTING ALL CONCERNED ABOUT LAWS FOR?
I MEAN ...
...UNTIL PRETTY RECENTLY, WOMEN HER AGE WERE STILL GIVING BIRTH.
SHE'S OUT OF YOUR LEAGUE.
GO TARGET SOMEONE ELSE.
WHAT?
HOW ARROGANT.
WHAT'S YOUR PROBLEM?
I MEANT WHAT I SAID.
THERE'S NO WAY YOUR FRIVOLOUS SELF CAN HANDLE HER.
GO FIND A SHALLOWER WOMAN.

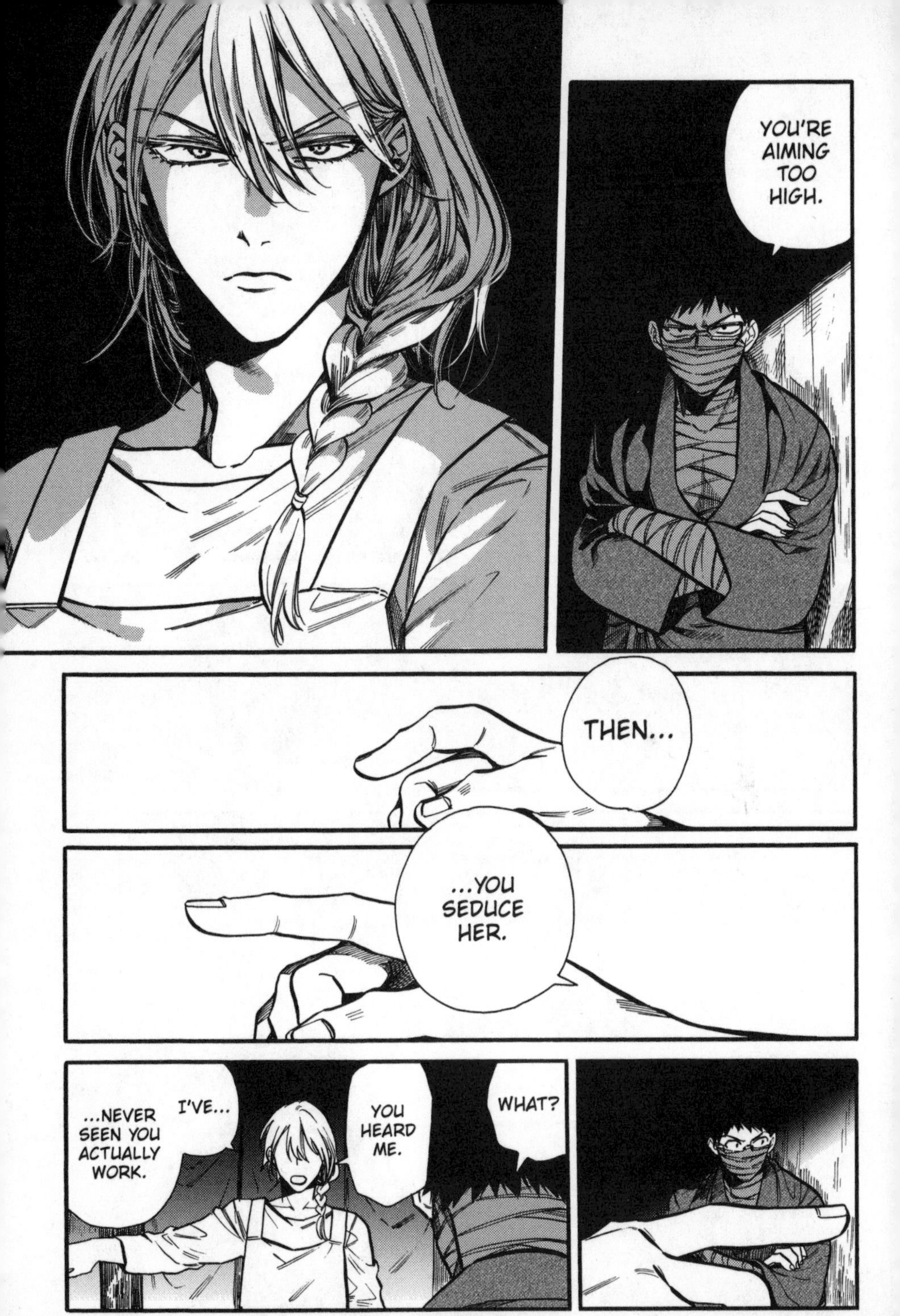
YOU'RE AIMING TOO HIGH.
THEN...
...YOU SEDUCE HER.
WHAT?
YOU HEARD ME.
I'VE...
...NEVER SEEN YOU ACTUALLY WORK.

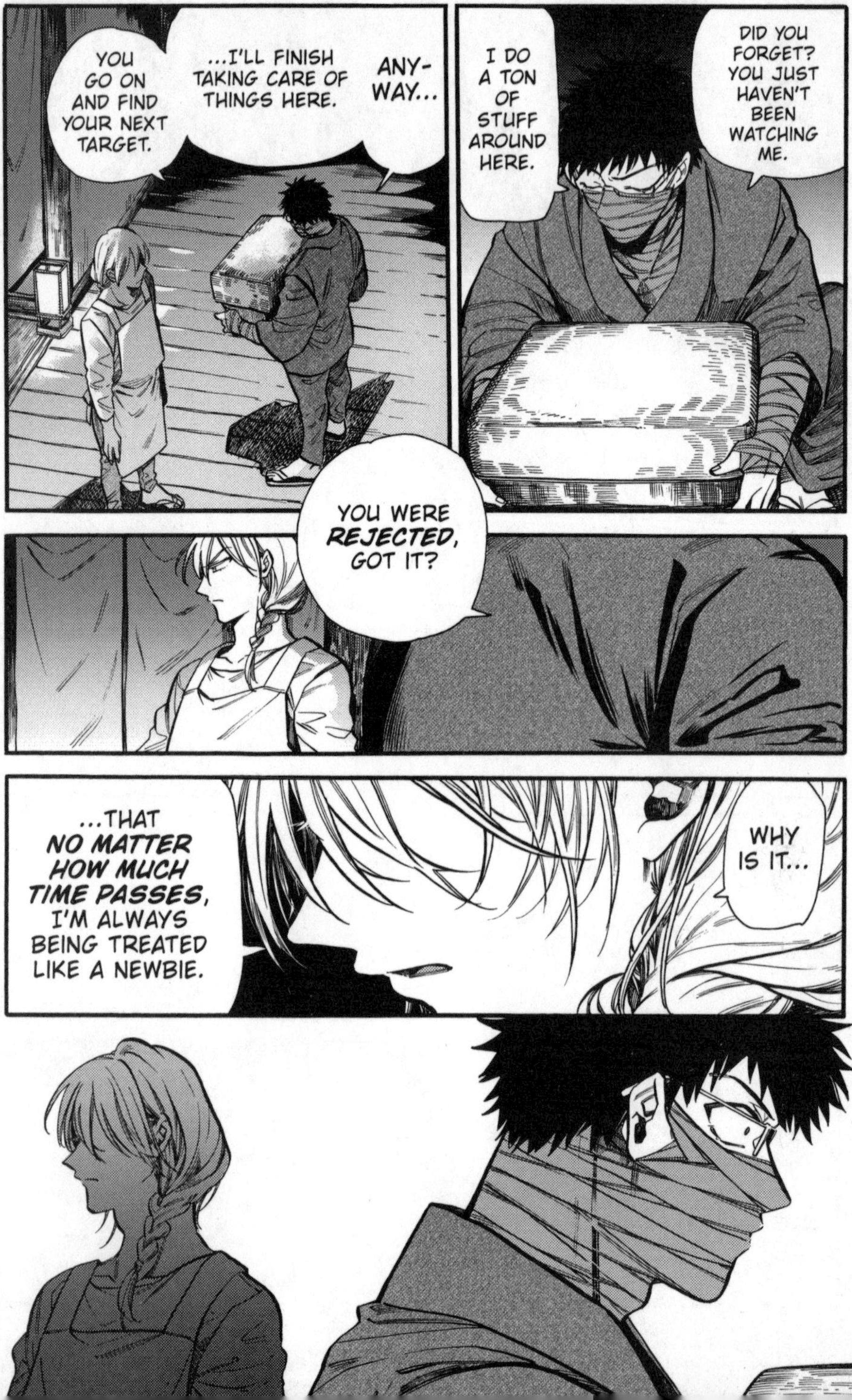
DID YOU FORGET? YOU JUST HAVEN'T BEEN WATCHING ME.
I DO A TON OF STUFF AROUND HERE.
ANY-WAY...
...I'LL FINISH TAKING CARE OF THINGS HERE.
YOU GO ON AND FIND YOUR NEXT TARGET.
YOU WERE ***REJECTED***, GOT IT?
WHY IS IT...
...THAT ***NO MATTER HOW MUCH TIME PASSES***, I'M ALWAYS BEING TREATED LIKE A NEWBIE.

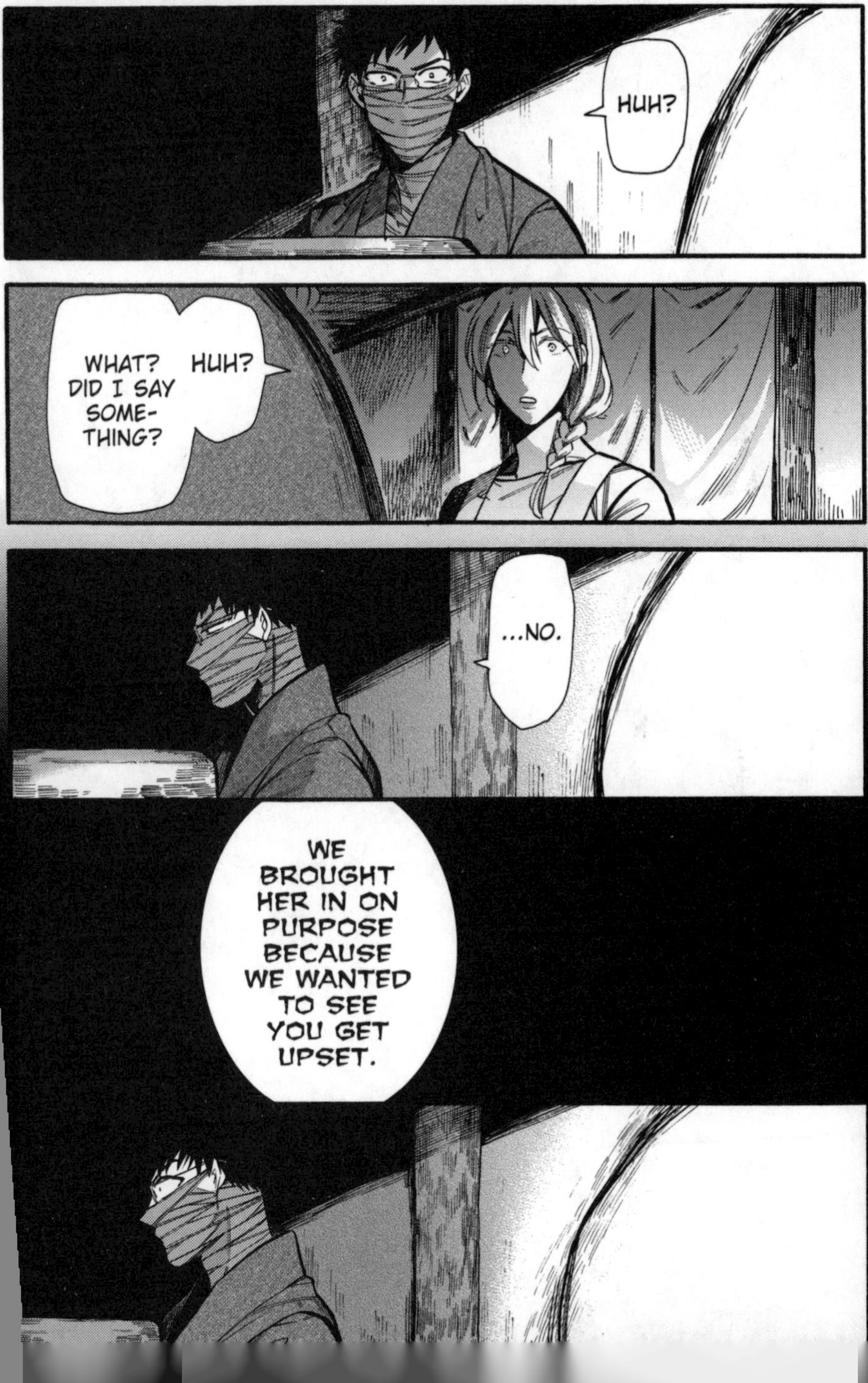
HUH?
HUH?
WHAT? DID I SAY SOME-THING?
...NO.
WE BROUGHT HER IN ON PURPOSE BECAUSE WE WANTED TO SEE YOU GET UPSET.

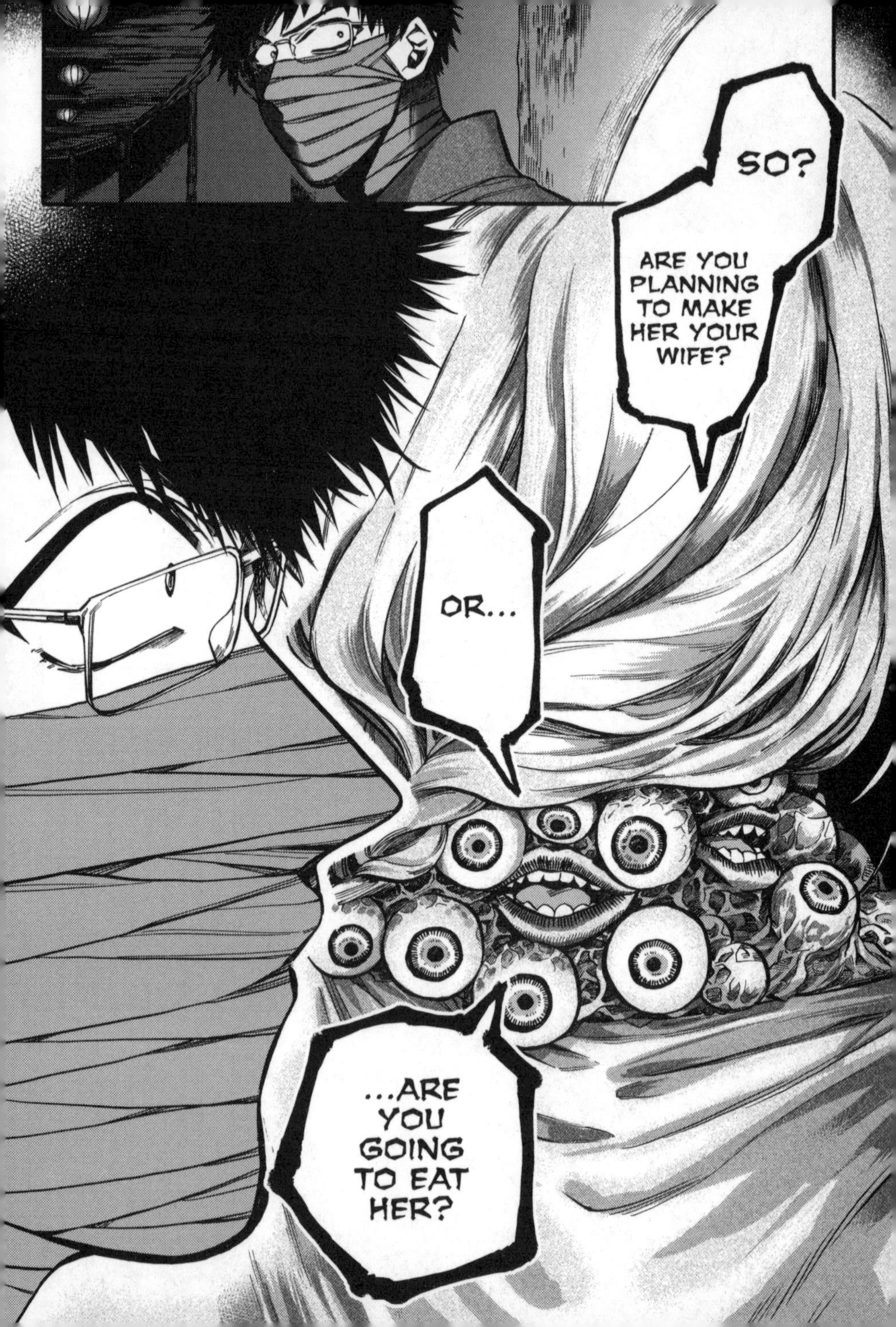
SO?
ARE YOU PLANNING TO MAKE HER YOUR WIFE?
OR...
...ARE YOU GOING TO EAT HER?

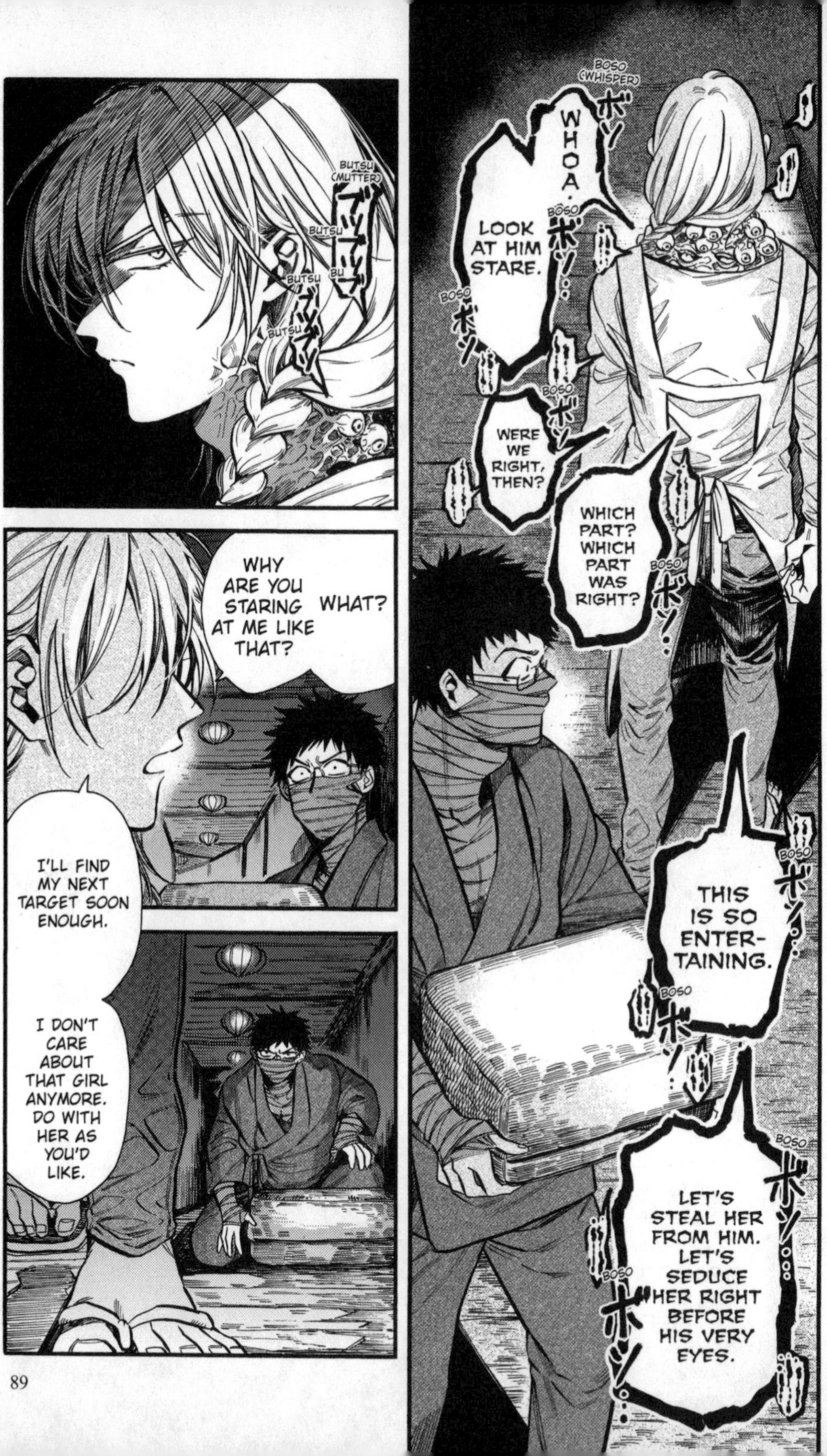
BOSO (WHISPER)
WHOA.
BOSO
LOOK AT HIM STARE.
BOSO
BOSO
WERE WE RIGHT, THEN?
WHICH PART? WHICH PART WAS RIGHT?
BOSO
BOSO
THIS IS SO ENTER-TAINING.
BOSO
BOSO
LET'S STEAL HER FROM HIM. LET'S SEDUCE HER RIGHT BEFORE HIS VERY EYES.
BOSO
BUTSU (MUTTER)
BUTSU
BU
BUTSU
BUTSU
WHAT?
WHY ARE YOU STARING AT ME LIKE THAT?
I'LL FIND MY NEXT TARGET SOON ENOUGH.
I DON'T CARE ABOUT THAT GIRL ANYMORE. DO WITH HER AS YOU'D LIKE.

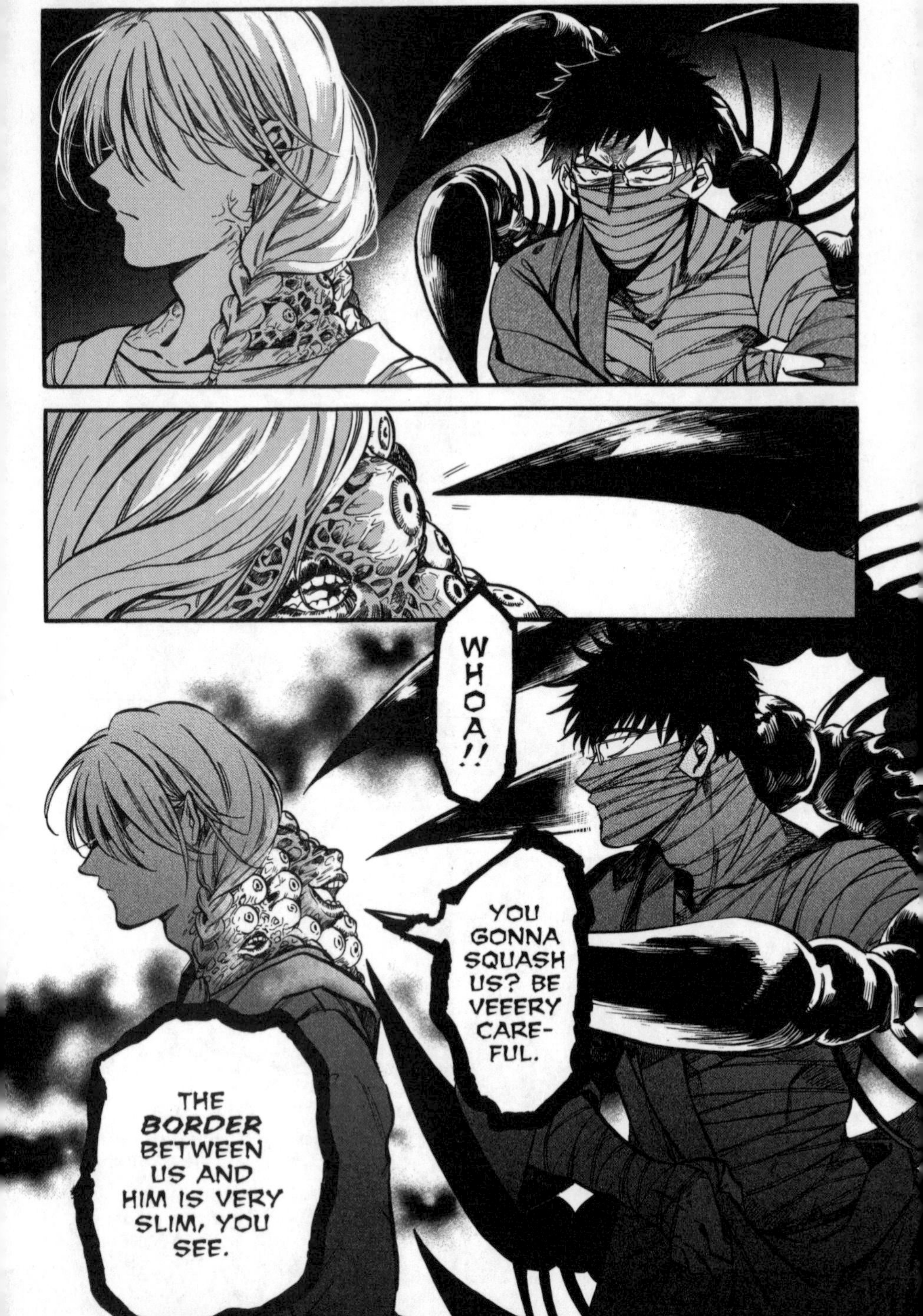
WHOA!!
YOU GONNA SQUASH US? BE VEEERY CARE-FUL.
THE *BORDER* BETWEEN US AND HIM IS VERY SLIM, YOU SEE.

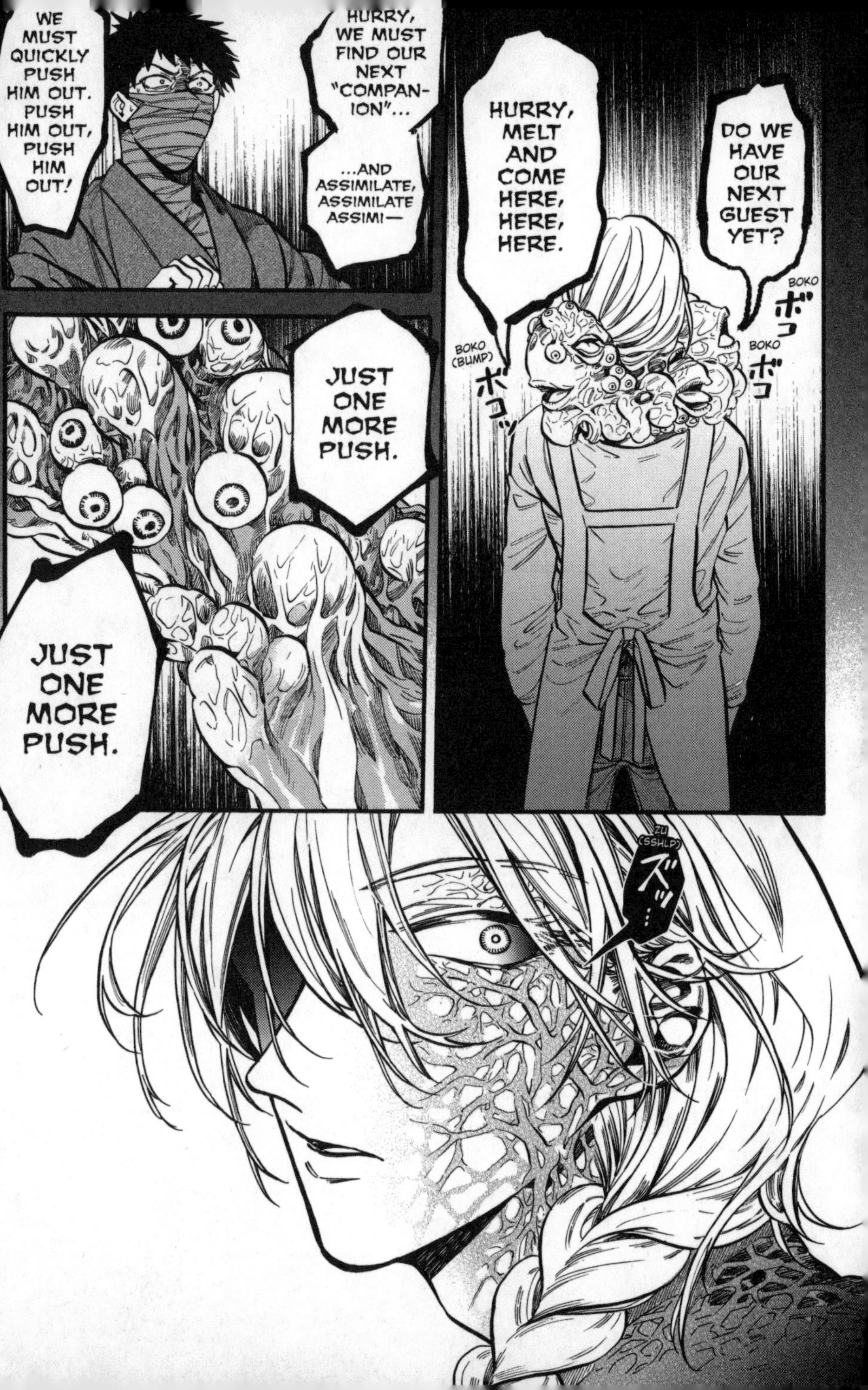
DO WE HAVE OUR NEXT GUEST YET?
BOKO
ボコ
BOKO
ボコ
HURRY, MELT AND COME HERE, HERE, HERE.
BOKO (BUMP)
ボコッ
HURRY, WE MUST FIND OUR NEXT "COMPANION"...
...AND ASSIMILATE, ASSIMILATE ASSIMI—
WE MUST QUICKLY PUSH HIM OUT. PUSH HIM OUT, PUSH HIM OUT!
JUST ONE MORE PUSH.
JUST ONE MORE PUSH.
ZU (SSHLP)
ズッ…

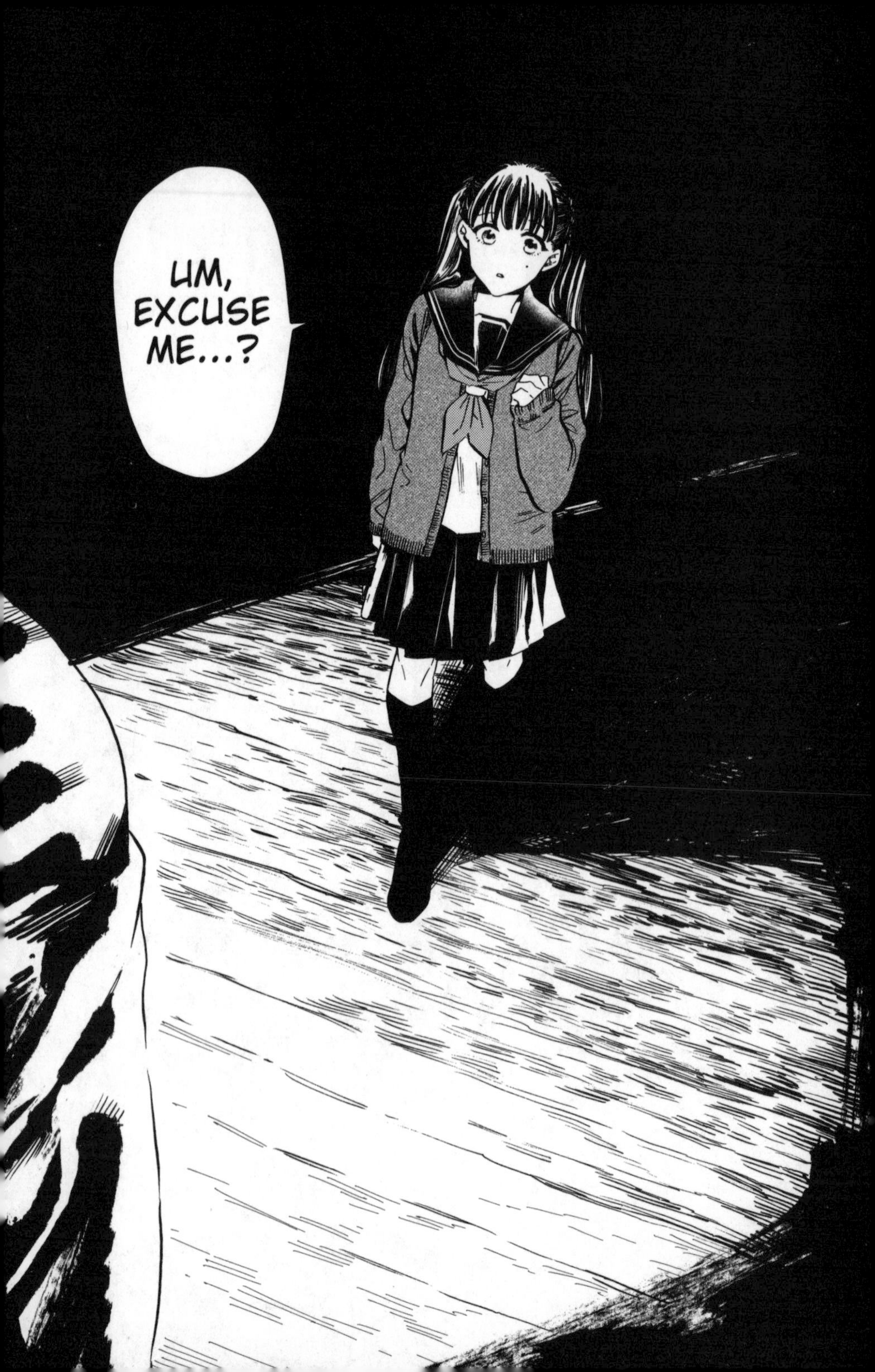
UM, EXCUSE ME...?

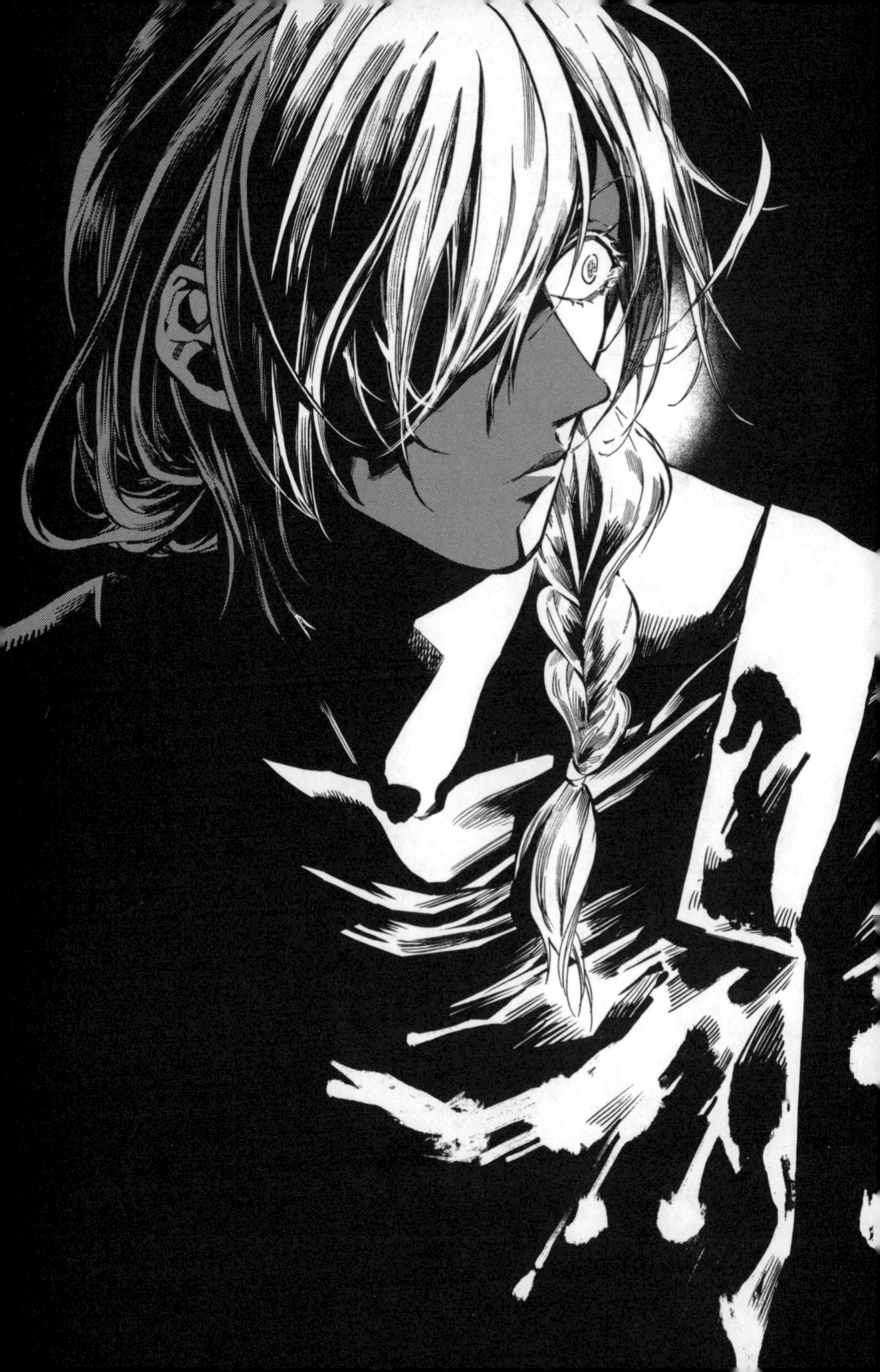

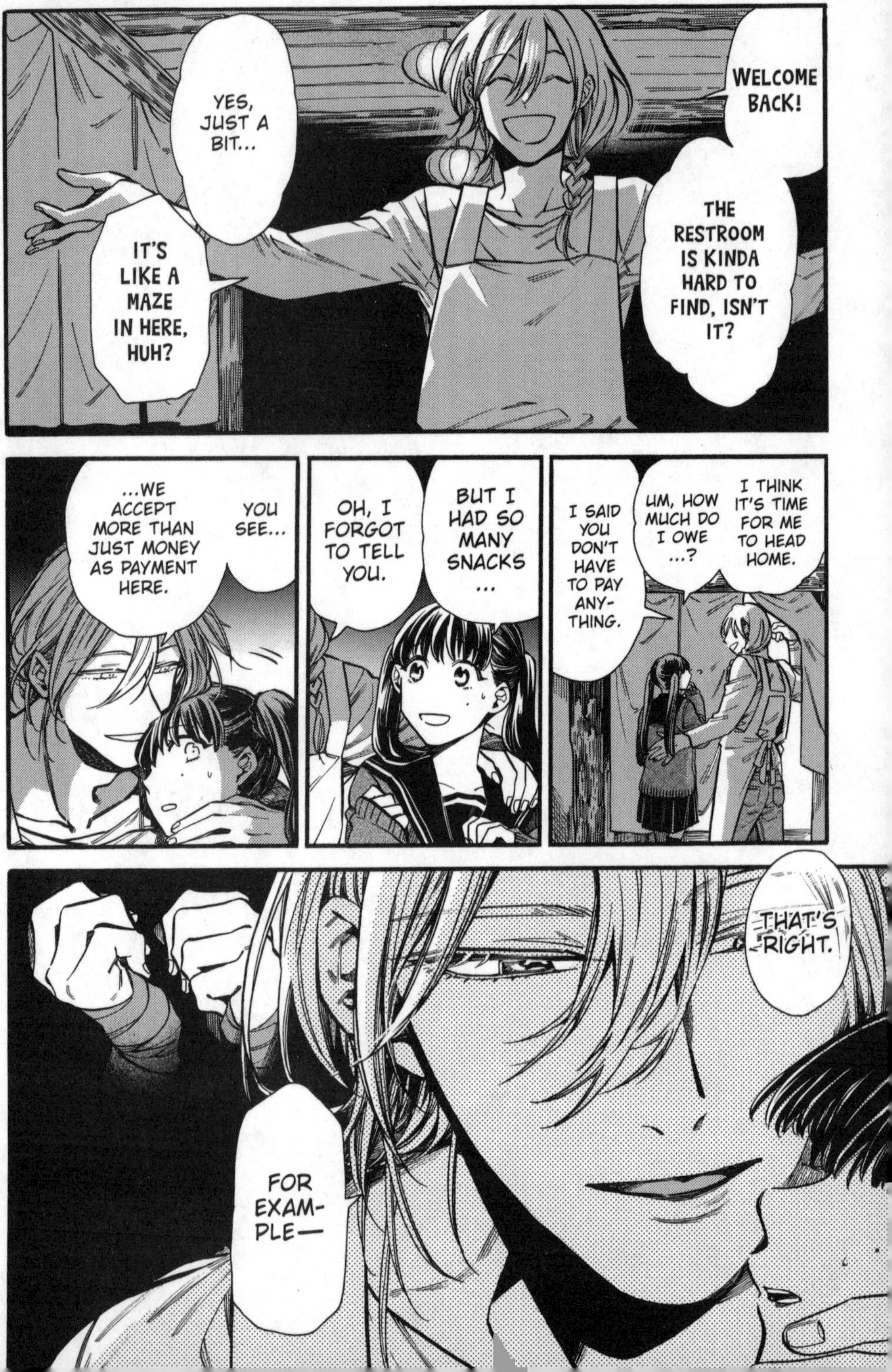
WELCOME BACK!
THE RESTROOM IS KINDA HARD TO FIND, ISN'T IT?
YES, JUST A BIT...
IT'S LIKE A MAZE IN HERE, HUH?
I THINK IT'S TIME FOR ME TO HEAD HOME.
UM, HOW MUCH DO I OWE ...?
I SAID YOU DON'T HAVE TO PAY ANY-THING.
BUT I HAD SO MANY SNACKS ...
OH, I FORGOT TO TELL YOU.
YOU SEE...
...WE ACCEPT MORE THAN JUST MONEY AS PAYMENT HERE.
THAT'S RIGHT.
FOR EXAMPLE—

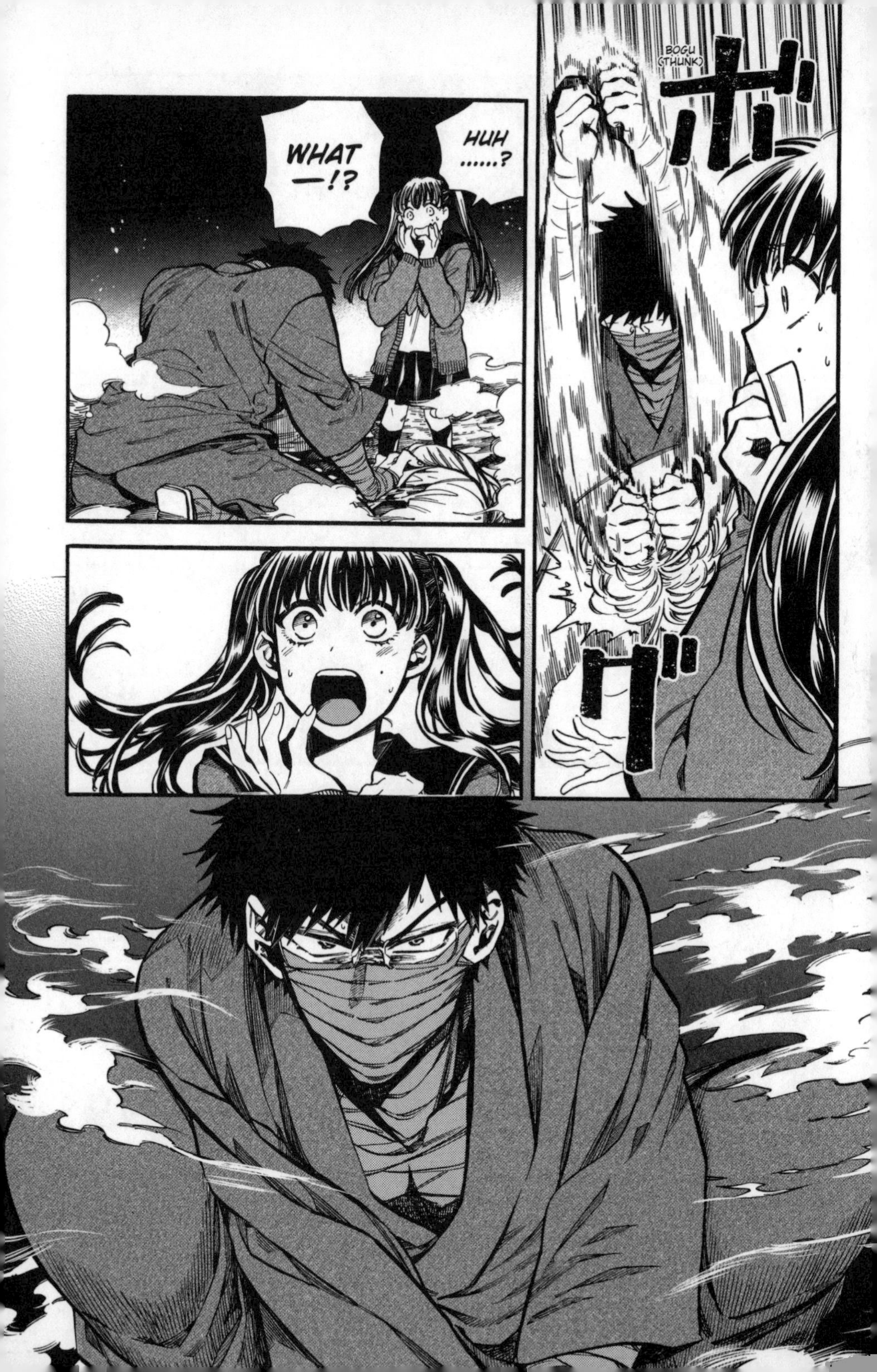
BOGU (THUNK)
HUH ......?
WHAT —!?

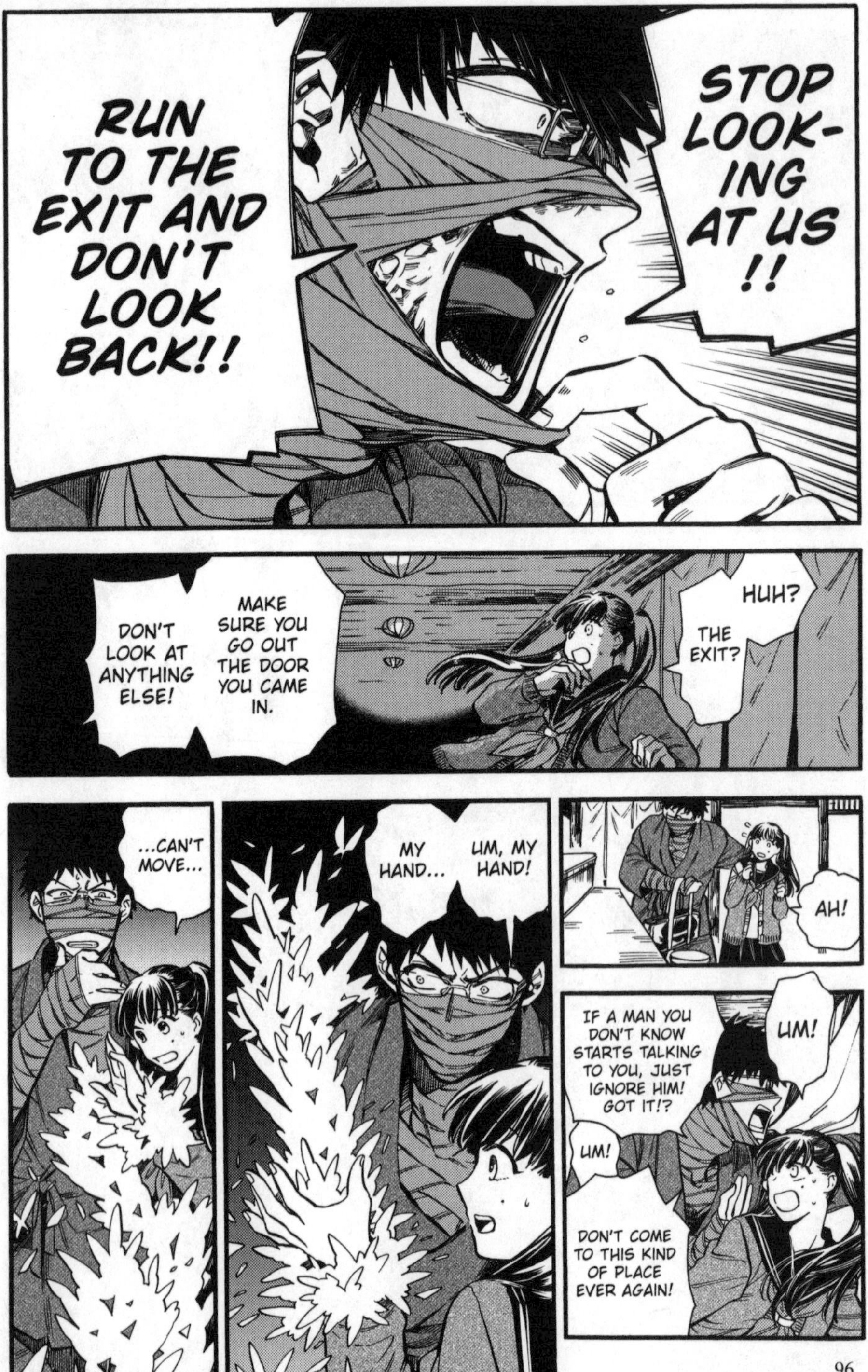
STOP LOOKING AT US!!
RUN TO THE EXIT AND DON'T LOOK BACK!!
HUH?
THE EXIT?
MAKE SURE YOU GO OUT THE DOOR YOU CAME IN.
DON'T LOOK AT ANYTHING ELSE!
AH!
UM!
IF A MAN YOU DON'T KNOW STARTS TALKING TO YOU, JUST IGNORE HIM! GOT IT!?
UM!
DON'T COME TO THIS KIND OF PLACE EVER AGAIN!
UM, MY HAND!
MY HAND...
...CAN'T MOVE...

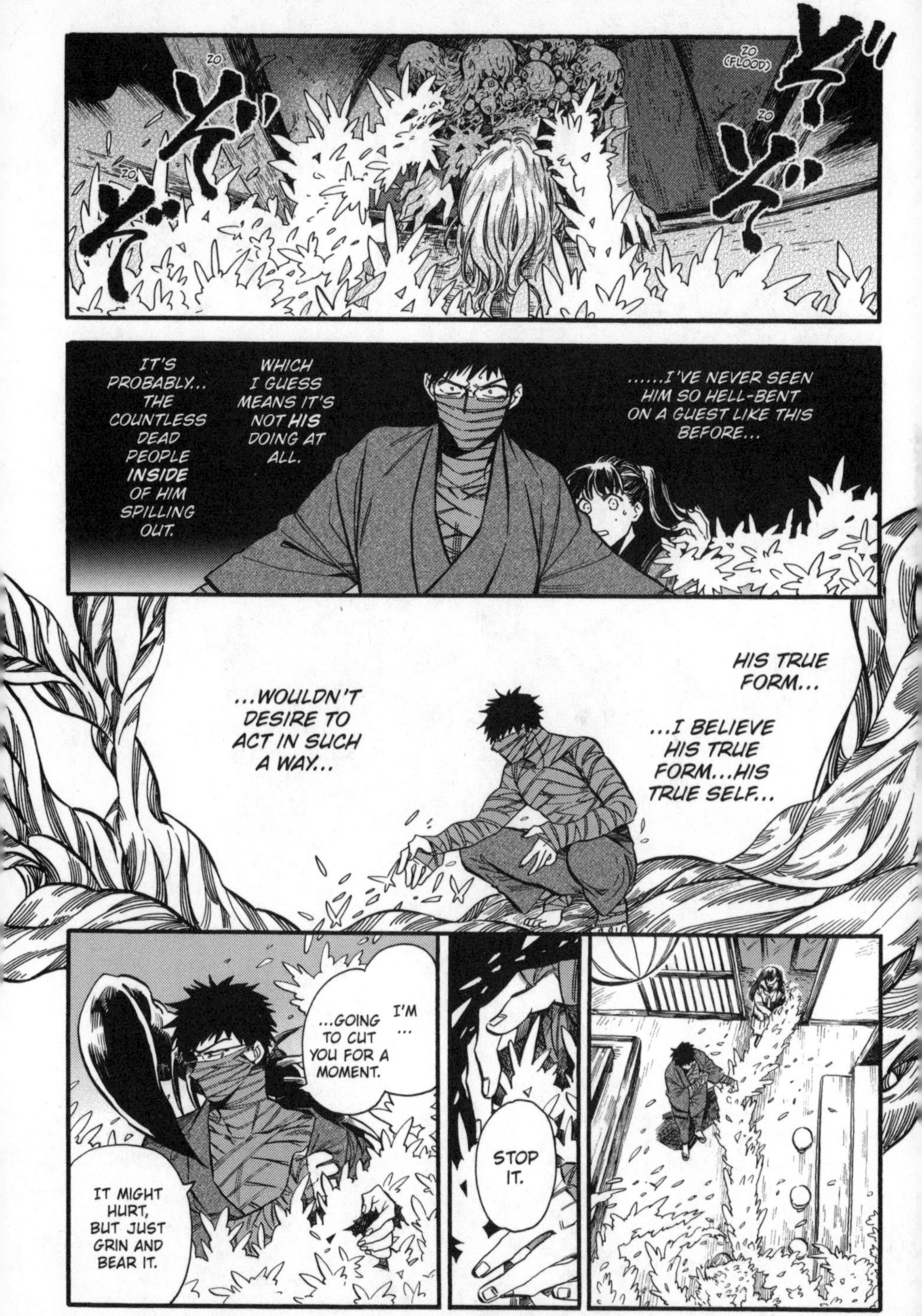
ZO (FLOOD)
ZO
ZO
ZO
......I'VE NEVER SEEN HIM SO HELL-BENT ON A GUEST LIKE THIS BEFORE...
IT'S PROBABLY... THE COUNTLESS DEAD PEOPLE INSIDE OF HIM SPILLING OUT.
WHICH I GUESS MEANS IT'S NOT HIS DOING AT ALL.
HIS TRUE FORM...
...I BELIEVE HIS TRUE FORM...HIS TRUE SELF...
...WOULDN'T DESIRE TO ACT IN SUCH A WAY...
STOP IT.
I'M ...
...GOING TO CUT YOU FOR A MOMENT.
IT MIGHT HURT, BUT JUST GRIN AND BEAR IT.

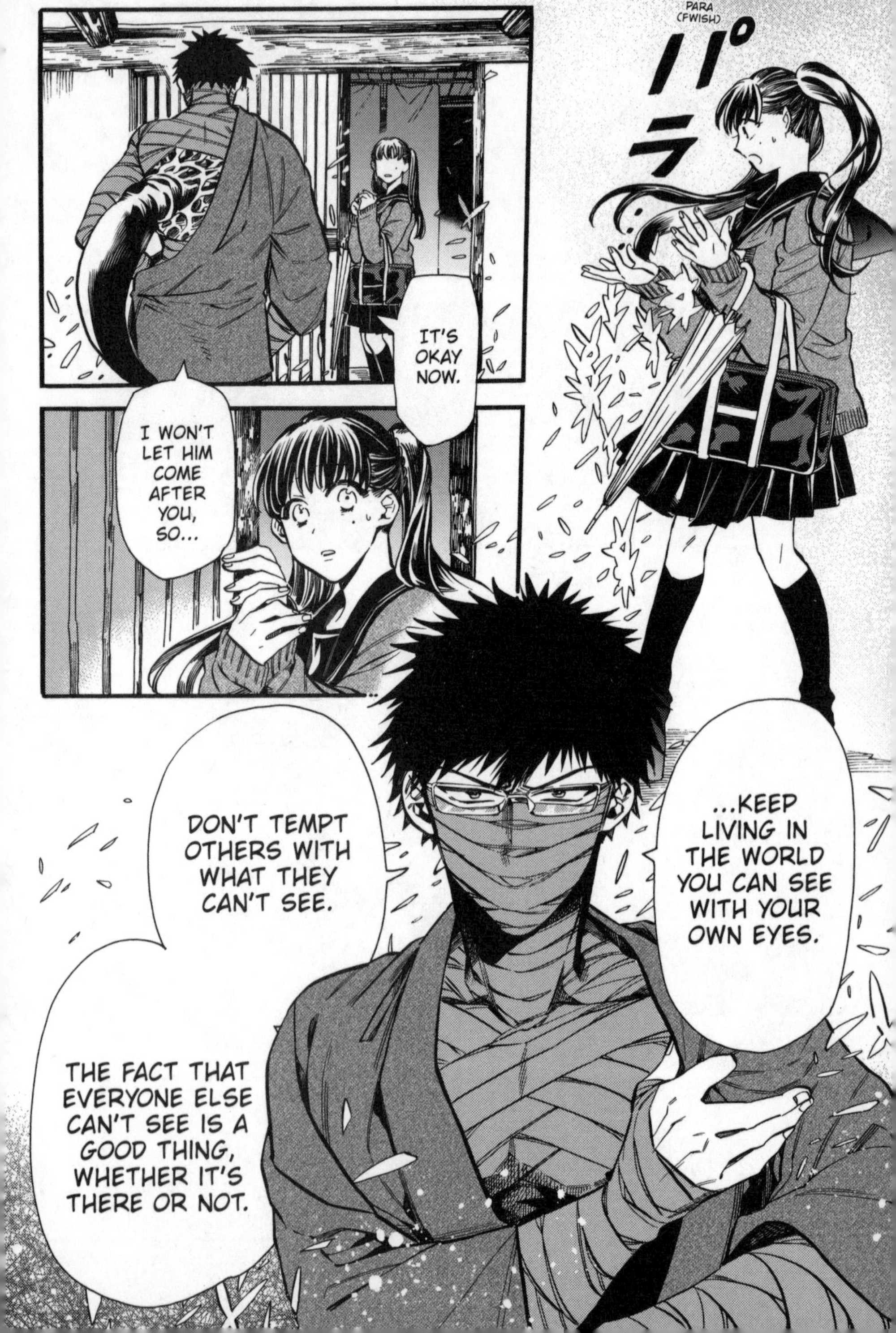
PARA (FWISH)
IT'S OKAY NOW.
I WON'T LET HIM COME AFTER YOU, SO...
...KEEP LIVING IN THE WORLD YOU CAN SEE WITH YOUR OWN EYES.
DON'T TEMPT OTHERS WITH WHAT THEY CAN'T SEE.
THE FACT THAT EVERYONE ELSE CAN'T SEE IS A GOOD THING, WHETHER IT'S THERE OR NOT.

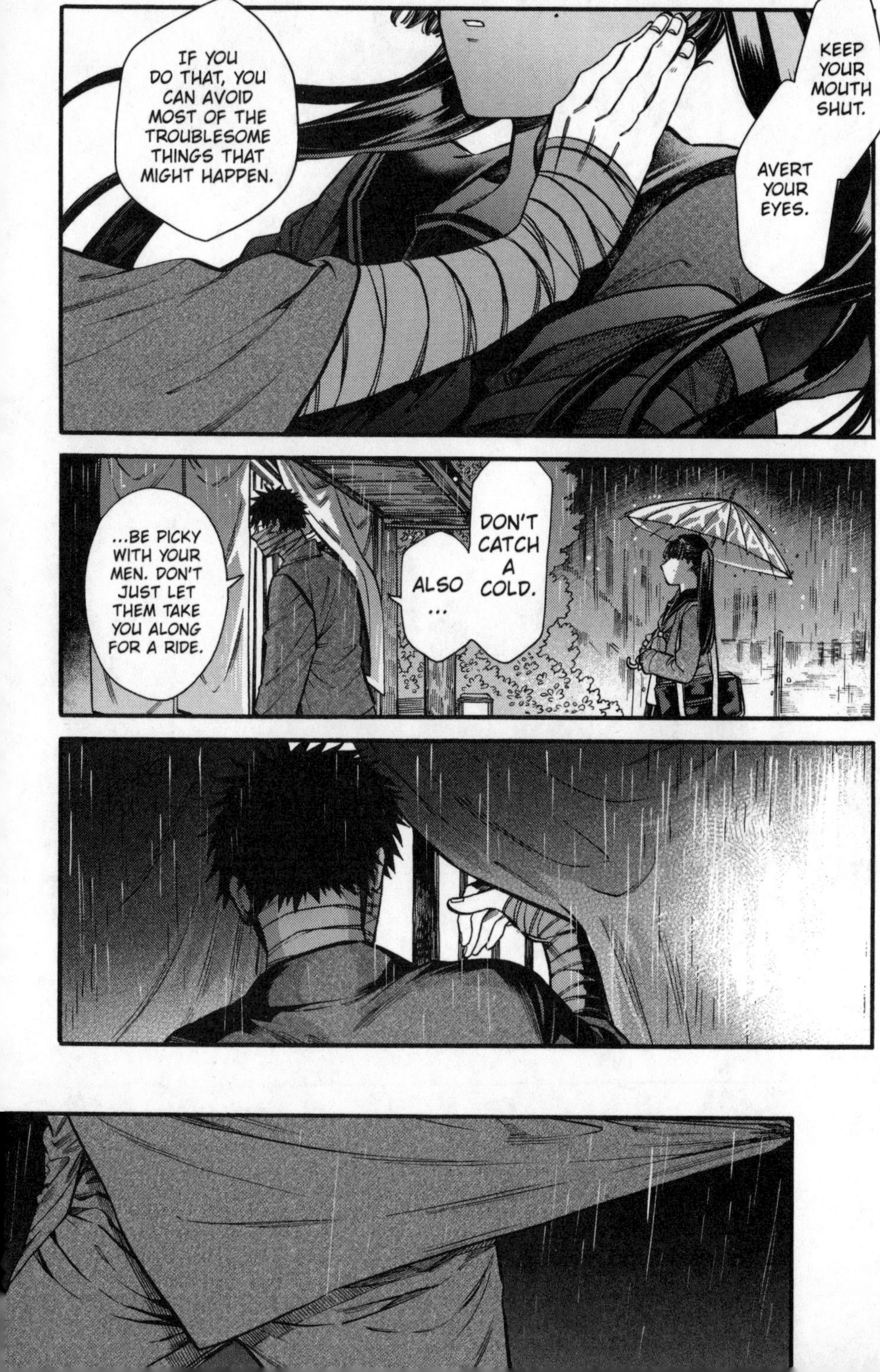
KEEP YOUR MOUTH SHUT.
AVERT YOUR EYES.
IF YOU DO THAT, YOU CAN AVOID MOST OF THE TROUBLESOME THINGS THAT MIGHT HAPPEN.
DON'T CATCH A COLD.
ALSO ...
...BE PICKY WITH YOUR MEN. DON'T JUST LET THEM TAKE YOU ALONG FOR A RIDE.

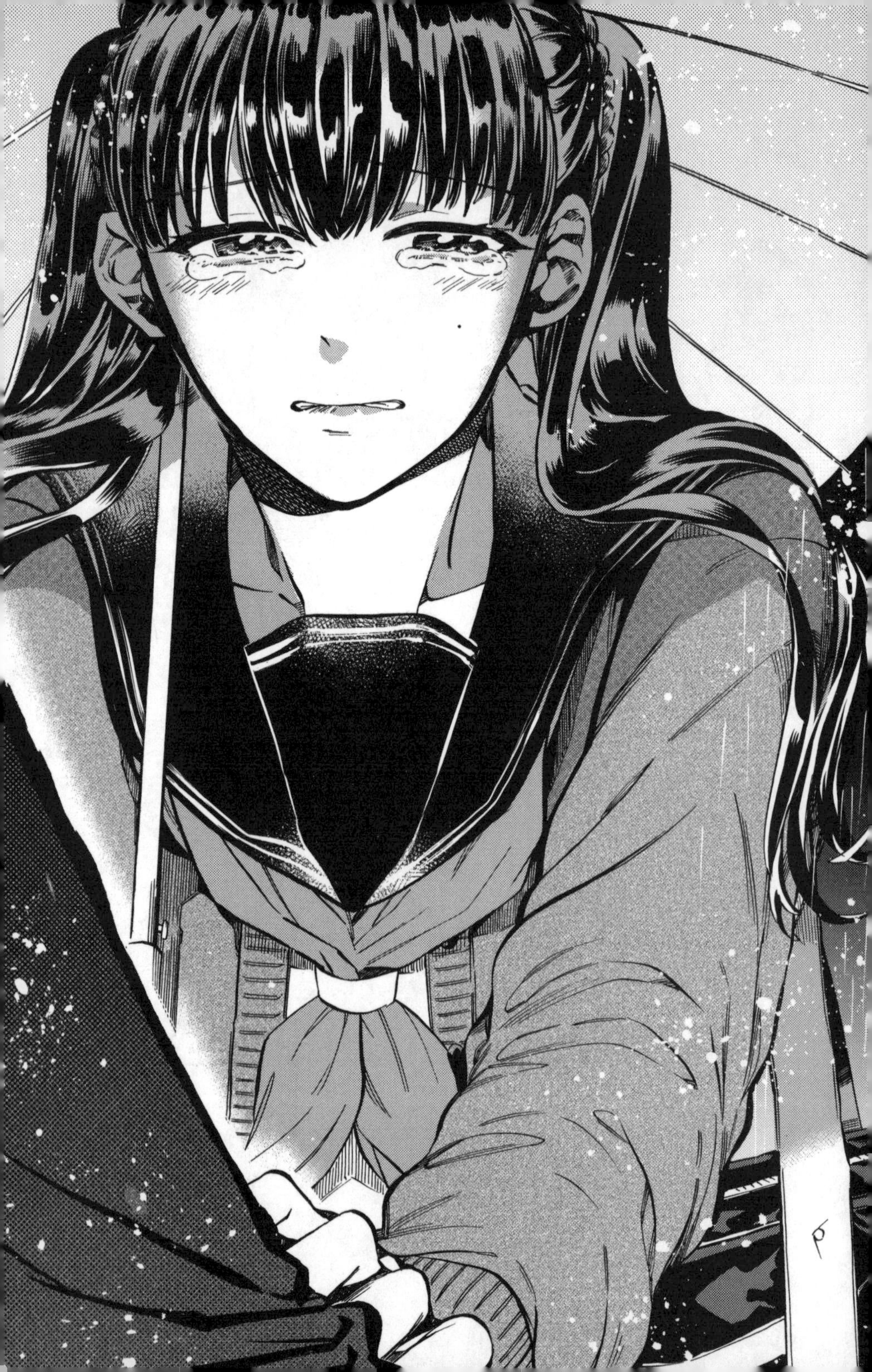

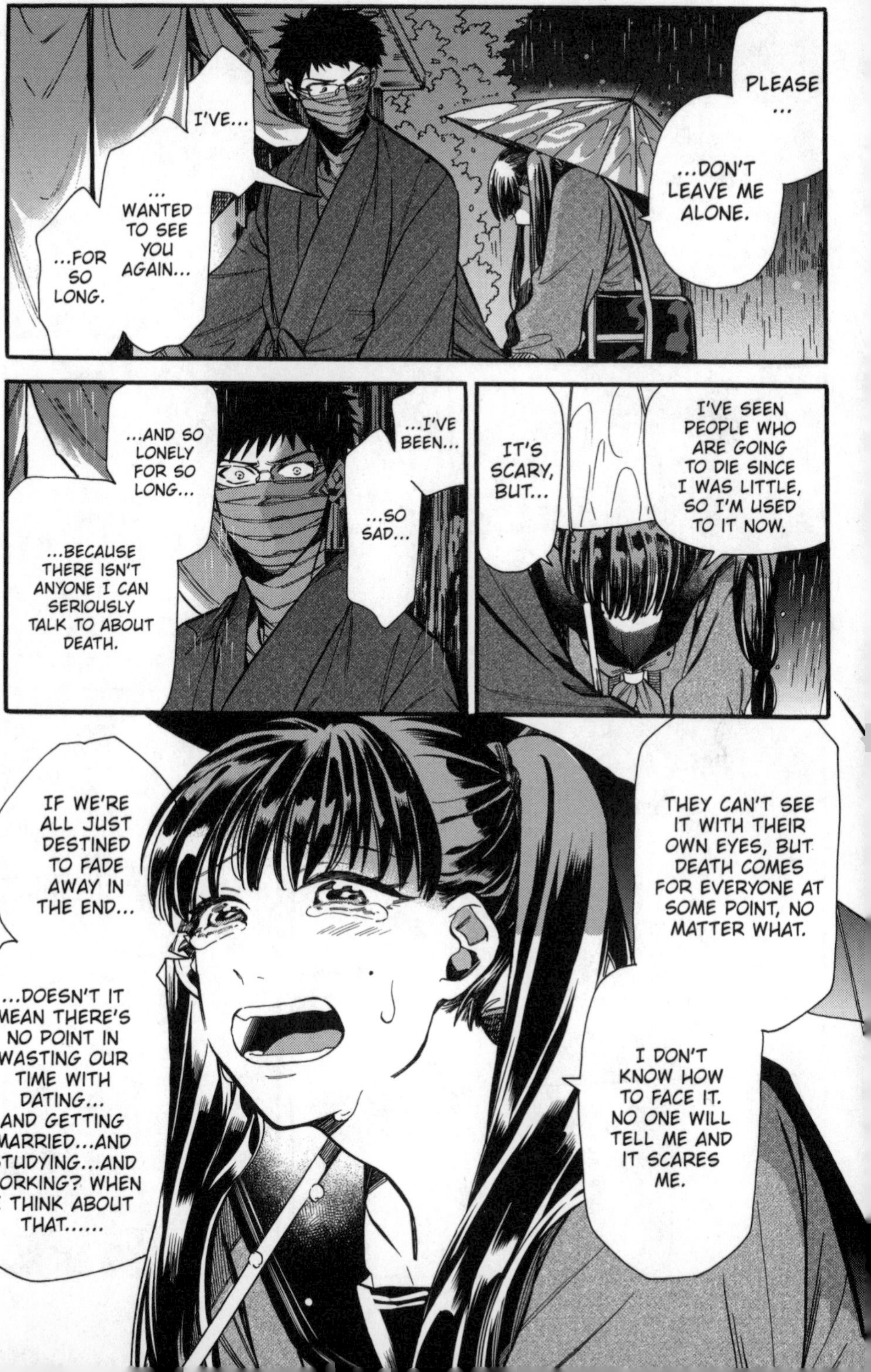
PLEASE...
...DON'T LEAVE ME ALONE.
I'VE...
...WANTED TO SEE YOU AGAIN...
...FOR SO LONG.
I'VE SEEN PEOPLE WHO ARE GOING TO DIE SINCE I WAS LITTLE, SO I'M USED TO IT NOW.
IT'S SCARY, BUT...
...I'VE BEEN...
...SO SAD...
...AND SO LONELY FOR SO LONG...
...BECAUSE THERE ISN'T ANYONE I CAN SERIOUSLY TALK TO ABOUT DEATH.
THEY CAN'T SEE IT WITH THEIR OWN EYES, BUT DEATH COMES FOR EVERYONE AT SOME POINT, NO MATTER WHAT.
I DON'T KNOW HOW TO FACE IT. NO ONE WILL TELL ME AND IT SCARES ME.
IF WE'RE ALL JUST DESTINED TO FADE AWAY IN THE END...
...DOESN'T IT MEAN THERE'S NO POINT IN WASTING OUR TIME WITH DATING... AND GETTING MARRIED...AND STUDYING...AND WORKING? WHEN I THINK ABOUT THAT......

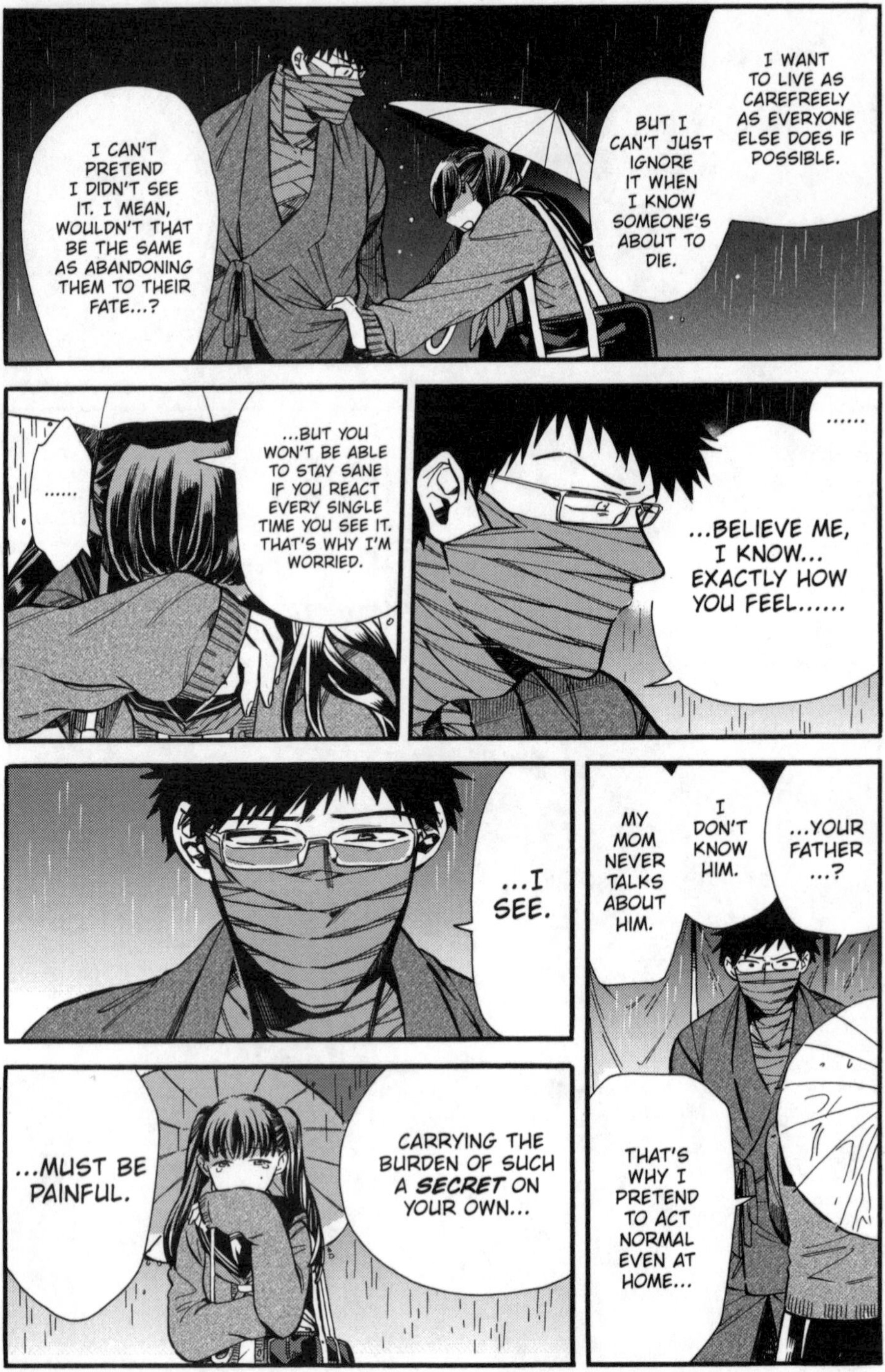
I WANT TO LIVE AS CAREFREELY AS EVERYONE ELSE DOES IF POSSIBLE.
BUT I CAN'T JUST IGNORE IT WHEN I KNOW SOMEONE'S ABOUT TO DIE.
I CAN'T PRETEND I DIDN'T SEE IT. I MEAN, WOULDN'T THAT BE THE SAME AS ABANDONING THEM TO THEIR FATE...?
......
...BELIEVE ME, I KNOW... EXACTLY HOW YOU FEEL......
...BUT YOU WON'T BE ABLE TO STAY SANE IF YOU REACT EVERY SINGLE TIME YOU SEE IT. THAT'S WHY I'M WORRIED.
......
...YOUR FATHER ...?
I DON'T KNOW HIM.
MY MOM NEVER TALKS ABOUT HIM.
THAT'S WHY I PRETEND TO ACT NORMAL EVEN AT HOME...
...I SEE.
CARRYING THE BURDEN OF SUCH A *SECRET* ON YOUR OWN...
...MUST BE PAINFUL.

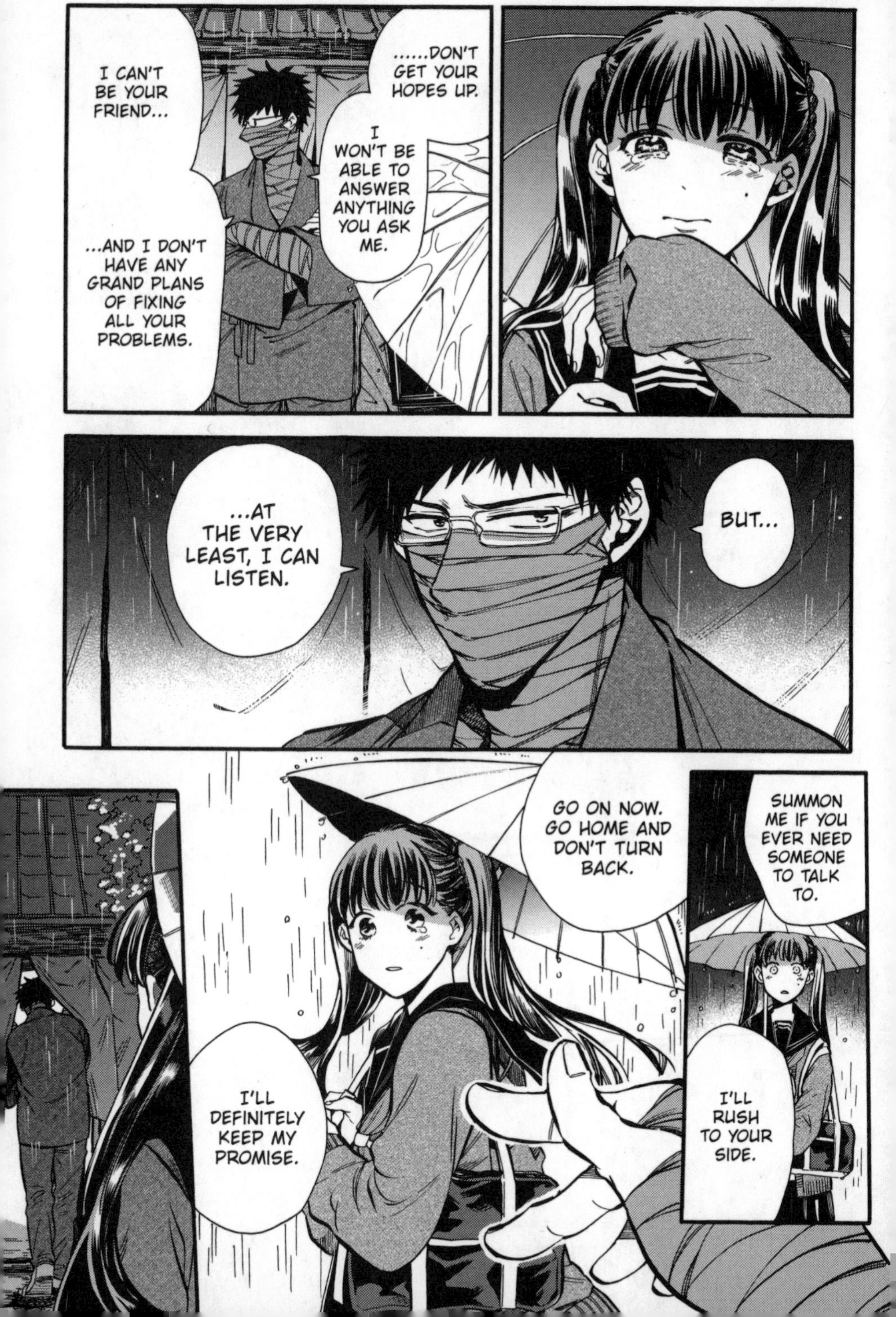
......DON'T GET YOUR HOPES UP.
I CAN'T BE YOUR FRIEND...
I WON'T BE ABLE TO ANSWER ANYTHING YOU ASK ME.
...AND I DON'T HAVE ANY GRAND PLANS OF FIXING ALL YOUR PROBLEMS.
BUT...
...AT THE VERY LEAST, I CAN LISTEN.
SUMMON ME IF YOU EVER NEED SOMEONE TO TALK TO.
I'LL RUSH TO YOUR SIDE.
GO ON NOW. GO HOME AND DON'T TURN BACK.
I'LL DEFINITELY KEEP MY PROMISE.

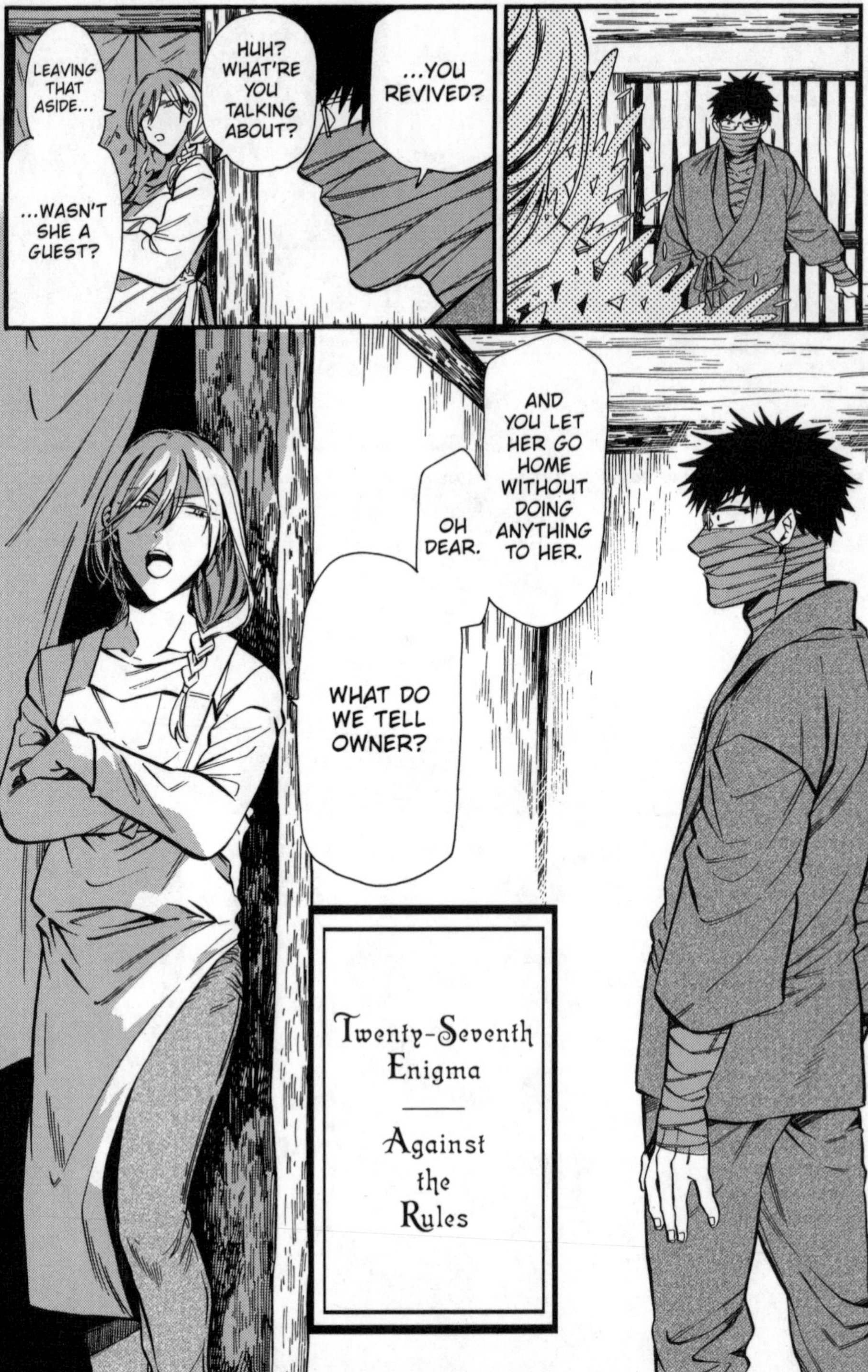
...YOU REVIVED?
HUH? WHAT'RE YOU TALKING ABOUT?
LEAVING THAT ASIDE...
...WASN'T SHE A GUEST?
AND YOU LET HER GO HOME WITHOUT DOING ANYTHING TO HER.
OH DEAR.
WHAT DO WE TELL OWNER?
Twenty-Seventh Enigma
Against the Rules

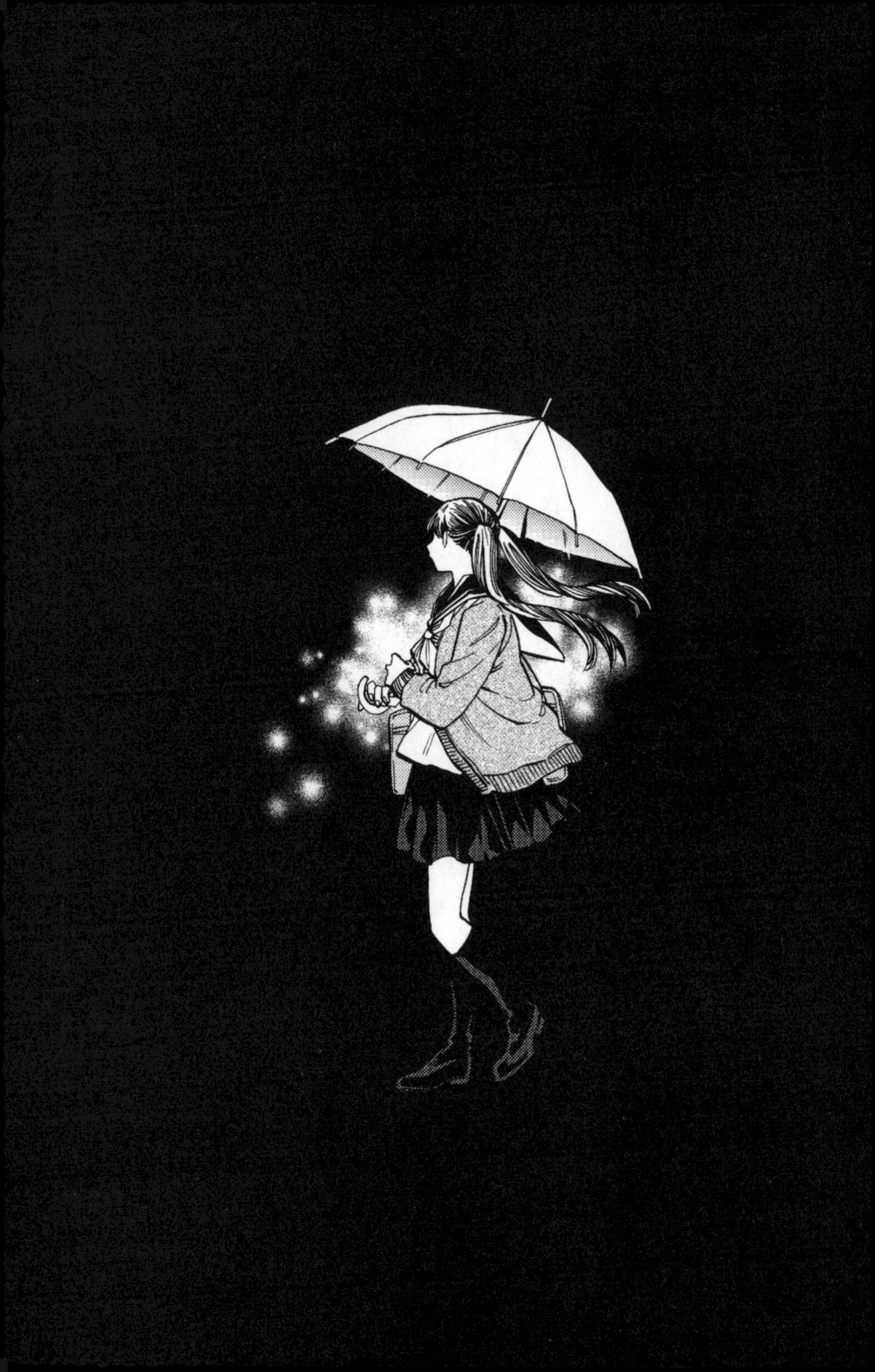

Phantom Tales of the Night

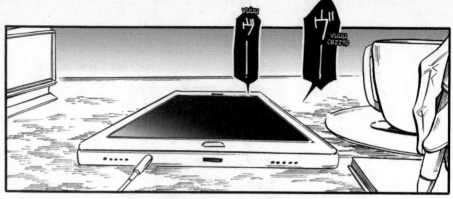

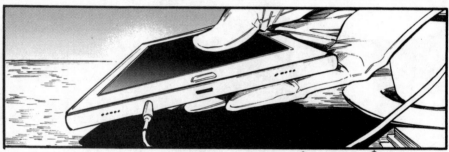

Um...

I have a boyfriend I'm thinking about marrying.

But it feels like...... we don't see eye-to-eye on a lot of things...

...and I'm not so sure about going forward with it anymore.

Can you please tell my fortune?

I ASSUME YOU READ THE EXPLANATION, BUT IT'S TWO HUNDRED EIGHTY YEN PER MINUTE, OKAY?

YES.

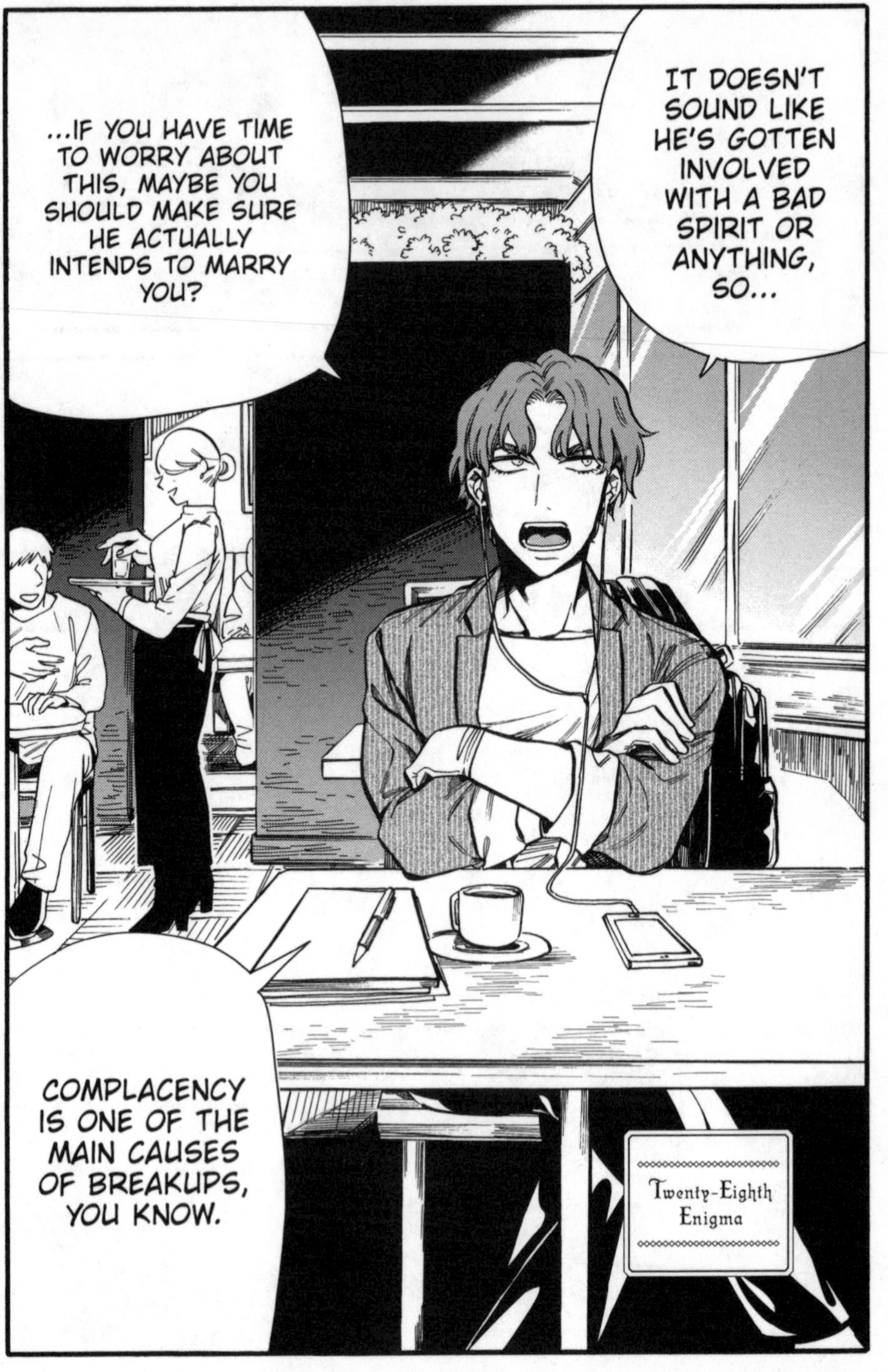
IT DOESN'T SOUND LIKE HE'S GOTTEN INVOLVED WITH A BAD SPIRIT OR ANYTHING, SO...
...IF YOU HAVE TIME TO WORRY ABOUT THIS, MAYBE YOU SHOULD MAKE SURE HE ACTUALLY INTENDS TO MARRY YOU?
Twenty-Eighth Enigma
COMPLACENCY IS ONE OF THE MAIN CAUSES OF BREAKUPS, YOU KNOW.

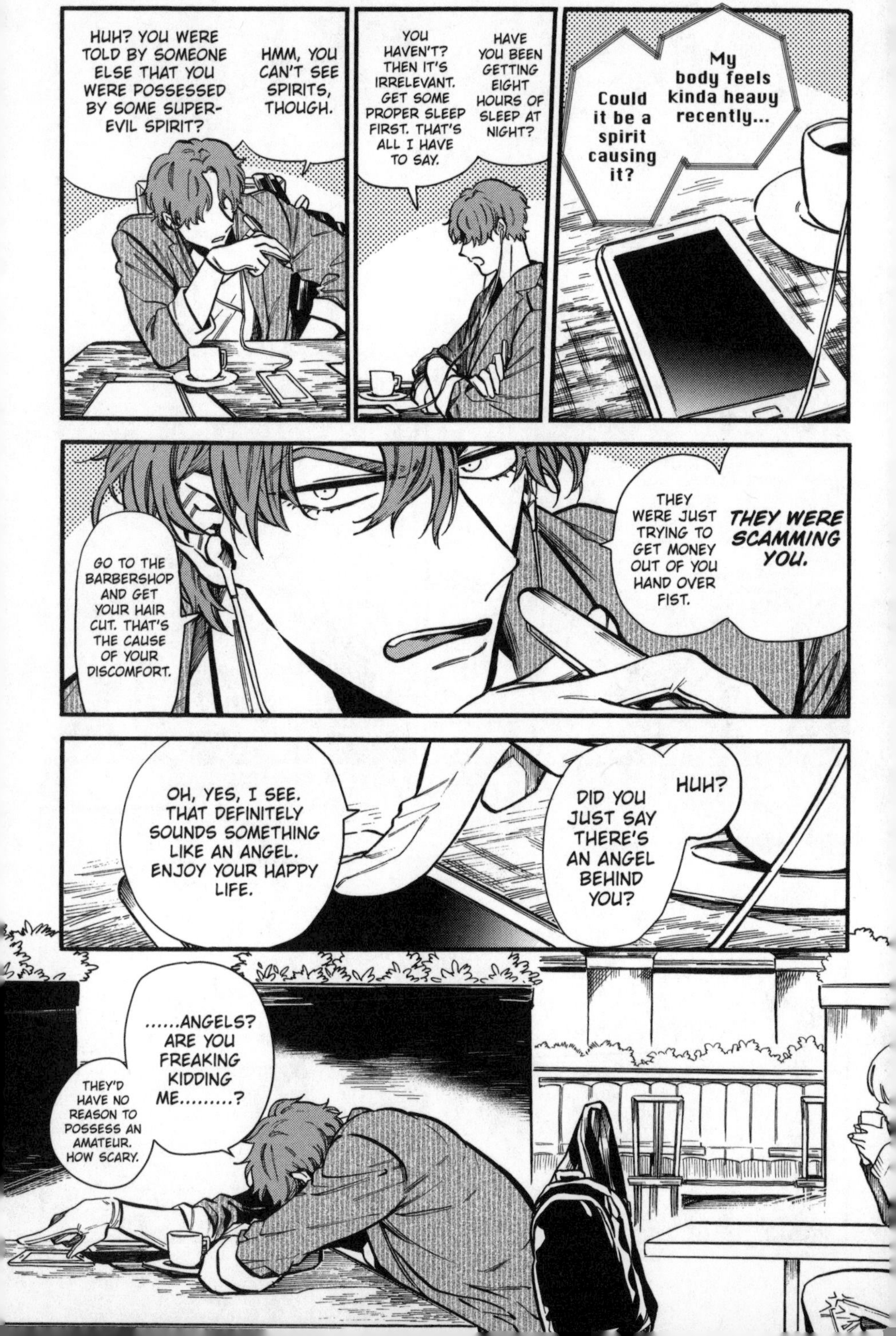
My body feels kinda heavy recently...
Could it be a spirit causing it?
HAVE YOU BEEN GETTING EIGHT HOURS OF SLEEP AT NIGHT?
YOU HAVEN'T? THEN IT'S IRRELEVANT. GET SOME PROPER SLEEP FIRST. THAT'S ALL I HAVE TO SAY.
HMM, YOU CAN'T SEE SPIRITS, THOUGH.
HUH? YOU WERE TOLD BY SOMEONE ELSE THAT YOU WERE POSSESSED BY SOME SUPER-EVIL SPIRIT?
THEY WERE SCAMMING YOU.
THEY WERE JUST TRYING TO GET MONEY OUT OF YOU HAND OVER FIST.
GO TO THE BARBERSHOP AND GET YOUR HAIR CUT. THAT'S THE CAUSE OF YOUR DISCOMFORT.
HUH?
DID YOU JUST SAY THERE'S AN ANGEL BEHIND YOU?
OH, YES, I SEE. THAT DEFINITELY SOUNDS SOMETHING LIKE AN ANGEL. ENJOY YOUR HAPPY LIFE.
......ANGELS? ARE YOU FREAKING KIDDING ME.........?
THEY'D HAVE NO REASON TO POSSESS AN AMATEUR. HOW SCARY.

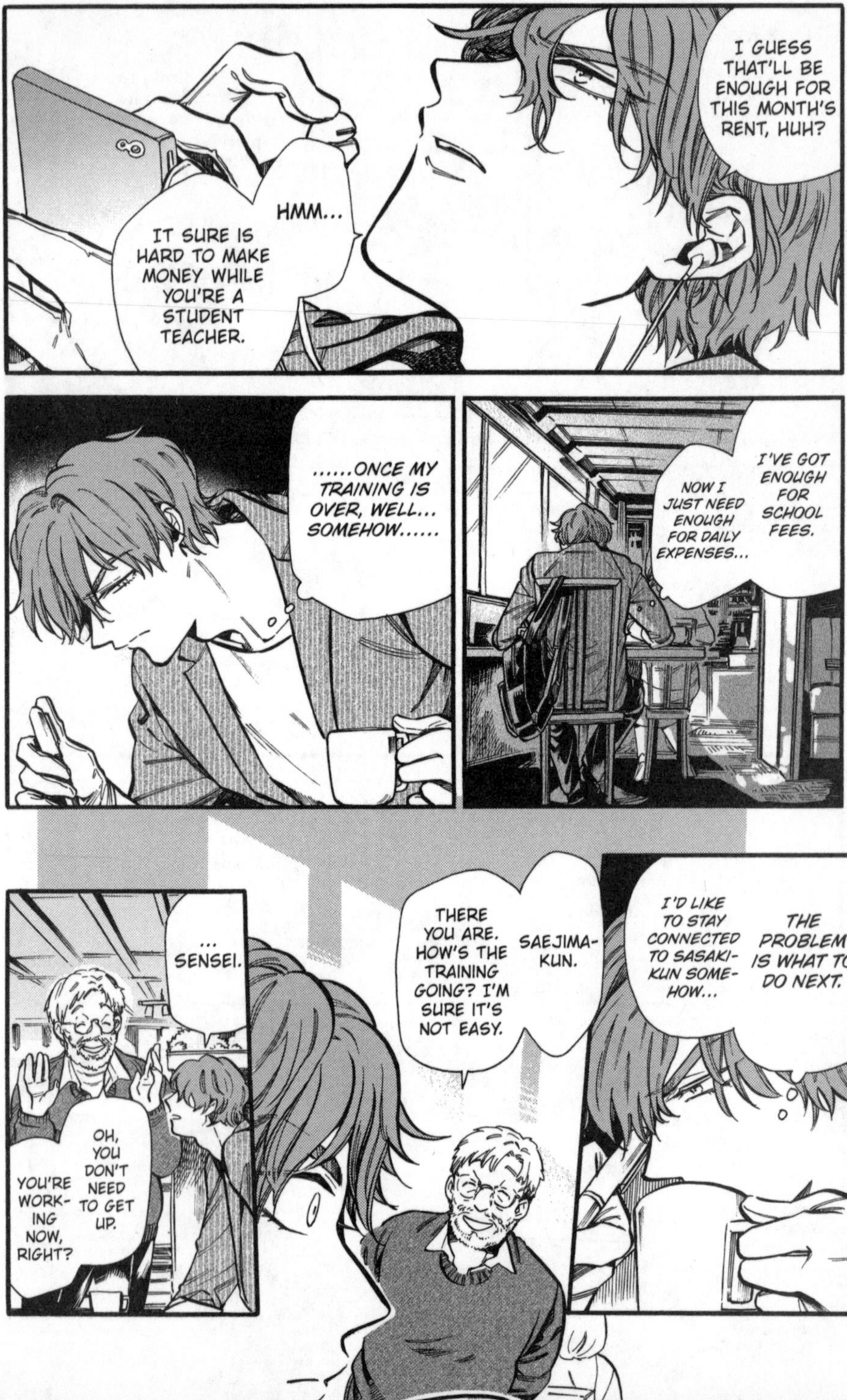
I GUESS THAT'LL BE ENOUGH FOR THIS MONTH'S RENT, HUH?
HMM...
IT SURE IS HARD TO MAKE MONEY WHILE YOU'RE A STUDENT TEACHER.
I'VE GOT ENOUGH FOR SCHOOL FEES.
NOW I JUST NEED ENOUGH FOR DAILY EXPENSES...
......ONCE MY TRAINING IS OVER, WELL... SOMEHOW......
THE PROBLEM IS WHAT TO DO NEXT.
I'D LIKE TO STAY CONNECTED TO SASAKI-KUN SOMEHOW...
SAEJIMA-KUN.
THERE YOU ARE. HOW'S THE TRAINING GOING? I'M SURE IT'S NOT EASY.
... SENSEI.
OH, YOU DON'T NEED TO GET UP.
YOU'RE WORKING NOW, RIGHT?

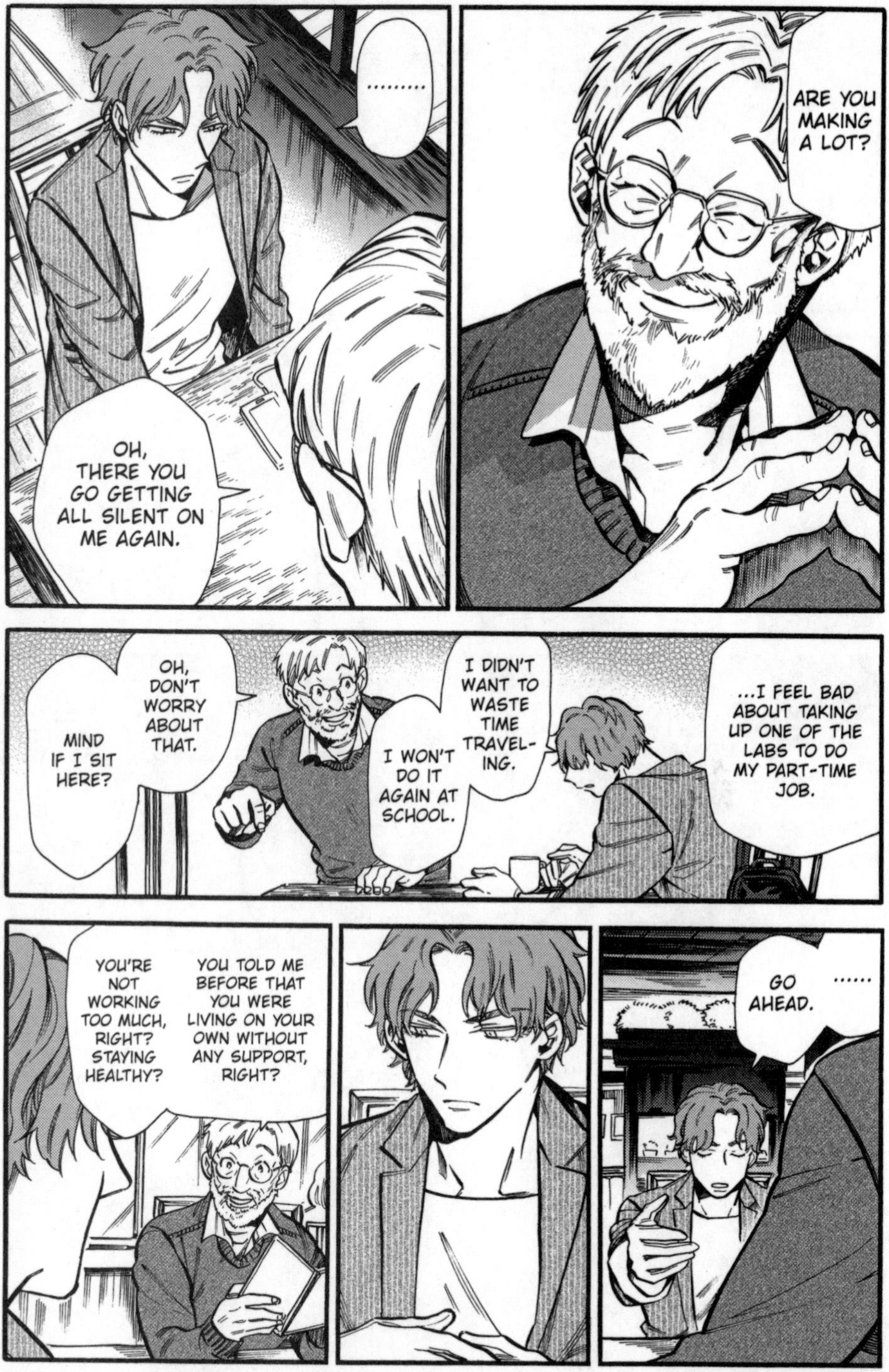
ARE YOU MAKING A LOT?
....
OH, THERE YOU GO GETTING ALL SILENT ON ME AGAIN.
...I FEEL BAD ABOUT TAKING UP ONE OF THE LABS TO DO MY PART-TIME JOB.
I DIDN'T WANT TO WASTE TIME TRAVELING.
I WON'T DO IT AGAIN AT SCHOOL.
OH, DON'T WORRY ABOUT THAT.
MIND IF I SIT HERE?
......
GO AHEAD.
YOU TOLD ME BEFORE THAT YOU WERE LIVING ON YOUR OWN WITHOUT ANY SUPPORT, RIGHT?
YOU'RE NOT WORKING TOO MUCH, RIGHT? STAYING HEALTHY?

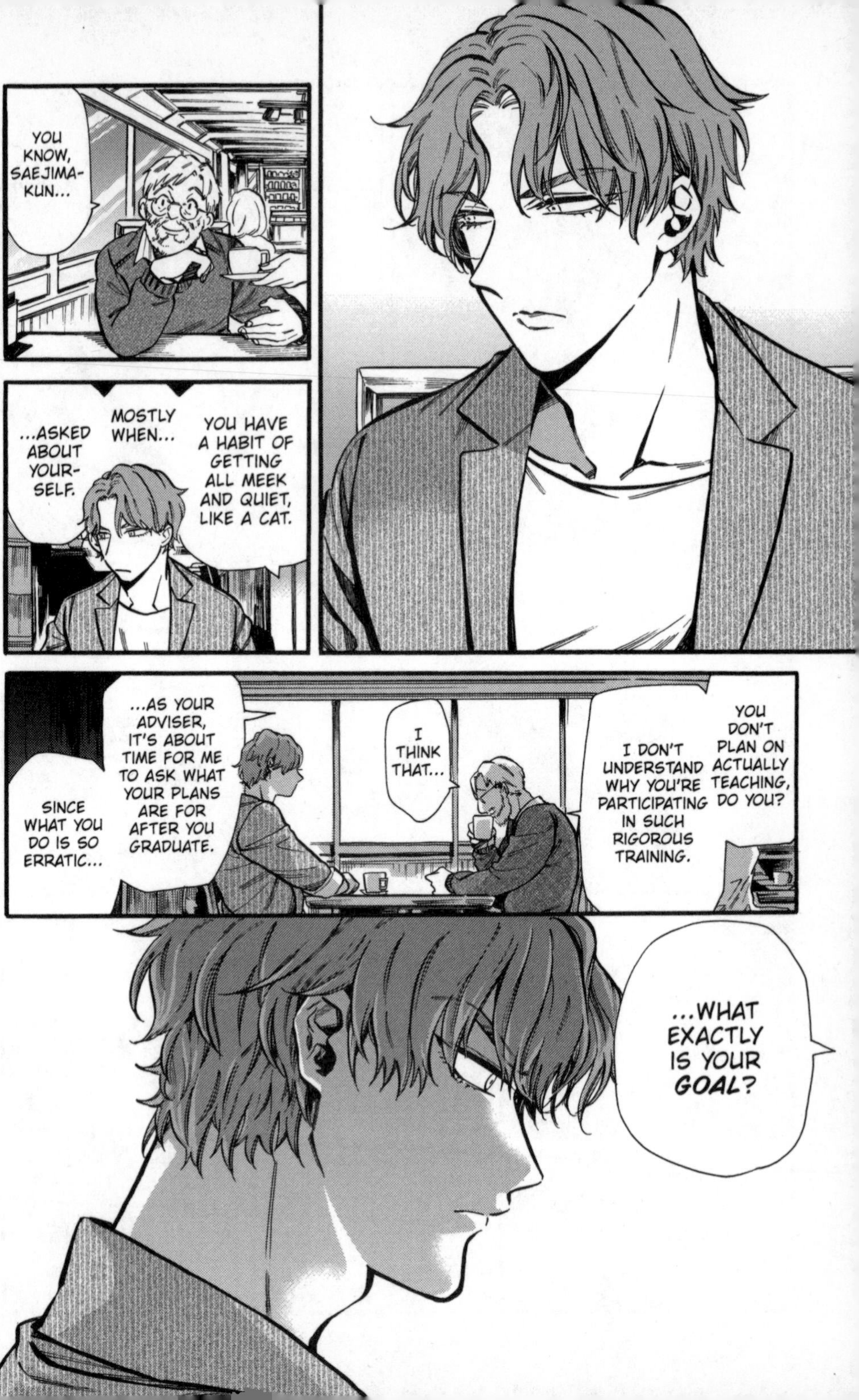
YOU KNOW, SAEJIMA-KUN...
YOU HAVE A HABIT OF GETTING ALL MEEK AND QUIET, LIKE A CAT.
MOSTLY WHEN...
...ASKED ABOUT YOURSELF.
YOU DON'T PLAN ON ACTUALLY TEACHING, DO YOU?
I DON'T UNDERSTAND WHY YOU'RE PARTICIPATING IN SUCH RIGOROUS TRAINING.
I THINK THAT...
...AS YOUR ADVISER, IT'S ABOUT TIME FOR ME TO ASK WHAT YOUR PLANS ARE FOR AFTER YOU GRADUATE.
SINCE WHAT YOU DO IS SO ERRATIC...
...WHAT EXACTLY IS YOUR ***GOAL***?

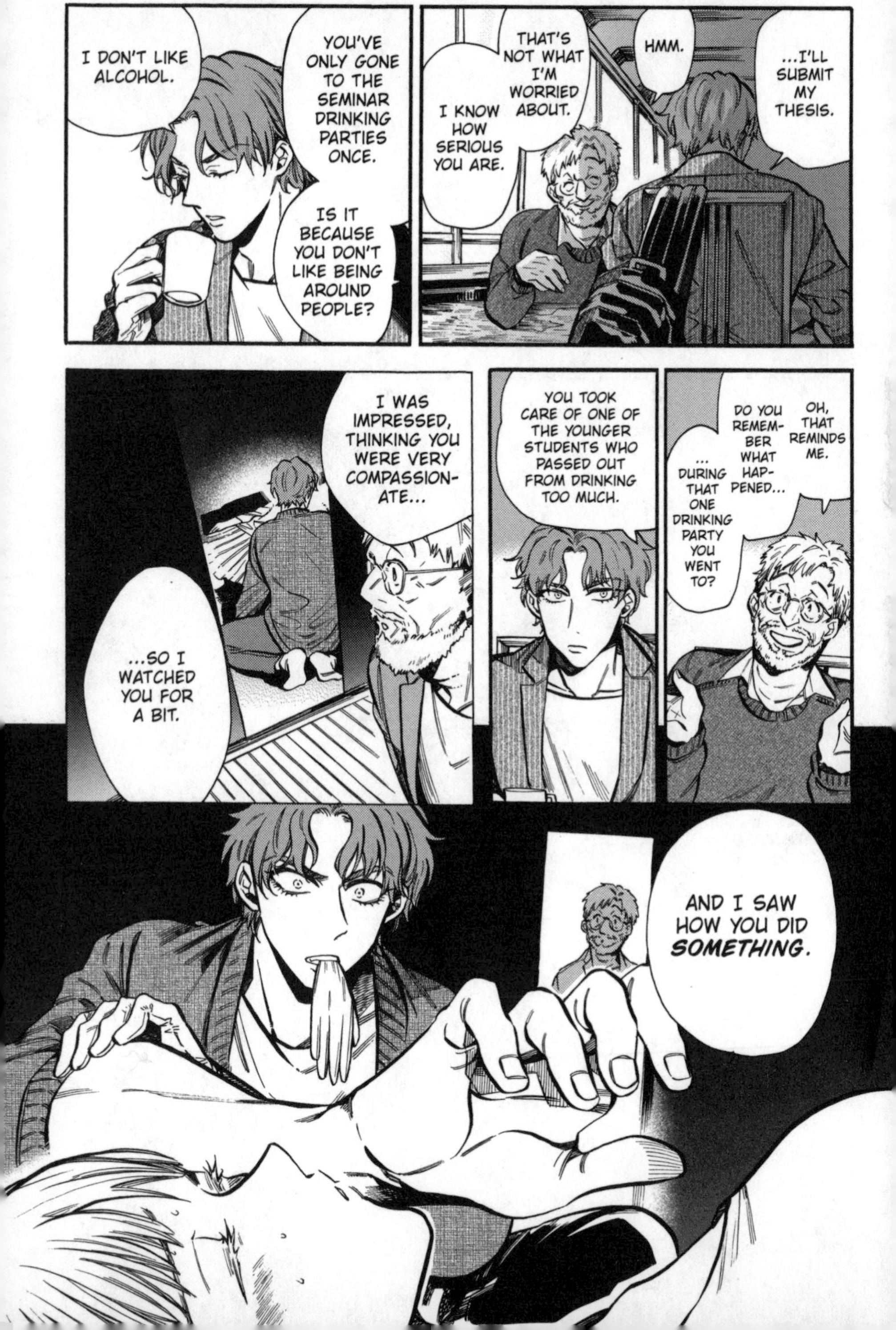
...I'LL SUBMIT MY THESIS.
HMM.
THAT'S NOT WHAT I'M WORRIED ABOUT.
I KNOW HOW SERIOUS YOU ARE.
YOU'VE ONLY GONE TO THE SEMINAR DRINKING PARTIES ONCE.
IS IT BECAUSE YOU DON'T LIKE BEING AROUND PEOPLE?
I DON'T LIKE ALCOHOL.
OH, THAT REMINDS ME.
DO YOU REMEMBER WHAT HAPPENED...
...DURING THAT ONE DRINKING PARTY YOU WENT TO?
YOU TOOK CARE OF ONE OF THE YOUNGER STUDENTS WHO PASSED OUT FROM DRINKING TOO MUCH.
I WAS IMPRESSED, THINKING YOU WERE VERY COMPASSIONATE...
...SO I WATCHED YOU FOR A BIT.
AND I SAW HOW YOU DID ***SOMETHING***.

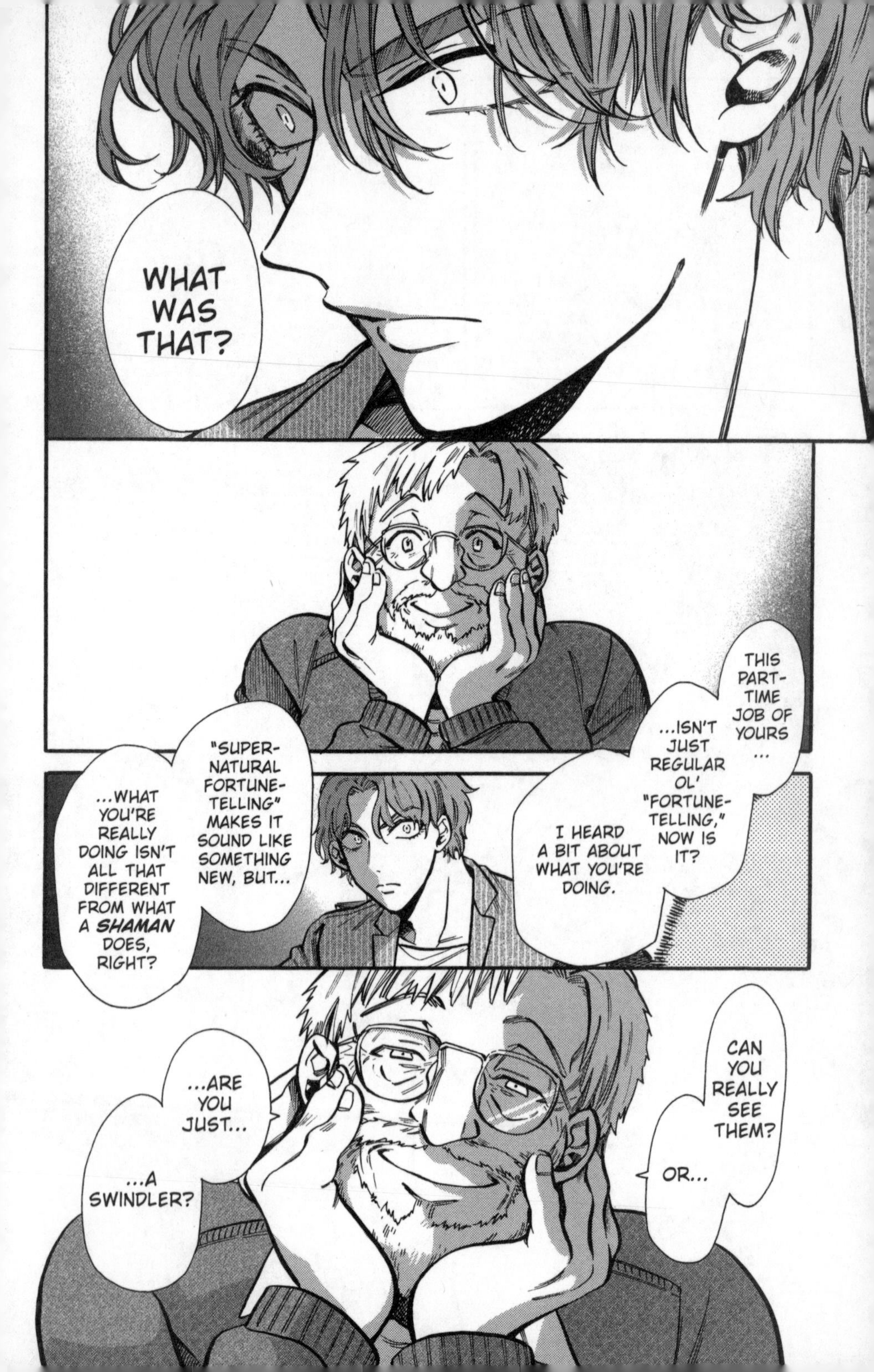
WHAT WAS THAT?
THIS PART-TIME JOB OF YOURS...
...ISN'T JUST REGULAR OL' "FORTUNE-TELLING," NOW IS IT?
I HEARD A BIT ABOUT WHAT YOU'RE DOING.
"SUPER-NATURAL FORTUNE-TELLING" MAKES IT SOUND LIKE SOMETHING NEW, BUT...
...WHAT YOU'RE REALLY DOING ISN'T ALL THAT DIFFERENT FROM WHAT A *SHAMAN* DOES, RIGHT?
CAN YOU REALLY SEE THEM?
OR...
...ARE YOU JUST...
...A SWINDLER?

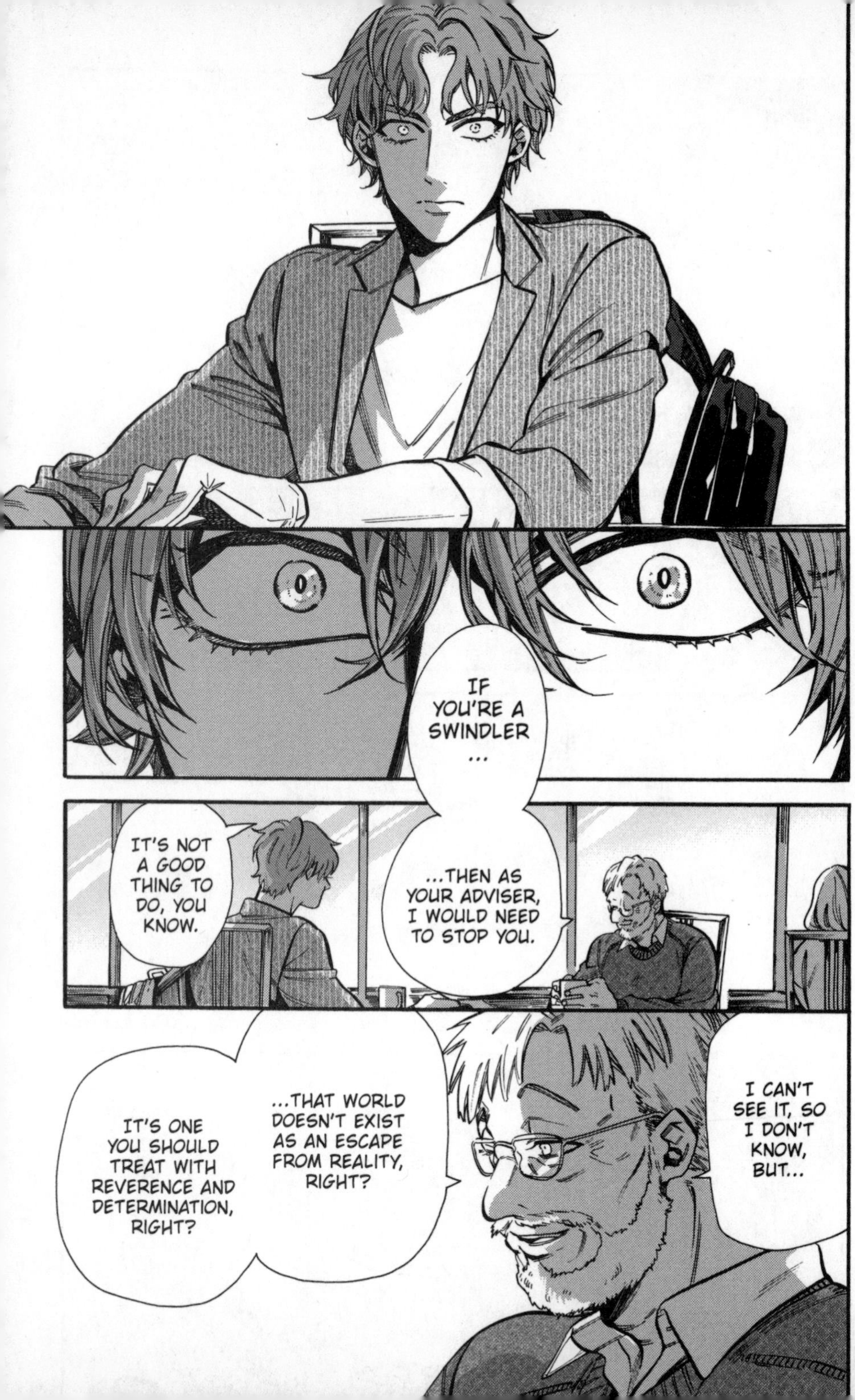
IF YOU'RE A SWINDLER...
...THEN AS YOUR ADVISER, I WOULD NEED TO STOP YOU.
IT'S NOT A GOOD THING TO DO, YOU KNOW.
I CAN'T SEE IT, SO I DON'T KNOW, BUT...
...THAT WORLD DOESN'T EXIST AS AN ESCAPE FROM REALITY, RIGHT?
IT'S ONE YOU SHOULD TREAT WITH REVERENCE AND DETERMINATION, RIGHT?

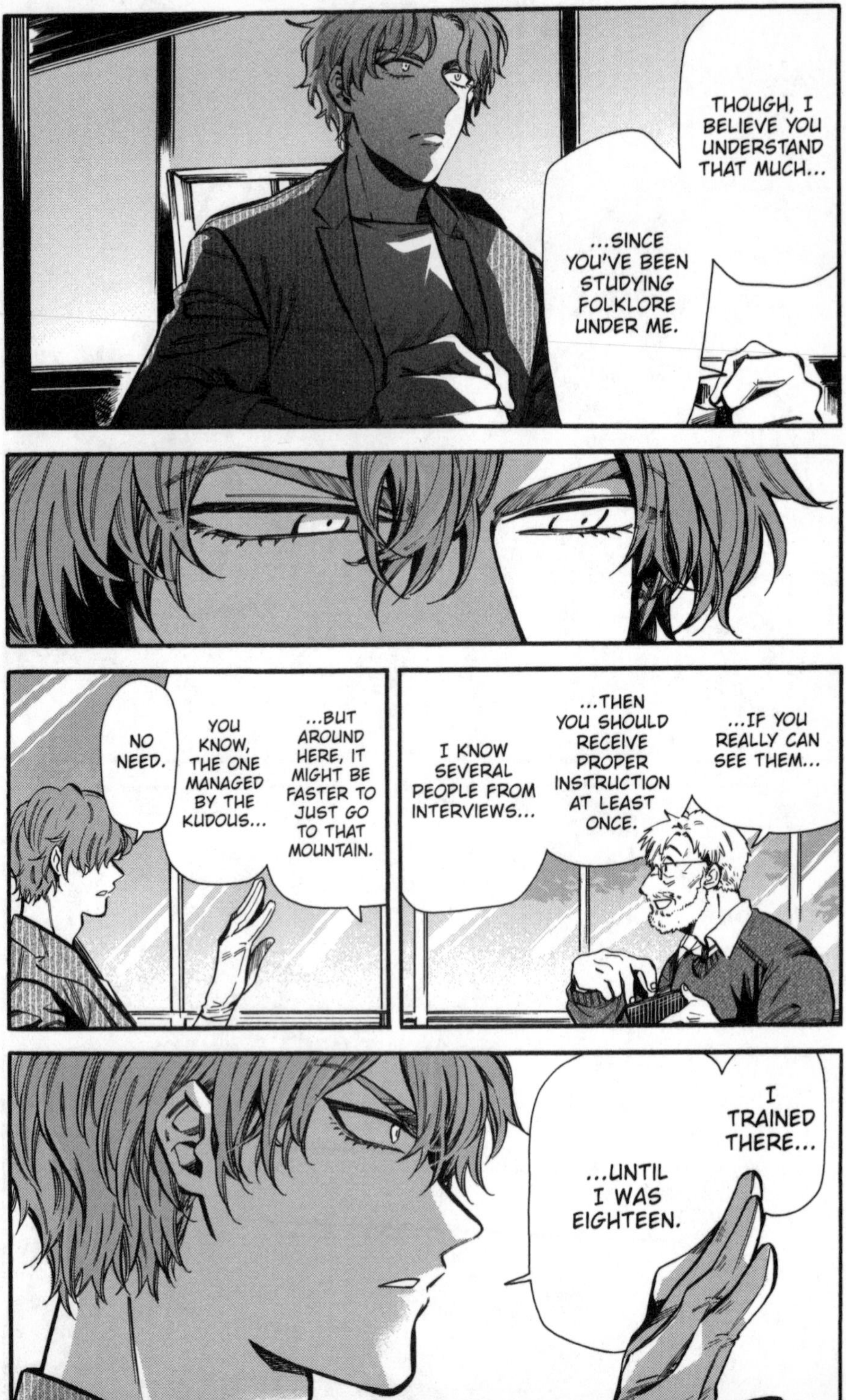
THOUGH, I BELIEVE YOU UNDERSTAND THAT MUCH...
...SINCE YOU'VE BEEN STUDYING FOLKLORE UNDER ME.
...IF YOU REALLY CAN SEE THEM...
...THEN YOU SHOULD RECEIVE PROPER INSTRUCTION AT LEAST ONCE.
I KNOW SEVERAL PEOPLE FROM INTERVIEWS...
...BUT AROUND HERE, IT MIGHT BE FASTER TO JUST GO TO THAT MOUNTAIN.
YOU KNOW, THE ONE MANAGED BY THE KUDOUS...
NO NEED.
I TRAINED THERE...
...UNTIL I WAS EIGHTEEN.

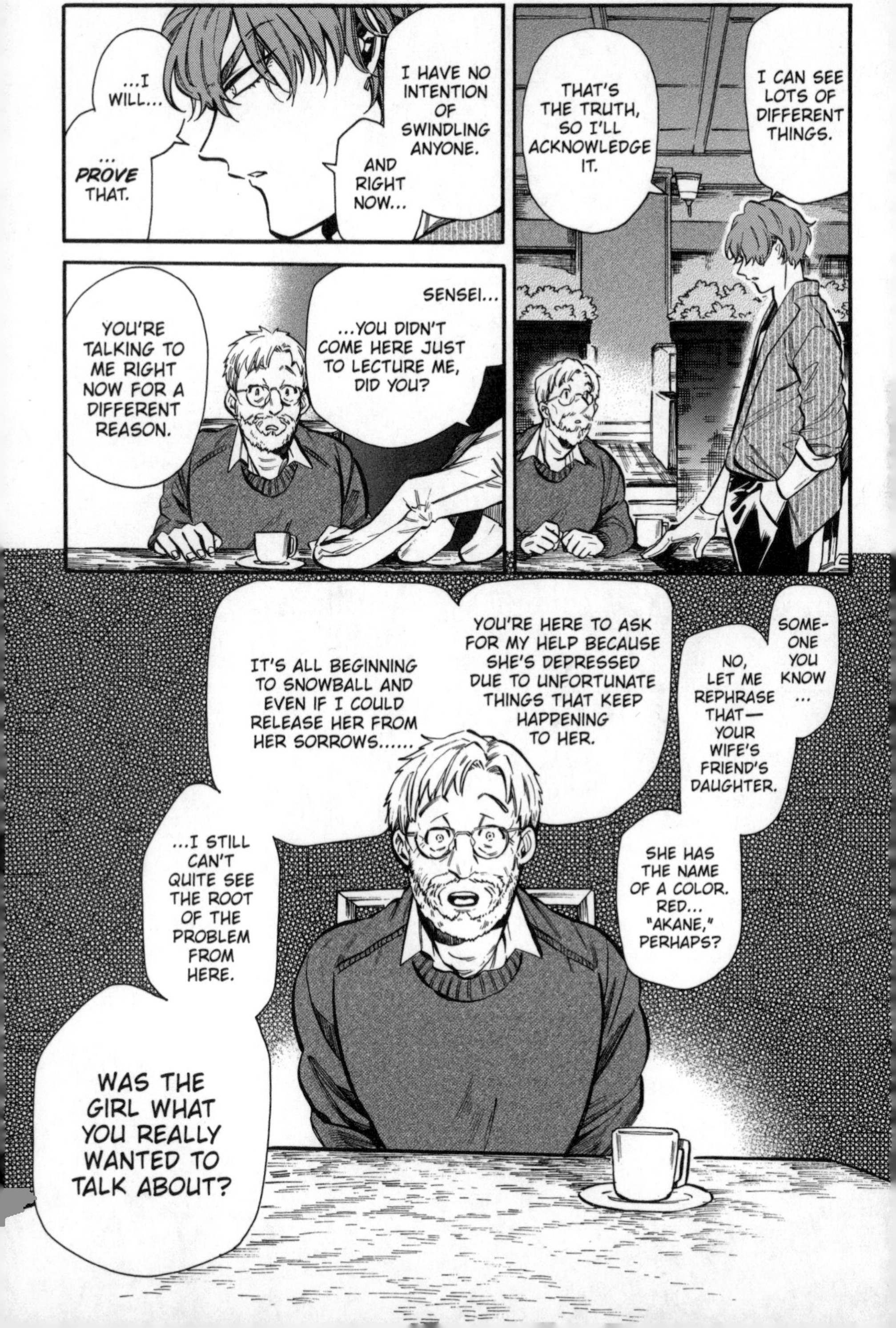
I CAN SEE LOTS OF DIFFERENT THINGS.
THAT'S THE TRUTH, SO I'LL ACKNOWLEDGE IT.
I HAVE NO INTENTION OF SWINDLING ANYONE.
AND RIGHT NOW...
...I WILL...
...*PROVE* THAT.
SENSEI...
...YOU DIDN'T COME HERE JUST TO LECTURE ME, DID YOU?
YOU'RE TALKING TO ME RIGHT NOW FOR A DIFFERENT REASON.
SOME-ONE YOU KNOW...
NO, LET ME REPHRASE THAT—YOUR WIFE'S FRIEND'S DAUGHTER.
YOU'RE HERE TO ASK FOR MY HELP BECAUSE SHE'S DEPRESSED DUE TO UNFORTUNATE THINGS THAT KEEP HAPPENING TO HER.
IT'S ALL BEGINNING TO SNOWBALL AND EVEN IF I COULD RELEASE HER FROM HER SORROWS......
SHE HAS THE NAME OF A COLOR. RED... "AKANE," PERHAPS?
...I STILL CAN'T QUITE SEE THE ROOT OF THE PROBLEM FROM HERE.
WAS THE GIRL WHAT YOU REALLY WANTED TO TALK ABOUT?

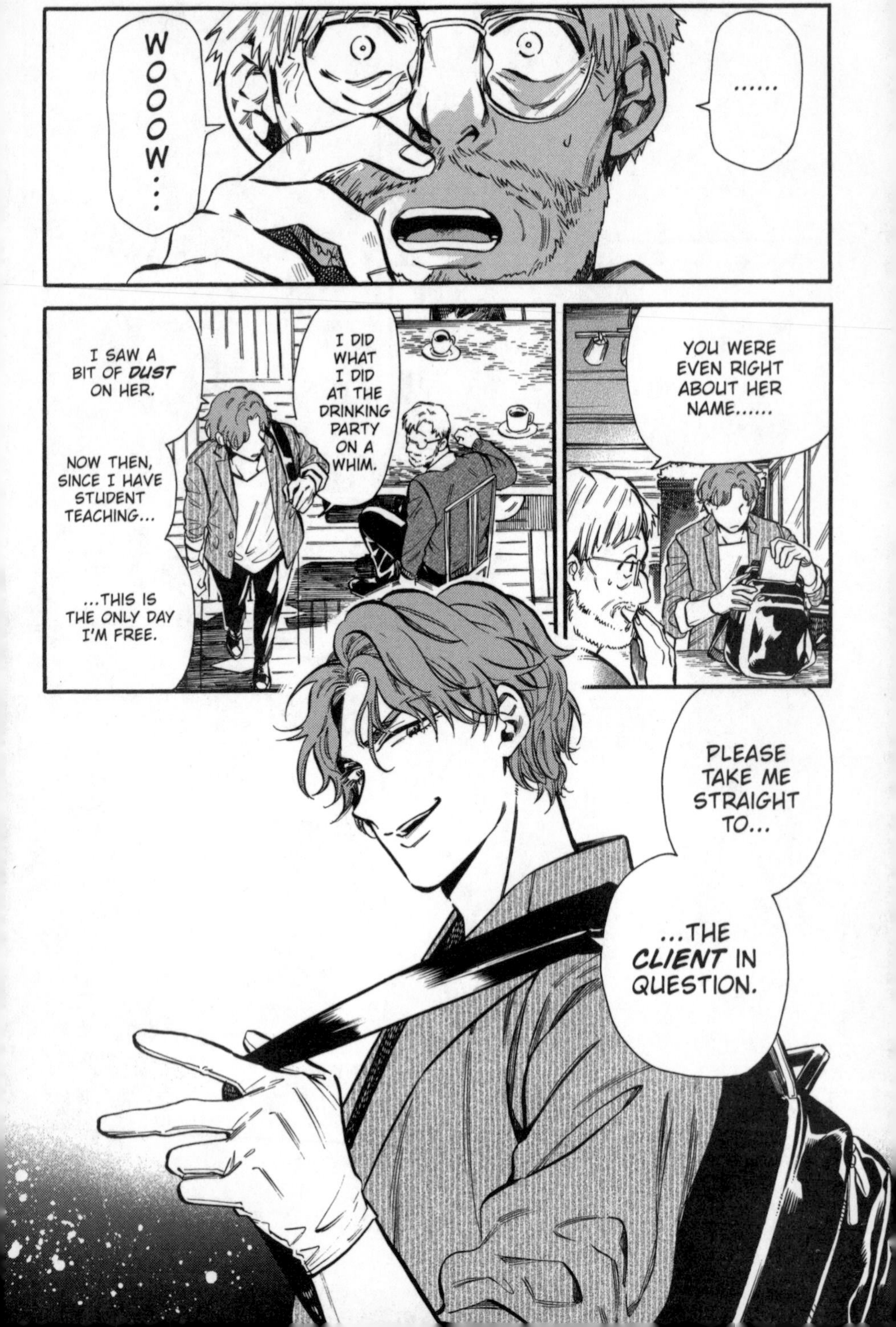
......
WOOOOW...
YOU WERE EVEN RIGHT ABOUT HER NAME......
I DID WHAT I DID AT THE DRINKING PARTY ON A WHIM.
I SAW A BIT OF *DUST* ON HER.
NOW THEN, SINCE I HAVE STUDENT TEACHING...
...THIS IS THE ONLY DAY I'M FREE.
PLEASE TAKE ME STRAIGHT TO...
...THE *CLIENT* IN QUESTION.

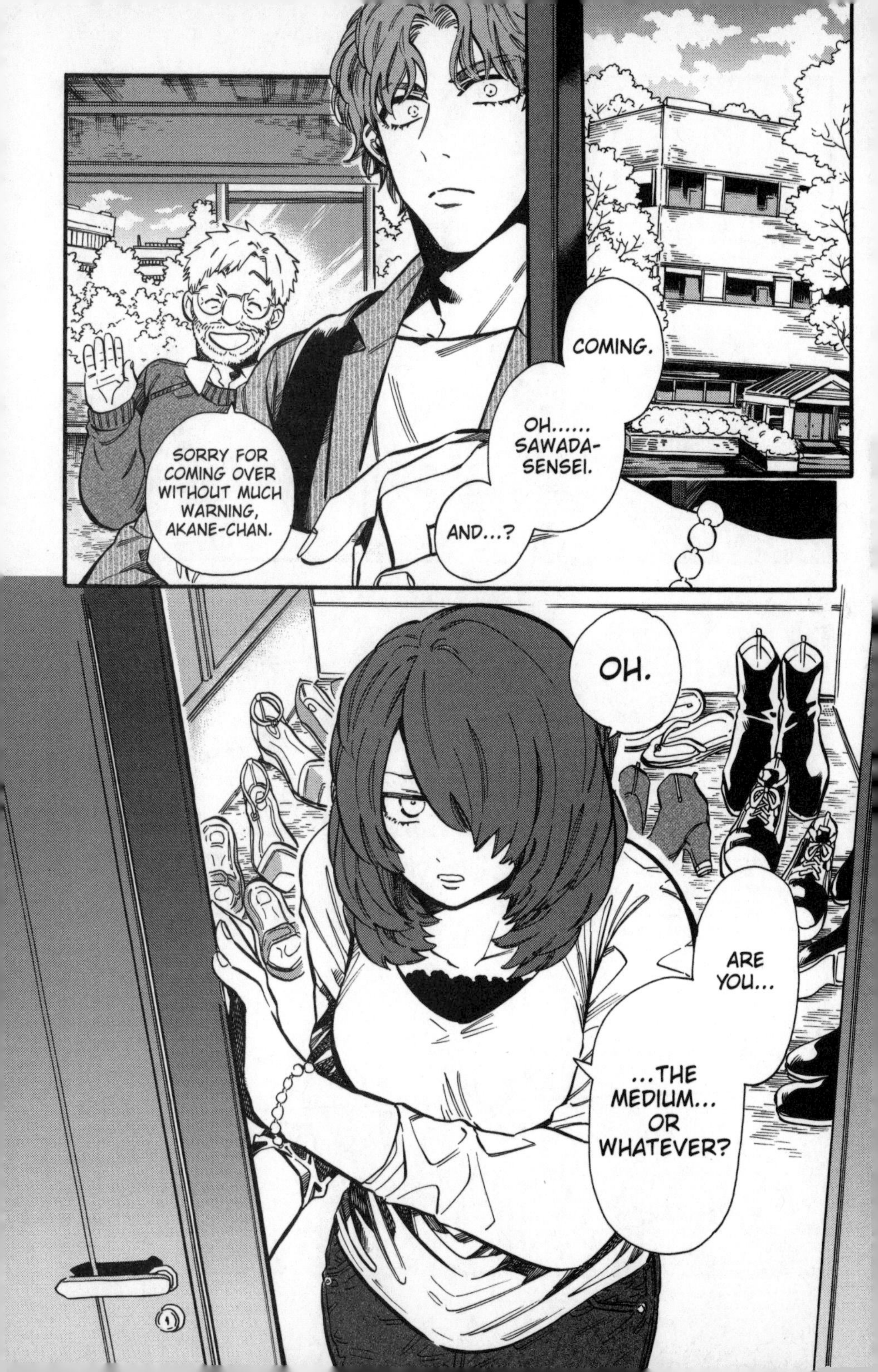
COMING.
OH...... SAWADA-SENSEI.
SORRY FOR COMING OVER WITHOUT MUCH WARNING, AKANE-CHAN.
AND...?
OH.
ARE YOU...
...THE MEDIUM... OR WHATEVER?

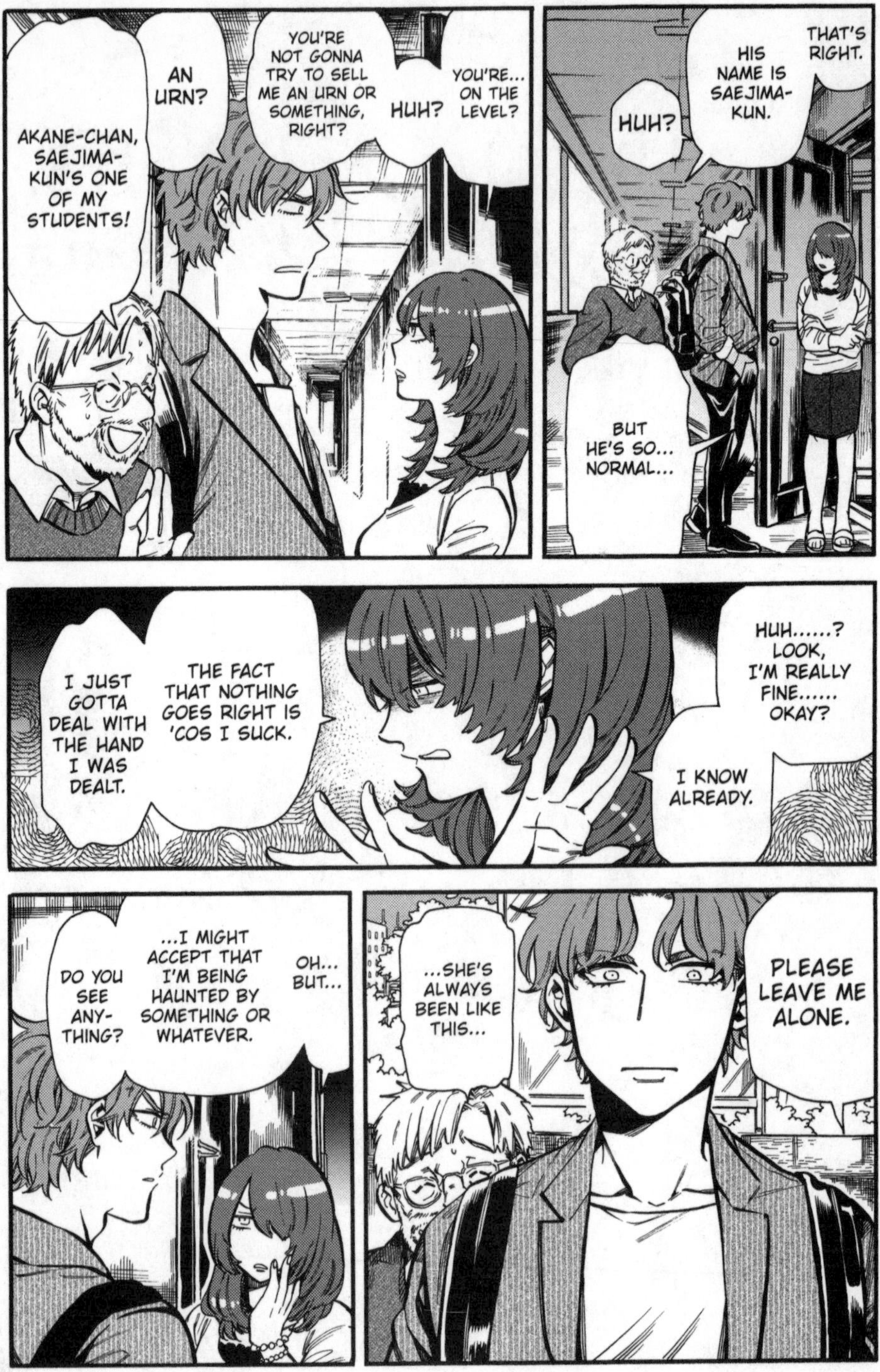
THAT'S RIGHT.
HIS NAME IS SAEJIMA-KUN.
HUH?
BUT HE'S SO... NORMAL...
YOU'RE... ON THE LEVEL?
HUH?
YOU'RE NOT GONNA TRY TO SELL ME AN URN OR SOMETHING, RIGHT?
AN URN?
AKANE-CHAN, SAEJIMA-KUN'S ONE OF MY STUDENTS!
HUH......? LOOK, I'M REALLY FINE...... OKAY?
I KNOW ALREADY.
THE FACT THAT NOTHING GOES RIGHT IS 'COS I SUCK.
I JUST GOTTA DEAL WITH THE HAND I WAS DEALT.
PLEASE LEAVE ME ALONE.
...SHE'S ALWAYS BEEN LIKE THIS...
OH... BUT...
...I MIGHT ACCEPT THAT I'M BEING HAUNTED BY SOMETHING OR WHATEVER.
DO YOU SEE ANYTHING?

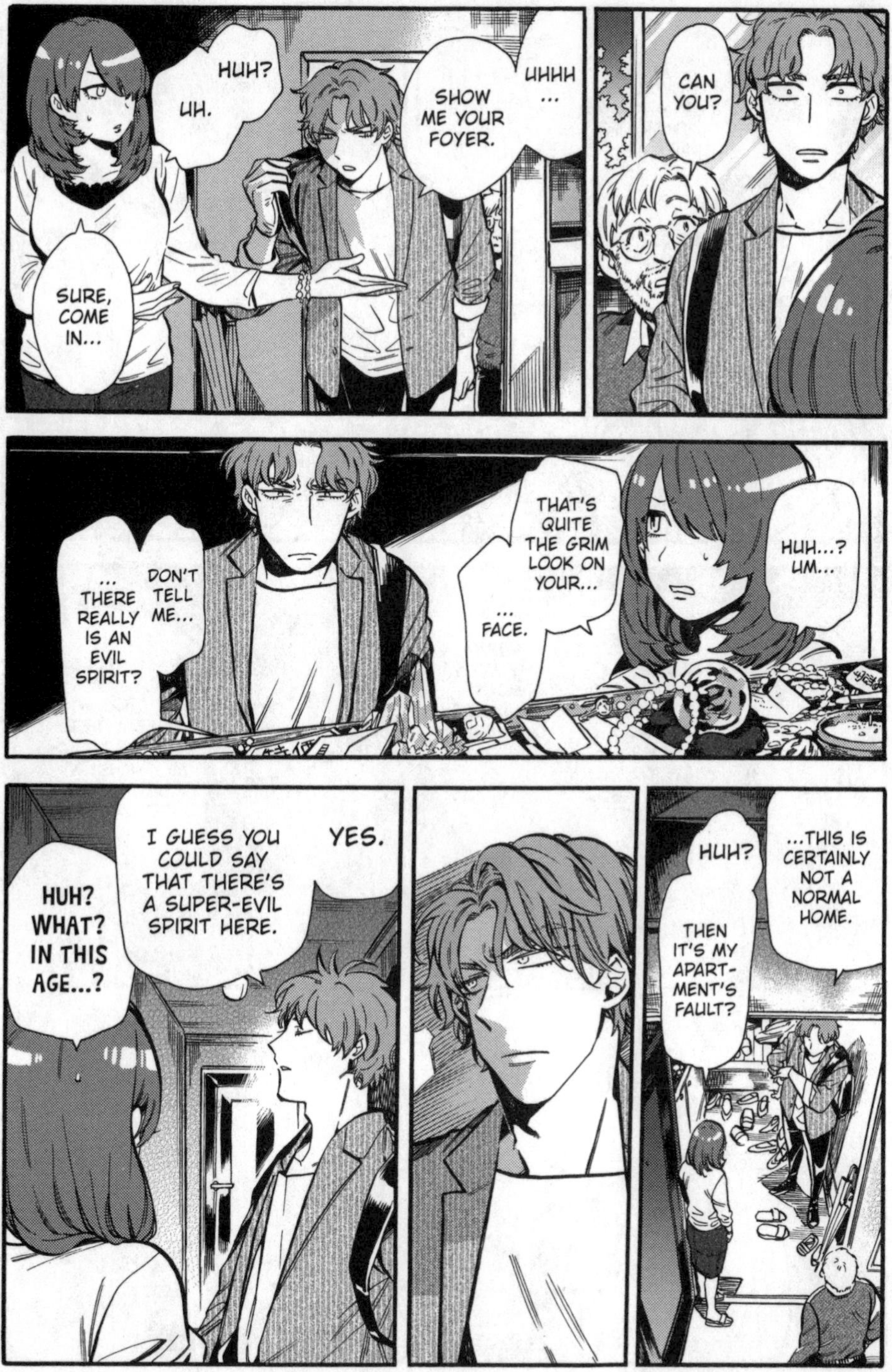
CAN YOU?
UHHH ...
SHOW ME YOUR FOYER.
HUH?
UH.
SURE, COME IN...
HUH...? UM...
THAT'S QUITE THE GRIM LOOK ON YOUR...
... FACE.
DON'T TELL ME...
... THERE REALLY IS AN EVIL SPIRIT?
...THIS IS CERTAINLY NOT A NORMAL HOME.
HUH?
THEN IT'S MY APART-MENT'S FAULT?
YES.
I GUESS YOU COULD SAY THAT THERE'S A SUPER-EVIL SPIRIT HERE.
HUH? WHAT? IN THIS AGE...?

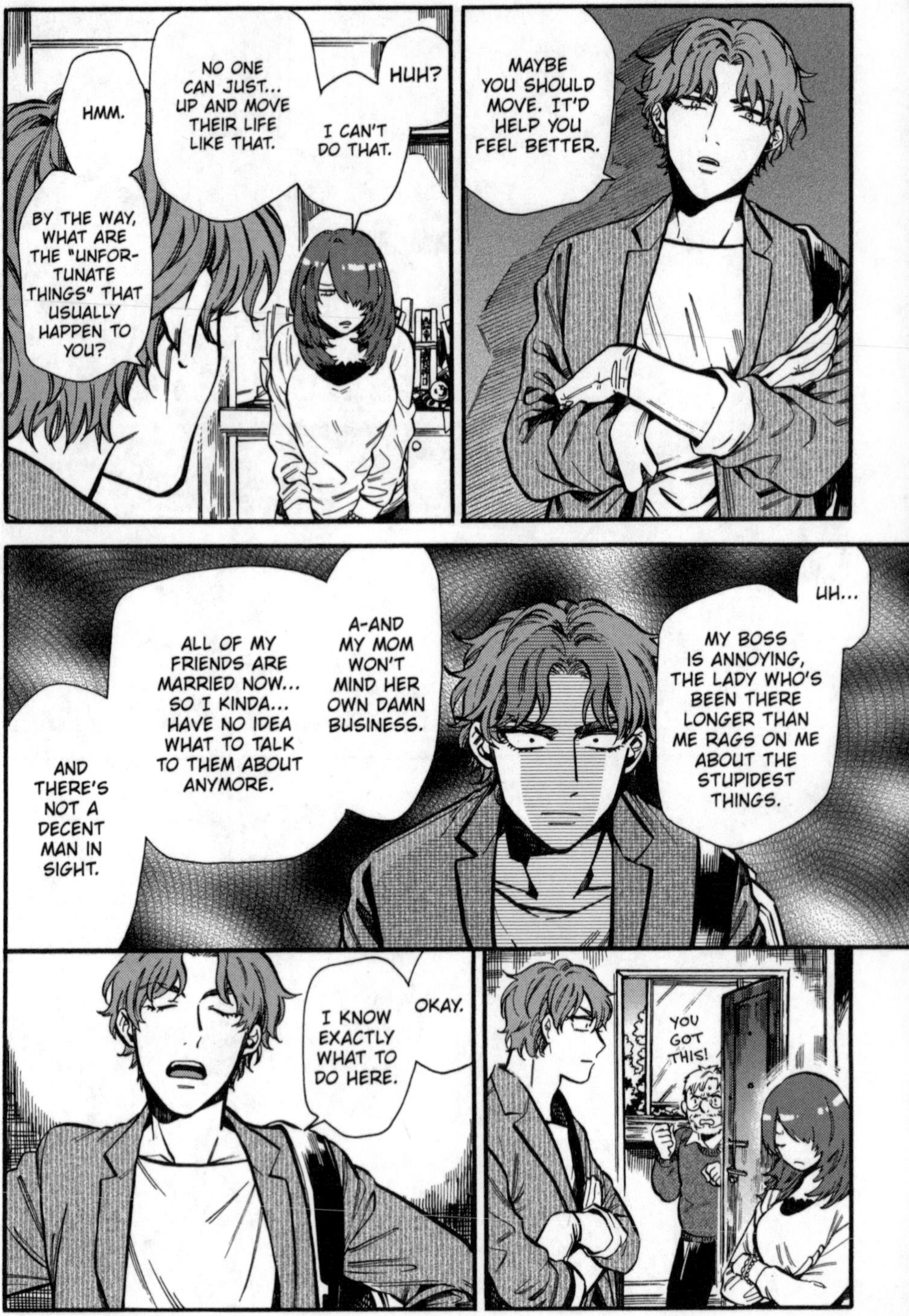
MAYBE YOU SHOULD MOVE. IT'D HELP YOU FEEL BETTER.
HUH?
I CAN'T DO THAT.
NO ONE CAN JUST... UP AND MOVE THEIR LIFE LIKE THAT.
HMM.
BY THE WAY, WHAT ARE THE "UNFORTUNATE THINGS" THAT USUALLY HAPPEN TO YOU?
UH...
MY BOSS IS ANNOYING, THE LADY WHO'S BEEN THERE LONGER THAN ME RAGS ON ME ABOUT THE STUPIDEST THINGS.
A-AND MY MOM WON'T MIND HER OWN DAMN BUSINESS.
ALL OF MY FRIENDS ARE MARRIED NOW... SO I KINDA... HAVE NO IDEA WHAT TO TALK TO THEM ABOUT ANYMORE.
AND THERE'S NOT A DECENT MAN IN SIGHT.
YOU GOT THIS!
OKAY.
I KNOW EXACTLY WHAT TO DO HERE.

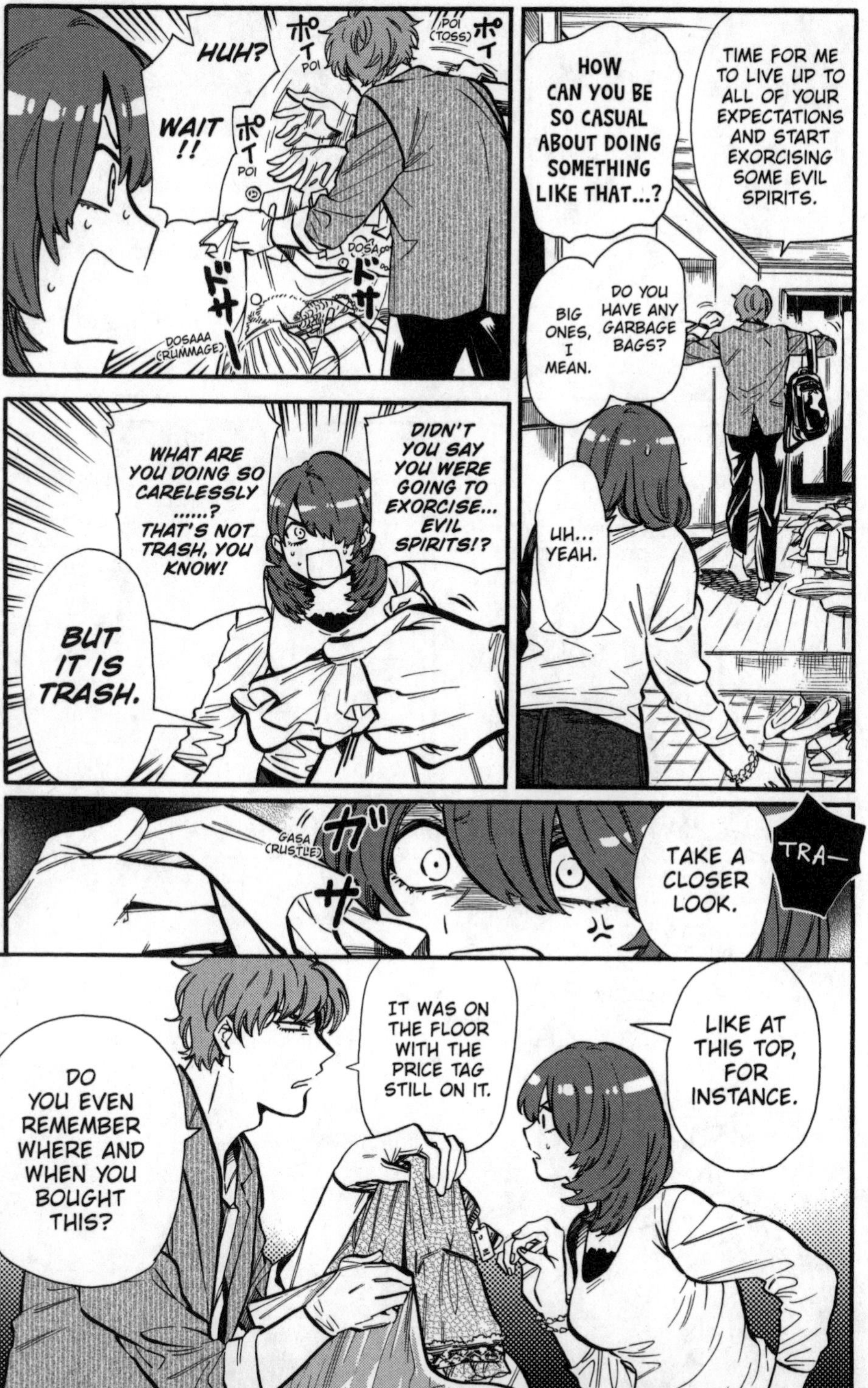
TIME FOR ME TO LIVE UP TO ALL OF YOUR EXPECTATIONS AND START EXORCISING SOME EVIL SPIRITS.
HOW CAN YOU BE SO CASUAL ABOUT DOING SOMETHING LIKE THAT...?
DO YOU HAVE ANY GARBAGE BAGS?
BIG ONES, I MEAN.
UH... YEAH.
ポイ
POI (TOSS)
ポイ
POI
HUH?
ポイ
POI
WAIT!!
ドサ
DOSA
ドサー
DOSAAA (RUMMAGE)
DIDN'T YOU SAY YOU WERE GOING TO EXORCISE... EVIL SPIRITS!?
WHAT ARE YOU DOING SO CARELESSLY ......? THAT'S NOT TRASH, YOU KNOW!
BUT IT IS TRASH.
TRA—
TAKE A CLOSER LOOK.
ガサ
GASA (RUSTLE)
LIKE AT THIS TOP, FOR INSTANCE.
IT WAS ON THE FLOOR WITH THE PRICE TAG STILL ON IT.
DO YOU EVEN REMEMBER WHERE AND WHEN YOU BOUGHT THIS?

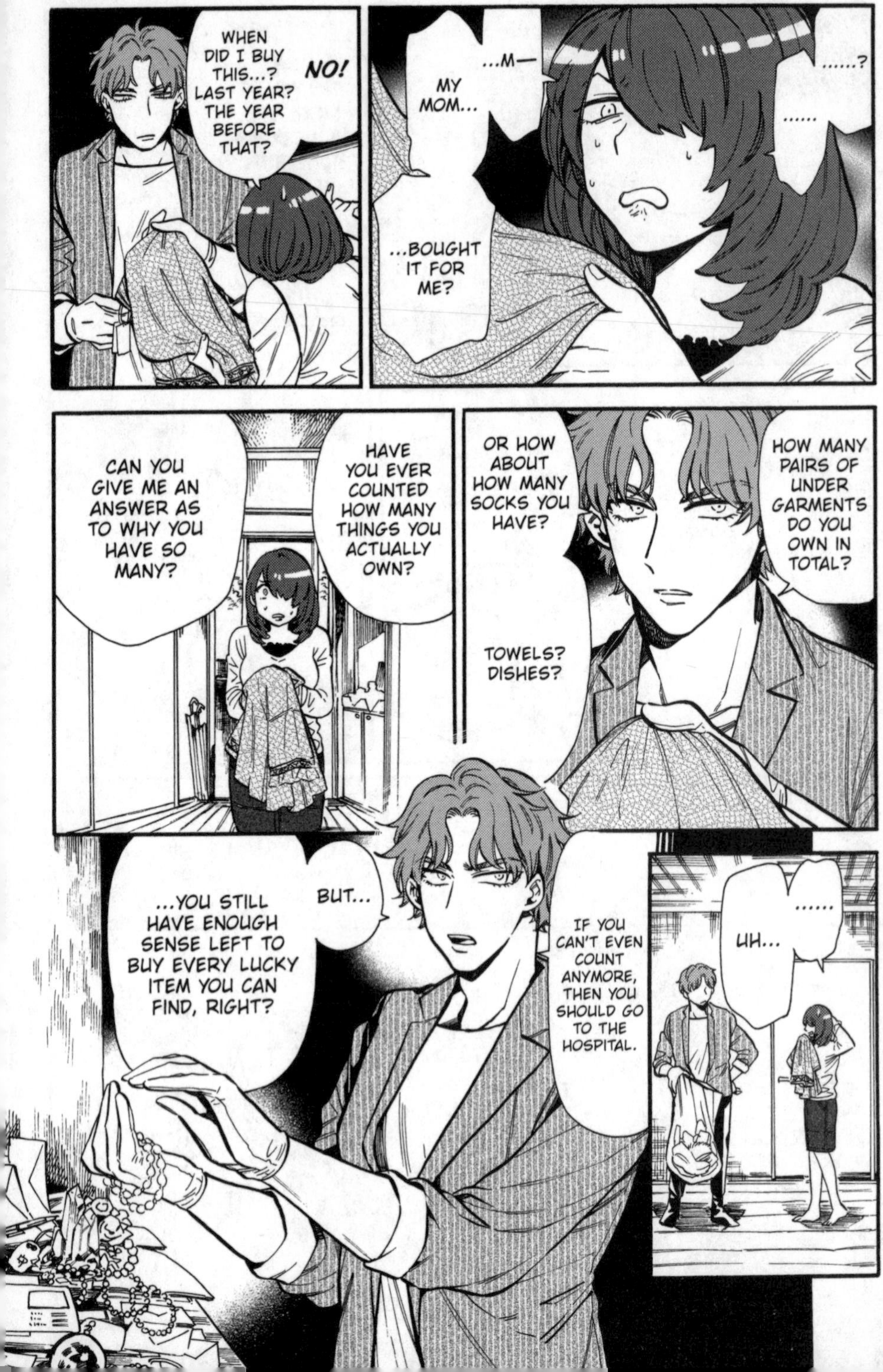
......?
......
...M—
MY MOM...
...BOUGHT IT FOR ME?
NO!
WHEN DID I BUY THIS...? LAST YEAR? THE YEAR BEFORE THAT?
HOW MANY PAIRS OF UNDER GARMENTS DO YOU OWN IN TOTAL?
OR HOW ABOUT HOW MANY SOCKS YOU HAVE?
TOWELS? DISHES?
HAVE YOU EVER COUNTED HOW MANY THINGS YOU ACTUALLY OWN?
CAN YOU GIVE ME AN ANSWER AS TO WHY YOU HAVE SO MANY?
......
UH...
IF YOU CAN'T EVEN COUNT ANYMORE, THEN YOU SHOULD GO TO THE HOSPITAL.
BUT...
...YOU STILL HAVE ENOUGH SENSE LEFT TO BUY EVERY LUCKY ITEM YOU CAN FIND, RIGHT?

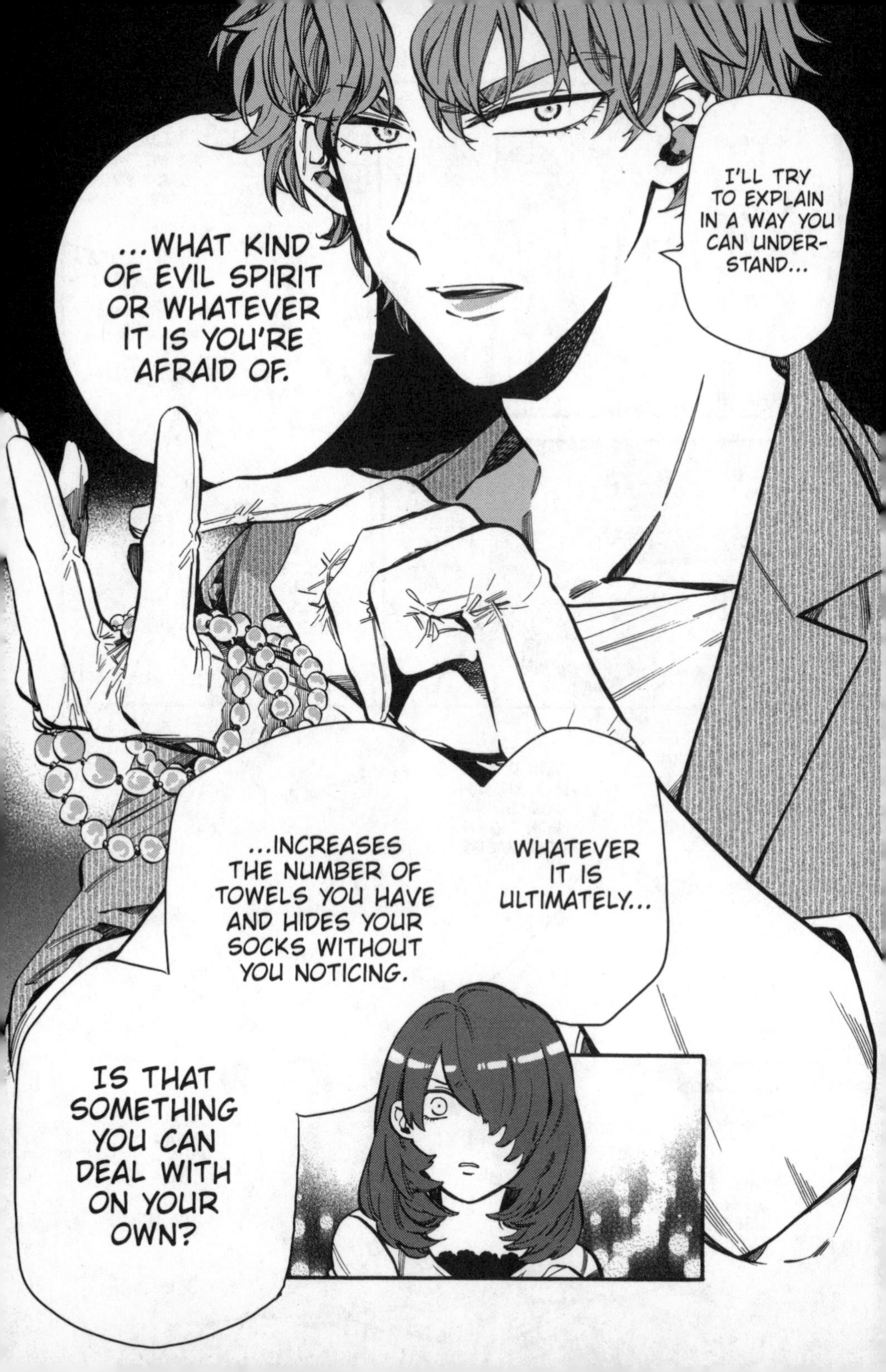
I'LL TRY TO EXPLAIN IN A WAY YOU CAN UNDER-STAND...
...WHAT KIND OF EVIL SPIRIT OR WHATEVER IT IS YOU'RE AFRAID OF.
WHATEVER IT IS ULTIMATELY...
...INCREASES THE NUMBER OF TOWELS YOU HAVE AND HIDES YOUR SOCKS WITHOUT YOU NOTICING.
IS THAT SOMETHING YOU CAN DEAL WITH ON YOUR OWN?

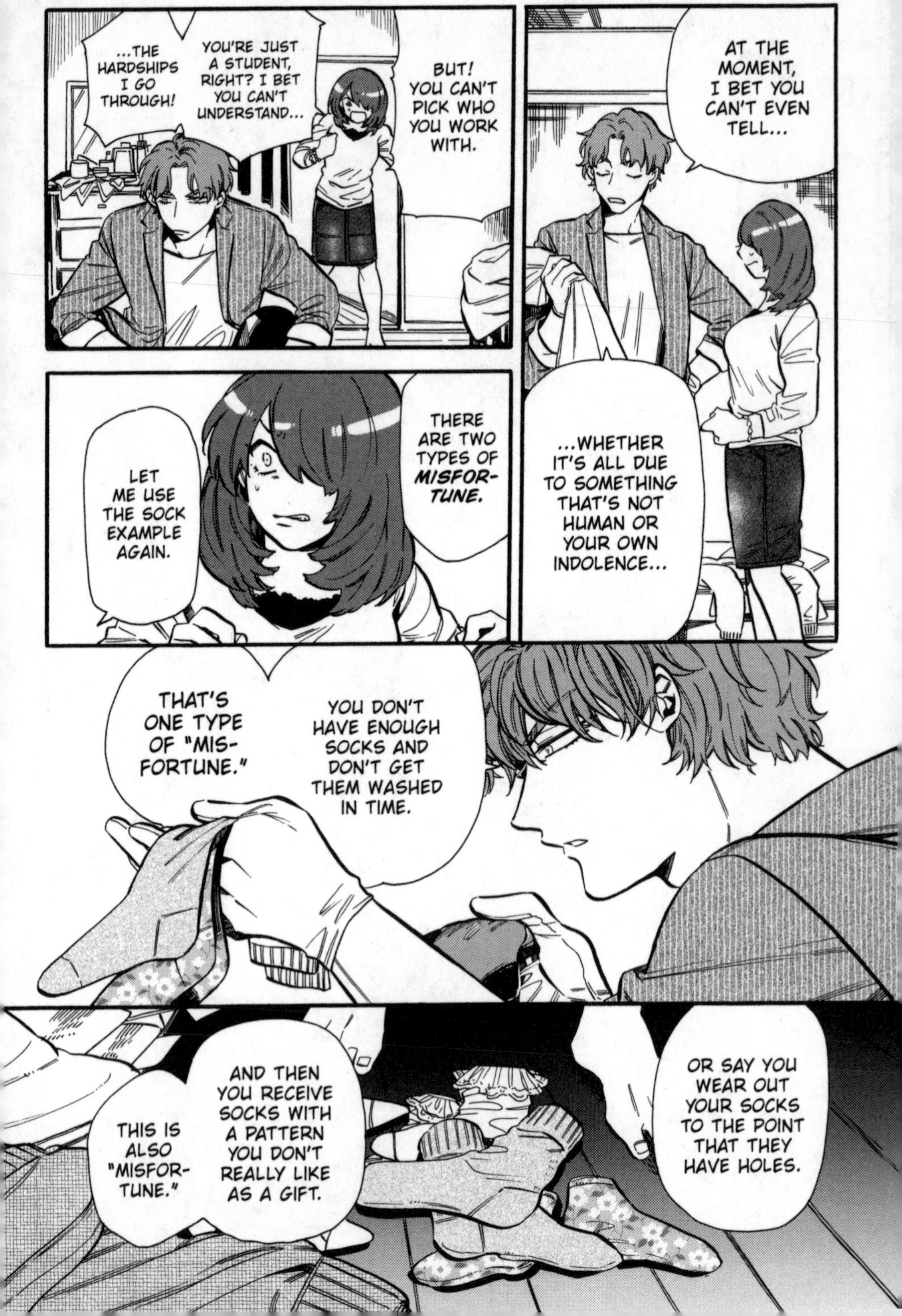
BUT! YOU CAN'T PICK WHO YOU WORK WITH.
YOU'RE JUST A STUDENT, RIGHT? I BET YOU CAN'T UNDERSTAND...
...THE HARDSHIPS I GO THROUGH!
AT THE MOMENT, I BET YOU CAN'T EVEN TELL...
...WHETHER IT'S ALL DUE TO SOMETHING THAT'S NOT HUMAN OR YOUR OWN INDOLENCE...
THERE ARE TWO TYPES OF *MISFORTUNE.*
LET ME USE THE SOCK EXAMPLE AGAIN.
YOU DON'T HAVE ENOUGH SOCKS AND DON'T GET THEM WASHED IN TIME.
THAT'S ONE TYPE OF "MISFORTUNE."
OR SAY YOU WEAR OUT YOUR SOCKS TO THE POINT THAT THEY HAVE HOLES.
AND THEN YOU RECEIVE SOCKS WITH A PATTERN YOU DON'T REALLY LIKE AS A GIFT.
THIS IS ALSO "MISFORTUNE."

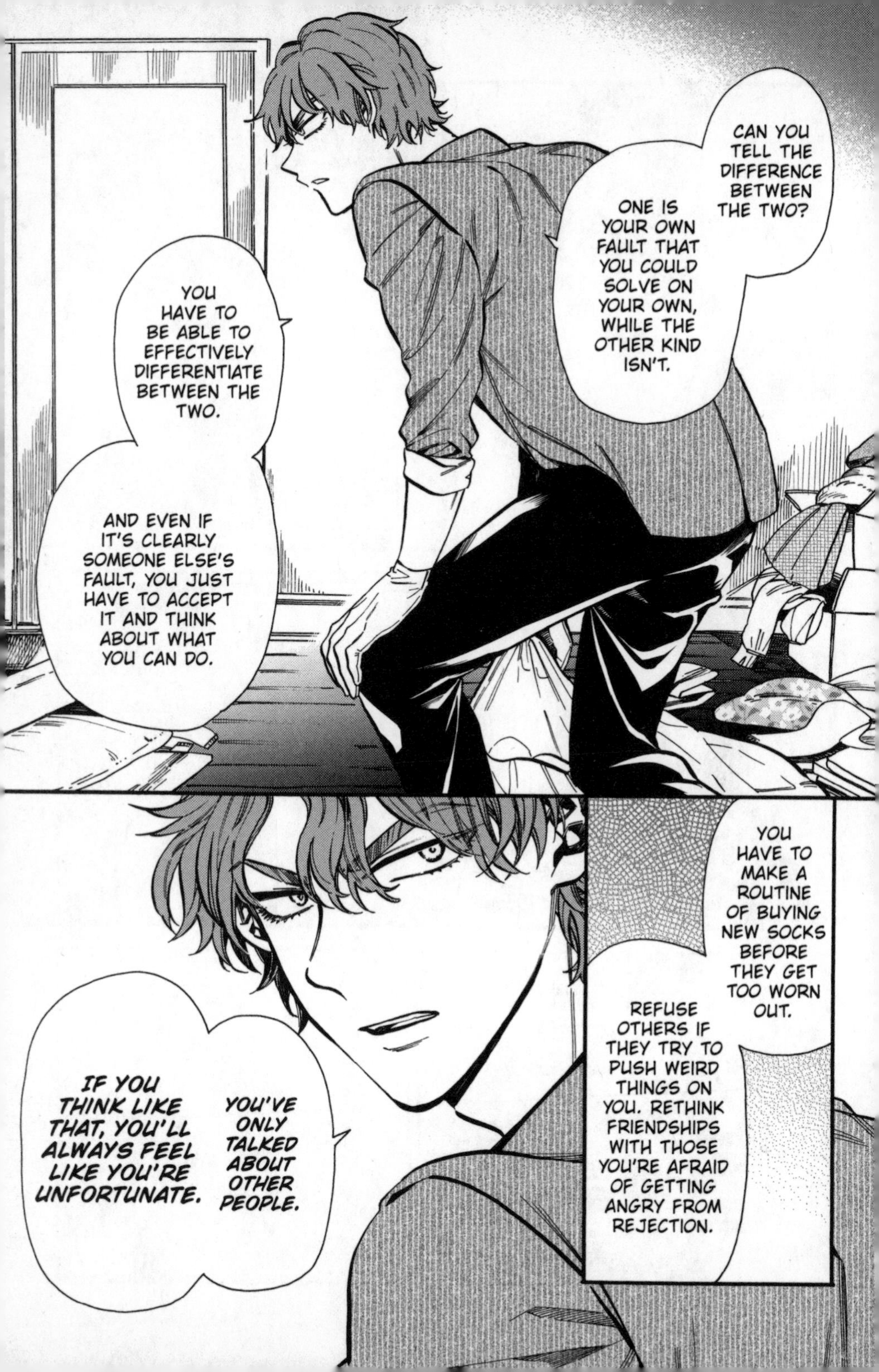
CAN YOU TELL THE DIFFERENCE BETWEEN THE TWO?
ONE IS YOUR OWN FAULT THAT YOU COULD SOLVE ON YOUR OWN, WHILE THE OTHER KIND ISN'T.
YOU HAVE TO BE ABLE TO EFFECTIVELY DIFFERENTIATE BETWEEN THE TWO.
AND EVEN IF IT'S CLEARLY SOMEONE ELSE'S FAULT, YOU JUST HAVE TO ACCEPT IT AND THINK ABOUT WHAT YOU CAN DO.
YOU HAVE TO MAKE A ROUTINE OF BUYING NEW SOCKS BEFORE THEY GET TOO WORN OUT.
REFUSE OTHERS IF THEY TRY TO PUSH WEIRD THINGS ON YOU. RETHINK FRIENDSHIPS WITH THOSE YOU'RE AFRAID OF GETTING ANGRY FROM REJECTION.
YOU'VE ONLY TALKED ABOUT OTHER PEOPLE.
IF YOU THINK LIKE THAT, YOU'LL ALWAYS FEEL LIKE YOU'RE UNFORTUNATE.

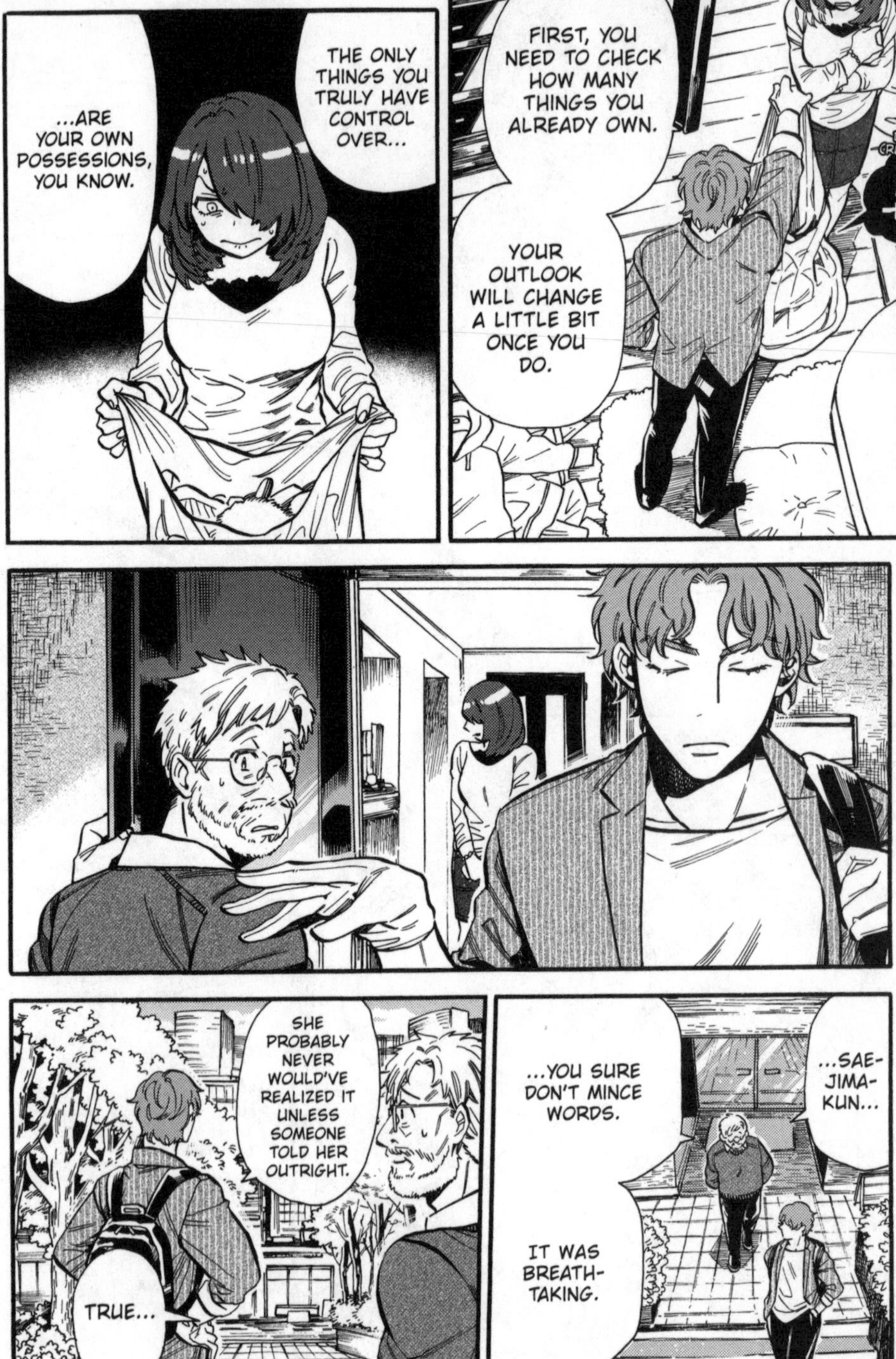
FIRST, YOU NEED TO CHECK HOW MANY THINGS YOU ALREADY OWN.
YOUR OUTLOOK WILL CHANGE A LITTLE BIT ONCE YOU DO.
DOSA (RUSTLE)
ドサ
THE ONLY THINGS YOU TRULY HAVE CONTROL OVER...
...ARE YOUR OWN POSSESSIONS, YOU KNOW.
...SAE-JIMA-KUN...
...YOU SURE DON'T MINCE WORDS.
IT WAS BREATH-TAKING.
SHE PROBABLY NEVER WOULD'VE REALIZED IT UNLESS SOMEONE TOLD HER OUTRIGHT.
TRUE...

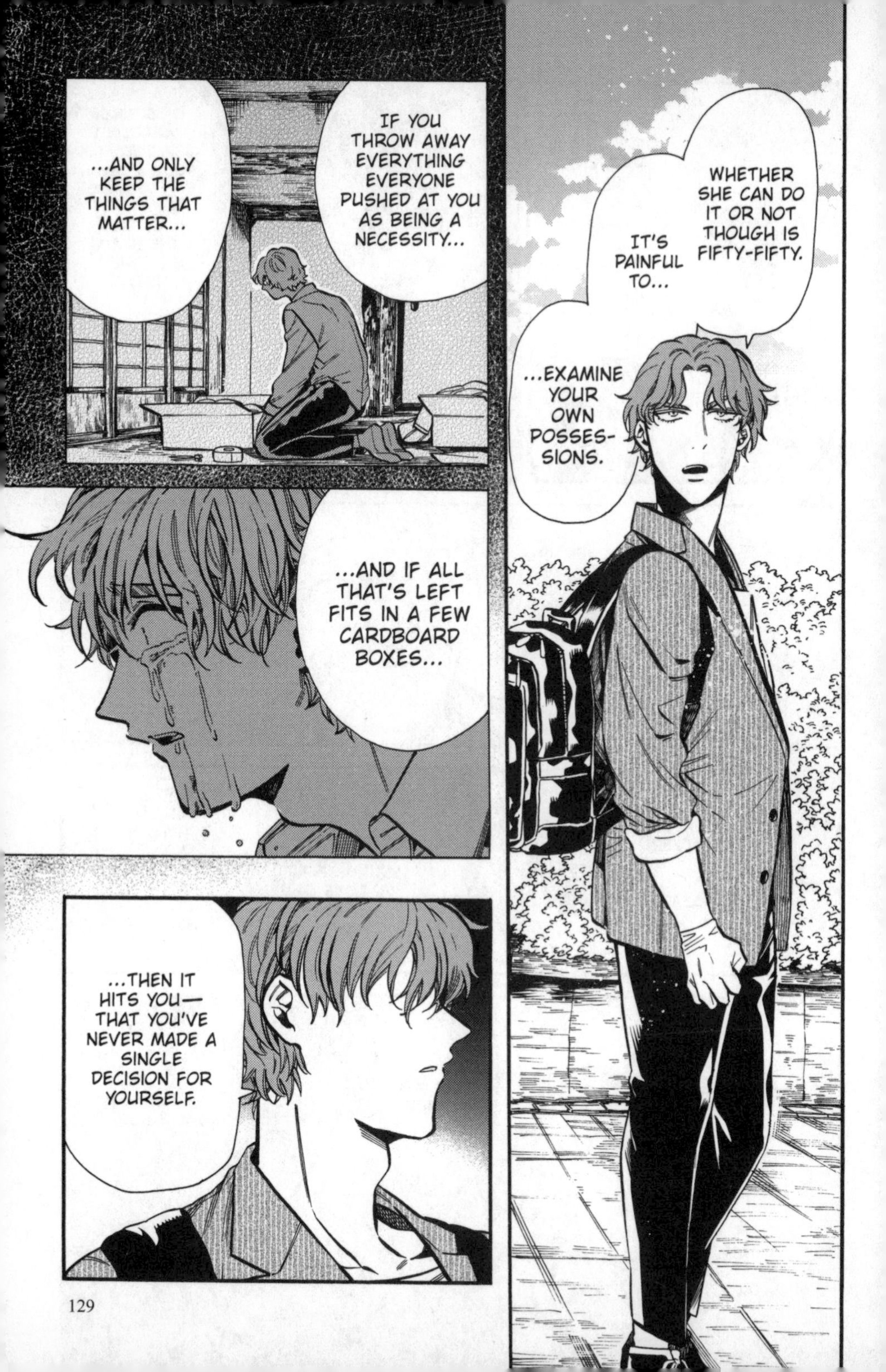
WHETHER SHE CAN DO IT OR NOT THOUGH IS FIFTY-FIFTY.
IT'S PAINFUL TO...
...EXAMINE YOUR OWN POSSES-SIONS.
IF YOU THROW AWAY EVERYTHING EVERYONE PUSHED AT YOU AS BEING A NECESSITY...
...AND ONLY KEEP THE THINGS THAT MATTER...
...AND IF ALL THAT'S LEFT FITS IN A FEW CARDBOARD BOXES...
...THEN IT HITS YOU—THAT YOU'VE NEVER MADE A SINGLE DECISION FOR YOURSELF.

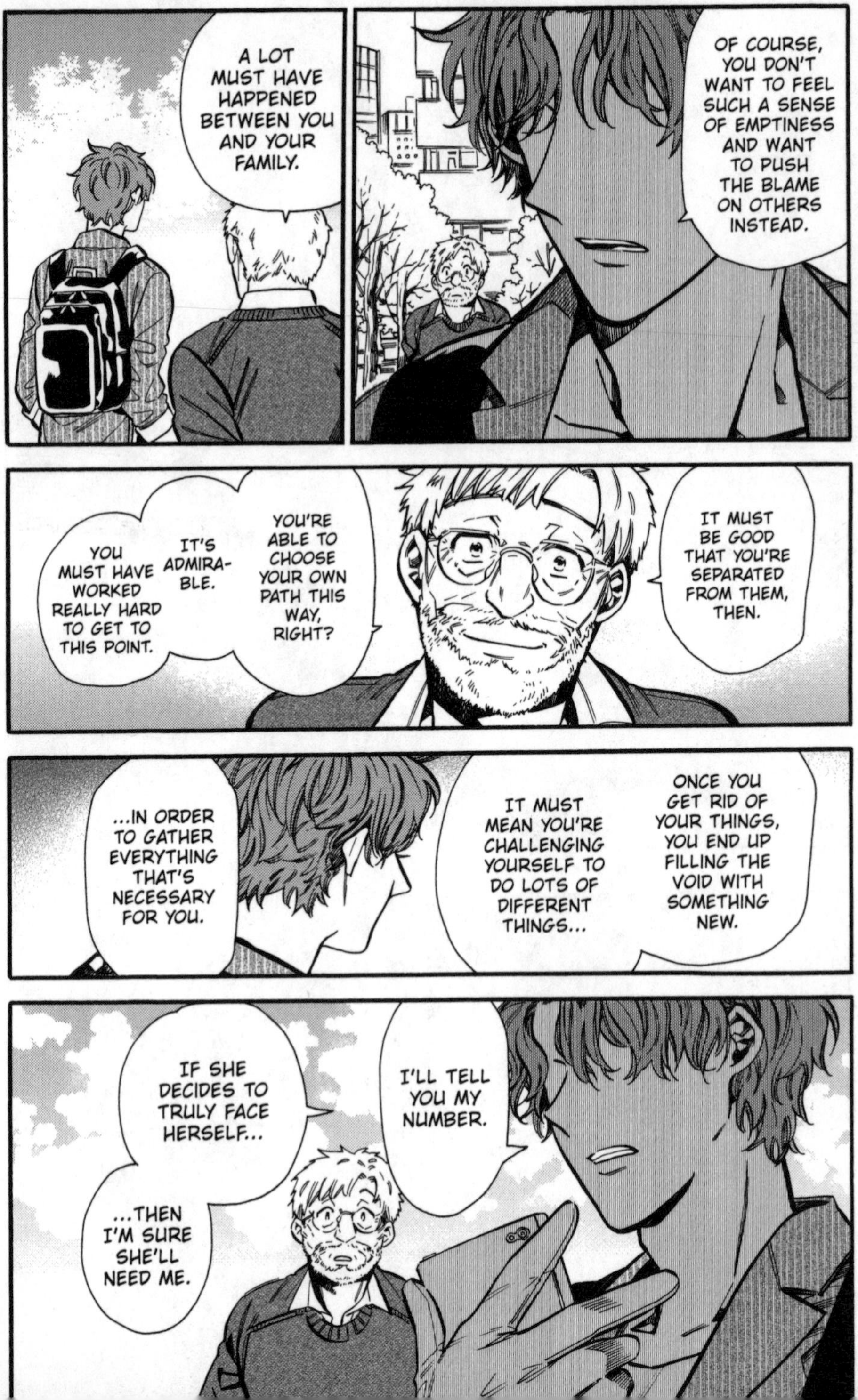
OF COURSE, YOU DON'T WANT TO FEEL SUCH A SENSE OF EMPTINESS AND WANT TO PUSH THE BLAME ON OTHERS INSTEAD.
A LOT MUST HAVE HAPPENED BETWEEN YOU AND YOUR FAMILY.
IT MUST BE GOOD THAT YOU'RE SEPARATED FROM THEM, THEN.
YOU'RE ABLE TO CHOOSE YOUR OWN PATH THIS WAY, RIGHT?
IT'S ADMIRA-BLE.
YOU MUST HAVE WORKED REALLY HARD TO GET TO THIS POINT.
ONCE YOU GET RID OF YOUR THINGS, YOU END UP FILLING THE VOID WITH SOMETHING NEW.
IT MUST MEAN YOU'RE CHALLENGING YOURSELF TO DO LOTS OF DIFFERENT THINGS...
...IN ORDER TO GATHER EVERYTHING THAT'S NECESSARY FOR YOU.
I'LL TELL YOU MY NUMBER.
IF SHE DECIDES TO TRULY FACE HERSELF...
...THEN I'M SURE SHE'LL NEED ME.

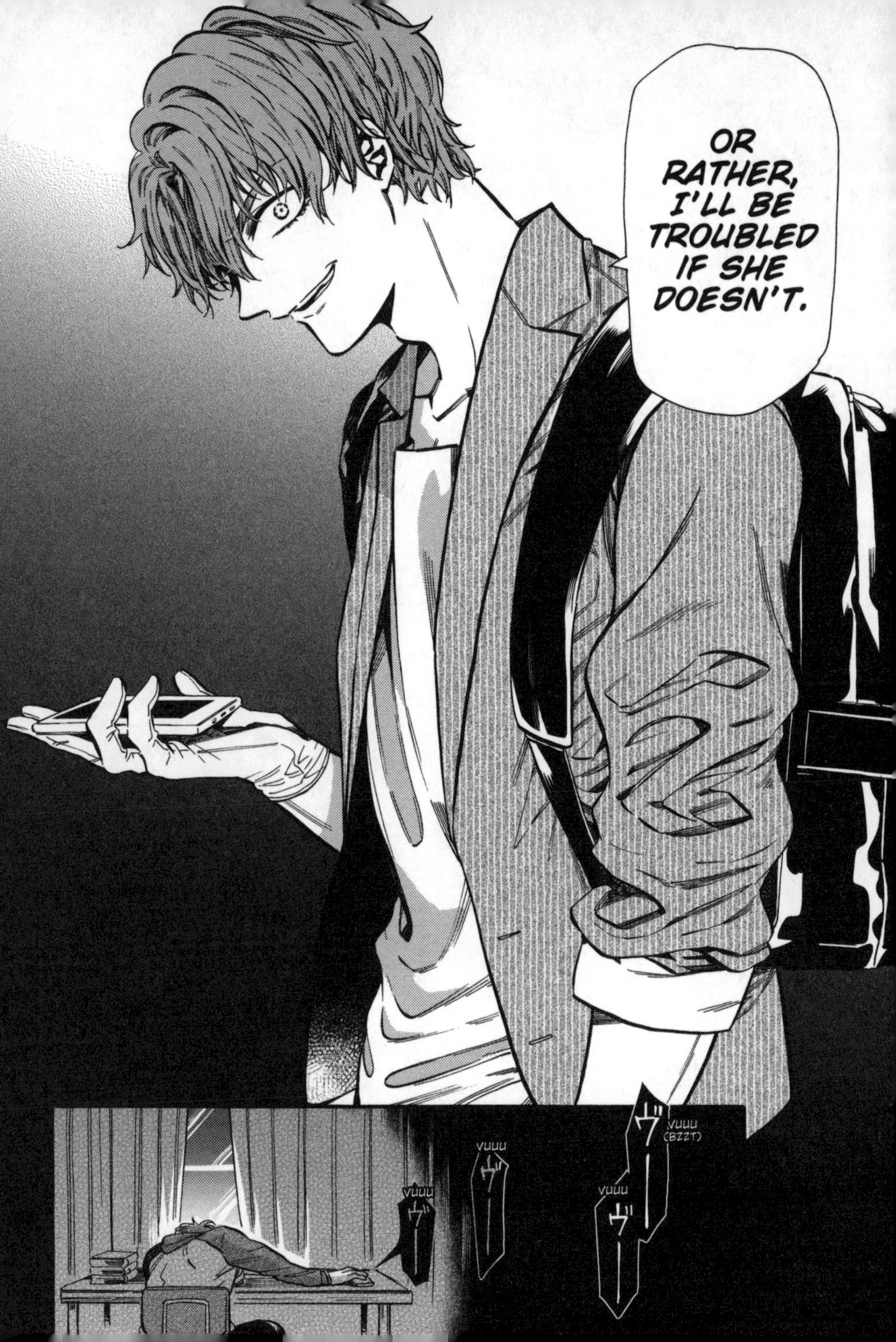
OR RATHER, I'LL BE TROUBLED IF SHE DOESN'T.
ヴー
VUUU (BZZT)
VUUU
ヴー
VUUU
ヴー
VUUU
ヴー

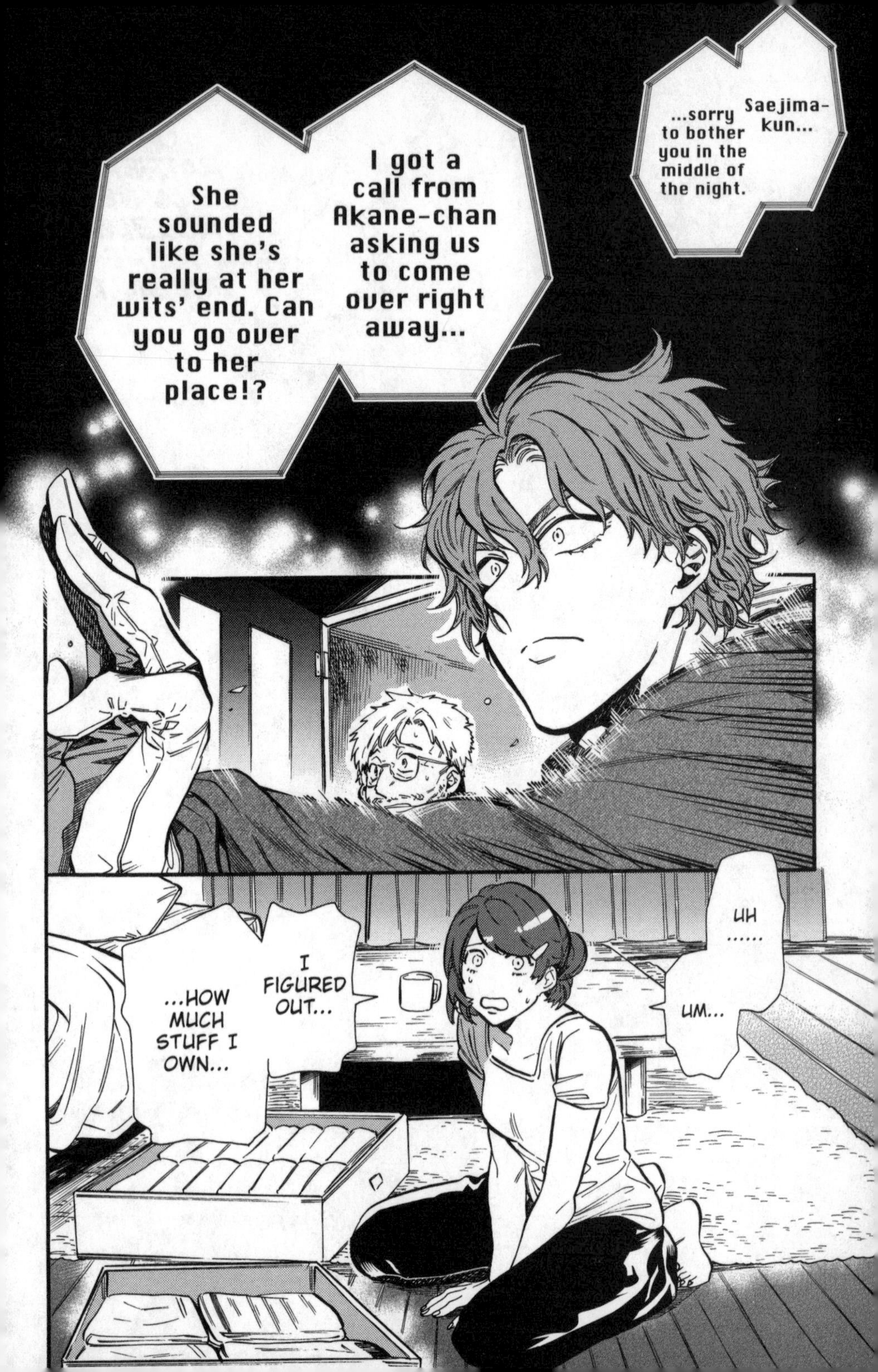
Saejima-kun...
...sorry to bother you in the middle of the night.
I got a call from Akane-chan asking us to come over right away...
She sounded like she's really at her wits' end. Can you go over to her place!?
UH ......
UM...
I FIGURED OUT...
...HOW MUCH STUFF I OWN...

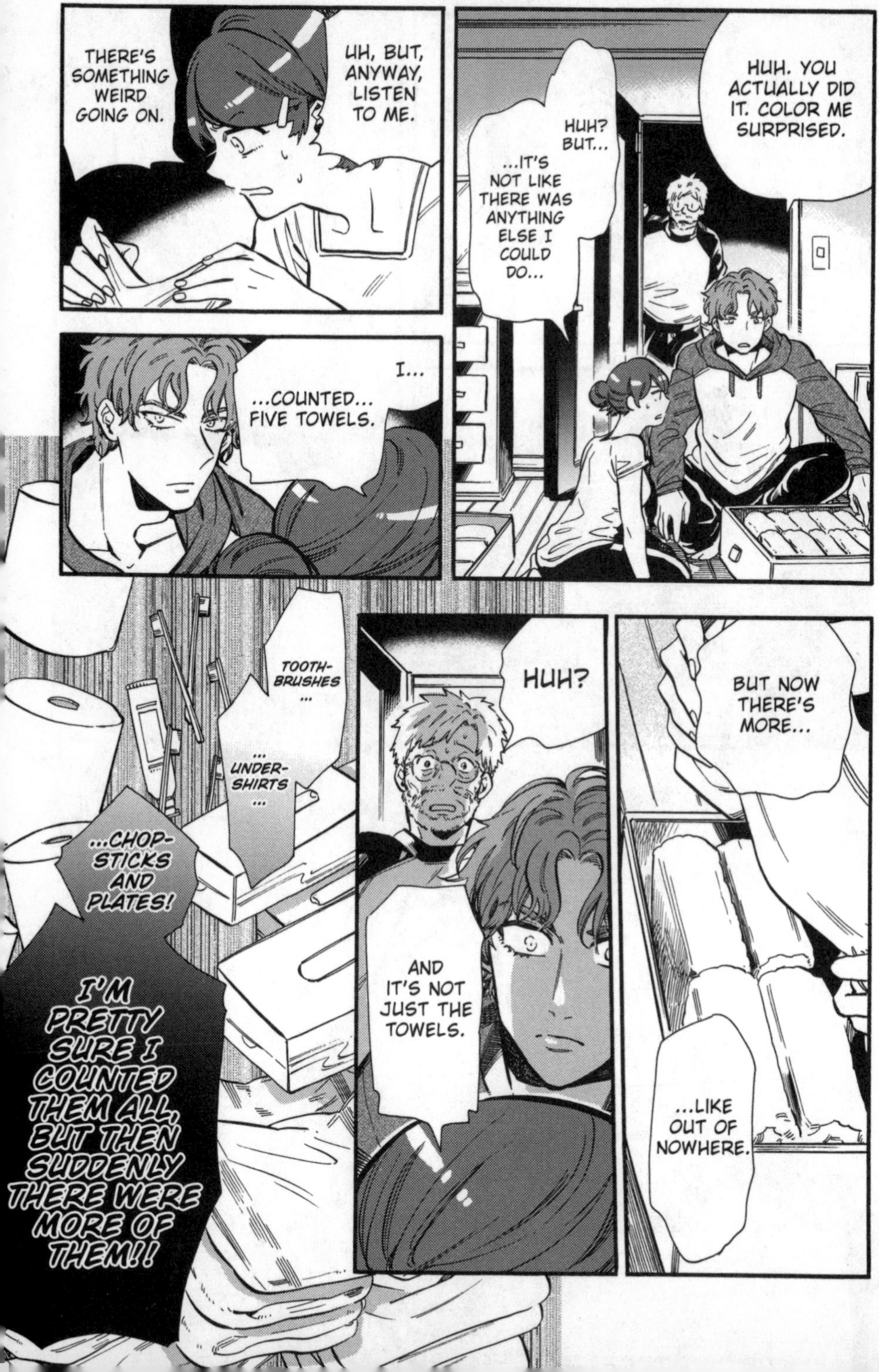
HUH. YOU ACTUALLY DID IT. COLOR ME SURPRISED.
HUH? BUT...
...IT'S NOT LIKE THERE WAS ANYTHING ELSE I COULD DO...
UH, BUT, ANYWAY, LISTEN TO ME.
THERE'S SOMETHING WEIRD GOING ON.
I...
...COUNTED... FIVE TOWELS.
BUT NOW THERE'S MORE...
...LIKE OUT OF NOWHERE.
HUH?
AND IT'S NOT JUST THE TOWELS.
TOOTH-BRUSHES...
...UNDER-SHIRTS...
...CHOP-STICKS AND PLATES!
I'M PRETTY SURE I COUNTED THEM ALL, BUT THEN SUDDENLY THERE WERE MORE OF THEM!!

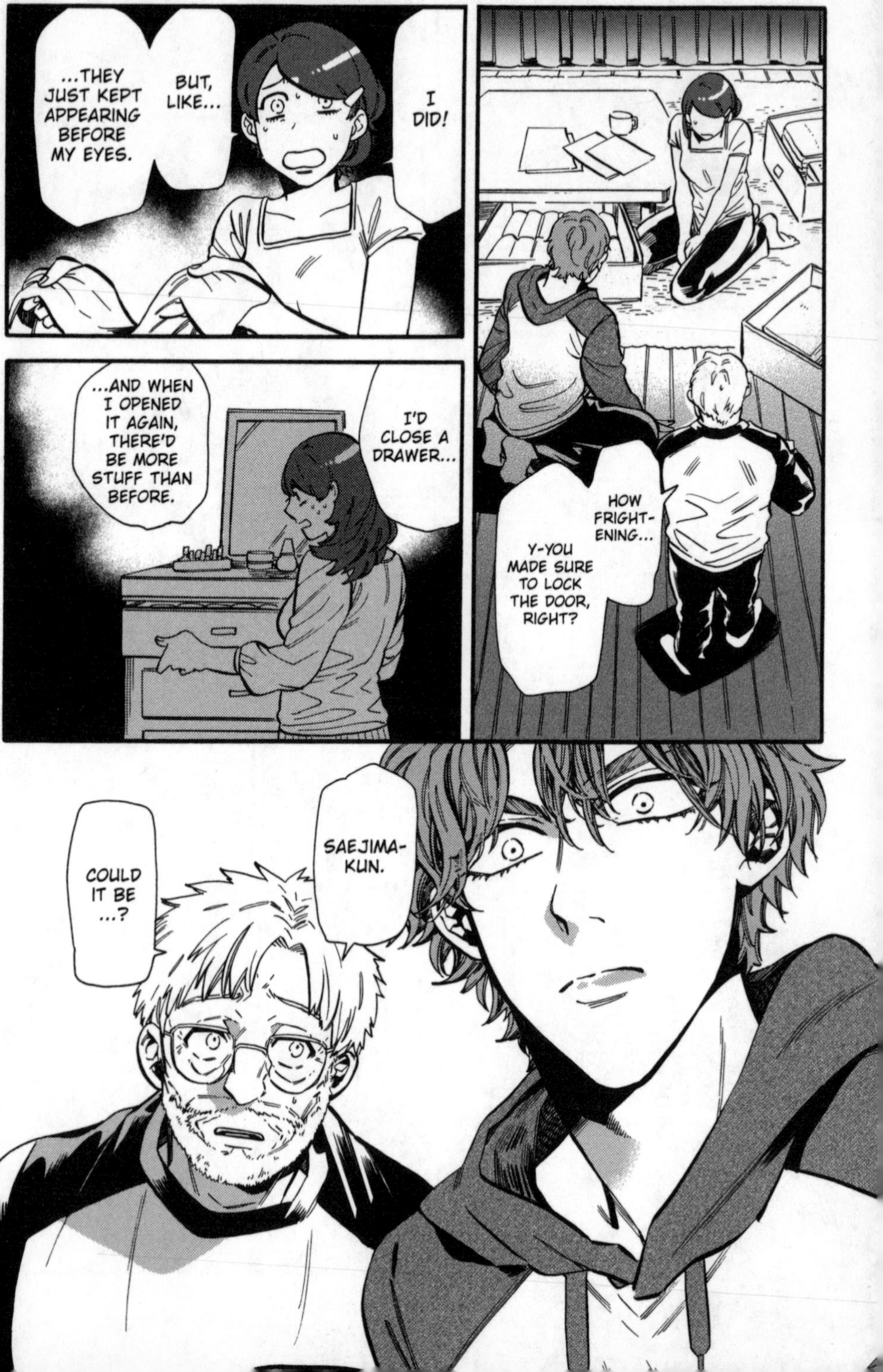
HOW FRIGHTENING...
Y-YOU MADE SURE TO LOCK THE DOOR, RIGHT?
I DID!
BUT, LIKE...
...THEY JUST KEPT APPEARING BEFORE MY EYES.
I'D CLOSE A DRAWER...
...AND WHEN I OPENED IT AGAIN, THERE'D BE MORE STUFF THAN BEFORE.
SAEJIMA-KUN.
COULD IT BE ...?

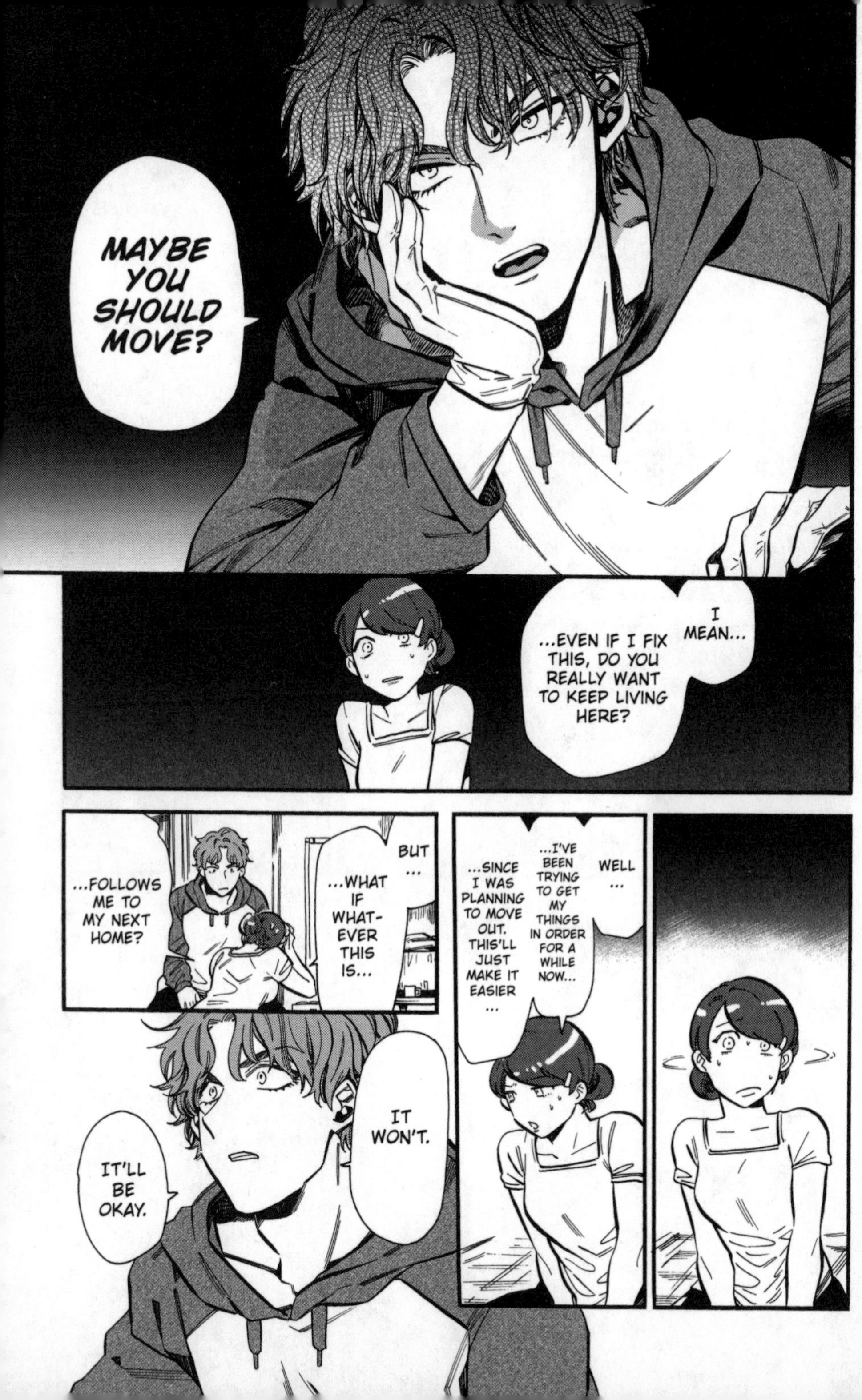
MAYBE YOU SHOULD MOVE?
I MEAN...
...EVEN IF I FIX THIS, DO YOU REALLY WANT TO KEEP LIVING HERE?
WELL ...
...I'VE BEEN TRYING TO GET MY THINGS IN ORDER FOR A WHILE NOW...
...SINCE I WAS PLANNING TO MOVE OUT. THIS'LL JUST MAKE IT EASIER ...
BUT ...
...WHAT IF WHATEVER THIS IS...
...FOLLOWS ME TO MY NEXT HOME?
IT WON'T.
IT'LL BE OKAY.

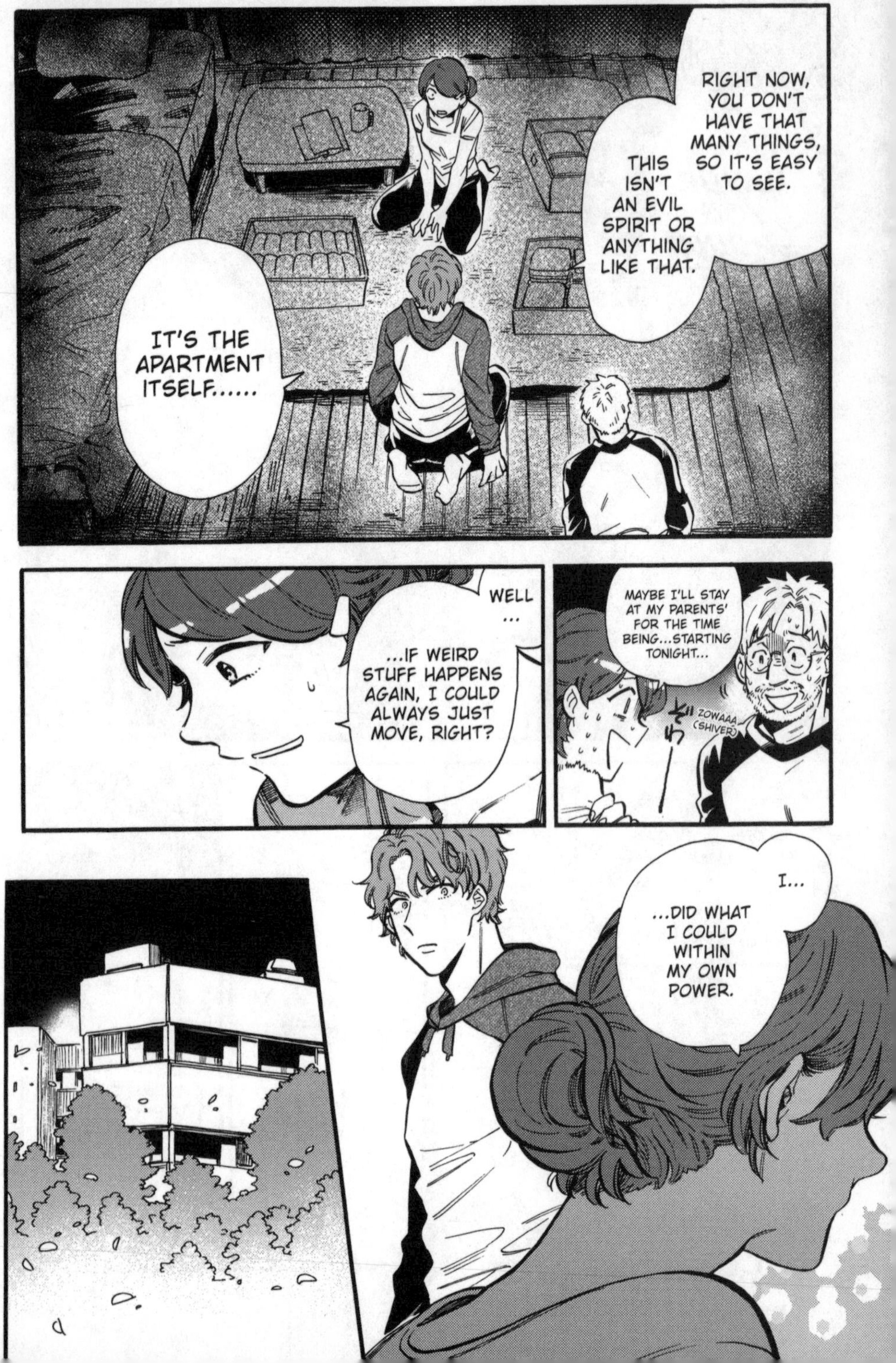
RIGHT NOW, YOU DON'T HAVE THAT MANY THINGS, SO IT'S EASY TO SEE.
THIS ISN'T AN EVIL SPIRIT OR ANYTHING LIKE THAT.
IT'S THE APARTMENT ITSELF......
MAYBE I'LL STAY AT MY PARENTS' FOR THE TIME BEING...STARTING TONIGHT...
ZOWAAA (SHIVER)
WELL...
...IF WEIRD STUFF HAPPENS AGAIN, I COULD ALWAYS JUST MOVE, RIGHT?
I...
...DID WHAT I COULD WITHIN MY OWN POWER.

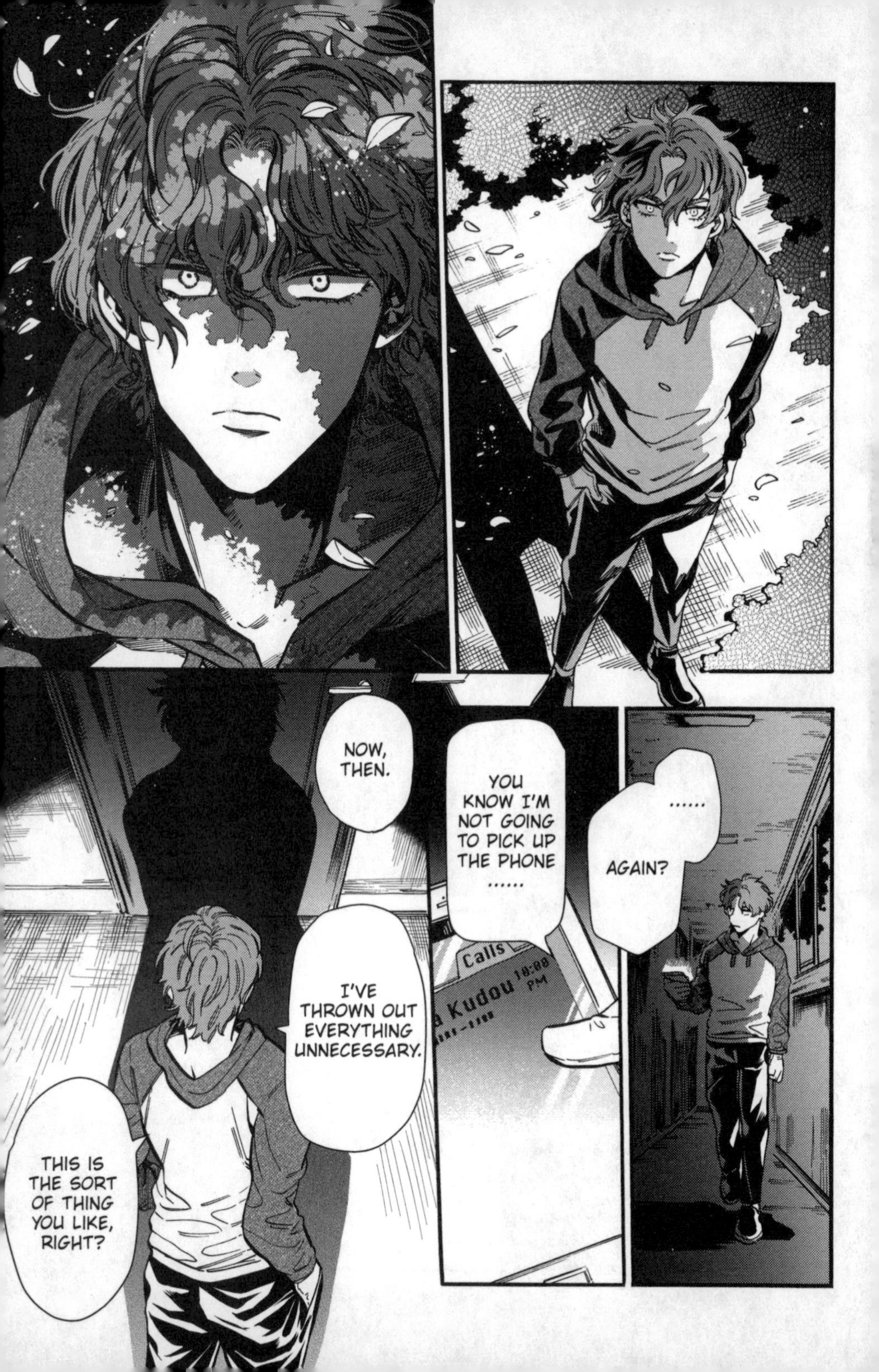
......
AGAIN?
YOU KNOW I'M NOT GOING TO PICK UP THE PHONE ......
Calls
Kudou
10:00 PM
NOW, THEN.
I'VE THROWN OUT EVERYTHING UNNECESSARY.
THIS IS THE SORT OF THING YOU LIKE, RIGHT?

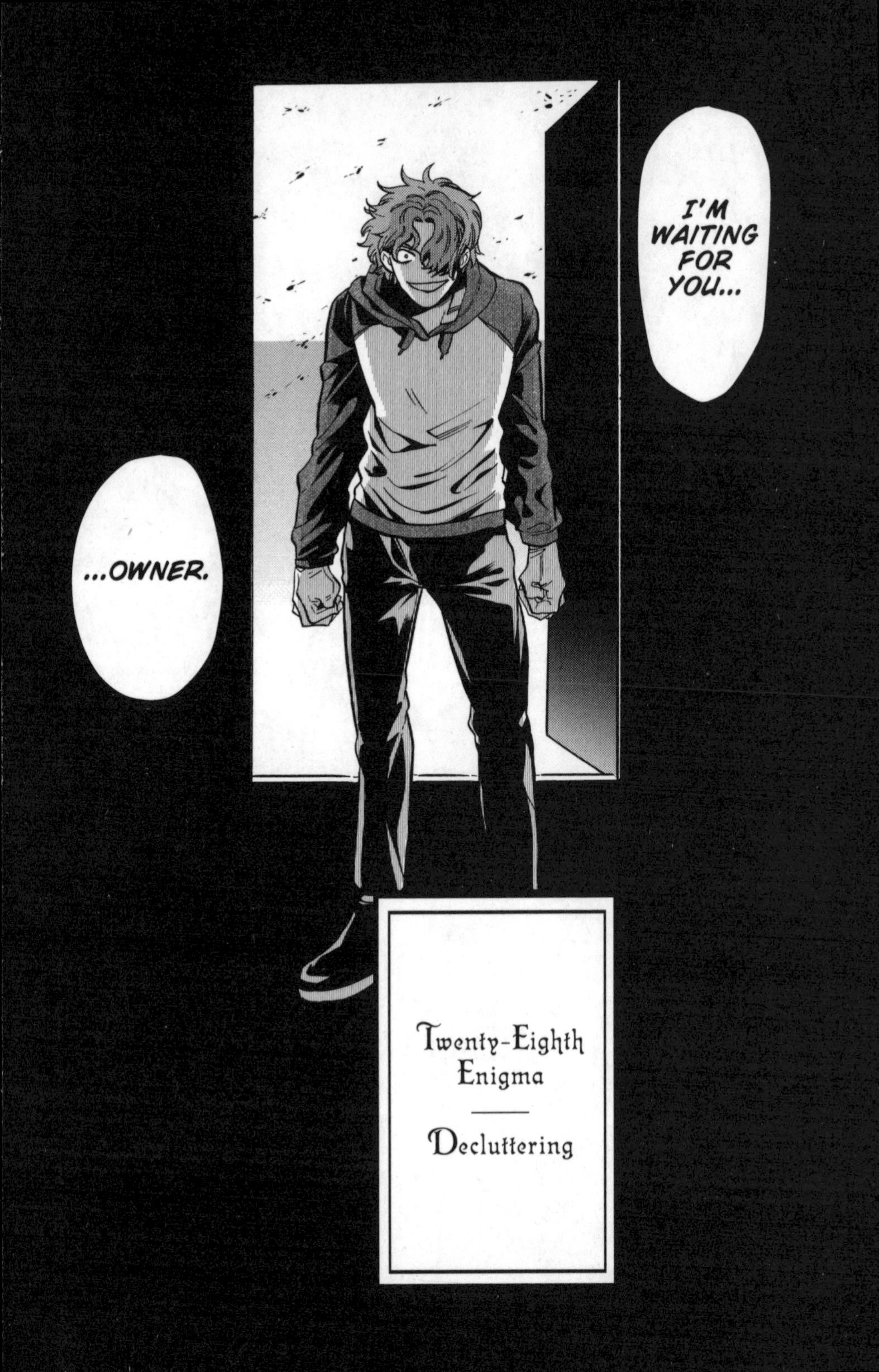
I'M WAITING FOR YOU...
...OWNER.
Twenty-Eighth Enigma
Decluttering

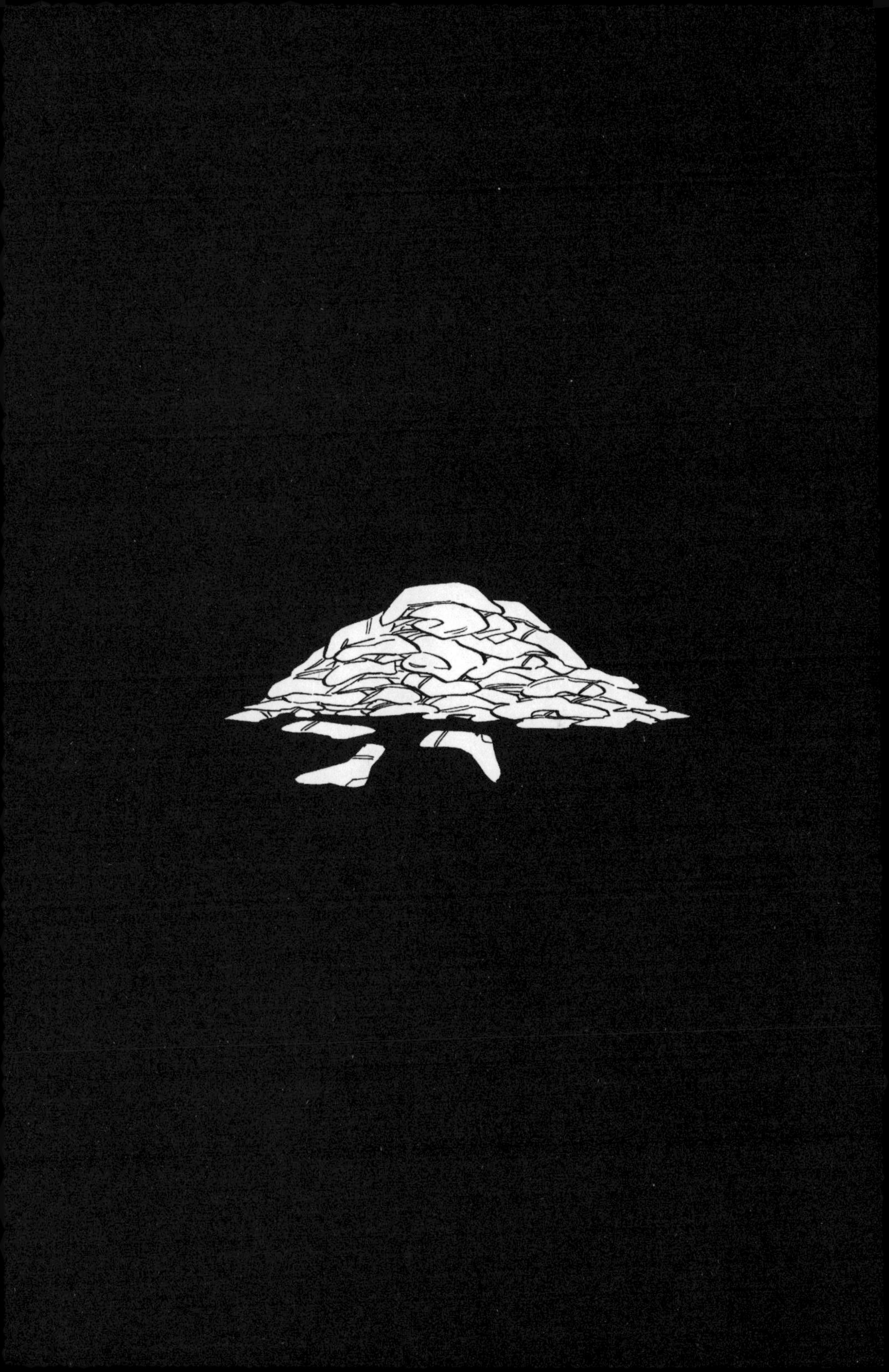

Phantom Tales of the Night

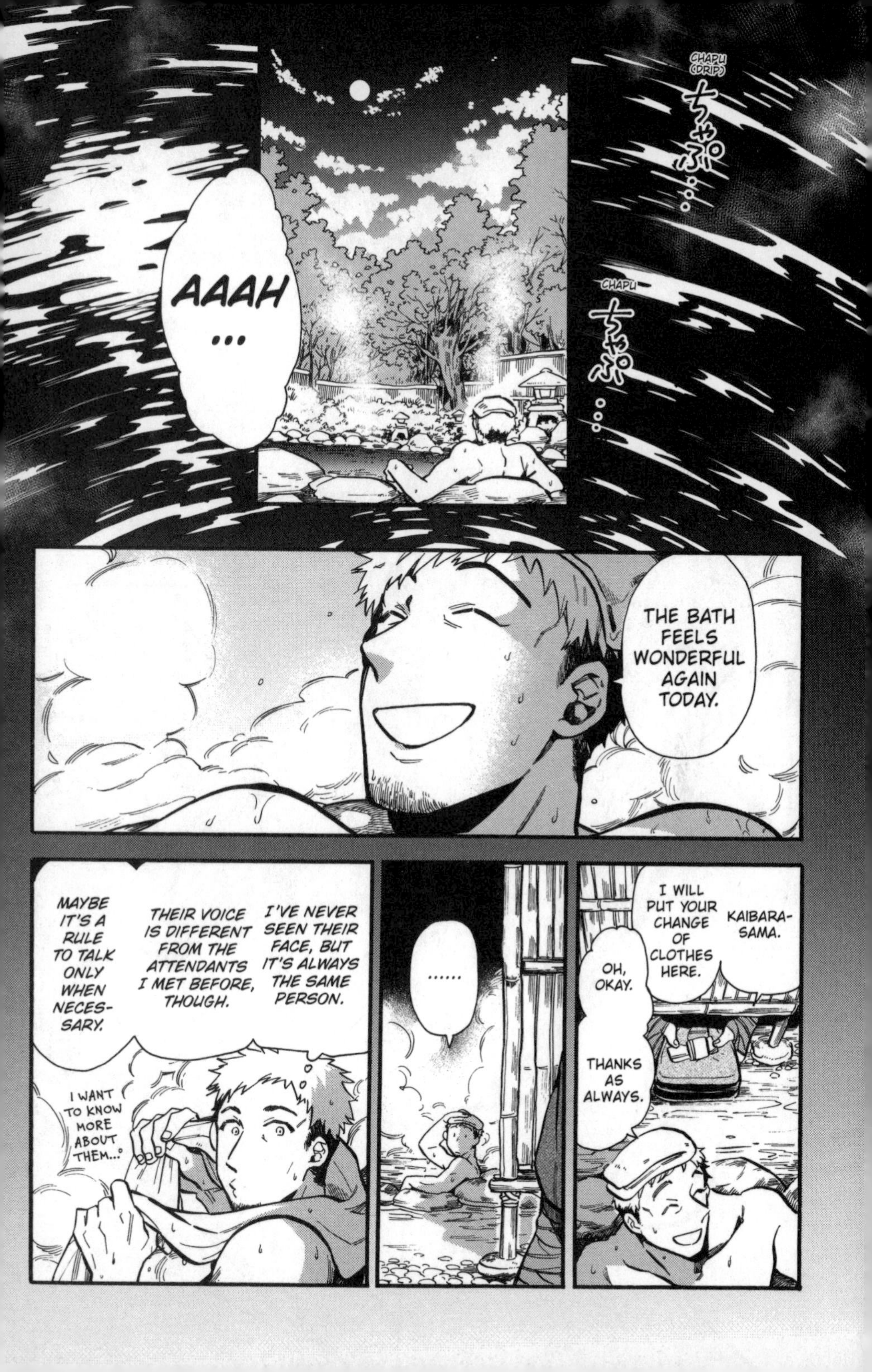
CHAPU (DRIP)
ちゃぷ…
CHAPU
ちゃぷ…
AAAH ...
THE BATH FEELS WONDERFUL AGAIN TODAY.
KAIBARA-SAMA.
I WILL PUT YOUR CHANGE OF CLOTHES HERE.
OH, OKAY.
THANKS AS ALWAYS.
......
I'VE NEVER SEEN THEIR FACE, BUT IT'S ALWAYS THE SAME PERSON.
THEIR VOICE IS DIFFERENT FROM THE ATTENDANTS I MET BEFORE, THOUGH.
MAYBE IT'S A RULE TO TALK ONLY WHEN NECES-SARY.
I WANT TO KNOW MORE ABOUT THEM...

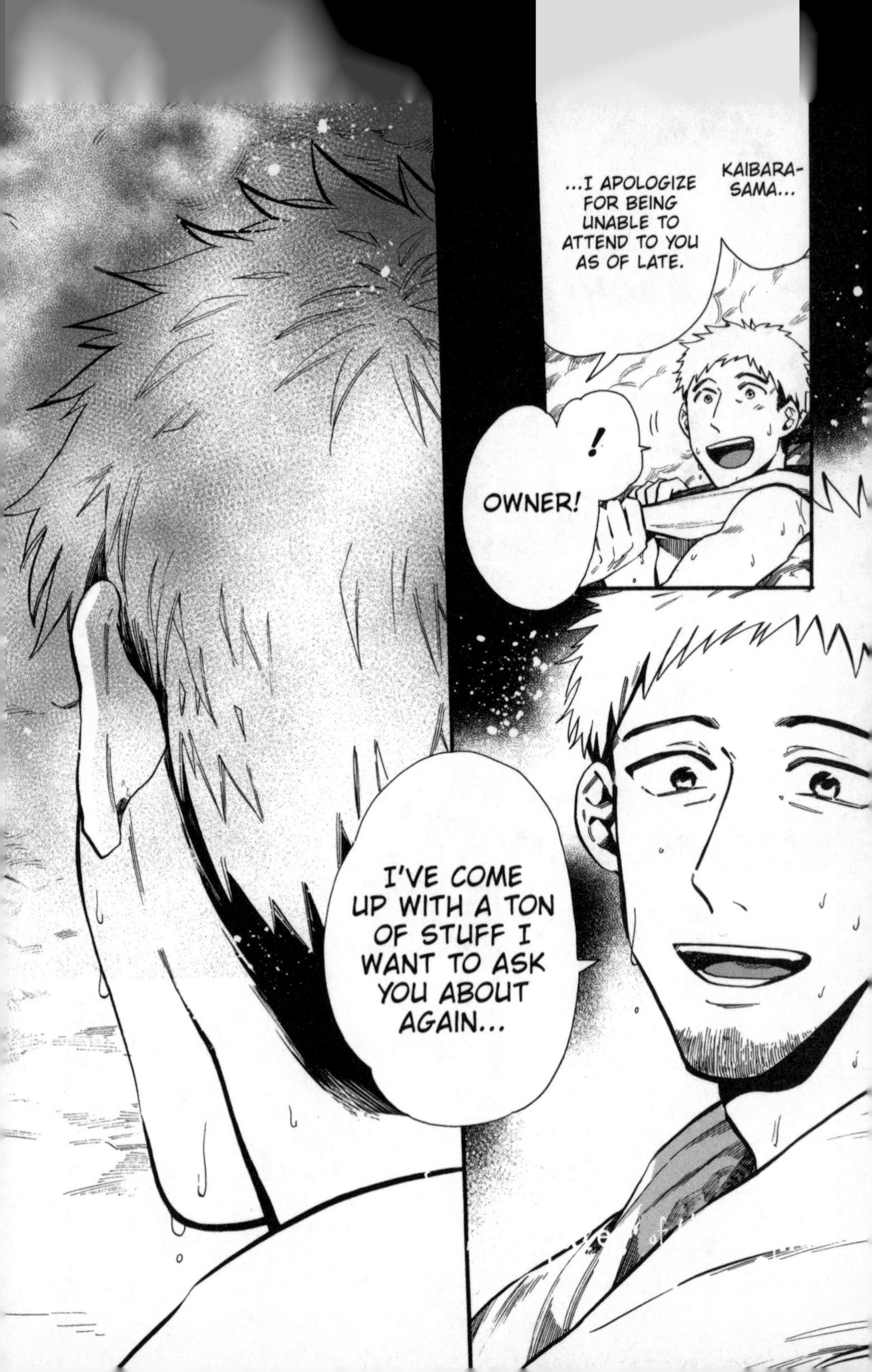
KAIBARA-SAMA...
...I APOLOGIZE FOR BEING UNABLE TO ATTEND TO YOU AS OF LATE.
!
OWNER!
I'VE COME UP WITH A TON OF STUFF I WANT TO ASK YOU ABOUT AGAIN...

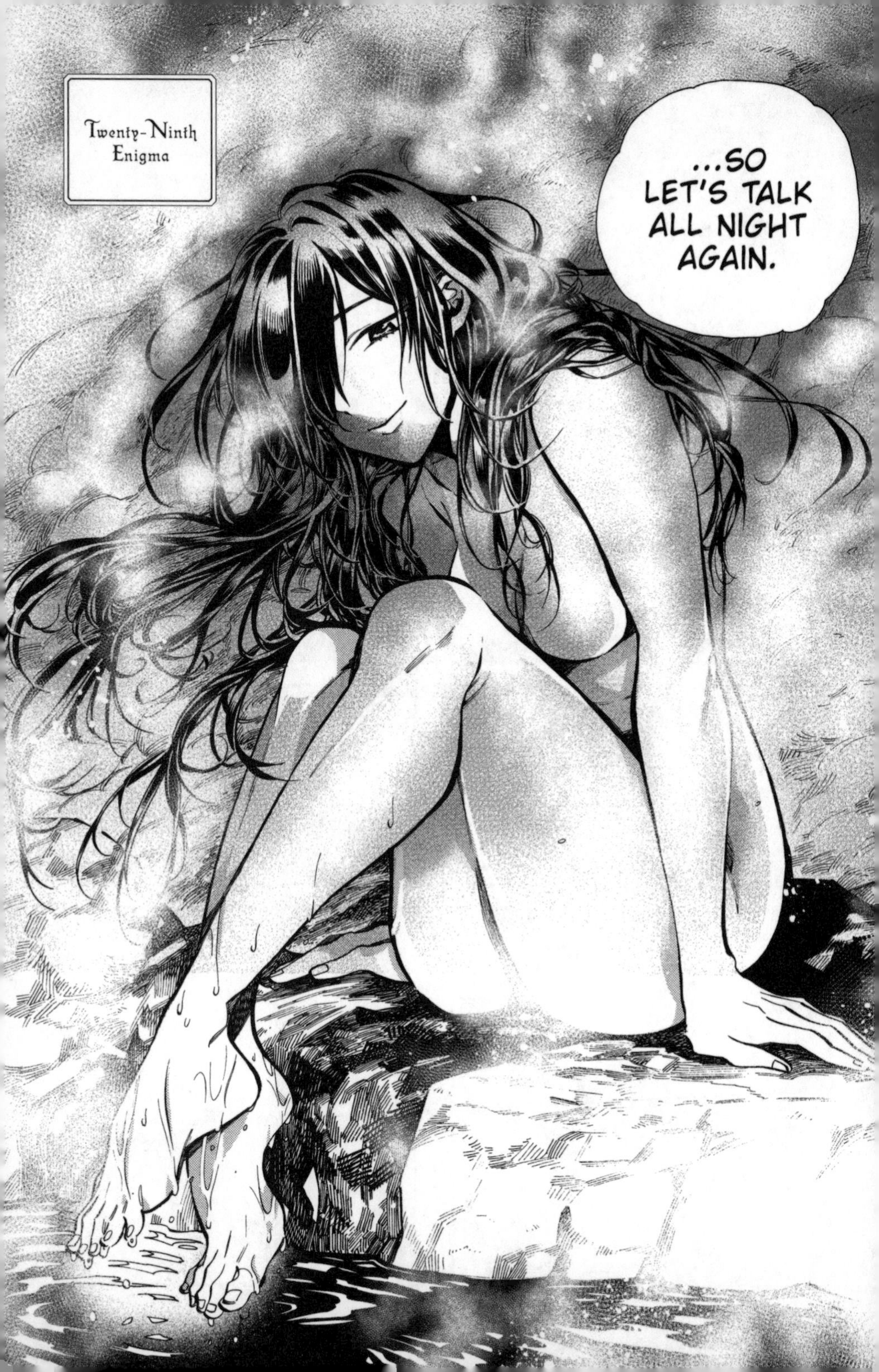
...SO LET'S TALK ALL NIGHT AGAIN.
Twenty-Ninth Enigma

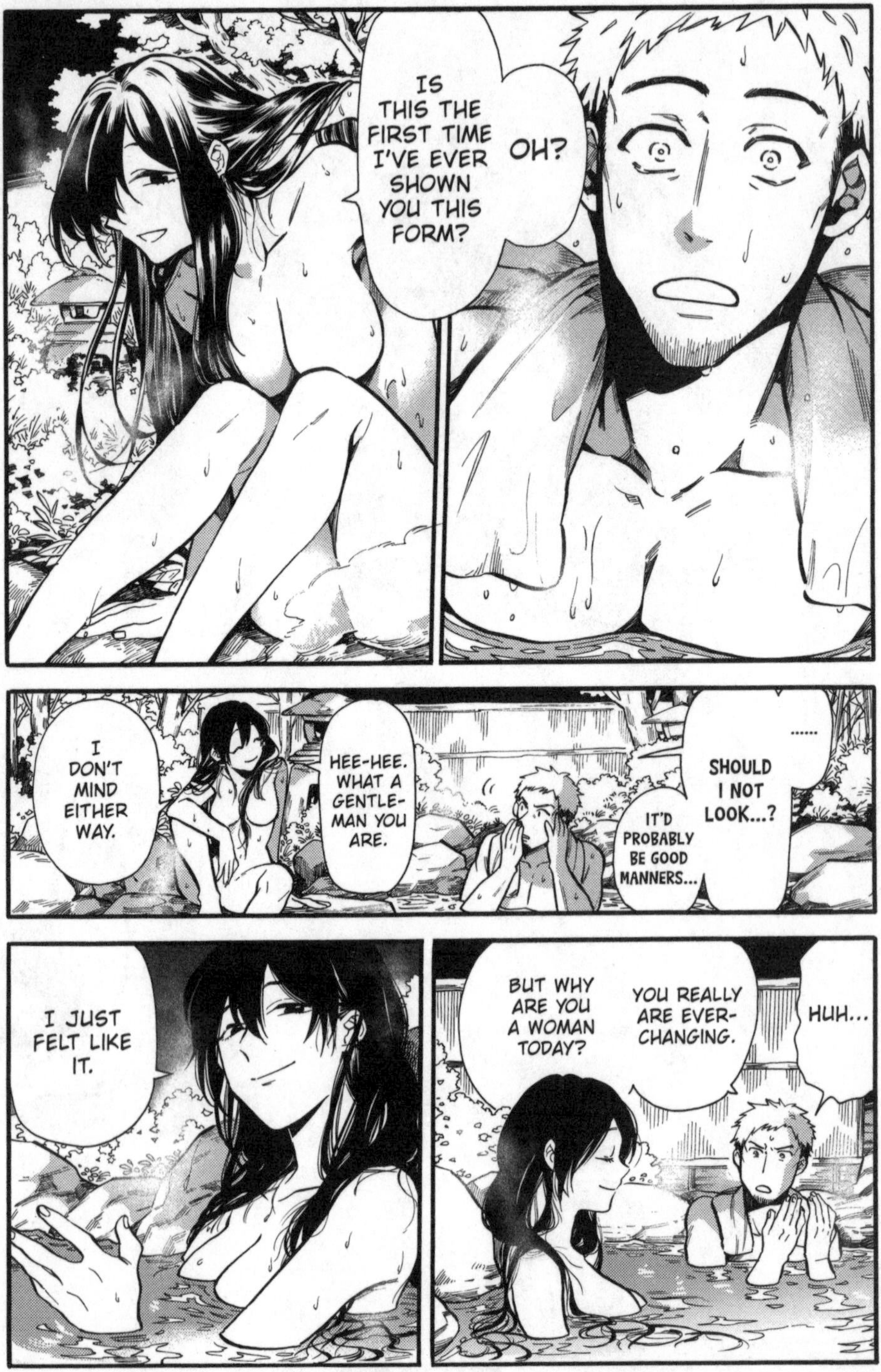
OH?
IS THIS THE FIRST TIME I'VE EVER SHOWN YOU THIS FORM?
......
SHOULD I NOT LOOK...?
IT'D PROBABLY BE GOOD MANNERS...
HEE-HEE. WHAT A GENTLE-MAN YOU ARE.
I DON'T MIND EITHER WAY.
HUH...
YOU REALLY ARE EVER-CHANGING.
BUT WHY ARE YOU A WOMAN TODAY?
I JUST FELT LIKE IT.

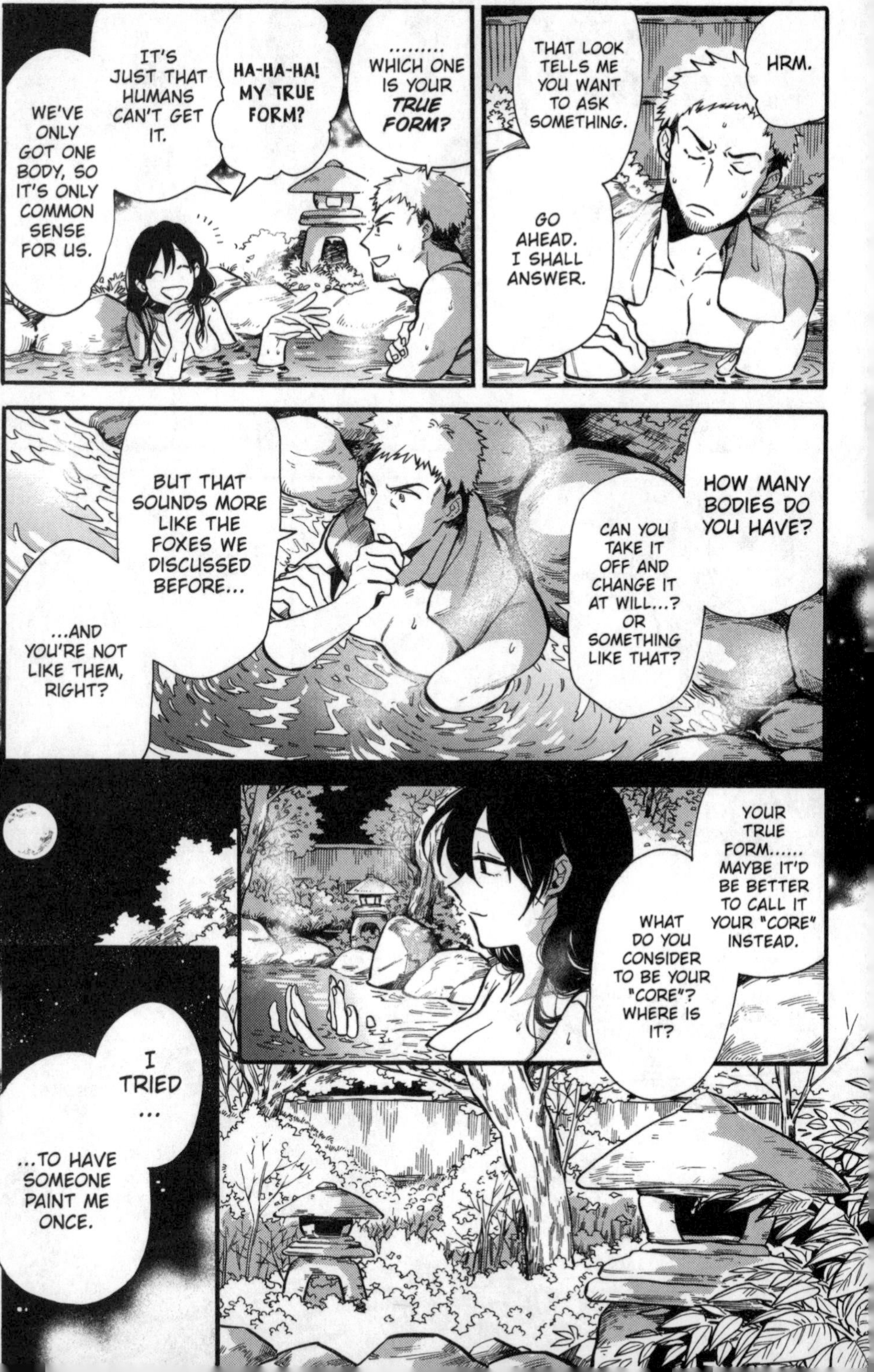
HRM.
THAT LOOK TELLS ME YOU WANT TO ASK SOMETHING.
GO AHEAD. I SHALL ANSWER.
.... WHICH ONE IS YOUR *TRUE FORM?*
HA-HA-HA! MY TRUE FORM?
IT'S JUST THAT HUMANS CAN'T GET IT.
WE'VE ONLY GOT ONE BODY, SO IT'S ONLY COMMON SENSE FOR US.
HOW MANY BODIES DO YOU HAVE?
CAN YOU TAKE IT OFF AND CHANGE IT AT WILL...? OR SOMETHING LIKE THAT?
BUT THAT SOUNDS MORE LIKE THE FOXES WE DISCUSSED BEFORE...
...AND YOU'RE NOT LIKE THEM, RIGHT?
YOUR TRUE FORM...... MAYBE IT'D BE BETTER TO CALL IT YOUR "CORE" INSTEAD.
WHAT DO YOU CONSIDER TO BE YOUR "CORE"? WHERE IS IT?
I TRIED...
...TO HAVE SOMEONE PAINT ME ONCE.

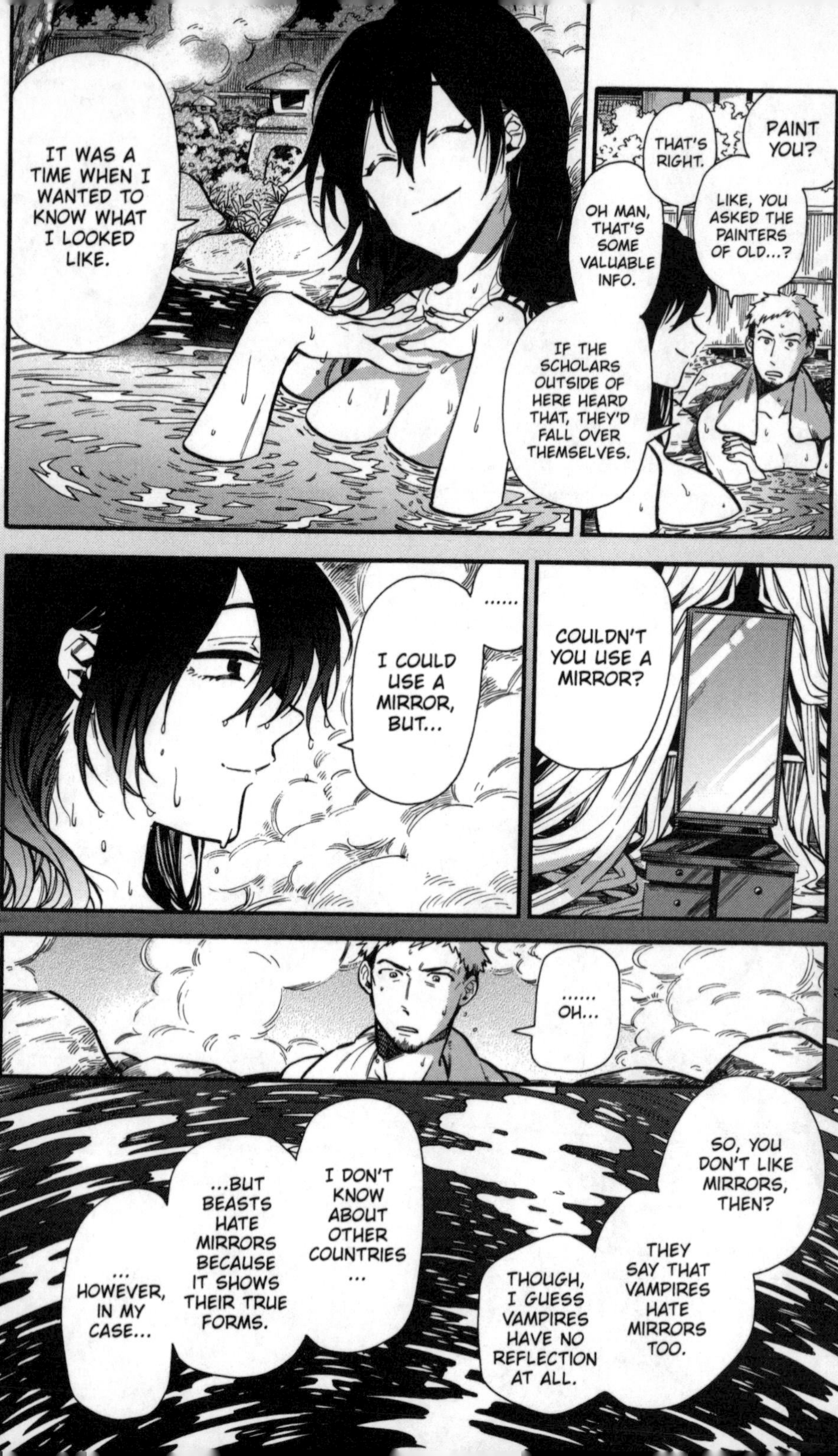
PAINT YOU?
LIKE, YOU ASKED THE PAINTERS OF OLD...?
THAT'S RIGHT.
OH MAN, THAT'S SOME VALUABLE INFO.
IF THE SCHOLARS OUTSIDE OF HERE HEARD THAT, THEY'D FALL OVER THEMSELVES.
IT WAS A TIME WHEN I WANTED TO KNOW WHAT I LOOKED LIKE.
COULDN'T YOU USE A MIRROR?
......
I COULD USE A MIRROR, BUT...
...... OH...
SO, YOU DON'T LIKE MIRRORS, THEN?
THEY SAY THAT VAMPIRES HATE MIRRORS TOO.
THOUGH, I GUESS VAMPIRES HAVE NO REFLECTION AT ALL.
I DON'T KNOW ABOUT OTHER COUNTRIES ...
...BUT BEASTS HATE MIRRORS BECAUSE IT SHOWS THEIR TRUE FORMS.
... HOWEVER, IN MY CASE...

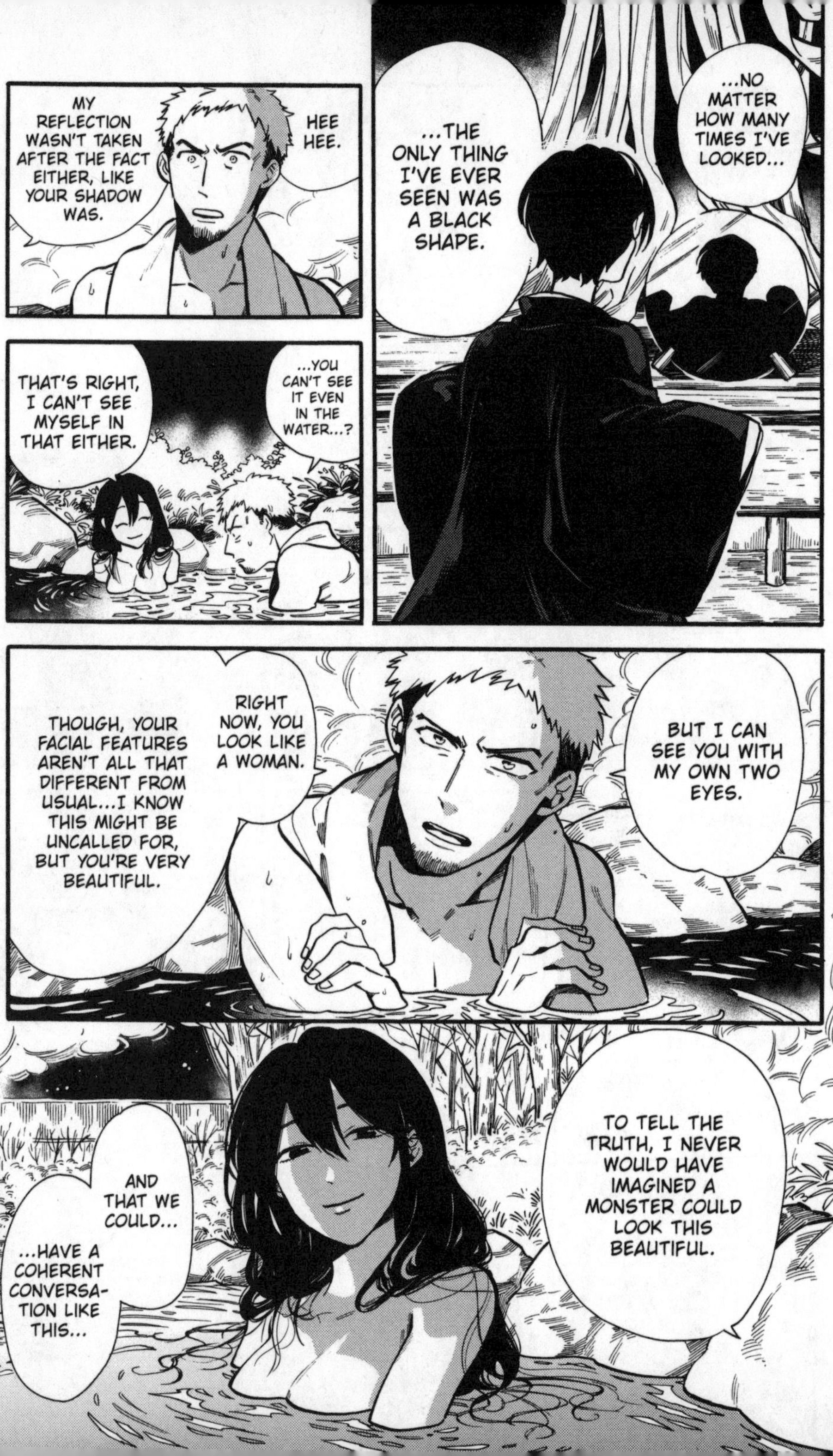
...NO MATTER HOW MANY TIMES I'VE LOOKED...
...THE ONLY THING I'VE EVER SEEN WAS A BLACK SHAPE.
HEE HEE.
MY REFLECTION WASN'T TAKEN AFTER THE FACT EITHER, LIKE YOUR SHADOW WAS.
...YOU CAN'T SEE IT EVEN IN THE WATER...?
THAT'S RIGHT, I CAN'T SEE MYSELF IN THAT EITHER.
BUT I CAN SEE YOU WITH MY OWN TWO EYES.
RIGHT NOW, YOU LOOK LIKE A WOMAN.
THOUGH, YOUR FACIAL FEATURES AREN'T ALL THAT DIFFERENT FROM USUAL...I KNOW THIS MIGHT BE UNCALLED FOR, BUT YOU'RE VERY BEAUTIFUL.
TO TELL THE TRUTH, I NEVER WOULD HAVE IMAGINED A MONSTER COULD LOOK THIS BEAUTIFUL.
AND THAT WE COULD...
...HAVE A COHERENT CONVERSATION LIKE THIS...

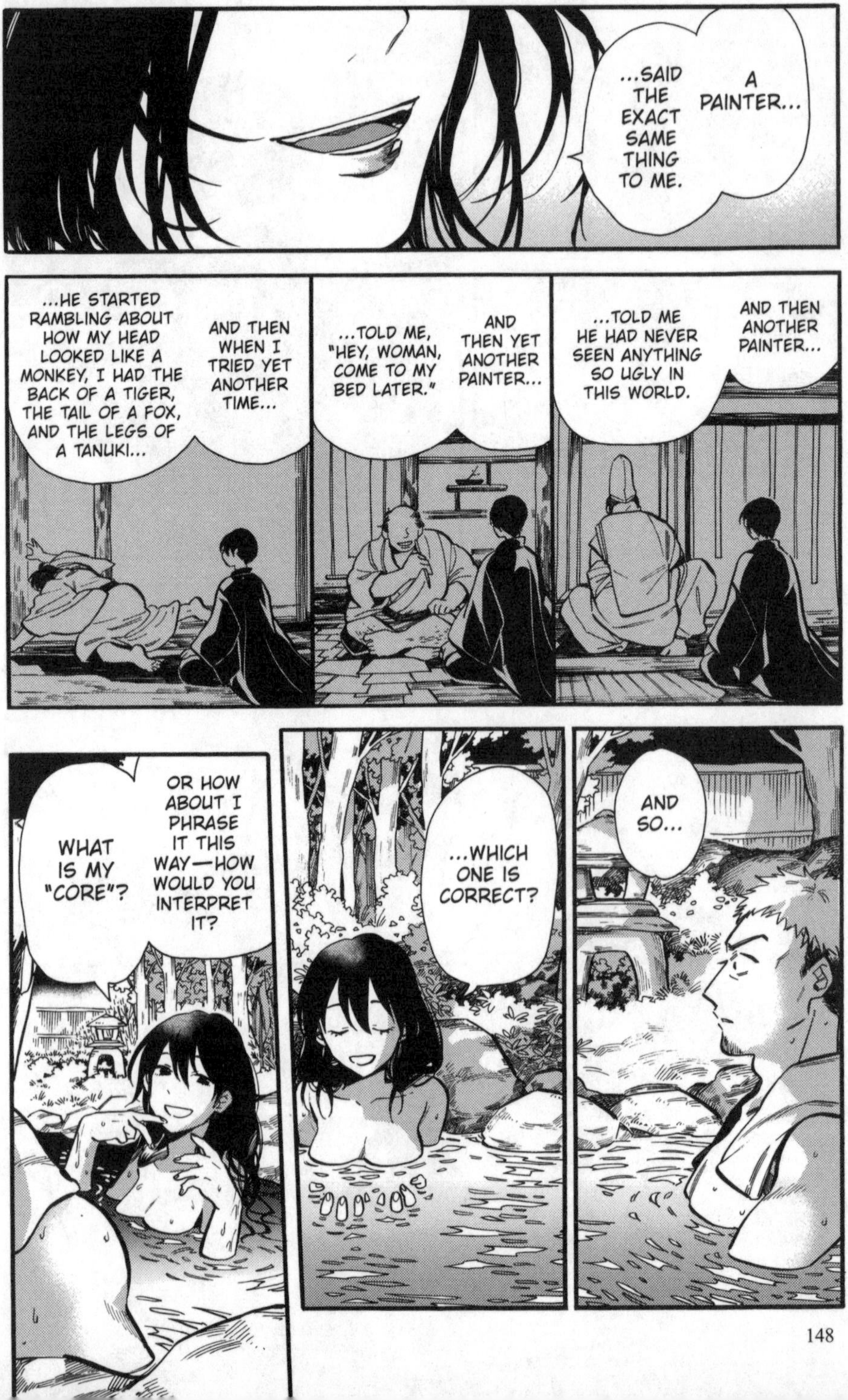
A PAINTER...
...SAID THE EXACT SAME THING TO ME.
AND THEN ANOTHER PAINTER...
...TOLD ME HE HAD NEVER SEEN ANYTHING SO UGLY IN THIS WORLD.
AND THEN YET ANOTHER PAINTER...
...TOLD ME, "HEY, WOMAN, COME TO MY BED LATER."
AND THEN WHEN I TRIED YET ANOTHER TIME...
...HE STARTED RAMBLING ABOUT HOW MY HEAD LOOKED LIKE A MONKEY, I HAD THE BACK OF A TIGER, THE TAIL OF A FOX, AND THE LEGS OF A TANUKI...
AND SO...
...WHICH ONE IS CORRECT?
OR HOW ABOUT I PHRASE IT THIS WAY—HOW WOULD YOU INTERPRET IT?
WHAT IS MY "CORE"?

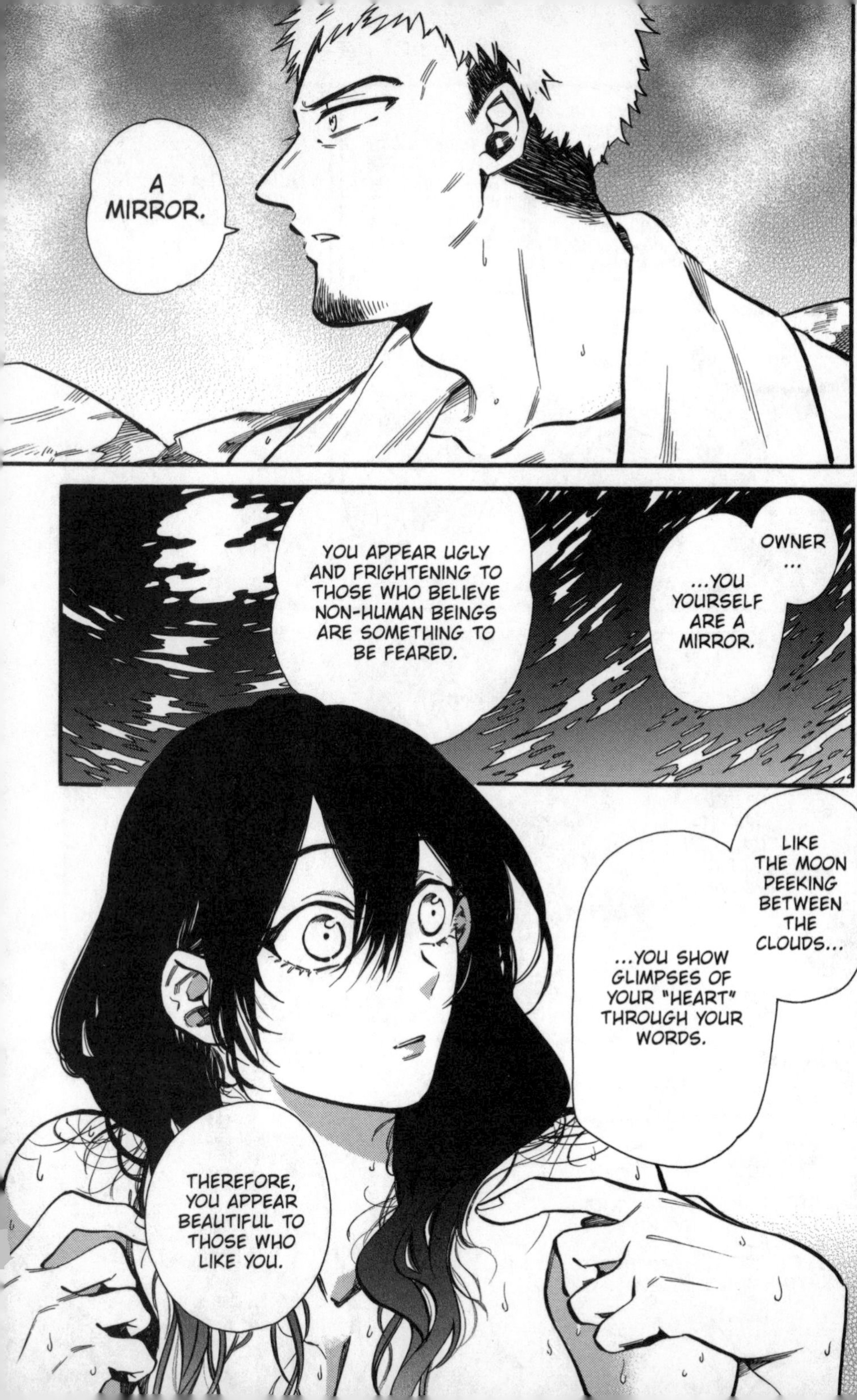
A MIRROR.
OWNER...
...YOU YOURSELF ARE A MIRROR.
YOU APPEAR UGLY AND FRIGHTENING TO THOSE WHO BELIEVE NON-HUMAN BEINGS ARE SOMETHING TO BE FEARED.
LIKE THE MOON PEEKING BETWEEN THE CLOUDS...
...YOU SHOW GLIMPSES OF YOUR "HEART" THROUGH YOUR WORDS.
THEREFORE, YOU APPEAR BEAUTIFUL TO THOSE WHO LIKE YOU.

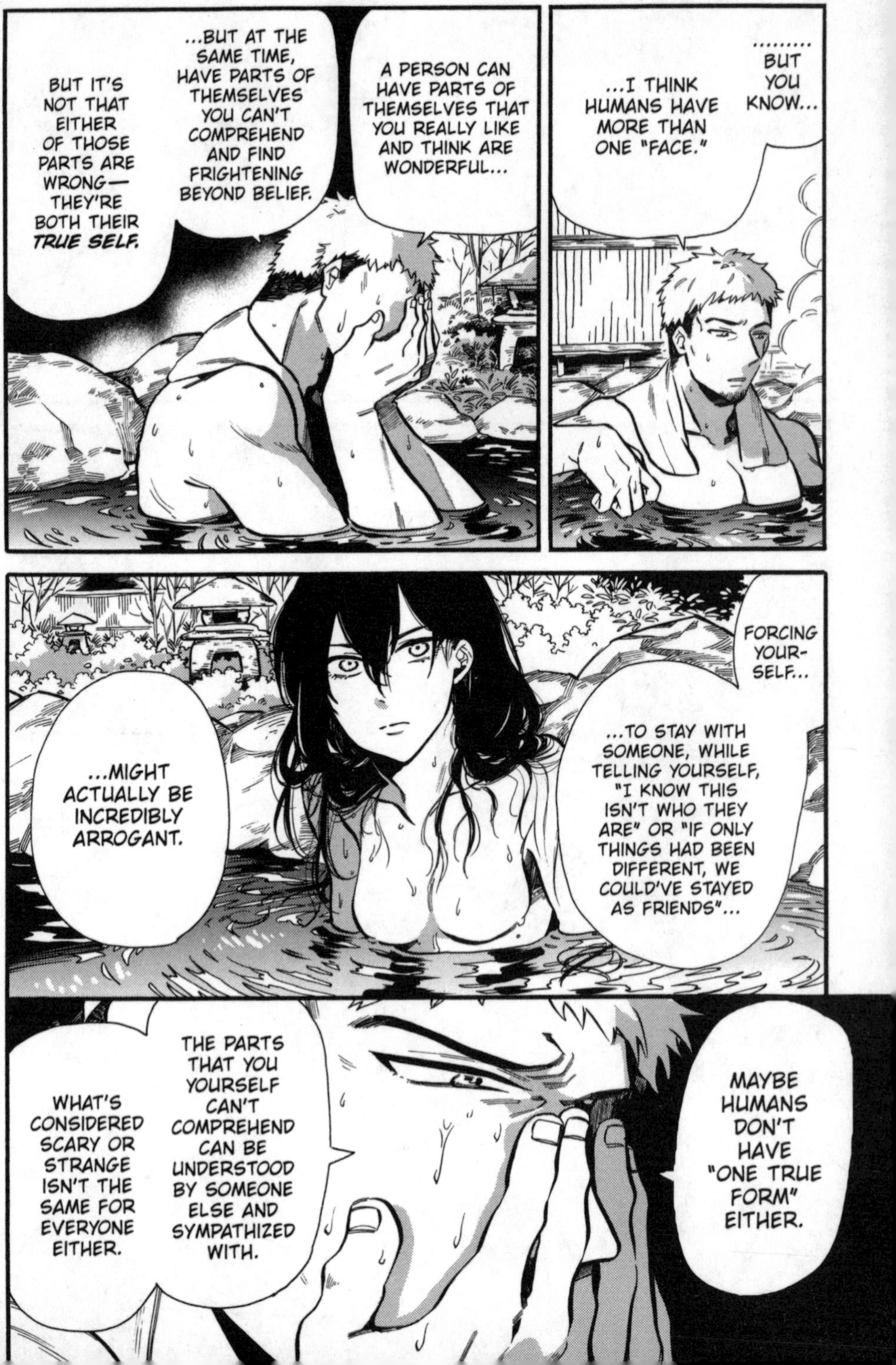
....
BUT YOU KNOW...
...I THINK HUMANS HAVE MORE THAN ONE "FACE."
A PERSON CAN HAVE PARTS OF THEMSELVES THAT YOU REALLY LIKE AND THINK ARE WONDERFUL...
...BUT AT THE SAME TIME, HAVE PARTS OF THEMSELVES YOU CAN'T COMPREHEND AND FIND FRIGHTENING BEYOND BELIEF.
BUT IT'S NOT THAT EITHER OF THOSE PARTS ARE WRONG—THEY'RE BOTH THEIR *TRUE SELF.*
FORCING YOURSELF...
...TO STAY WITH SOMEONE, WHILE TELLING YOURSELF, "I KNOW THIS ISN'T WHO THEY ARE" OR "IF ONLY THINGS HAD BEEN DIFFERENT, WE COULD'VE STAYED AS FRIENDS"...
...MIGHT ACTUALLY BE INCREDIBLY ARROGANT.
MAYBE HUMANS DON'T HAVE "ONE TRUE FORM" EITHER.
THE PARTS THAT YOU YOURSELF CAN'T COMPREHEND CAN BE UNDERSTOOD BY SOMEONE ELSE AND SYMPATHIZED WITH.
WHAT'S CONSIDERED SCARY OR STRANGE ISN'T THE SAME FOR EVERYONE EITHER.

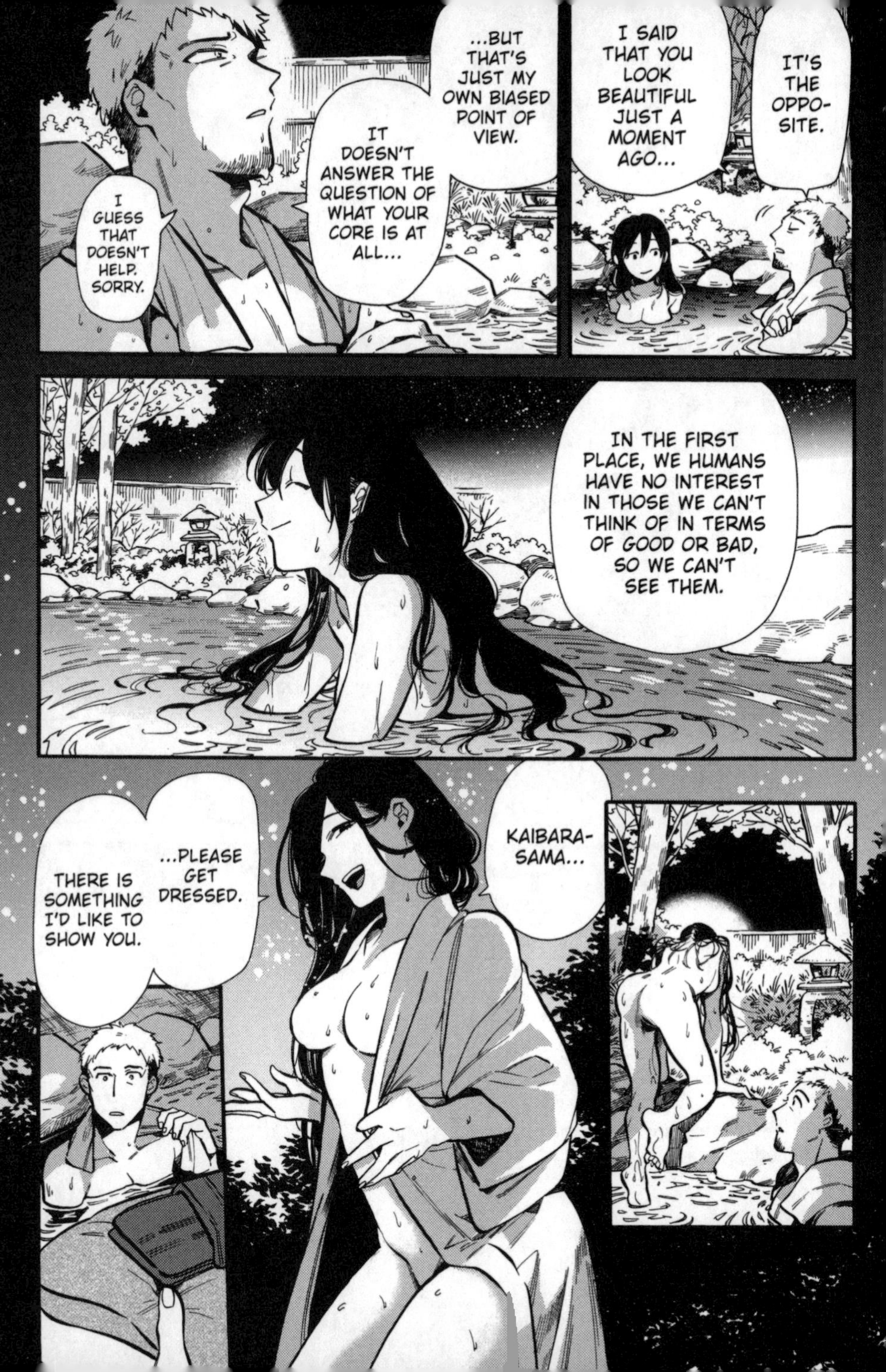
IT'S THE OPPO-SITE.
I SAID THAT YOU LOOK BEAUTIFUL JUST A MOMENT AGO...
...BUT THAT'S JUST MY OWN BIASED POINT OF VIEW.
IT DOESN'T ANSWER THE QUESTION OF WHAT YOUR CORE IS AT ALL...
I GUESS THAT DOESN'T HELP. SORRY.
IN THE FIRST PLACE, WE HUMANS HAVE NO INTEREST IN THOSE WE CAN'T THINK OF IN TERMS OF GOOD OR BAD, SO WE CAN'T SEE THEM.
KAIBARA-SAMA...
...PLEASE GET DRESSED.
THERE IS SOMETHING I'D LIKE TO SHOW YOU.

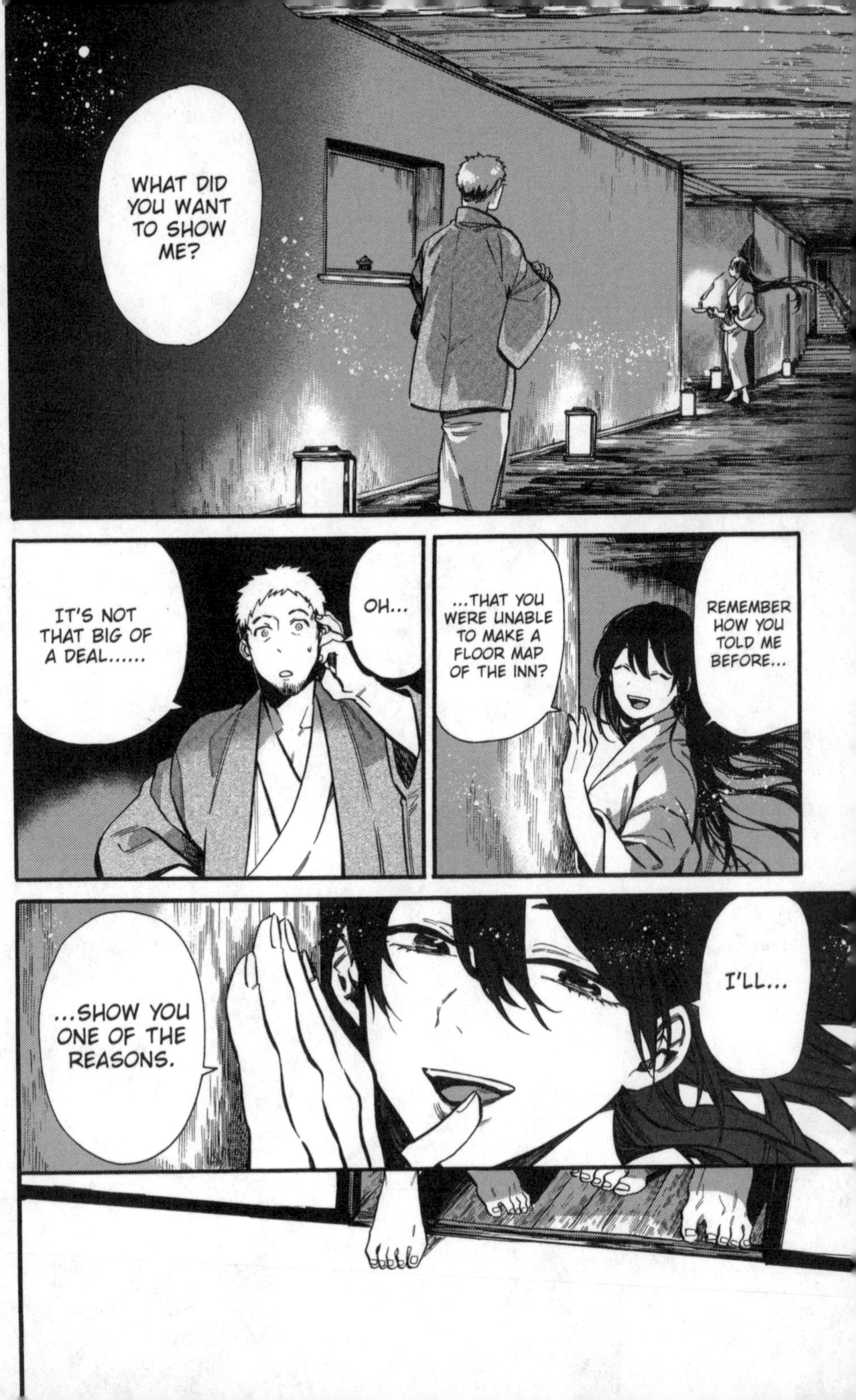
WHAT DID YOU WANT TO SHOW ME?
REMEMBER HOW YOU TOLD ME BEFORE...
...THAT YOU WERE UNABLE TO MAKE A FLOOR MAP OF THE INN?
OH...
IT'S NOT THAT BIG OF A DEAL......
I'LL...
...SHOW YOU ONE OF THE REASONS.

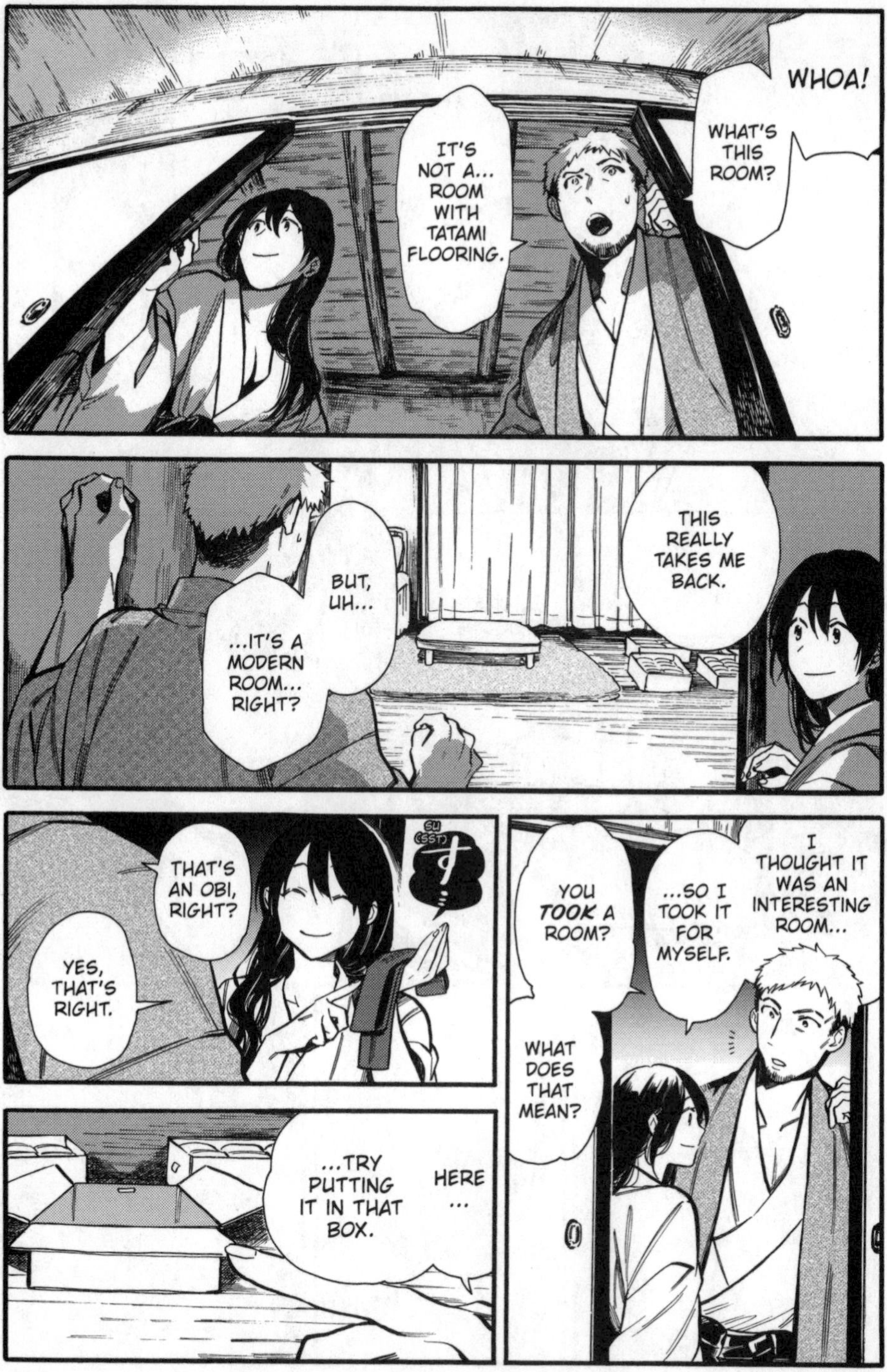
WHOA!
WHAT'S THIS ROOM?
IT'S NOT A... ROOM WITH TATAMI FLOORING.
THIS REALLY TAKES ME BACK.
BUT, UH...
...IT'S A MODERN ROOM... RIGHT?
I THOUGHT IT WAS AN INTERESTING ROOM...
...SO I TOOK IT FOR MYSELF.
YOU *TOOK* A ROOM?
WHAT DOES THAT MEAN?
SU (SST) す
THAT'S AN OBI, RIGHT?
YES, THAT'S RIGHT.
HERE...
...TRY PUTTING IT IN THAT BOX.

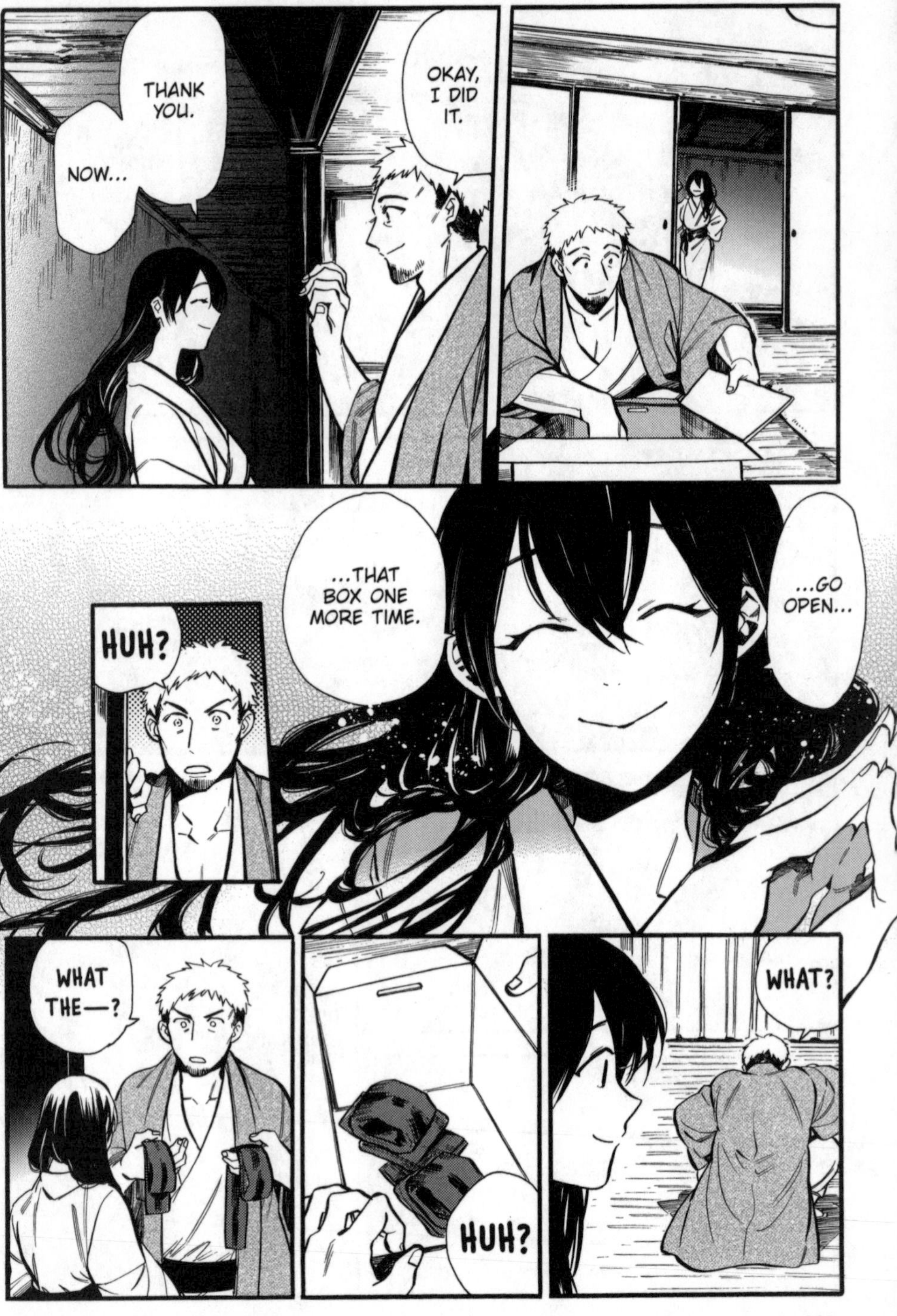
OKAY, I DID IT.
THANK YOU.
NOW...
...GO OPEN...
...THAT BOX ONE MORE TIME.
HUH?
WHAT?
HUH?
WHAT THE—?

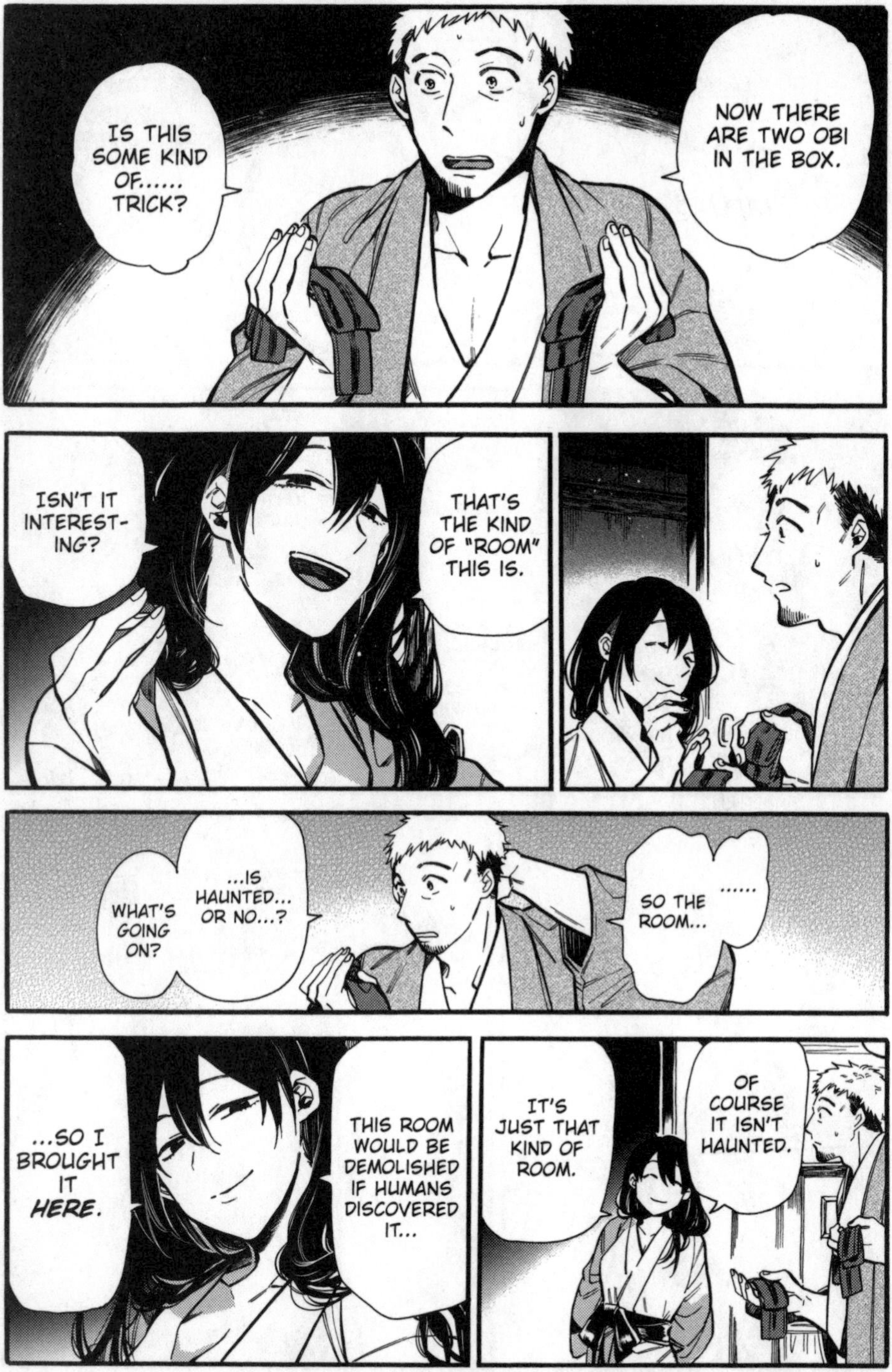
NOW THERE ARE TWO OBI IN THE BOX.
IS THIS SOME KIND OF...... TRICK?
THAT'S THE KIND OF "ROOM" THIS IS.
ISN'T IT INTEREST-ING?
......
SO THE ROOM...
...IS HAUNTED... OR NO...?
WHAT'S GOING ON?
OF COURSE IT ISN'T HAUNTED.
IT'S JUST THAT KIND OF ROOM.
THIS ROOM WOULD BE DEMOLISHED IF HUMANS DISCOVERED IT...
...SO I BROUGHT IT *HERE*.

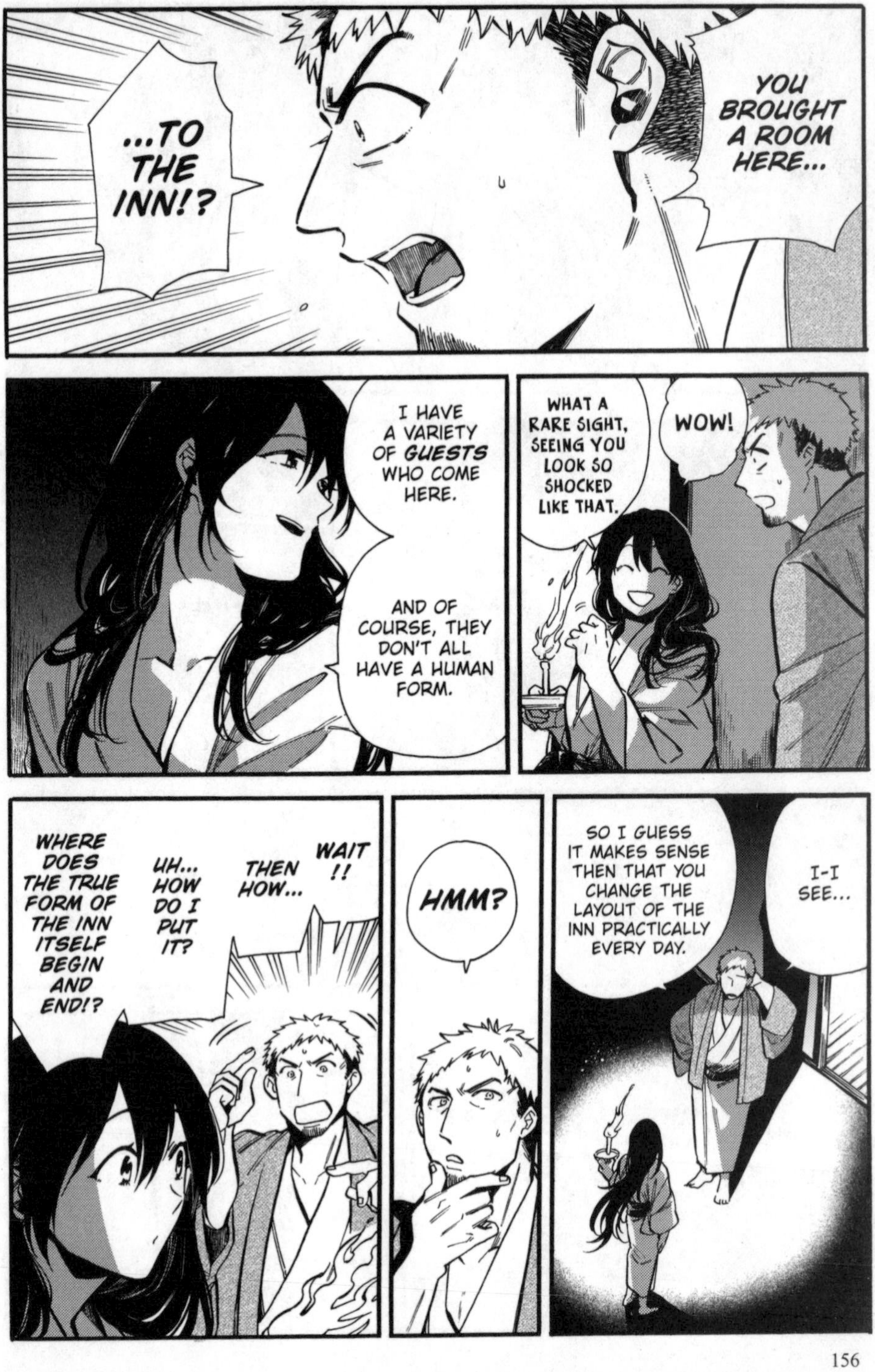
YOU BROUGHT A ROOM HERE...
...TO THE INN!?
WOW!
WHAT A RARE SIGHT, SEEING YOU LOOK SO SHOCKED LIKE THAT.
I HAVE A VARIETY OF GUESTS WHO COME HERE.
AND OF COURSE, THEY DON'T ALL HAVE A HUMAN FORM.
I-I SEE...
SO I GUESS IT MAKES SENSE THEN THAT YOU CHANGE THE LAYOUT OF THE INN PRACTICALLY EVERY DAY.
HMM?
WAIT!!
THEN HOW...
UH... HOW DO I PUT IT?
WHERE DOES THE TRUE FORM OF THE INN ITSELF BEGIN AND END!?

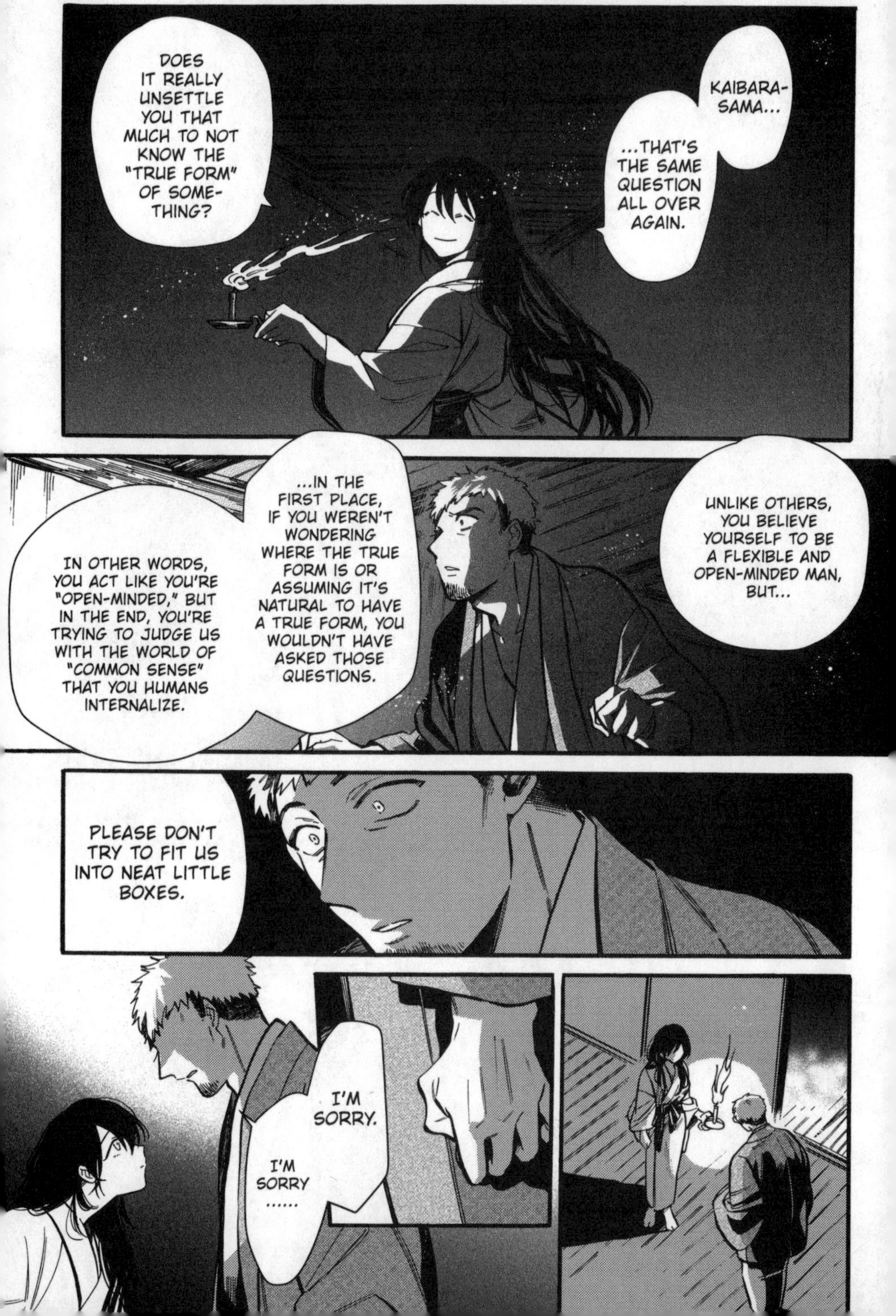
KAIBARA-SAMA...
...THAT'S THE SAME QUESTION ALL OVER AGAIN.
DOES IT REALLY UNSETTLE YOU THAT MUCH TO NOT KNOW THE "TRUE FORM" OF SOME-THING?
UNLIKE OTHERS, YOU BELIEVE YOURSELF TO BE A FLEXIBLE AND OPEN-MINDED MAN, BUT...
...IN THE FIRST PLACE, IF YOU WEREN'T WONDERING WHERE THE TRUE FORM IS OR ASSUMING IT'S NATURAL TO HAVE A TRUE FORM, YOU WOULDN'T HAVE ASKED THOSE QUESTIONS.
IN OTHER WORDS, YOU ACT LIKE YOU'RE "OPEN-MINDED," BUT IN THE END, YOU'RE TRYING TO JUDGE US WITH THE WORLD OF "COMMON SENSE" THAT YOU HUMANS INTERNALIZE.
PLEASE DON'T TRY TO FIT US INTO NEAT LITTLE BOXES.
I'M SORRY.
I'M SORRY ......

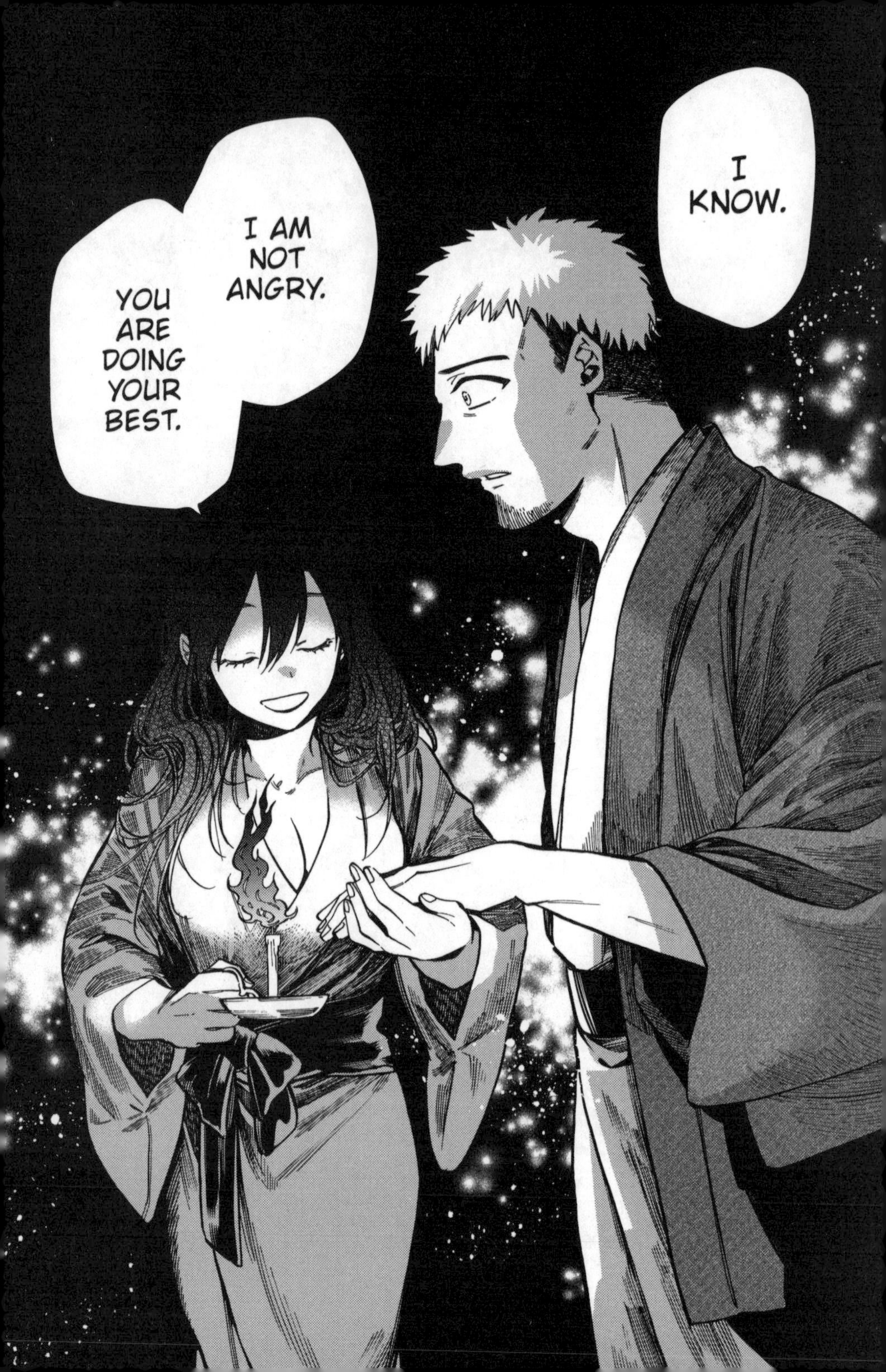
I KNOW.
I AM NOT ANGRY.
YOU ARE DOING YOUR BEST.

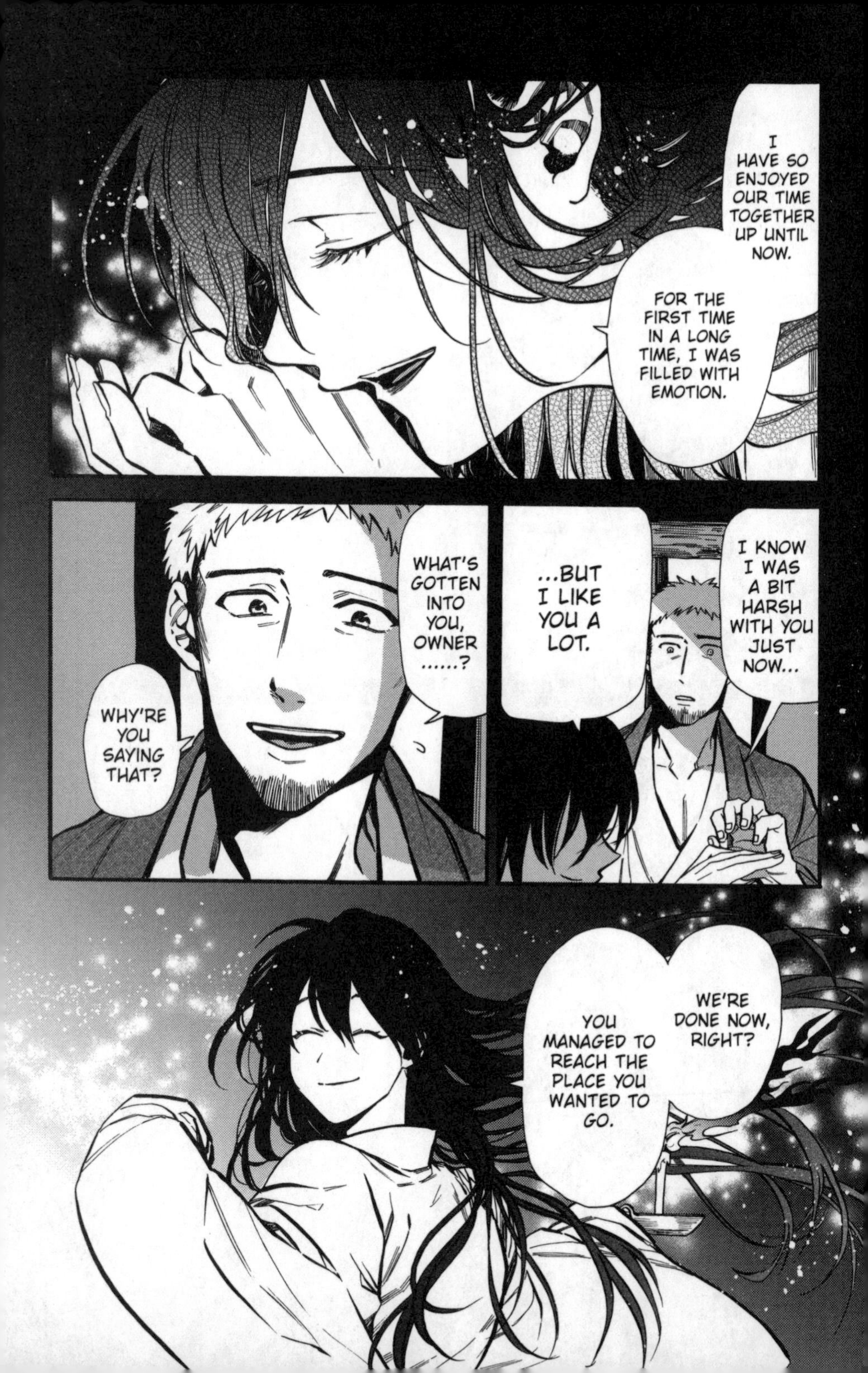
I HAVE SO ENJOYED OUR TIME TOGETHER UP UNTIL NOW.
FOR THE FIRST TIME IN A LONG TIME, I WAS FILLED WITH EMOTION.
I KNOW I WAS A BIT HARSH WITH YOU JUST NOW...
...BUT I LIKE YOU A LOT.
WHAT'S GOTTEN INTO YOU, OWNER ......?
WHY'RE YOU SAYING THAT?
WE'RE DONE NOW, RIGHT?
YOU MANAGED TO REACH THE PLACE YOU WANTED TO GO.

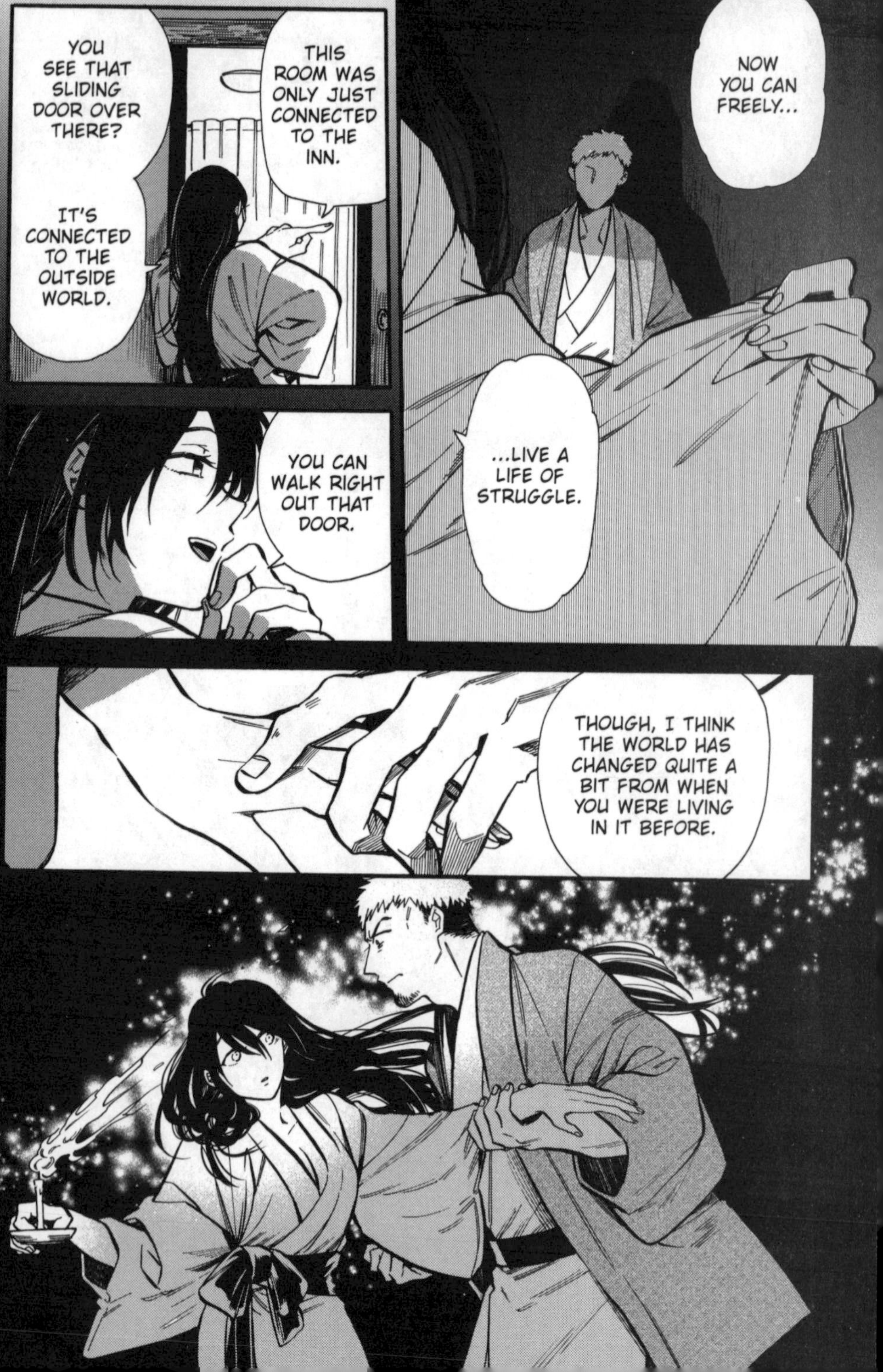
NOW YOU CAN FREELY...
...LIVE A LIFE OF STRUGGLE.
THIS ROOM WAS ONLY JUST CONNECTED TO THE INN.
YOU SEE THAT SLIDING DOOR OVER THERE?
IT'S CONNECTED TO THE OUTSIDE WORLD.
YOU CAN WALK RIGHT OUT THAT DOOR.
THOUGH, I THINK THE WORLD HAS CHANGED QUITE A BIT FROM WHEN YOU WERE LIVING IN IT BEFORE.

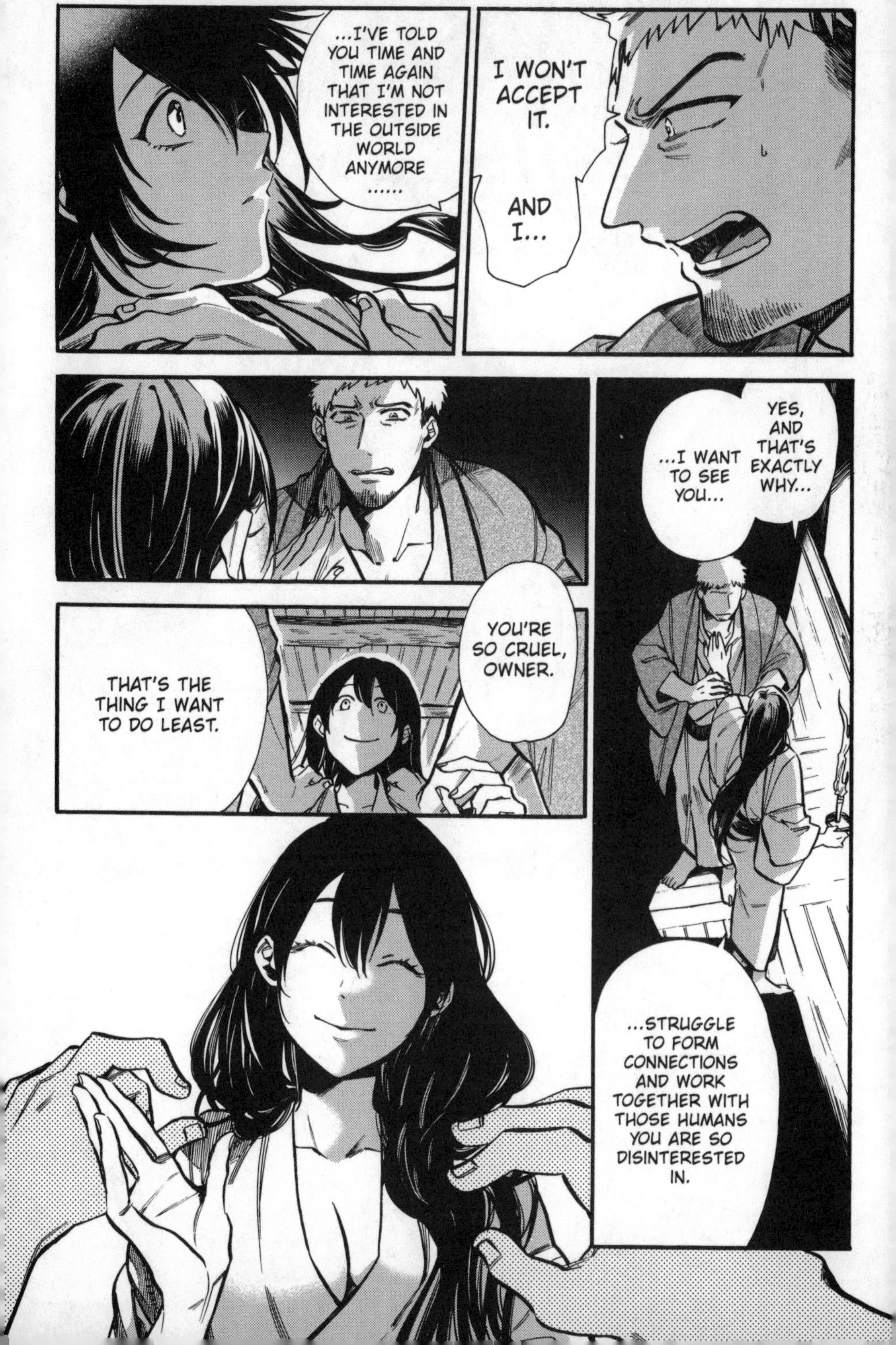
I WON'T ACCEPT IT.
AND I...
...I'VE TOLD YOU TIME AND TIME AGAIN THAT I'M NOT INTERESTED IN THE OUTSIDE WORLD ANYMORE ......
YES, AND THAT'S EXACTLY WHY...
...I WANT TO SEE YOU...
YOU'RE SO CRUEL, OWNER.
THAT'S THE THING I WANT TO DO LEAST.
...STRUGGLE TO FORM CONNECTIONS AND WORK TOGETHER WITH THOSE HUMANS YOU ARE SO DISINTERESTED IN.

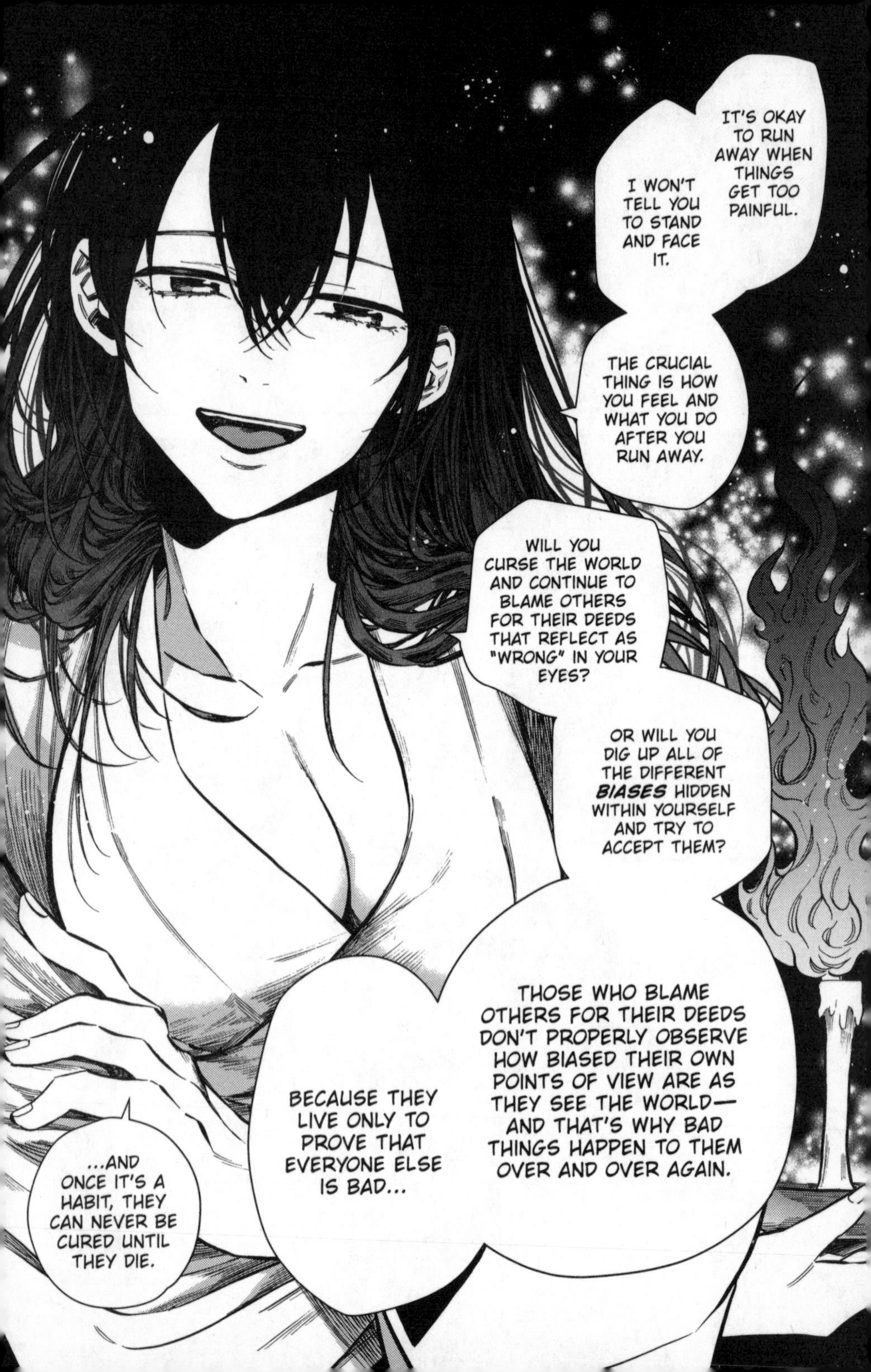
IT'S OKAY TO RUN AWAY WHEN THINGS GET TOO PAINFUL.
I WON'T TELL YOU TO STAND AND FACE IT.
THE CRUCIAL THING IS HOW YOU FEEL AND WHAT YOU DO AFTER YOU RUN AWAY.
WILL YOU CURSE THE WORLD AND CONTINUE TO BLAME OTHERS FOR THEIR DEEDS THAT REFLECT AS "WRONG" IN YOUR EYES?
OR WILL YOU DIG UP ALL OF THE DIFFERENT BIASES HIDDEN WITHIN YOURSELF AND TRY TO ACCEPT THEM?
THOSE WHO BLAME OTHERS FOR THEIR DEEDS DON'T PROPERLY OBSERVE HOW BIASED THEIR OWN POINTS OF VIEW ARE AS THEY SEE THE WORLD—AND THAT'S WHY BAD THINGS HAPPEN TO THEM OVER AND OVER AGAIN.
BECAUSE THEY LIVE ONLY TO PROVE THAT EVERYONE ELSE IS BAD...
...AND ONCE IT'S A HABIT, THEY CAN NEVER BE CURED UNTIL THEY DIE.

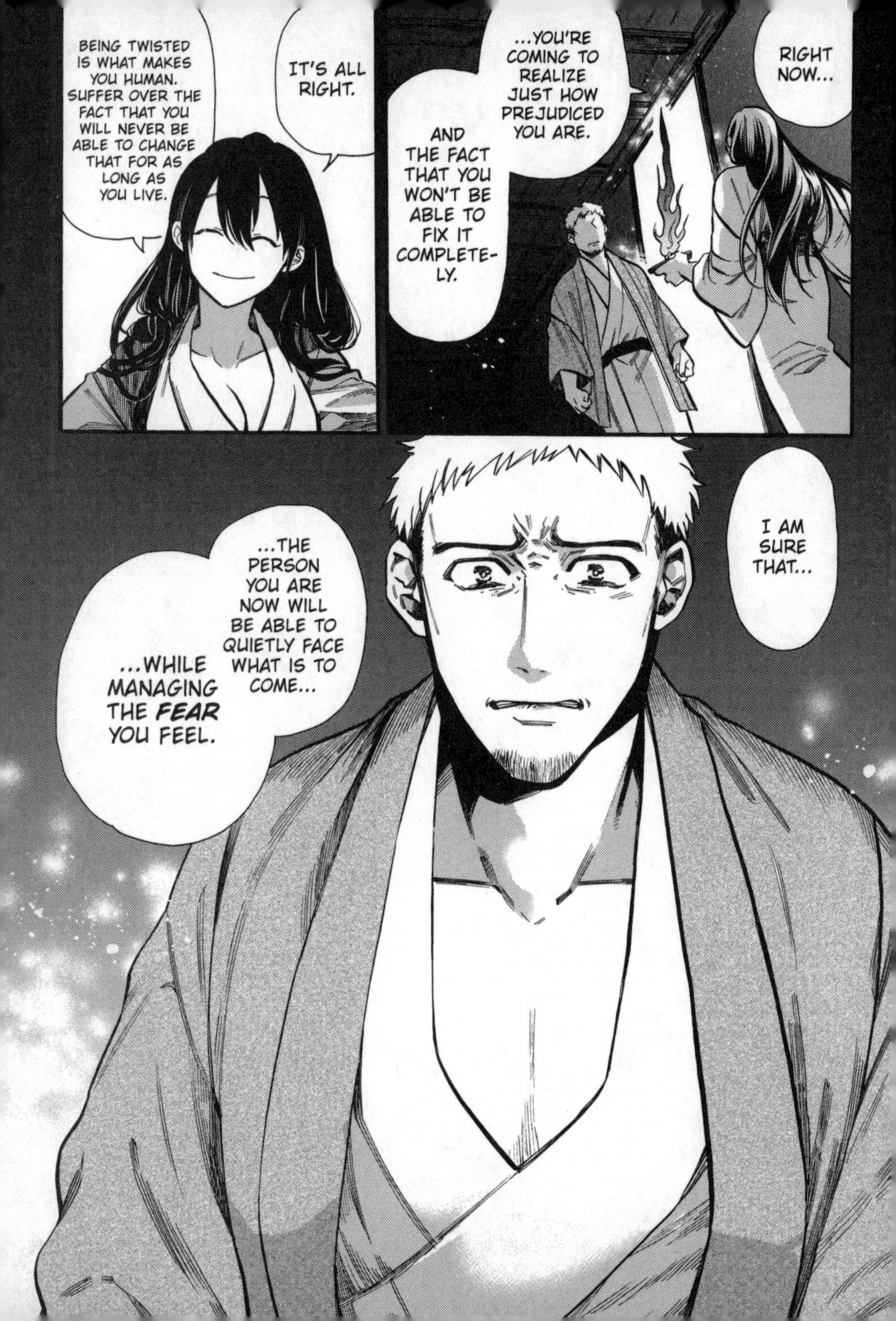
RIGHT NOW...
...YOU'RE COMING TO REALIZE JUST HOW PREJUDICED YOU ARE.
AND THE FACT THAT YOU WON'T BE ABLE TO FIX IT COMPLETE-LY.
IT'S ALL RIGHT.
BEING TWISTED IS WHAT MAKES YOU HUMAN. SUFFER OVER THE FACT THAT YOU WILL NEVER BE ABLE TO CHANGE THAT FOR AS LONG AS YOU LIVE.
I AM SURE THAT...
...THE PERSON YOU ARE NOW WILL BE ABLE TO QUIETLY FACE WHAT IS TO COME...
...WHILE MANAGING THE FEAR YOU FEEL.

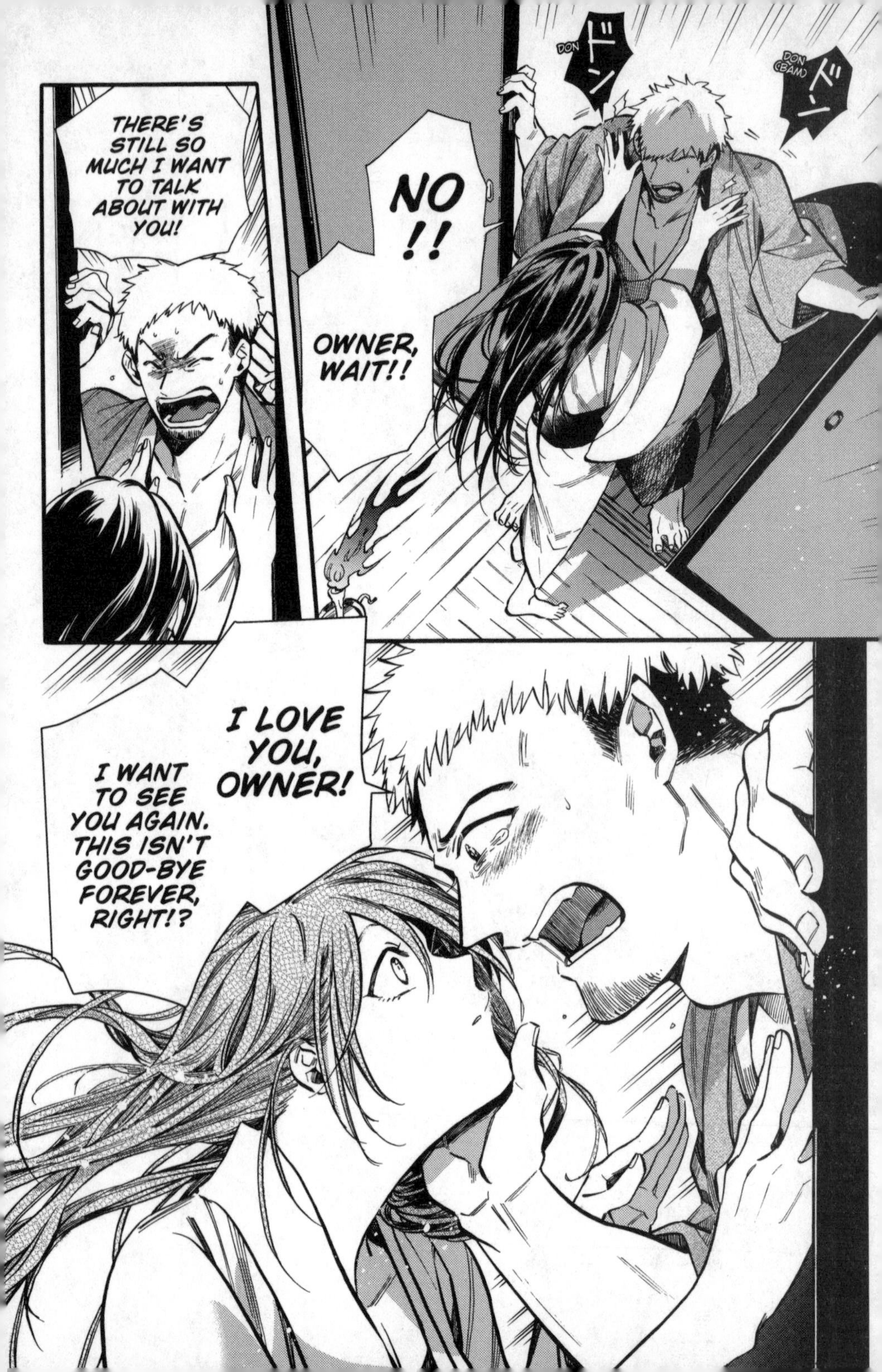
DON (BAM)
ドン
DON
ドン
NO!!
OWNER, WAIT!!
THERE'S STILL SO MUCH I WANT TO TALK ABOUT WITH YOU!
I LOVE YOU, OWNER!
I WANT TO SEE YOU AGAIN. THIS ISN'T GOOD-BYE FOREVER, RIGHT!?

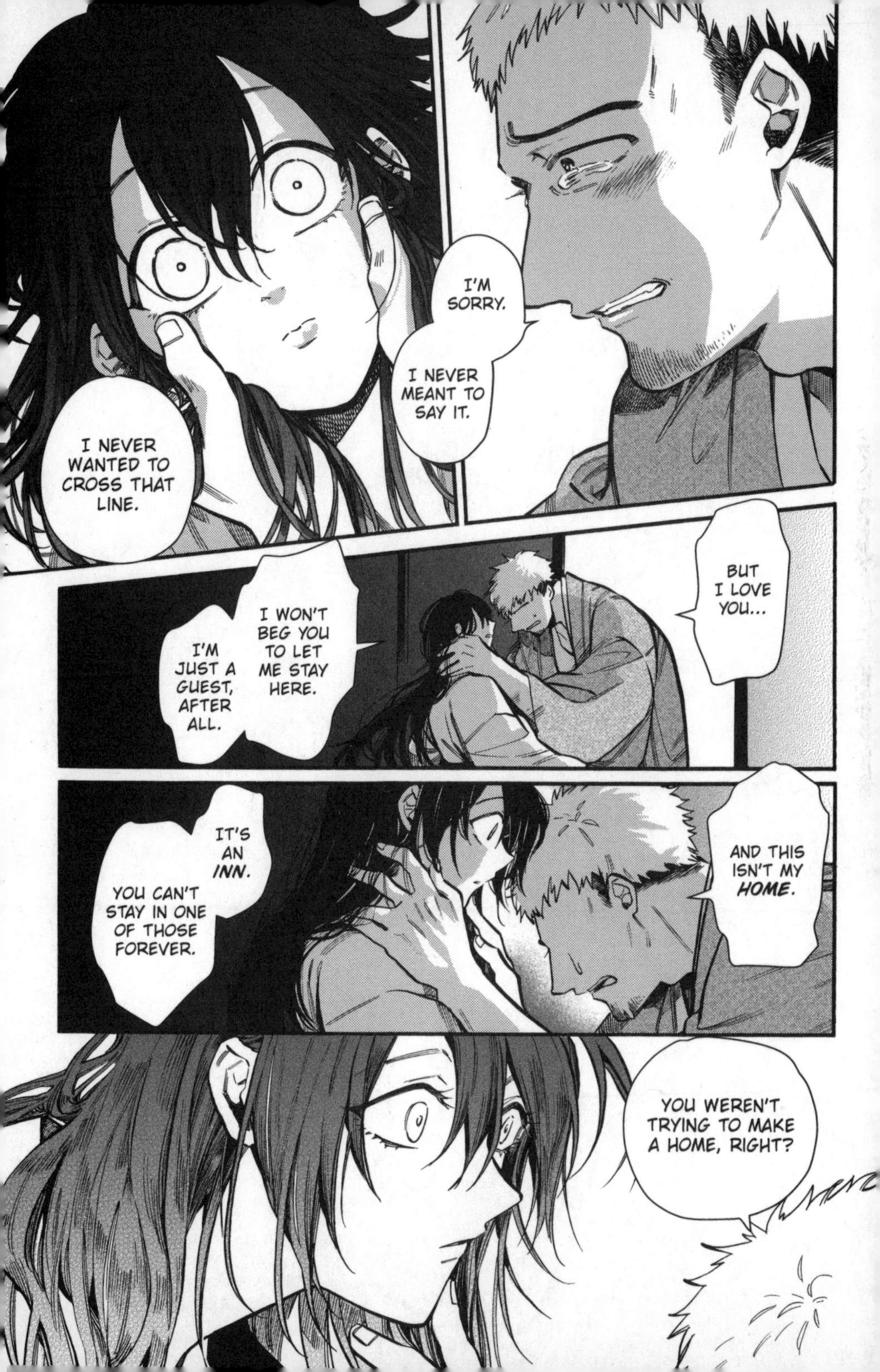
I'M SORRY.
I NEVER MEANT TO SAY IT.
I NEVER WANTED TO CROSS THAT LINE.
BUT I LOVE YOU...
I WON'T BEG YOU TO LET ME STAY HERE.
I'M JUST A GUEST, AFTER ALL.
AND THIS ISN'T MY *HOME*.
IT'S AN *INN*.
YOU CAN'T STAY IN ONE OF THOSE FOREVER.
YOU WEREN'T TRYING TO MAKE A HOME, RIGHT?

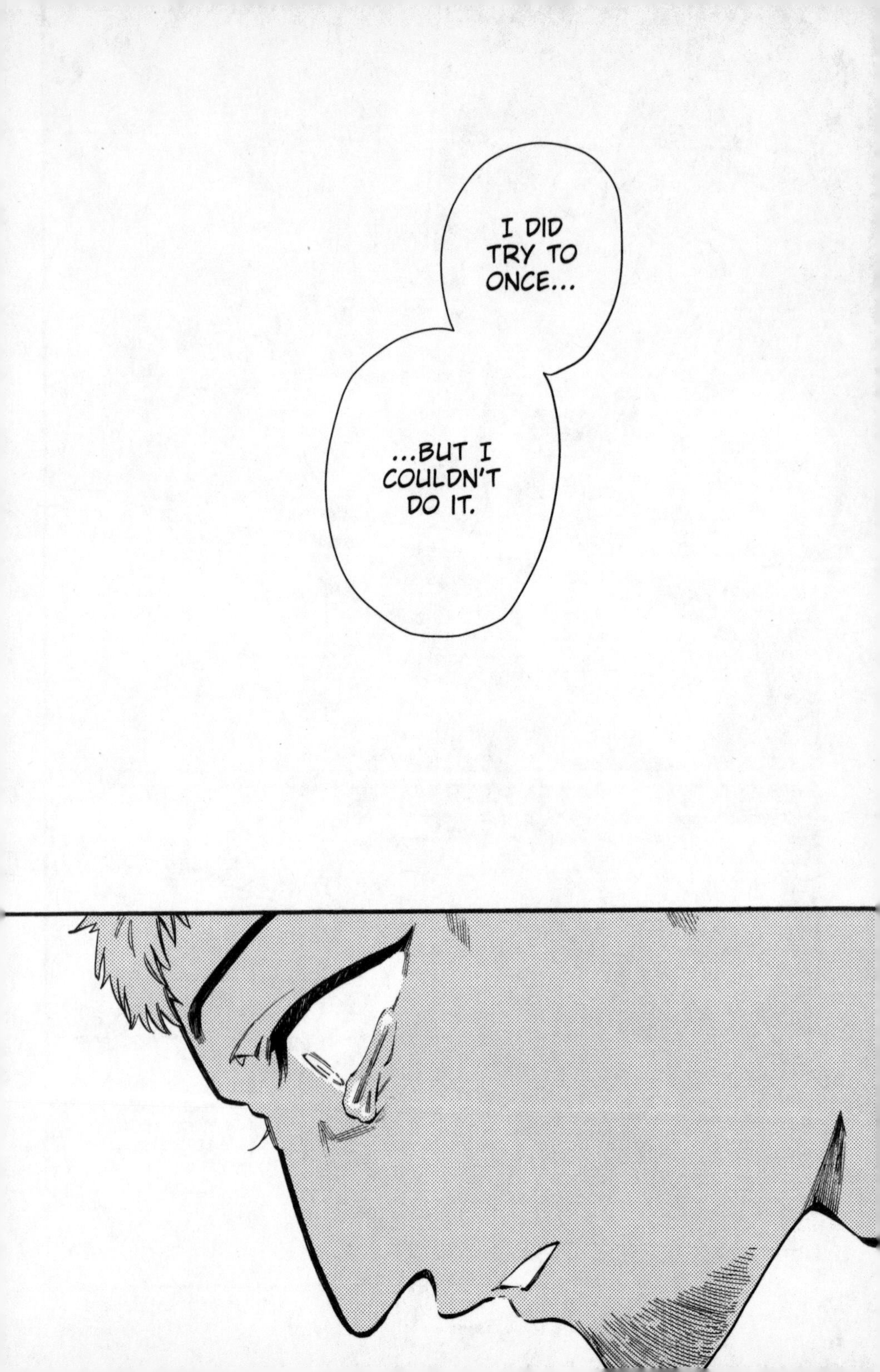
I DID TRY TO ONCE...
...BUT I COULDN'T DO IT.

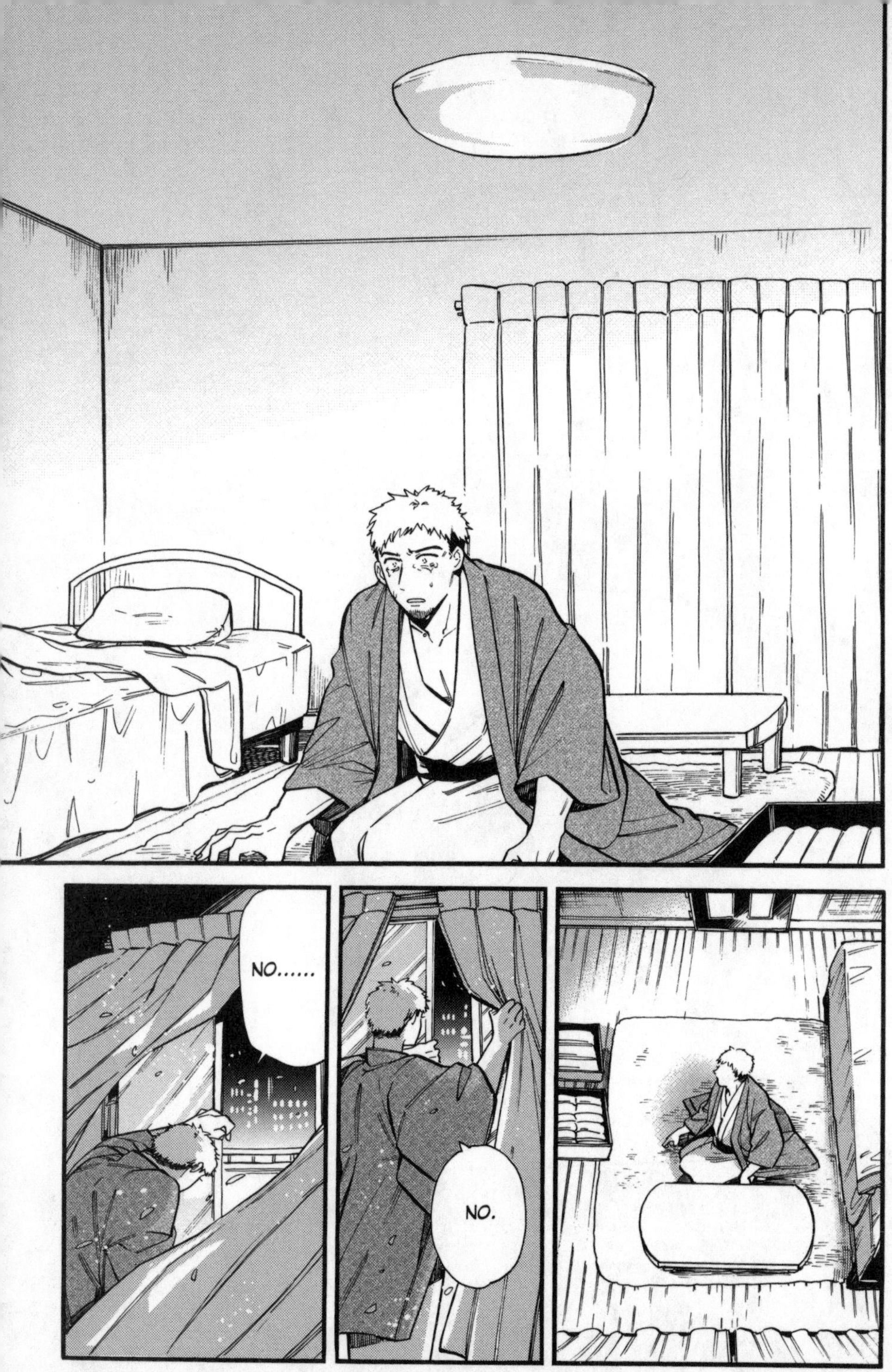
NO.
NO......

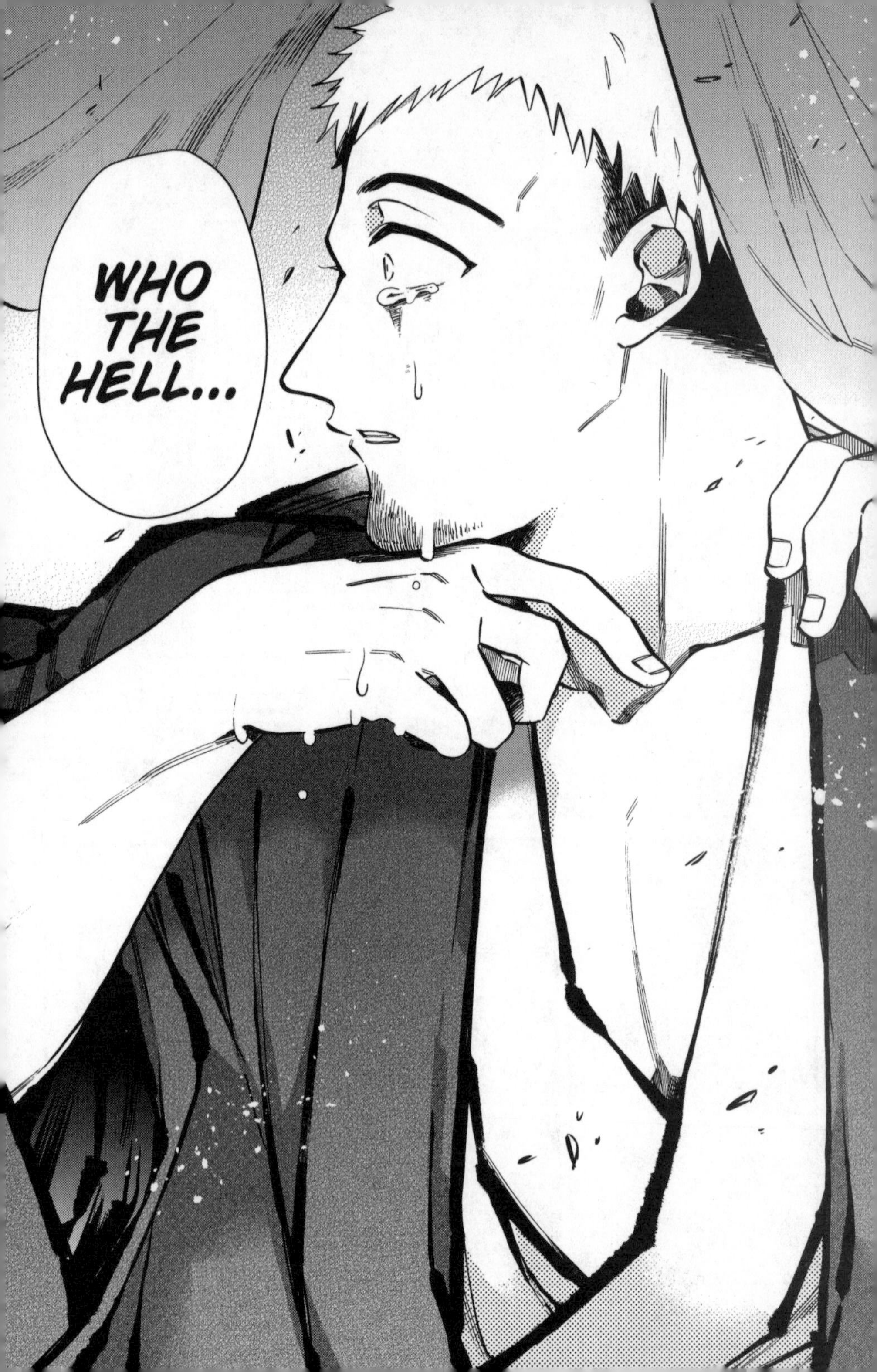
WHO THE HELL...

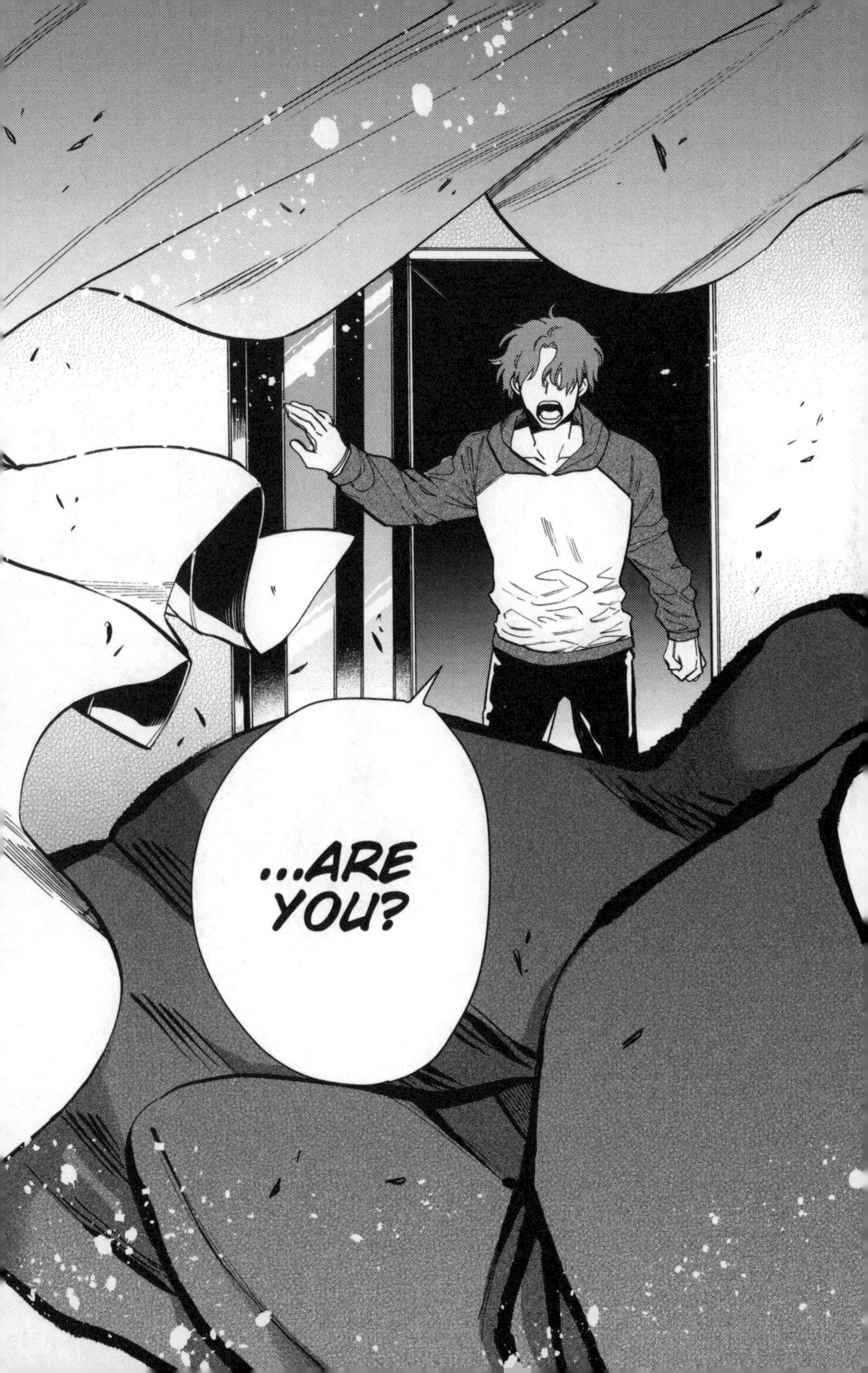
...ARE YOU?

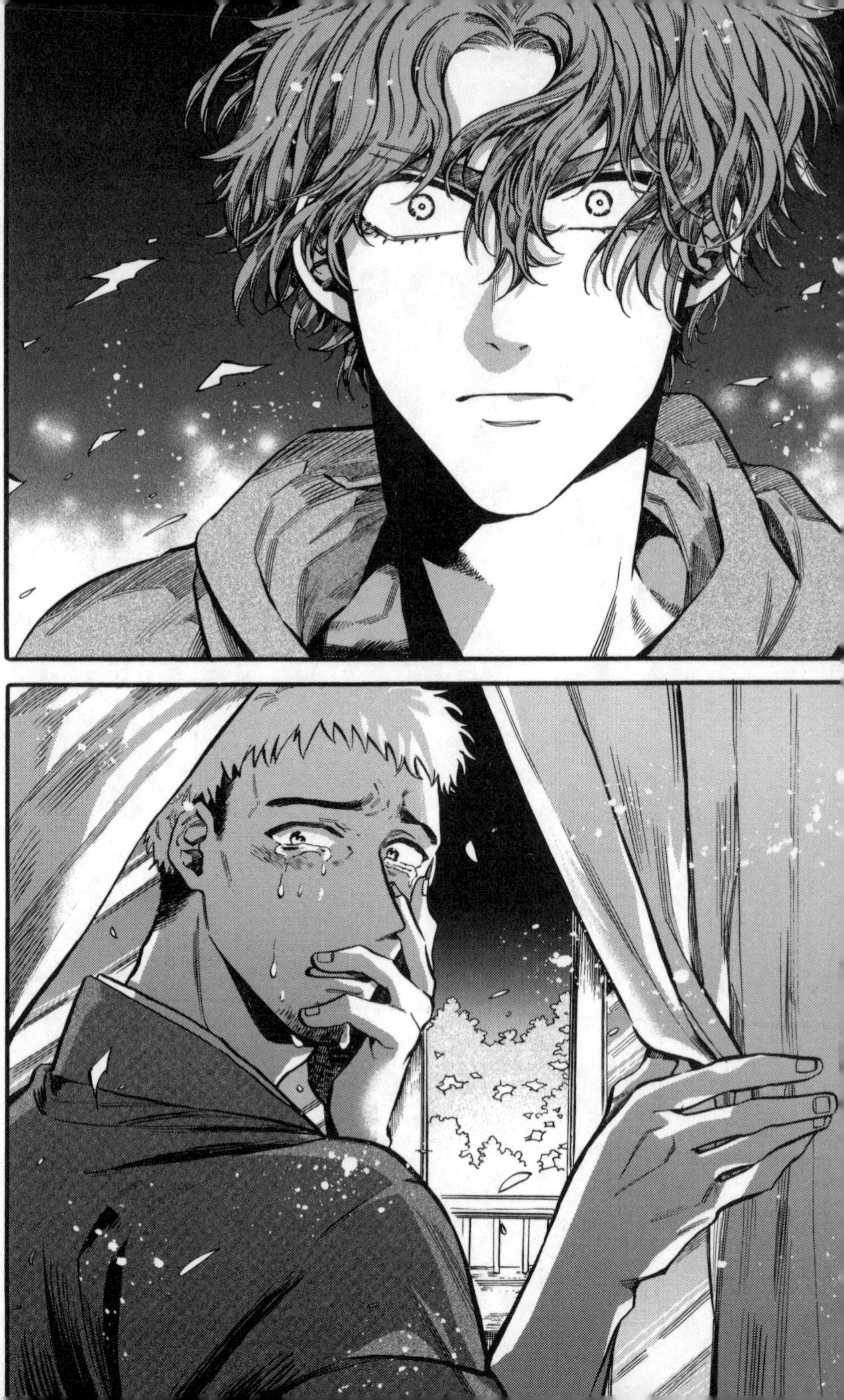

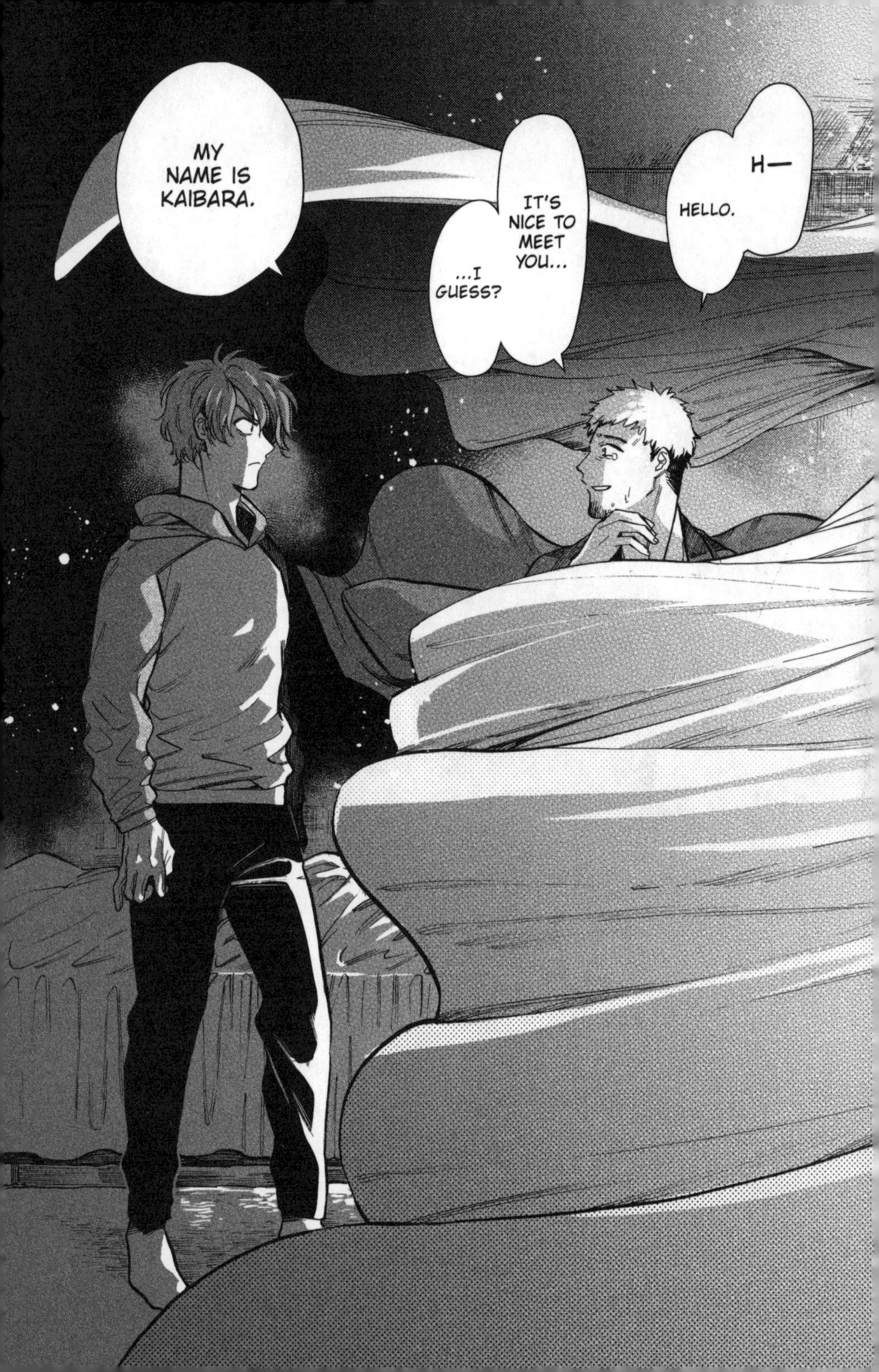
H—
HELLO.
IT'S NICE TO MEET YOU...
...I GUESS?
MY NAME IS KAIBARA.

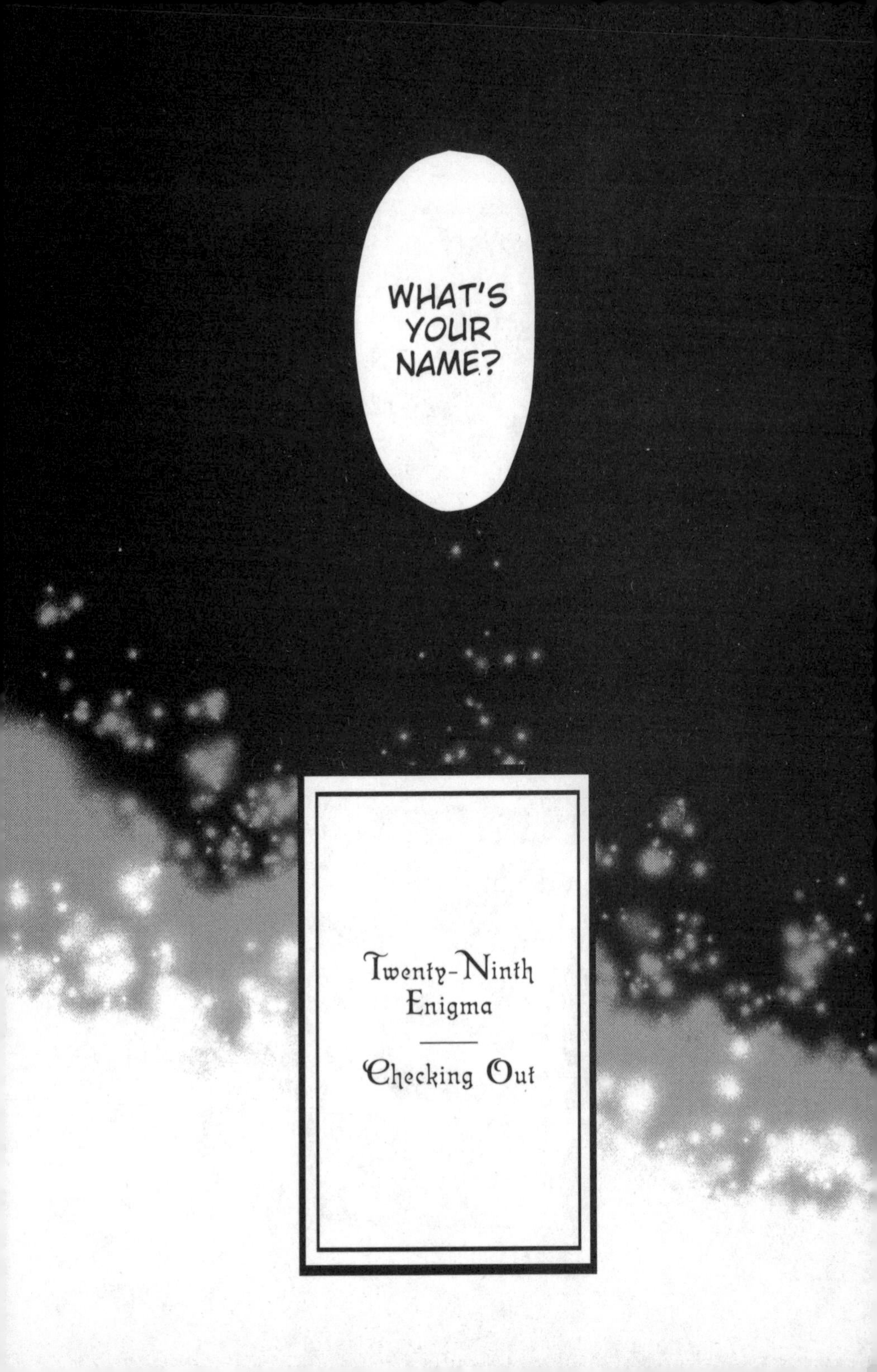
WHAT'S YOUR NAME?

Twenty-Ninth Enigma

Checking Out

Phantom Tales of the Night

To be continued in Volume 7

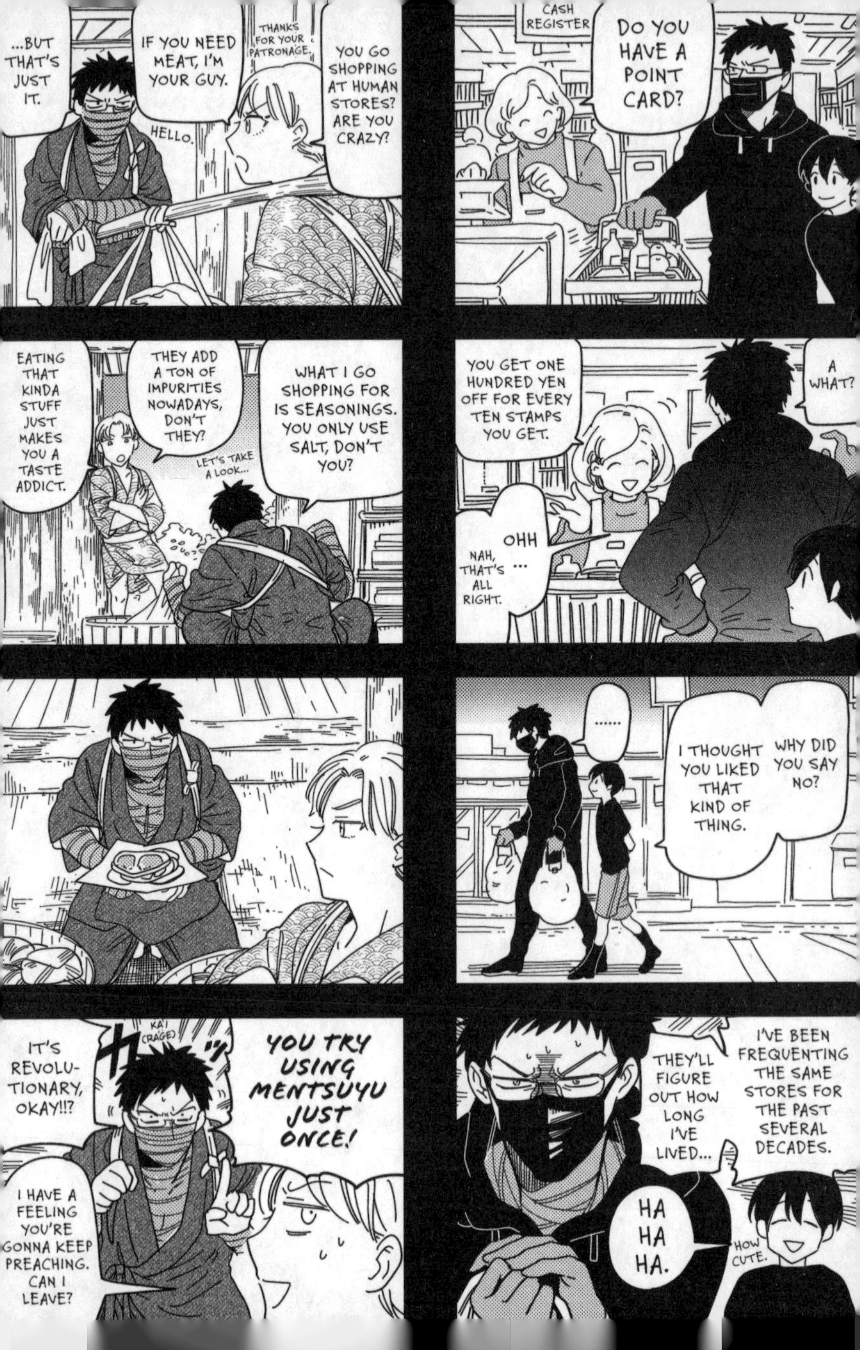
CASH REGISTER
DO YOU HAVE A POINT CARD?
A WHAT?
YOU GET ONE HUNDRED YEN OFF FOR EVERY TEN STAMPS YOU GET.
OHH...
NAH, THAT'S ALL RIGHT.
......
WHY DID YOU SAY NO?
I THOUGHT YOU LIKED THAT KIND OF THING.
I'VE BEEN FREQUENTING THE SAME STORES FOR THE PAST SEVERAL DECADES.
THEY'LL FIGURE OUT HOW LONG I'VE LIVED...
HA HA HA.
HOW CUTE.
YOU GO SHOPPING AT HUMAN STORES? ARE YOU CRAZY?
THANKS FOR YOUR PATRONAGE.
IF YOU NEED MEAT, I'M YOUR GUY.
HELLO.
...BUT THAT'S JUST IT.
WHAT I GO SHOPPING FOR IS SEASONINGS. YOU ONLY USE SALT, DON'T YOU?
LET'S TAKE A LOOK...
THEY ADD A TON OF IMPURITIES NOWADAYS, DON'T THEY?
EATING THAT KINDA STUFF JUST MAKES YOU A TASTE ADDICT.
YOU TRY USING MENTSUYU JUST ONCE!
KA! (RAGE)
IT'S REVOLUTIONARY, OKAY!!?
I HAVE A FEELING YOU'RE GONNA KEEP PREACHING. CAN I LEAVE?

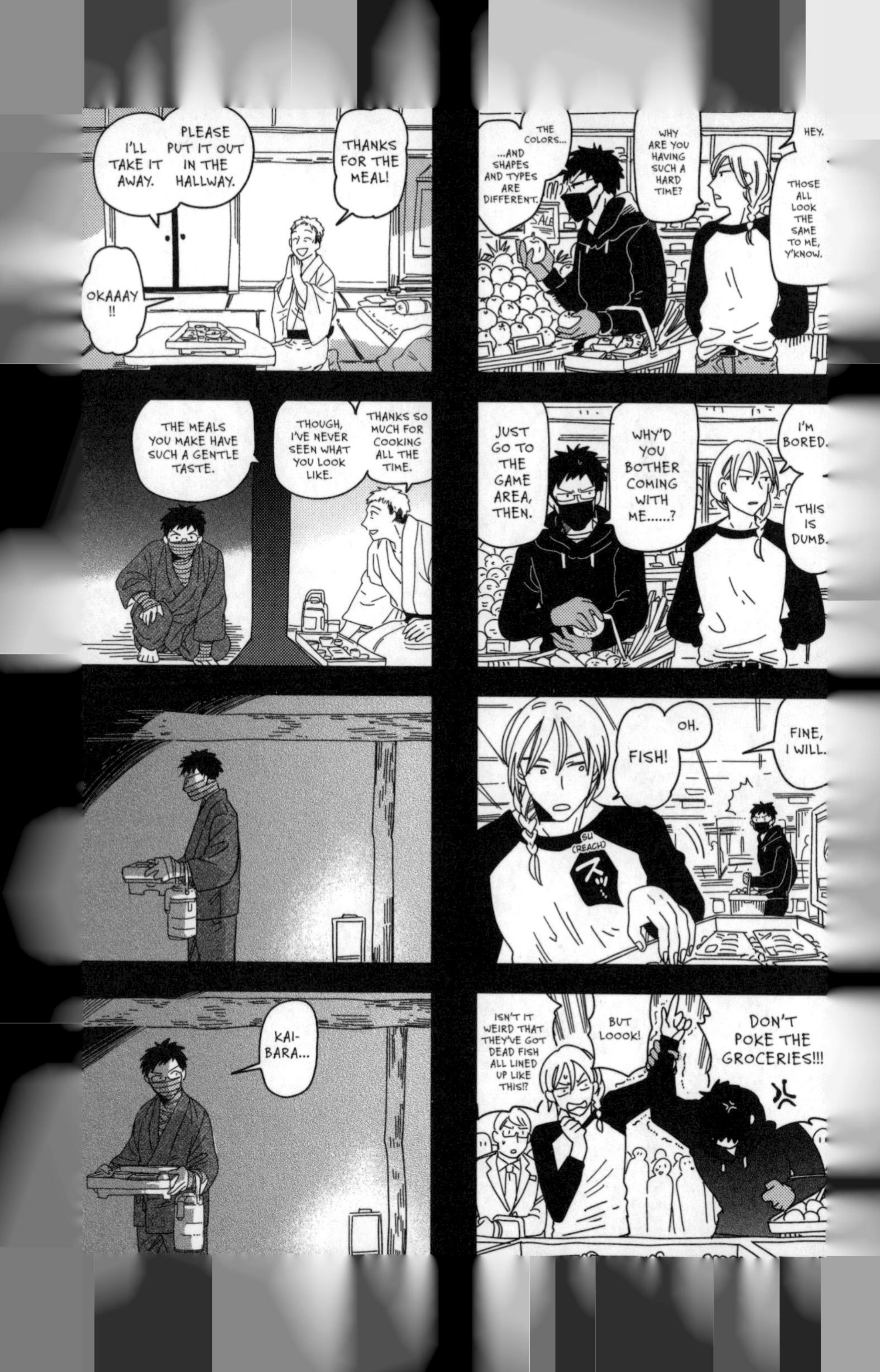
HEY.
THOSE ALL LOOK THE SAME TO ME, Y'KNOW.
WHY ARE YOU HAVING SUCH A HARD TIME?
THE COLORS...
...AND SHAPES AND TYPES ARE DIFFERENT.
I'M BORED.
THIS IS DUMB.
WHY'D YOU BOTHER COMING WITH ME......?
JUST GO TO THE GAME AREA, THEN.
FINE, I WILL.
OH.
FISH!
SU (REACH)
スッ
DON'T POKE THE GROCERIES!!!
BUT LOOOK!
ISN'T IT WEIRD THAT THEY'VE GOT DEAD FISH ALL LINED UP LIKE THIS!?
THANKS FOR THE MEAL!
PLEASE PUT IT OUT IN THE HALLWAY.
I'LL TAKE IT AWAY.
OKAAAY!!
THANKS SO MUCH FOR COOKING ALL THE TIME.
THOUGH, I'VE NEVER SEEN WHAT YOU LOOK LIKE.
THE MEALS YOU MAKE HAVE SUCH A GENTLE TASTE.
KAI-BARA...

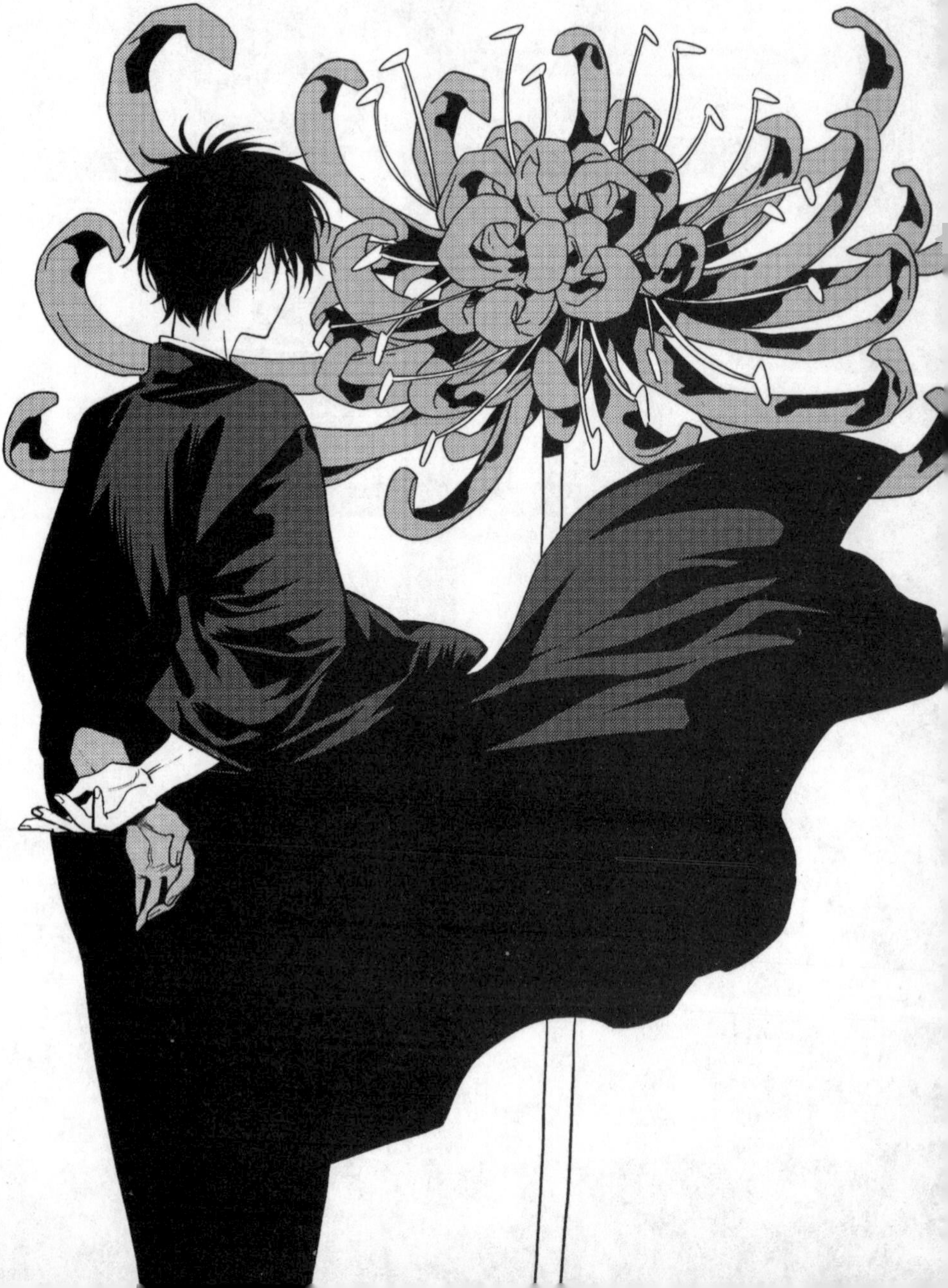

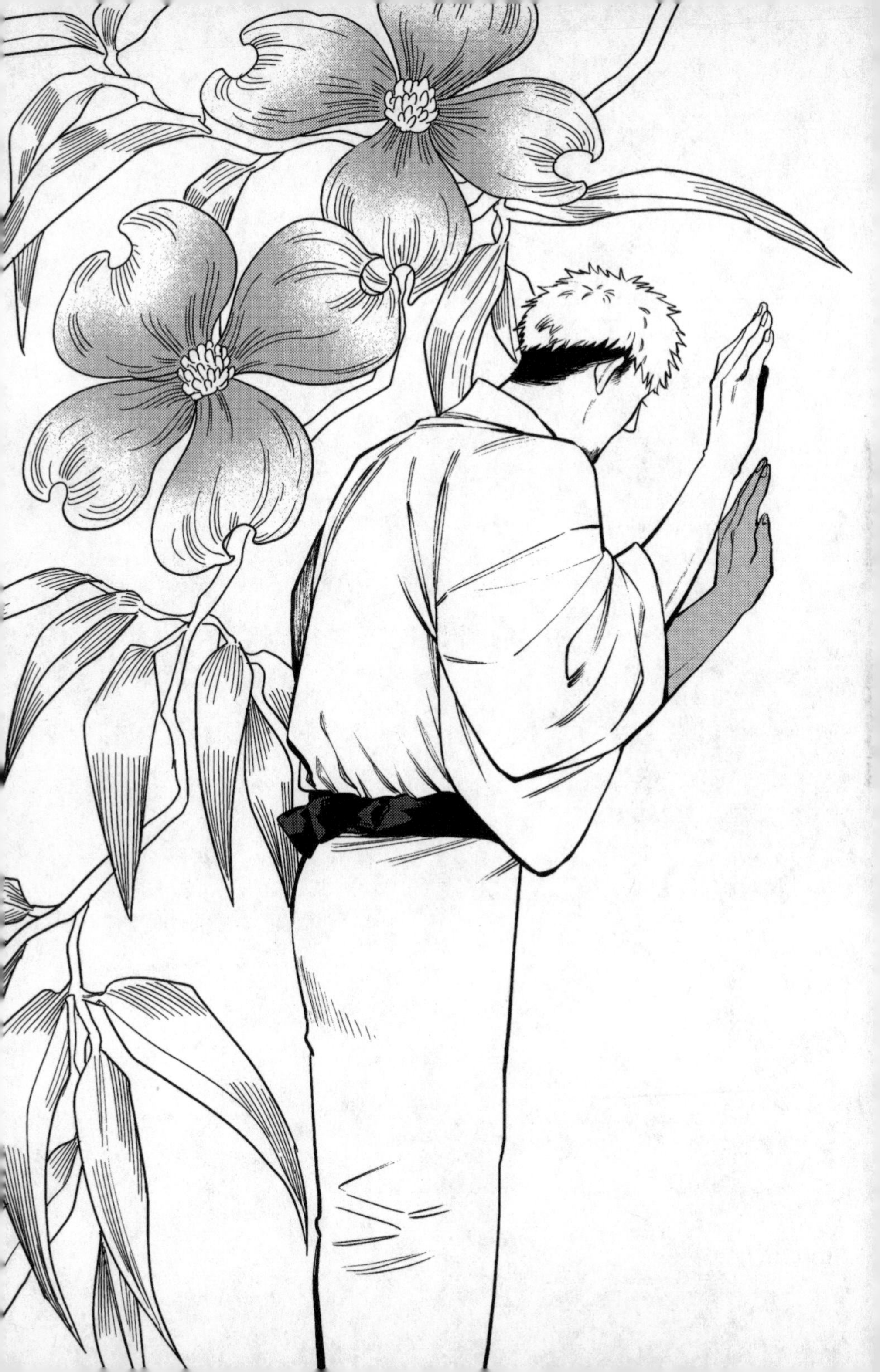

Translation Notes

Common Honorifics

no honorific: Indicates familiarity or closeness; if used without permission or reason, addressing someone in this manner would constitute an insult.

-san: The Japanese equivalent of Mr./Mrs./Miss. If a situation calls for politeness, this is the fail-safe honorific.

-kun: Used most often when referring to boys, this indicates affection or familiarity. Occasionally used by older men among their peers, but it may also be used by anyone referring to a person of lower standing.

-chan: An affectionate honorific indicating familiarity used mostly in reference to girls; also used in reference to cute persons or animals of either gender.

-sensei: A respectful term for teachers, artists, or high-level professionals.

-sama: Conveys great respect; may also indicate that the social status of the speaker is lower than that of the addressee.

(o)nee: Japanese equivalent to "older sister."

(o)nii: Japanese equivalent to "older brother."

General

Youkai are a class of Japanese supernatural being, translated variously in English as "ghosts," "demons," "monsters," etc.

Page 5

When Bone Monk calls the woman a **fox**, he's actually referring to a type of *youkai* known as a *kitsune*. *Kitsune* are infamously known in Japanese folklore as dangerous tricksters with the power to shape-shift into human form. They often take the guise of a beautiful woman.

Page 7

In Japanese, the **Owner** is called *Taishou*, a term used to refer to the owners of traditional Japanese restaurants and inns. It generally means "boss" or "chief."

Page 12

According to Japanese folklore, **800-year nun** gained immortality after her father unknowingly fed her mermaid meat and she stopped growing old. Eventually, she became a nun and wandered the world, finally dying at 800 years old.

Page 14

Sashimi refers to a type of popular Japanese cuisine consisting of thinly sliced raw meat—often fish—served as the first course in a formal Japanese meal, or as the main entree with rice and *miso* (fermented soybean) soup. The word *sashimi* originated in the Muromachi period (1336–1573) from the words *sashi*, meaning "cut" or "pierce," and *mi* meaning "body" or "meat." This dish is not to be confused with *sushi*, which in fact actually refers to the vinegar rice over which raw fish is placed and not the actual raw fish itself.

According to Japanese folklore, dining on **mermaid flesh** can grant the consumer powers of eternal life. One of the most famous legends about consuming mermaid flesh is that of the **800-year nun**, or *Yao Bikuni*. One of the versions goes as follows: a man was invited over to a fisherman's house to eat a rare fish—a mermaid—caught in the nets. Not wishing to eat a fish with a human face, the man avoided the meat. However, the fisherman insisted he bring the mermaid flesh home, where his daughter ate it without knowing what it was. As those around her grew old and died, she stayed eternally youthful. After everyone she knew perished, she traveled the world for eight hundred years before enshrining herself in a cave by the sea in Wakasa-Obama (Fukui Prefecture) area. Supposedly, the camellia tree she planted near the entrance would wither when she died. To this day, it is believed the tree still hasn't withered.

Page 21

In Japanese, the word used for **huntsmen** is *momonjiya*, meat vendors active in the Edo period (1603–1838) who specialized in large game.

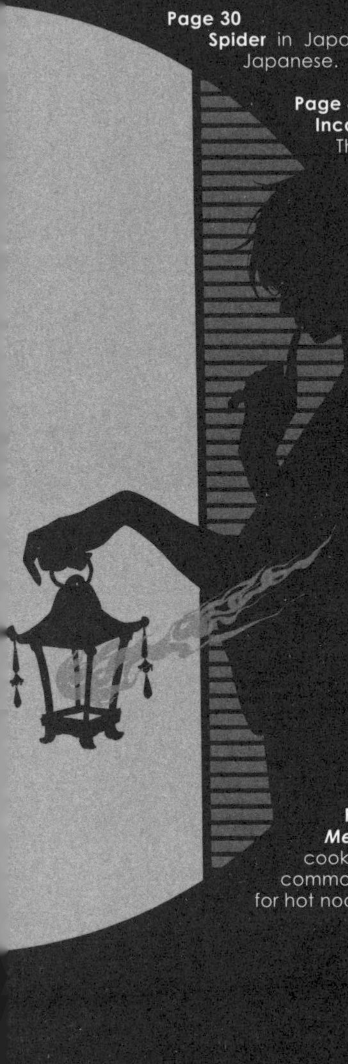

Page 24

Tengu are one of Japan's most famous *youkai* and are often associated with mountainous areas. Although the word *tengu* roughly translates to "heaven hounds," *tengu* were originally depicted as birdlike creatures with wings, a beaked mouth, and the ability to fly. However, during the Edo period (1603–1867), depictions of *tengu* changed to that of a tall, monk-like figure with a long, bulbous red nose. *Tengu* play three major roles in Japanese folklore—as harbingers of misfortune, as teachers of secret martial arts techniques, and as the culprits of "spiriting away." The phrase "spiriting away" or *kamikakushi* refers to the phenomenon of children being abducted by supernatural forces, often appearing far away with no memory of where they had been or what they were doing.

Page 30

Spider in Japanese is *kumo*, and the character is referred to as such in Japanese.

Page 41

Incarnate Butterflies is a translation of the Japanese *chou keshin*. The literal translation is "incarnation butterfly," so it was translated into English as "Incarnate Butterflies" since Butterfly is made of incarnated souls.

Page 76

Daikon radish is a mild-flavored winter radish often used in Japanese cooking. It is characterized by its fast-growing leaves and long, white root.

Page 77

Spring onion is a translation of the Japanese word *negi*, which refers to a type of scallion. This particular species of scallion is also known as the Welsh onion, bunching onion, or long green onion and is characterized by its long, white stem with green tip.

Soboro refers to ground meat, fish or eggs that are cooked into fine, crumbled pieces.

Page 107

1 US dollar = approximately 106 Japanese yen.

Page 115

Akane means "deep red" or "madder red"—madder being a type of plant.

Page 148

Tanuki are a species of omnivorous mammals native to East Asia that look like a cross between a raccoon and a possum.

Page 174

Mentsuyu is a soup base made with soy sauce, *mirin* (a rice-based cooking wine), bonito flakes, and *kombu* (a type of kelp). It is most commonly used as a dipping sauce for cold noodles or to make broth for hot noodle soup dishes.

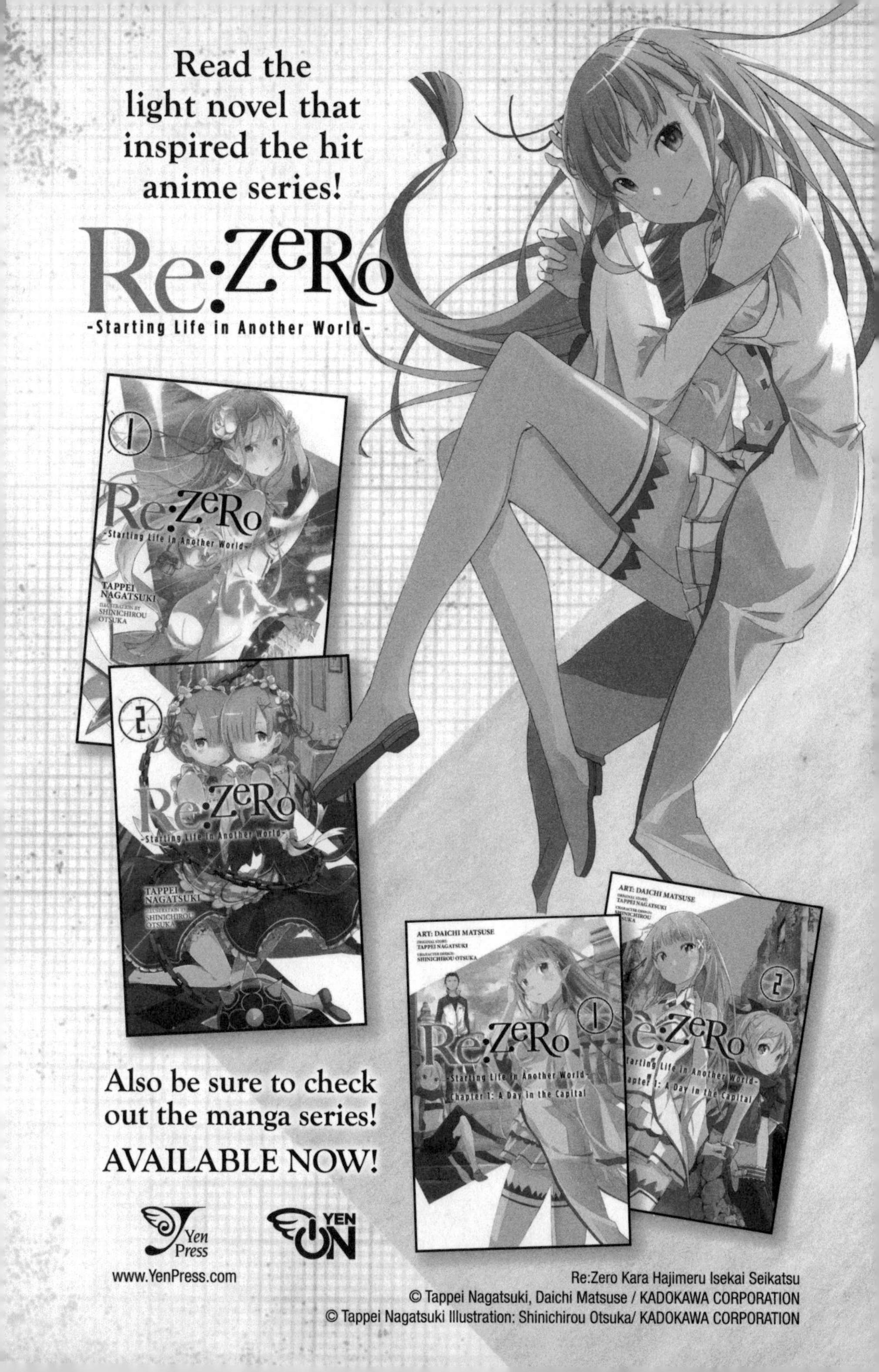
Read the light novel that inspired the hit anime series!
Re:ZeRo -Starting Life in Another World-
Re:ZeRo -Starting Life in Another World-
TAPPEI NAGATSUKI
ILLUSTRATION BY SHINICHIROU OTSUKA
Re:ZeRo -Starting Life in Another World-
TAPPEI NAGATSUKI
ILLUSTRATION BY SHINICHIROU OTSUKA
ART: DAICHI MATSUSE
ORIGINAL STORY: TAPPEI NAGATSUKI
CHARACTER DESIGN: SHINICHIROU OTSUKA
Re:ZeRo -Starting Life in Another World- Chapter 1: A Day in the Capital
Re:ZeRo -Starting Life in Another World- Chapter 1: A Day in the Capital
Also be sure to check out the manga series!
AVAILABLE NOW!
Yen Press
YEN ON
www.YenPress.com
Re:Zero Kara Hajimeru Isekai Seikatsu
© Tappei Nagatsuki, Daichi Matsuse / KADOKAWA CORPORATION
© Tappei Nagatsuki Illustration: Shinichirou Otsuka/ KADOKAWA CORPORATION

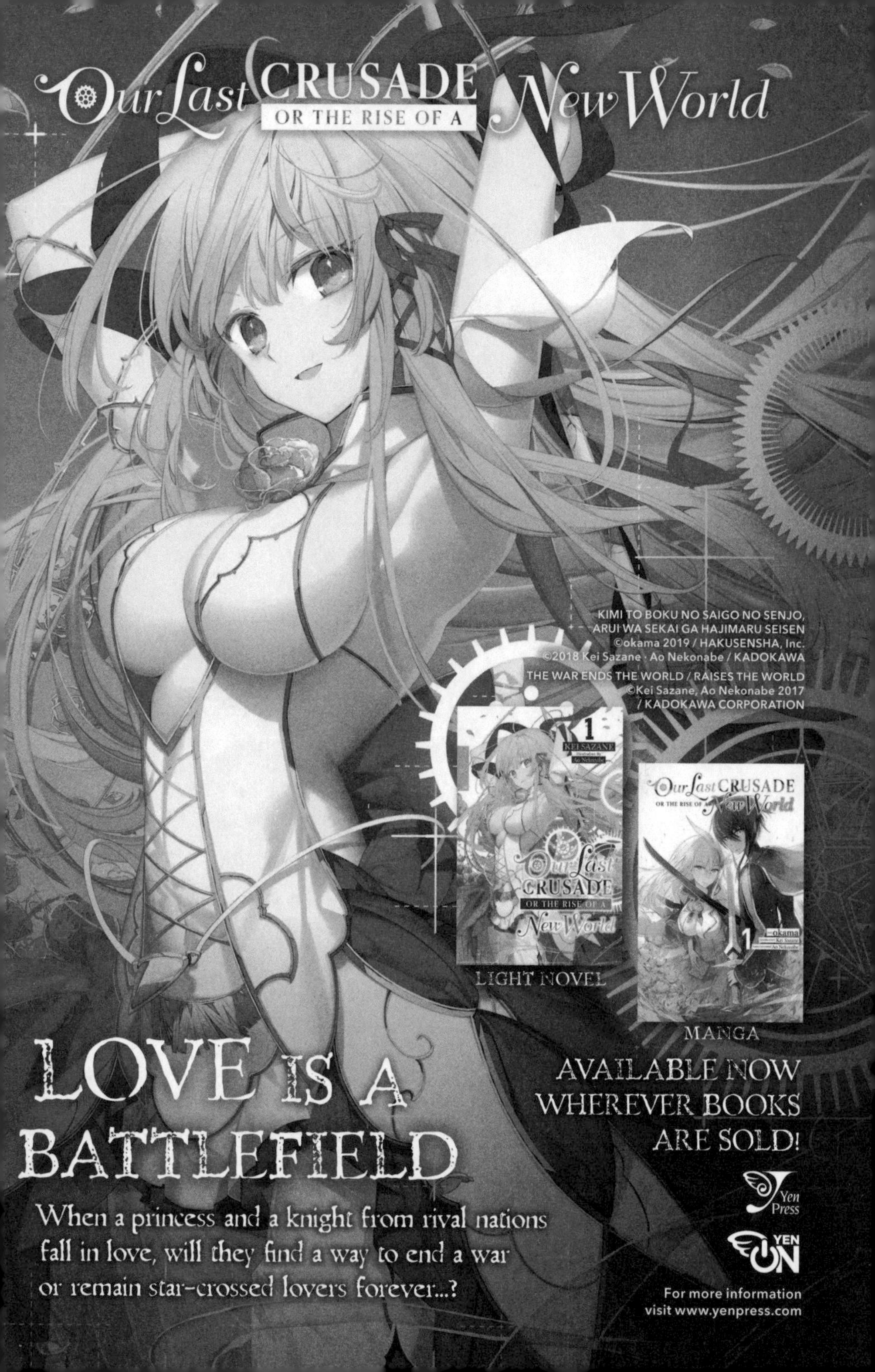
Our Last CRUSADE OR THE RISE OF A New World
KIMI TO BOKU NO SAIGO NO SENJO, ARUI WA SEKAI GA HAJIMARU SEISEN ©okama 2019 / HAKUSENSHA, Inc. ©2018 Kei Sazane · Ao Nekonabe / KADOKAWA
THE WAR ENDS THE WORLD / RAISES THE WORLD ©Kei Sazane, Ao Nekonabe 2017 / KADOKAWA CORPORATION
LIGHT NOVEL
MANGA
AVAILABLE NOW WHEREVER BOOKS ARE SOLD!
LOVE IS A BATTLEFIELD
When a princess and a knight from rival nations fall in love, will they find a way to end a war or remain star-crossed lovers forever...?
Yen Press
YEN ON
For more information visit www.yenpress.com

Phantom Tales of the Night 6
Matsuri

Translation: Julie Goniwich
Lettering: Chiho Christie

BAKEMONO YAWA ZUKUSHI vol. 6
©Matsuri 2019
First published in Japan in 2019 by KADOKAWA CORPORATION, Tokyo. English translation rights arranged with KADOKAWA CORPORATION, Tokyo through TUTTLE-MORI AGENCY, INC., Tokyo.

Yen Press
150 West 30th Street, 19th Floor
New York, NY 10001

Visit us at yenpress.com
facebook.com/yenpress
twitter.com/yenpress
yenpress.tumblr.com
instagram.com/yenpress

First Yen Press Edition: November 2020

Yen Press is an imprint of Yen Press, LLC.
The Yen Press name and logo are trademarks of Yen Press, LLC.

The publisher is not responsible for websites (or their content) that are not owned by the publisher.

Library of Congress Control Number: 2019942895

ISBNs: 978-1-9753-1745-4 (paperback)
        978-1-9753-1746-1 (ebook)

10 9 8 7 6 5 4 3 2 1

WOR

Printed in the United States of America